SUPPLEMENTA

HUMANISTICA LOVANIENSIA

XXIII

SUPPLEMENTA HUMANISTICA LOVANIENSIA



*Editorial Correspondence*: Seminarium Philologiae Humanisticae
Blijde-Inkomststraat 21 (Box 3316)
B-3000 Leuven (Belgium)

SUPPLEMENTA

HUMANISTICA LOVANIENSIA

XXIII

# «CUI DONO LEPIDUM NOVUM LIBELLUM?»

## DEDICATING LATIN WORKS AND MOTETS IN THE SIXTEENTH CENTURY

PROCEEDINGS OF THE INTERNATIONAL CONFERENCE HELD AT THE ACADEMIA BELGICA, ROME, 18-20 AUGUST 2005

Edited by Ignace BOSSUYT, Nele GABRIËLS, Dirk SACRÉ & Demmy VERBEKE

LEUVEN UNIVERSITY PRESS

2008

ISBN 978 90 5867 669 6
D/2008/1869/32
NUR 635

## CONTENTS

# FOREWORD

In 2001, the Katholieke Universiteit Leuven provided a grant for an interdisciplinary research project concerning 'The Latin Dedications of the Motet Editions of the Franco-Flemish Polyphonists from the Second Half of the Sixteenth Century as Musical and Literary Sources'. Based on the realisation that Renaissance editions of music as a rule contained dedicatory letters and/or other liminary texts which are a mine of information for both musicological and Neo-Latin research but were largely neglected in modern scholarship, the project embarked on a systematic interdisciplinary examination of these texts, combining Latin philological and musicological expertise.

The corpus was restricted to *Einzeldrucke* with motets by Franco-Flemish composers of the second half of the sixteenth century, resulting in some three hundred books (including reprints), although not all of these contain Latin liminary texts. The more than two hundred Latin letters and poems which appeared in the corpus were edited, translated, annotated and analysed in their literary-historical context. Starting from and in conjunction with this philological research undertaken, the musicological part set out to examine possible relations between the dedicatory letters and other liminary texts on the one hand and the musical content of the respective print on the other. In addition to this investigation into the relations between literary and musical items in the motet books, the study of these liminary texts also revealed biographical data and information about the relations between composer, printer, patron and other figures, and exposed contemporary views on religion, culture and music as well as developments in the status of composers and in the increasing market-oriented music business.

The international conference *Cui dono lepidum novum libellum? Dedicating Latin Works and Motets in the Sixteenth Century: Theory and Practice*, which took place at the *Academia Belgica* in Rome from 18 to 20 August 2005, was the conclusion and coronation of four years of intense and fertile research. We are pleased to present to you the proceedings of this meeting which brought together scholars from diverse disciplines to reflect on the many-sided problem of dedications and other liminary texts in the sixteenth century.

The dedication project and its conference were successfully undertaken thanks to the engagement of various people and organisations.

First of all, we wish to express our gratitude to our collaborators Nele Gabriëls and Demmy Verbeke, who have concentrated during four years on a theme of great challenge and full of risk, for, in the absence of any existing research, we did not know what we were beginning nor where we would end up. The results, however, were fruitful: a doctorate in classical philology by Verbeke, various papers at colloquia and congresses and articles in national and international journals. We thank them for their loyal collaboration, their unflinching commitment and their irrepressible enthusiasm.

Besides, we wish to thank all those who accepted our invitation to present a paper at the conference within their area of expertise. Since the offer was greater than the demand, we were regrettably obliged to refuse a number of papers. We are especially indebted to our colleague musicologist prof. Mary Lewis (University of Pittsburgh), for her willingness to present the conference concluding remarks and introduce the publication at hand.

We are also particularly grateful to prof. Walter Geerts, director of the *Academia Belgica*, and his team, for their spontaneous hospitality. The conference's splendid location was particularly appropriate for a theme that finds its ultimate origin in Rome.

Last but not least, we express our gratitude to the Fonds voor Wetenschappelijk Onderzoek Vlaanderen for its financial support for the organisation of the conference, thereby allowing the publication of these proceedings.

Ignace Bossuyt
Musicology
Katholieke Universiteit Leuven
Blijde-Inkomststraat 21
B-3000 Leuven
ignace.bossuyt@arts.kuleuven.be

Dirk Sacré
Literary Studies: Latin Literature & Seminarium Philologiae Humanisticae
Katholieke Universiteit Leuven
Blijde-Inkomststraat 21
B-3000 Leuven
dirk.sacre@arts.kuleuven.be

# INTRODUCTION
# THE DEDICATION AS PARATEXT

Mary S. Lewis

The essays in this volume all deal with aspects of dedications of Latin writings and motets. In most cases, the writers have examined the dedications in the larger context of the overall paratextual apparatus of the publication in question — that is, as related to titles, title pages, illustrations, dedications, poetry, tables of contents, headings, and notes.

The term *paratext* was first coined by the French literary theorist Gérard Genette in his *Seuils* of 1987.[1] He used the term to describe all visual and verbal elements that are included with the texts and that present the texts to the public. Paratexts are frames that interact with the text itself. When studied from this point of view, dedications and other liminary material aid our understanding of the main text by revealing previously hidden funds of information regarding the main text and its contexts. While Genette was concerned particularly with French fiction of the nineteenth and twentieth centuries, scholars have expanded the use of the term to apply it to a much wider spectrum of publications. In the case of the present volume, the concept of paratext has served as a powerful tool in the study of Latin writings and motets of the fifteenth and sixteenth centuries.

In the twenty years since Genette's introduction of the term, the study of paratexts has become an important component of literary studies. In music, paratextual analysis has also taken hold, especially in the fields of music printing and publishing. One earlier study, that by Raimund Redeker, is devoted wholly to Latin dedications to mass and motet prints of the first half of the sixteenth century, and is particularly relevant to the subject of our conference,[2] as is another by Dagmar Schnell on a similar

[1] Gérard Genette, *Seuils* (Paris: Seuil, 1987); English translation by Jane E. Lewis as *Paratexts: Thresholds of Interpretation* (Cambridge: Cambridge University Press, 1997).

[2] Raimund Redeker, *Lateinische Widmungsvorreden zu Mess- und Motettendrucken der ersten Hälfte des 16. Jahrhunders* (Eisenach: Karl Dieter Wagner, 1995).

repertory from a century later.[3] As a rule, though, discussions of dedications and other paratexts have found their way into more general studies of music printing and publishing, or into specialized accounts of particular repertories or of certain composers.[4]

In the field of literary theory, studies of paratexts have become increasingly influential as the critical relevance of these materials becomes apparent. A sampling of writings on paratexts by literary critics and theorists reminds us of the importance of staying in touch with such parallel fields.[5] We can see then that the conference that produced the papers in this volume was firmly in step with the growing awareness by literary and musical scholars that every element of a book is of critical importance.

As Genette has maintained, the paratexts are the thresholds to the book, and this is particularly true of dedications. They let us know "what we imagine we are doing when we pick up and make our way into a printed book";[6] they prepare us to think of the book in a certain way. Paratexts bring the reader to the book and invite him in by giving important information about the book. According to Genette, the paratext "enables a text to become a book and to be offered as such to its readers and, more generally to the public."[7]

Paratexts also "play a crucial role in shaping the relationships between authors, texts, contexts and readers."[8] Before we can truly analyze and

[3] Dagmar Schnell, *In lucem edidit. Der deutsche Notendruck der ersten Hälfte des 17. Jahrhunderts als Kommunikationsmedium. Dargestellt an der Vorreden* (Osnabrück: Der Andere Verlag, 2003).

[4] See, for example, Susan Lewis Hammond, *Editing Music in Early Modern Germany* (Aldershot: Ashgate, 2007); Kate van Orden (ed.), *Music and the Cultures of Print* (New York: Garland, 2000); Martha Feldman, *City Culture and the Madrigal at Venice* (Berkeley: University of California Press, 1995); Cristle Collins Judd, *Reading Renaissance Music Theory: Hearing with the Eyes* (New York: Cambridge University Press, 2000); and Rebecca Oettinger, *Music as Propaganda in the German Reformation* (Aldershot: Ashgate, 2001).

[5] Sabrina Alcorn Baron, Eric N. Lindquist, and Eleanor F. Shevlin (eds.), *Agent of Change: Print Culture Studies after Elizabeth L. Eisenstein* (Boston: University of Massachusetts Press, 2007); Adrian Armstrong and Malcolm Quainton (eds.), *Book and Text in France, 1400-1600: Poetry on the Page* (Aldershot: Ashgate, 2007); A. A. den Hollander, U. B. Schmid, and W. F. Smelik (eds.), *Paratext and Megatext as Channels of Jewish and Christian Traditions: The Textual Markers of Contextualization* (Leiden-Boston: Brill, 2003).

[6] Willliam H. Sherman, 'On the Threshold: Architecture, Paratext, and Early Print Culture', in *Agent of Change*, p. 67.

[7] Genette, *Paratexts*, p. 1.

[8] Adrian Armstrong, 'Introduction', in *Book and Text in France*, p. 2.

understand a book, we must perceive its contexts, and paratexts are invaluable in providing those insights.

Paratexts locate authorial agency in printed works, whether that be the printer-publisher, the author, the editor, or even readers (who exercise agency when they write corrections in the texts).[9] A dedication written by the author furthered his or her agency. Likewise, other paratexts, if they interpreted, contextualized, or focused the author's text, furthered that agency. A dedication by a printer/publisher, on the other hand, might transfer agency from the author to the writer of the dedication.

Paratexts certainly influence the reception of the text and the strategies of the author or editor.[10] We can also see, particularly where dedications are concerned, that, in Natalie Zemon Davis's words, books are "carriers of relationships."[11] Paratexts can also represent political agendas, and function often as tropes on the texts themselves.

Paratexts also served to provide evidence that the authority of a writer or composer was justified.[12] The presence of a privilege on the title page was one way to provide that justification. Another was the protection of a powerful patron. Even the presence of the author's name on the title page was evidence of his importance and his right to be published. Sometimes the authority of the edition itself was proclaimed by a statement that the contents had been diligently corrected, thus including the editor in the process of justification, and perhaps distinguishing the work from that of other publishers.[13]

Scholars of paratexts have developed a variety of classifications for liminary material. Guyda Armstrong divides them into authorial, organizational, visual, and editorial paratexts.[14] Authorial paratexts include above all the dedication if it is signed by the author, as well as subtitles, liturgical assignments of motets, rubrics and similar material. Organizational paratexts include the title-page material and the index or table of contents. Visual paratexts consist of decorative elements including illustrations,

[9] Baron, Lindquist, and Shevlin, 'Part I. Agents, Agency, and Print in Early Modern Europe', in *Agent of Change*, p. 18.

[10] Armstrong, 'Introduction', pp. 6, 13.

[11] Cited in Armstrong, 'Introduction', note 14.

[12] François Rigolot, 'Paratextual Strategy and Sexual Politics: Louise Labé's *Œuvres lyonnaises*', in Armstrong and Quainton, *Book and Text*, p. 170.

[13] Hammond, *Editing Music*, p. 18.

[14] Guyda Armstrong, 'Paratexts and Their Functions in Seventeenth-Century English *Decamerons*', *Modern Language Review*, 102/1 (January 2007), 40-57 (at pp. 41-2).

heraldry, printers' marks, scribal devices, and ornaments such as leaves, borders and the like. Finally, editorial paratexts can include the dedication if written by someone other than the author, laudatory poems by friends, statements by the printer or editor, and similar non-authorial textual material.

Raimund Redeker, in his work on Latin dedications to mass and motet prints, has proposed a different categorization, based on authorship.[15] In his first category, he includes dedications by printers and editors. His subsequent categories include dedications by theologians, and then dedications by composers. He also includes a category of dedications by printers in Wittenberg, Nürnberg, and Augsburg as a special group germane to his study, though not one that is generally applicable.

While the papers in this book are concerned above all with dedications, many deal with other sorts of paratexts. The first paratext that usually meets the eye is the title page, which prepares the reader's expectations and thus his focus in his reading. Among its several functions, the title page places the book geographically, chronologically, and socially. That placement can be effected through the statement on the title page of the name of the printer and the date and city of publication, identification of the author's position (if given) and the presence or absence of a privilege.[16] Further geographical and chronological positioning may also come from a date and place given as part of the signature to the dedication. The typographical arrangement of the title page, including the size of fonts assigned to various words and names, as well as the presence of any heraldic devices or printer's marks, are also meaningful.

As the commercialization of music printing grew in the sixteenth century, title pages of anthologies frequently advertised the presence of music by a famous composer, even though his works might have made up only a fraction of the contents. In such cases, anthology title pages can be of particular interest in revealing both the tastes of the editor and publisher as well as their reading of the public's preferences. Agency would seem to lie with editor and publisher, in these instances, rather than with any one composer.

[15] Redeker, *Lateinische Widmungsvorreden*, pp. IX-XIII.

[16] In my experience (mostly with Italian prints), the statement of privilege (e.g. *Con gratia et privilegio*) appeared on the title page. In a very few publications, such as the early prints of Antonio Gardano, the privilege was spelled out in the colophon, but that practice was soon dropped. In either case, the statement of a privilege carries with it connotations of importance.

Titles of anthologies were also important means of identifying the work with a kind of catch phrase, such as *Mottetti del fiore* or *Novum et insigne opus musicum*, to be used in the first and subsequent editions to attract the public.[17] Such titles strengthened the notion of the anthology as a container of musical objects.[18]

In a great majority of cases, title pages featured some sort of art work. Most often this was a printer's mark which itself carried a message about the quality and ideals of the printing house. At other times, a woodcut or engraving of a more specific sort referred to a patron. This could be a coat of arms, the representation of a saint or of a mythical figure, or some other pictorial representation, often draped with a banner containing a motto of some sort. Such an artistic reference automatically lent importance and significance to the publication, and encouraged the reader to turn immediately to the dedicatory page for further details. At other times, a portrait of the author or composer appeared on the title page or soon afterwards. Illustrations sometimes occurred elsewhere in the book as well, and thus added a further dimension to the volume's paratexts.

But above all, it is dedications that provide us with a doorway into the contents of the book, its context, and the motivations of the author. The essays in this volume reveal a wide spectrum of strategies used by authors and publishers to further their personal ambitions and promote causes through their astute use of dedicatory material.

Readers of dedications today are often deceived by the inclusion of standard phrases and topics in the books of the sixteenth century that may obscure the significant meaning of some of the dedication's language. But prefaces and dedications may position the books for us socially, economically and culturally, and we must look beyond the jargon-laden formulas to extract the specific information that provides the keys to the text itself.

[17] Examples include *Primus liber cum quinque vocibus. Mottetti del frutto* (Venice: Gardano, 1538; RISM 1538[4]); *Primus liber cum sex vocibus. Mottetti del frutto a sei voci* (Venice: Gardano, 1539; RISM 1539[3]); *Primus liber cum quatuor vocibus. Mottetti del frutto a quatro* (Venice: Gardano, 1539; RISM 1539[13]); *Liber primus Musarum cum quatuor vocibus...* (Venice: Rampazzetto, 1563; RISM 1563[3]); *Libro terzo delle Muse a quattro voci...* (Venice: Rampazetto, 1563; RISM 1563[9]); *Novum et insigne opus musicum ... cantionum sex vocum* (Nürnberg: Berg & Neuber, 1558; RISM 1558[4]); *Secunda pars magni operis musici ...Quinque vocum ...* (Nürnberg: Berg & Neuber, 1559; RISM 1559[1]); *Tertia pars magni operis musici ... quatuor vocum ...* (Nürnberg: Berg & Neuber, 1559; RISM 1559[2]).

[18] Redeker, *Lateinische Widmungsvorreden*, p. 24.

Each dedication began with some sort of salutation to the patron (usually in large type), thereby establishing from the outset the legitimization of the contents under the name of an esteemed personage. The dedication concluded with an offer of servitude and devotion to the patron, proclaiming humility, and reminding the reader once again of the protection of the dedicatee and the gratitude of the author (or whoever actually signed the dedication).

Within the body of the letter, the author went about the business of making it clear to the reader that his writings were worthy, and thus creating the tension between humility and self-promotion so characteristic of the sixteenth-century dedication, and noticeable even in dedications of antiquity. Such declarations were often preceded by humble protestations that the work was only brought before the public at the request of friends, the patron, or worthy colleagues. In this way they pre-emptively defended themselves from critics in a move that Genette has called *paratonnerres* (lightning rods).[19] Frequently a reference was made to ancient writers and musicians, from Minerva to Orpheus to Jubal, and to music as one of the liberal arts. Authors often gave guidance to the readers in dealing with the text, or spoke of its cultural, religious, or social value.

Reading the central text along with its surrounding material, the authors of the essays in this volume tie together threads of meaning, a web of causality and intention, that might not otherwise be obvious to us. The relationship of the work to its world becomes clearer as it is framed in the network of gratitude, flattery, justification, false humility, self seeking, self aggrandizement, and propaganda that often forms a prominent part of the paratexts.

The practice of dedicating a book to someone goes back to antiquity, as Harm-Jan van Dam shows us. In his essay, van Dam points out the similarities between ancient and modern practice, as well as the differences inherent when the book is produced in manuscript rather than print. He concentrates on Latin literature, and shows us the ways in which an author may dedicate a work in that genre. He also traces the early history of dedicatory practice, starting with poetry and proceeding to prose, and then the emergence of the dedicatory letter. Van Dam further investigates the identity of dedicators and dedicatees, and the motivations for dedications during antiquity and the early middle ages. His writing on the

[19] Genette, *Paratexts*, p. 192.

various themes and *topoi* of the dedications is of particular value in revealing the mindsets of both authors and dedicatees. Van Dam's paper establishes connections with later early modern practices and serves as a foundation for the essays that follow.

The next paper in this volume, that by Karl A. E. Enenkel, is closely related to van Dam's in its study of fifteenth- and sixteenth-century writings on antiquity and its literature. He proposes that dedications were a way for authors in that new field to legitimize their work and to organize and administer the knowledge acquired in their studies. His paper looks at ten representative dedications from landmark publications between 1446 and 1612. Enenkel first points out the importance of the dedications to the understanding of the text, an importance overlooked by scholars of the nineteenth and early twentieth centuries. He then investigates the way these dedications functioned as interactions between the author, the dedicatee, and the general reader. Enenkel calls attention to the way the dedication locates the text in a system of power. Even more importantly, he emphasizes the fact that the dedication functioned as the "official act of publication," a point often overlooked by most scholars. The dedicatee in fact determines who may speak, who is an author. Prof. Enenkel's analysis of the ten dedications amplifies our understanding of the role of the dedication and the dedicatee for the fifteenth- and sixteenth-century "Artes antiquitatis" in mediating the message of the text.

The two following papers are concerned with motets and their dedications. They are of particular importance to musicologists, for motet texts that at first glance seem innocuous and straightforwardly tied to the liturgical calendar can be shown through paratexts to be part of a complex pattern of identification with a patron or an event. Mysterious or enigmatic references in a poem or motet text may be clarified when read in light of dedicatory material. Biographies of authors and dedicatees become easier to construct, while the identities of others are called into question.

Demmy Verbeke looks at preliminary material in sixteenth century motet editions by composers from the Low Countries. He concentrates on the period between the first half of the sixteenth and the first half of the seventeenth centuries, the era not covered by Redeker and Schnell.[20] His work covers a corpus of 261 editions which he has examined for the presence of dedications and related materials. After a statistical study of

[20] Redeker, *Lateinische Widmungsvorreden*; Schnell, *In lucem edidit*.

this corpus, he delves into practices involving reprints, language choice, and the different forms of the paratexts, as well as the identity of authors (composers, printers, or others). The examples that he provides furnish us with valuable material for further study of the motet repertory of this period.

Nele Gabriëls looks at the same repertory from the point of view of the information that can be mined from dedications. She presents five categories of knowledge that can be gained about the musical and socio-musical history of the motet in the second half of the sixteenth century. In addition, she suggests connections between the paratexts and the content of the motets in the prints — both texts and music. The implications of her findings on historical and factual material buried in dedicatory texts are amazing in their implications for those involved in the writing of a contextual as well as a musical history of motets. While she admits that information on music in the dedications is scarce, she still manages to unearth some solid statements on views of music and music theory among the corpus of motets. She ends with a discussion of the functions of the dedications and the ways they were viewed by the composers. Her paper is an exemplary study of the importance of paratextual material in our understanding of the motet and its history.

Thomas Schmidt-Beste turns to dedications in manuscripts, and discusses in particular the reasons why there are so few in motet manuscripts of the fifteenth and sixteenth centuries. At the same time, he discusses the circumstances and motivations behind those dedications that exist. He looks especially at presentation manuscripts, where dedications would have been more appropriate. His discussion of particular dedicated manuscripts reveals many details about the contexts that their paratexts provide, especially when it comes to implicit rather than explicit dedications. Since many of these manuscripts have been the objects of a great deal of scholarly attention, the information he provides is particularly welcome.

Jan Bloemendal is concerned with dedications of Neo-Latin plays in the Netherlands in the sixteenth and seventeenth centuries. He looks specifically at both the comedies of the sixteenth century and the tragedies of the seventeenth, taking into consideration the background of religious strife at the time. He also examines the differences between dedications for comedies meant to be performed at schools, and those for tragedies destined for university performance. His investigation pursues questions regarding the choice of dedicatees, the author of the dedications and prefaces, and differences in genre. By analyzing the contents of the dedications, he unearths considerable information about the context of the plays and their supporters. Bloemendal's article gives us valuable insight into the context of Neo-Latin plays.

In her paper on Latin laudatory motets, Victoria Panagl first makes important distinctions between the *Staatsmotet* and the laudatory motet, even though the two genres sometimes overlap. Her study treats the texts of the motets as one might usually treat paratexts, and goes beyond the usual approach of historical, sociological, and aesthetic discussion. Instead, she undertakes a philological analysis of the texts of the motets. Her consideration of laudatory motets for the Habsburgs considers the relationship between the composer and poet, the addressee, and the laudatory motet itself as a work of the Muses. In particular, using a number of motets as examples, she concentrates on the classical references in these texts and their meaning for both the person being praised and for the authors of the texts. Her study makes a valuable contribution to our understanding of the texts and functions of laudatory motets and serves as an example for further work.

Farkas Gábor Kiss takes up Latin dedications in Hungary and their functions for humanist scholars. In seeking to explain the linguistic tension created in the dedications between expressions of humility and the highly sophisticated language in which they were formulated, he turns to the examination of adages and proverbs in the dedications. He looks in particular at humanistic dedications of Hungarian authors, and at their adoption of Beroaldian or Ciceronian writing styles. In that light, he finds the Beroaldian style full of proverbs and adages which writers of dedications employed to good advantage. His article provides useful guidance to the understanding of the use and meaning of proverbs and adages in these texts.

Walter Kreyszig looks for the first time at the paratexts of the four volumes of the seminal music treatises by Franchino Gaffurio (1451-1522). Kreyszig points out that the number of paratexts — ranging from two to nine — in each volume depends on the complexity of the material presented. He then continues with detailed and rewarding critical analyses of the paratexts in the *Theorica music*e, the *Practica musicae*, and the *De harmonia* and how they help us understand the treatises. The author concludes by emphasizing that the paratexts point to "the magic triangle of author, opus and audience." Surely anyone studying the writings of Gaffurius from now on should take Kreyszig's article into consideration.

The dedication of the *De Orbe Novo* by Pierre Martyr d'Anghiera forms the subject of Brigitte Gauvin's contribution to this volume. She looks at the many letters and dedicatees of Martyr's writings on the New World and sees them at times producing a portrait of the writer. In a careful accounting of the contents, form, and styles of the letters, she is able to sort out the complex web of dedicatees, many of which change from one edition to another. She also investigates Martyr's motivations for choosing his dedicatees, and for his use of the usual characteristics of the dedications and prefaces of classical and late Antiquity. Her paper gives us a useful picture of the complexity of the dedicatory system in general, and of Martyr's in particular.

Latin inscriptions in books of music for vihuela are the subject of Paloma Otaola Gonzalez's article. She discusses the wealth of paratextual material in these editions, meant above all for the educated, aristocratic, and refined, but also highly popular with other segments of society. She shows that the books have a similar structure containing dedication, notice of privilege, letters to the benefactor and to the reader, and then instructions on the music, the tablature, tuning of the instrument, and similar matters. The prefaces all evoke the splendor and importance of the music of the Ancients. In addition, many of these books include engravings and emblems accompanied by inscriptions in Latin or in Castilian, as well as epigrams and poems. While the primary language of the books is Castilian, many of the paratexts are in Latin. Dr. Gonzalez proceeds to examine the Latin paratexts in a number of these publications in detail, dividing the Latin inscriptions eventually into three distinct categories — inscriptions for engravings of those of high rank in the form of Latin epigraphs on commemorative monuments, Biblical citations, and classical quotations. Her work provides us with new insight into the world of Spanish music and music printing in the sixteenth century.

Jeanine De Landtsheer's essay delineates Justus Lipsius's choice of patrons to further his career planning. She examines his selection of dedicatees for his treatises in light of their social status, and for their political importance. She shows that he made certain choices in order to ingratiate himself with rulers who might bestow remunerative titles on him. In other cases, he selected dedicatees who could offer protection against possible calumnies, or those whose piety and orthodoxy would protect him from criticism of his religious writings in his miracle treatises. Dr. De Landtsheer also discusses Lipsius's dedications to fellow humanists and their spirit of admiration or affection. She follows this analysis with a study of the formal aspects of the dedicatory letters, and in her conclusion takes note of the risks that might be involved in the selection of a dedicatee during a time of religious uncertainty. The article gives us a valuable insight into the motivations that could lie behind the choice of a dedicatee during the sixteenth century, and the ways in which those choices could affect a writer's career.

Biographical information on the composer René (Rinaldo) del Mel (ca. 1554-ca. 1598) is found almost entirely in the dedications of seven of his music books containing religious and secular music. Emilie Corswarem has examined these dedications and found that they provide us with information on the composer's biography, the chronology of his works, his ambitions, his employers, and to a certain extent, the reception of his music. She has read the composer's dedications with care, analysed their contents, and filled in their background, producing a study that adds depth and detail to the scant list of writings on this unjustly neglected composer.

Peter Poulos looks at the works of the Genoese composer and chapel master Simone Molinaro, and analyzes the information on the composer found in the dedications of Molinaro's first published work, the *Motetorum ... Liber primus* of 1597. At the same time, he discovers significant contextual information in the texts of the motets. He then goes beyond the *Motetorum... Liber primus* to look at dedications of four later books in which Molinaro offers tributes to the memory of his uncle, Giovanni Battista Dalla Gostena. Dr. Poulos's essay brings us many new details about Molinaro's life and music.

In conclusion, these fourteen essays present a prodigious variety of material and approaches to the study of paratextual material in publications of early modern Latin writings and motets. Anyone dealing with publications of the sixteenth century could profitably use these studies as models in viewing the works they are studying in their full context.

Department of Music
University of Pittsburgh
USA – Pittsburgh, PA 15260
lsm@pitt.edu

# *"VOBIS PAGINA NOSTRA DEDICATUR"*
# DEDICATION IN CLASSICAL ANTIQUITY

HARM-JAN VAN DAM

## Introduction

In the French novel *Le roman bourgeois* of 1666 an imaginary book in four volumes is introduced which offers a complete discussion of literary dedication. The curious reader, fobbed off with no more than its table of contents, learns that the second chapter is entitled 'whether dedication of a book is absolutely necessary. This question is answered in the negative, against the view of several ancient and modern authors'.[1] Although it is true that dedication of a book was not absolutely necessary in antiquity, most ancient authors (and readers) would consider it normal, indeed essential, for literature immortalizes both the author and the addressee, as Pliny states, to give just one instance.[2] That is the reason why the ninth-century encyclopaedist Photius in his *Bibliotheke*, a large collection of summaries of literary works, pays much attention to the question if a book was dedicated to someone.[3] Accordingly, a great many ancient

[1] Antoine Furetière, *Le roman bourgeois. Ouvrage comique* (Paris: *Éditions Porteret*, 1927), pp. 259-260: 'examen general de toutes les questions qui se peuvent faire touchant la dédicace des livres, divisée en quatre volumes', p. 260: 'Chapitre II: Si la dédicace est absolument necessaire à un livre. Question décidée en faveur de la négative, contre l'opinion de plusieurs autheurs anciens et modernes'.

[2] Plin. *nat. praef.* 25: "Apion quidem grammaticus ... immortalitate donari a se scripsit ad quos aliqua componebat"; also e.g. Lact. *epitoma inst. praef.* 1: "tibi epitomam fieri, Pentadi frater, desideras, credo ut ad te aliquid scribam tuumque nomen ... celebretur ...".

[3] The following, about Phrynichus and his (lost) work Σοφιστικὴ παρασκευή, is a typical example: *Bibliotheke* 158: '(he) flourished during the reign of Marcus Aurelius and his son Commodus, to whom the work is dedicated and inscribed, "Phrynichus to Commodus Caesar, greeting". In the preface he exhorts Commodus to the pursuit of learning, at the same time praising his own work, of which he says that he had already composed thirty-seven books and dedicated them to the emperor ... In spite of his assertion that he dedicated the work to the emperor, he appears to have inscribed the separate books to different persons. Thus, the first, second, and third books are addressed to a certain Aristocles, in the hope that it may serve as an amusement and source of recreation for him on his birthday; the fourth to a certain Julian, a fellow-citizen and friend. The author adds that he had at first intended to dedicate the whole to Aristocles, but after by the royal decree he became a member of the great council at Rome, he decided to adopt Julian instead as

works are dedicated to someone: my provisional list of ancient dedications counts a few hundred books while leaving out many late authors and virtually all Christian ones.

Ancient and modern books do not only differ in the frequency of their dedication, there is a qualitative difference as well: Gérard Genette distinguishes between *dédier*, dedicate a work to someone, and *dédicacer*, to dedicate a single copy. In modern books the dedication of a work is generally characterized by typographical convention as *paratexte*, something outside the 'real' text: it is the only text on an otherwise empty page; yet this dedication is part of the (printed) book, reproduced by the printing process in every copy of one edition. We may inscribe a *particular* copy of the text to a particular friend.[4] Recently a writer in a letter to the editor asked what to do when you notice one of your books being offered in an internet auction extra expensive because it bears your personal dedication to an old friend who is still alive.[5] In antiquity this situation would not have been possible: although the dedication of an ancient work may be either part of the text itself or *paratexte*, the relation between single copy and work is different without the printing press. I will return to this point. In other respects, however, there are similarities between ancient and modern practice: ancient dedication, too, is done before the text gets underway, or at least in its beginning, mentioning a name is essential, and dedication is a public gesture even without the printing press. For, in a certain sense, the dedicatee is co-author of the work; this is a point made by Genette, and it is especially true of antiquity: the

his friend and associate in his labours and to make use of his services as the judge and critic of his writings. In spite of this promise, he dedicates the fifth book to a learned friend of his, named Menodorus, who had previously censured him for not having adequately investigated the inflexion of words…' (tr. by J.H. Freese (1920), cf. http://www.tertullian.org/fathers/photius_03bibliotheca.htm). Many aspects mentioned here will recur in the following, such as the dedicatee as judge, the dedication as an exhortation, multiple dedication, dedication of lost works etc.

[4] On *paratexte* and its importance for the dedication, and also on dedication of texts in general, see Gérard Genette, *Seuils* (Paris: Éd. du Seuil, 1987). On *dédier* (*dédicace d'oeuvre)* versus *dédicacer* (*dédicace d'exemplaire*) pp. 110-133; cf. also R.R. Nauta, *Poetry for Patrons. Literary Communication in the Age of Domitian* (Leiden: Brill, 2002), pp. 120 ff., and Demmy Verbeke, *"Ad musicae patronos" — Latijnse dedicaties en inleidende teksten in motettenbundels van componisten uit de Nederlanden (ca. 1550 – ca. 1600)*, 4 vols (PhD diss. Katholieke Universiteit Leuven, 2005), I, 12 ff.

[5] He was advised to buy the book and offer it to this friend a second time, now inscribing it with the wish that his financial problems would soon be over, see *De Groene Amsterdammer* of 01.VII.2005, p. 45.

work is for someone and it is for him because it is also "by him", he inspired it, or must approve of it, or *will* inspire it.[6]

The aim of this contribution is just to offer some general information concerning ancient dedication of texts: when, why and how did classical authors dedicate, what works, to whom and in what terms? Thus I hope to sketch a background for the more detailed studies on the dedication of Latin works and motets in the sixteenth century which form the real subject of this book. On the one hand I will try to give a general picture, on the other hand, I will draw attention to variation and complication. In this, I shall concentrate on the Roman world and focus on Latin literature, if only because almost all relevant material is from the first century BC and later — though much of it is actually written in Greek. The origins of classical dedication, however, lie in classical Greece.[7]

## Ways to dedicate

Basically an author can dedicate a work in one of three ways: by naming the dedicatee, by presenting him with the work, or by asking him for correction. These devices are often combined, but every single one is enough to convey to dedicatee and public: "this book is for so-and-so, for he is a special person". The author must put this into writing (for otherwise the dedication could not be known and is useless to the dedicatee), and he may do so by 1) addressing the dedicatee and stating that

[6] Genette, *Seuils*, p. 126. Him, for I do not know a book dedicated to a woman in antiquity (the love elegy is a different matter).

[7] On dedication of books in antiquity, see the older studies by Rudolfus Graefenhain, *De more libros dedicandi apud scriptores graecos et romanos obvio* (Marpurgi Cattorum, 1892) and Ioannes Ruppert, *Quaestiones ad historiam dedicationis librorum pertinentes* (Lipsiae, 1911) (earlier literature on pp. 7-8 there), as well as more recent work on both prefaces and dedications, also in medieval and renaissance literature: G. Simon, 'Untersuchungen zur Topik der Widmungsbriefe mittelalterlicher Geschichtsschreiber bis zum Ende des 12. Jahrhunderts', *Archiv für Diplomatik*, 4 (1958), 52-119; 5-6 (1959-60), 73-153, Tore Janson, *Latin prose prefaces. Studies in literary conventions*, Studia Latina Stockholmiensia, 13 (Stockholm: Almqvist och Wiksell, 1964), Zoja Pavlovskis, 'From Statius to Ennodius. A Brief History of Prose-Prefaces to Poems', *Rendiconti Istituto Lombardo delle Scienze e Lettere*, 101 (1967), 535-567, Peter White, 'The Presentation and Dedication of the *Silvae* and the Epigrams', *Journal of Roman Studies*, 64 (1974), 40-61, Raymond J. Starr, 'The circulation of literary texts in the Roman world', *Classical Quarterly*, 37 (1987), 213-223, Fritz Felgentreu, *Claudians* praefationes. *Bedingungen, Beschreibungen und Wirkungen einer poetischen Kleinform* (Stuttgart-Leipzig: Teubner, 1999), Nauta, *Poetry for patrons*, pp. 98-99, 103, 113, 120-131, 280-290, 374-378, Verbeke, *"Ad musicae patronos"*, now on http://hdl.handle.net/1979/160.

he presents him with this work and/or 2) that he requests criticism of his draft, or 3) by just mentioning the dedicatee's name in the beginning of his work.

In addressing the dedicatee and presenting him with the book, the author will use the terminology of dedication — unless he just mentions the name in the vocative. Unexpectedly perhaps, the Latin word *dedicare* is relatively rare in dedications, just as its Greek example ἀνατιθέναι.[8] *Dedicare* is first used by Phaedrus to dedicate the third book of his *Fables* (probably somewhere in the thirties A.D.) to Eutychus, then also by Pliny the Elder and by Statius in a prose-letter.[9] The quotation from Martial which is the title of my paper (Mart. 5.2.2) is actually not quite what we mean by dedication. *Dedicare* is, in fact, a technical expression for parting with an object on behalf of a religious instance and inscribing that object with the details of this cession[10], so its use in dedicating books is a rather violent metaphor. Apart from deifying the dedicatee, the word expresses at the same time that the author gives up his work, that it is not his any more, and indeed, by formally dedicating their work ancient authors did cede their 'copyright'. Similar terms are *emittere*, to send away, and *mittere* (Greek πέμπειν, ἀποστέλλειν), also *ferre*, *edere* (Greek φέρω, ἐκδιδόναι), publish, but in fact 'let go', *publicare*, make public. But *dedicare* also means that the author makes a present of his work (or pays his debts), and words like *dare*, *donare* (Greek δοῦναι), *donum*, *munus* are frequent.[11]

The other method of dedicating is, as I said, adressing someone. Greek προσφωνεῖν, 'to address, direct', is frequent: Photius uses it virtually exclusively. Cicero in his Letters once has the noun προσφώνησις in the sense of 'dedication' and elsewhere the Latin translation

[8] See *ThLL* V1 260, 60 ff. Not all forms of the word fit the hexameter, but enough of them do. On ἀνατιθέναι, see Graefenhain, *De more*, pp. 6, 29, 31.

[9] Phaedr. 3.1.30: "honori et meritis dedicans illum (librum) tuis", Plin. *nat. praef.* 12, Stat. *silv.* 4 *praef.* 1 (but in Quint. *inst. praef.* 4, 1 *dicare* must be read, not *dedicare*).

[10] 'Dedicatio', in *Paulys Realencyclopädie der classischen Altertumswissenschaft*, ed. Georg Wissowa, IV.2 (Stuttgart: A. Druckenmüller, 1901), 2356-2359 (Wissowa).

[11] *emittere* Quint. *inst. ep. ad* Trypho, *mittere* Catull. 65.15-16: "Sed tamen in tantis maeroribus, Ortale, mitto/ haec expressa tibi carmina Battiadae", Cic. *Att.* 12.6: "Tuus est enim profecto, quoniam quidem est missus ad te", Cens. 1.1. See also Meleager *AP* IV 1: "Μοῦσα φίλη, τίνι τάνδε φέρεις πάγκαρπον ἀοίδαν;", Vitruv. *Praef.*: "edere non audebam ... de architectura scripta ...", Stat. *silv. Praef.* 4: "epistola quam ad illum de editione Thebaidos meae publicavi". On the terminology of dedication (including the terms quoted below), see Graefenhain, *De more*, pp. 5-10, 27-32, on *dare, donare, mittere, ferre* and cognates in Martial's epigrams, see Nauta, *Poetry for Patrons*, p. 123 n. 108.

*adfatus.*[12] The Greek terms ἀναγράφειν and especially γράφειν πρὸς correspond to Latin *scribere ad*, which is probably the most common Latin term, regularly used by Cicero, like *tibi scribere.*[13]

Even just mentioning a name in the form of address, is enough to ensure that a book is dedicated to someone: in the first place, it is unclear what else this vocative could mean if not a dedication, but that mere address is a signal of dedication is proved by the elder Cato's famous phrase, repeatedly quoted in Latin literature *Orator est, Marce fili, vir bonus dicendi peritus.*[14] The late lexicographer Nonius Marcellus (who dedicated his own work to his son) informs us that the book to which this sentence belonged was actually called *On oratory to his son* (*Ad filium ... de oratore*). The use of the vocative case is also the point of an anecdote told by the younger Pliny: during a recitation the poet Passennus Paulus, a remote descendant of Propertius, opened a poem with the words *Prisce, iubes* ('Priscus, you ask me'), whereupon a certain Iavolenus Priscus cried out: 'I don't ask anything!'. This was a ridiculous remark, according to Pliny, who even doubts Priscus' mental sanity. Obviously Paulus had wished to dedicate a poem to Priscus, who failed to understand this social convention. Longer poems and books of poetry often bear a dedication in this form.[15]

[12] Cic. *Att.* 13.12.3 (= Shackleton Bailey 320.3): "iam Varro mihi denuntiaverat magnam sane et gravem προσφώνησιν", *Brut.* 13: "An mihi potuit, inquam, esse aut gratior ulla salutatio aut ad hoc tempus aptior quam illius libri, quo me hic adfatus quasi iacentem excitavit?" [dedication of Atticus' lost *liber annalis* to Cicero].

[13] Cic. *Lael.* 4: "in Catone Maiore, qui est scriptus ad te de senectute ... tum ad senem senex de senectute, sic hoc libro ad amicum", Lact. *epitoma inst.*,Varro *rust.* 1 *praef.* 1: "scribam tibi", Vitruv. *praef.* 3: "tibi scribere coepi".

[14] Cato *Ad fil. frg.* 14 J, quoted in Sen. *contr.* 1 *praef.* 9, Quint. *inst.* 12.1, cf. Plin. *epist.* 4.7.5, *al.* See Non. 143.7.

[15] Plin. *epist.* 6.15. Cf. e.g. Cic. *Brut.* 1: "Utrum difficilius aut maius esset negare tibi saepius idem roganti an efficere id quod rogares diu multumque, Brute, dubitavi" [cf. Statius to Stella in note 43], *Lael.* 4: "Cum enim saepe mecum ageres ut de amicitia scriberem aliquid... Itaque feci non invitus ut prodessem multis rogatu tuo", Hor. *epist.* 1.1.3-4: "quaeris, Maecenas", Sen. *dial.* 3.1: "exegisti a me, Novate", Scribon. *Praef.* 12: "Fateor itaque libenter unicas me tibi gratias agere, quod et prius quam rogaveris consummasti", Donatus *Commentarius in Vergilium Praef.*: "id quod nobis praescripseras", Hier. *epist.* 1.1: "postulasti, Innocenti carissime", Sidon *epist.* 9.1-2: "Exigis, domine fili, ... Quae iubes". On the request as a theme in prefaces and dedications, and expressions for requesting, see Janson, *Latin prose prefaces*, pp. 116-120; but his claim that *iubere* is a strong word only used in later antiquity (for instance Aus. *praefatiuncula* 3, 8) is incorrect. For address in poetry see e.g. Prop. 1.1.9: "Milanion nullos fugiendo, *Tulle*, labores / saevitiam durae contudit Iasidos", *Culex* 1: "Lusimus, *Octavi*, gracili modulante Thalia", Hor. *carm.* 1.1.1: *Maecenas*, atavis edite regibus (my italics: HJvD).

On the other hand, not *every* address means dedication — apart from the general address to the reader, which is obviously a different matter anyhow. In the beginning of Hesiod's *Works and Days*, the author announces his desire to tell (μυθησαίμην) true things to his brother Perses, and somewhat further on he addresses him,[16] but only in order to admonish him, for, as the poem makes clear, the two brothers had fallen out. In this case there can be no question of dedication, perhaps also because in archaic Greece dedication of a work of literature to an individual is less probable: dedication presupposes a certain level of literacy in society *and* a view of author and reader as individuals rather than as part of society or members of a group. Genette draws attention to addressing the Muses as an opening device from Homer onwards, but for the older period this does not represent a dedication: rather the archaic Muse is omniscient, inspires and dictates the work. Finally, we must distinguish between the dedication of single poems, such as that to Priscus for instance, and of books of poetry: many individual poems in Horace and the elegists, and even more in Statius and Martial are addressed and dedicated to a patron, but the book as such can be dedicated to one of them only, generally in a clear way.[17]

Two speeches or pamphlets by Isocrates, *Nicocles* and *Euagoras*, composed around 370 BC, may be seen as the earliest dedications: they address the ruler, the king of Cyprus, by name, at the outset, in a kind of introduction, and speak of giving and receiving and, at the end, of honouring.[18] The oldest special dedicatory device is probably the letter to the dedicatee: among the earliest examples of dedication after Isocrates are the letters preceding the book on *Conics* by the mathematician Apollonius of Perge, written around 245 BC and addressed to King Eudemus of

[16] I accept the reading Πέρσῃ, dative, in 10, not Πέρση, vocative, as it is in 27.

[17] Though there is some relationship between inspiration and dedication, see Genette, *Seuils*, p. 126. On the differences between dedicating or addressing a poem and dedicating a book, see Nauta, *Poetry for patrons*, pp. 91 ff., 106 ff., 128-129, 279 ff., and below.

[18] Ruppert, *Quaestiones*, pp. 8-16 in discussing the origins of dedication finds its first example in an elegy by Dionysius Chalcus addressed to a certain Theodorus (around 450 BC), preserved in Athen. 15.669D. However, longer and more formal dedications, to a superior or an equal, rather seem to be Hellenistic, taking their origin in the 4th Cent., see Isocrates *Nicocles* (*Orat*. 2) 1.1: "When men are in the habit, *Nicocles*, of bringing to you king's garments or brass or wrought gold … 22.2 Now, I thought that it would be the noblest and most profitable *gift* (δῶρον) and one most becoming me to *give* and you to *receive* (δοῦναι, λαβεῖν)… (end of the work: 54) Now I have exhorted you to the extent of my knowledge, and I *honour* you by these means" (tr. J.A. Freese, my italics: HJvD), *Euagoras* (*Orat*. 9) 1.

Pergamon (the first three books) and his successor Attalus, and those which the physicist Archimedes attached to some technical treatises, addressed to a certain Dositheus and to Gelo II tyrant of Syracuse around 220 BC.[19]

Such a letter of dedication may originally be a separate text, sent (or rather, presented) together with a copy of the work, which became attached to and copied together with the text. Or, more often, the author himself began his work with a short preface in the form of a letter and then, after a concluding formula like ἔρρωσο or *vale*, continued with the 'real' subject. These different formats cannot be discerned any more in our textual tradition. Moreover, there is no essential difference between dedicatory preface (*praefatio*) and dedicatory letter as far as content or *topoi* are concerned; such a preface may, or may not, take the form of a letter. On the other hand, there *is* a difference in kind between dedication and preface: both introduce a work, but a preface concentrates on why and how, a dedication on whom; a preface may but does not have to include a dedication.[20]

A given text can be called a letter if it has an opening formula such as "Greetings", or "Dear so-and-so", secondly the name of the addressee (in Latin letters this is often combined by a superscription in the form: A to B, A greets B), thirdly if it is in the form of an address (vocative case, 2nd person verbs), and fourthly if it ends with a formula.[21] In practice, either the opening or the closing formula or both may be left out in dedicatory letters. A metrical treatise by Servius, the commentator of Vergil, is introduced by a short letter with address and valediction. But some books have only an opening, such as those of the elder Seneca

[19] *De quadratura parabolae* and *Arenarius / Psammites*.

[20] "pourquoi et comment": Genette, *Seuils*, pp. 182 ff. In this respect my aims and scope are different from that of Janson in his *Latin prose prefaces*: Janson's corpus consists of prefaces defined as 'the introductory part of a long text...' and only of those in prose (pp. 9, 12-13), without distinguishing between those prefaces which are dedications and those which are not. Thus he recognises two main types of prefaces, the epistolary and the rhetorical, either of which may or may not be dedicatory (pp. 14-23). As a matter of course, the texts we study overlap, just as some strategies and topoi do, but see his p. 117: "the dedication is not treated here as a section of its own, and what little I have to say of the problems connected with it will appear below". Dramatic prologues, which have no dedication, are ignored by me, but included by Janson. On prologues and prefaces, see also Felgentreu, *Claudians* praefationes, chapters 1-2.

[21] Cf. e.g. Paolo Cugusi, *Evoluzione e forme dell'epistolografia latina nella tarda repubblica e nei primi due secoli dell'impero, con cenni sull'epistolografia preciceroniania* (Roma: Herder, 1983), pp. 47-67.

addressing his sons, or the work on prescriptions by the first-century pharmocologist Scribonius Largus dedicated to L. Cornelius Balbus, or that of the third-century encyclopaedist Solinus. This is also true of the well-known, elaborate letter by which the elder Pliny dedicated his *Natural History* to the Emperor Titus, with only the formula *Gaius Plinius Secundus Vespasiano suo Salutem*, but no formal ending. Pliny himself does qualify the text as a letter twice, in the beginning, and at the end when he states that he has added a table of content 'to this letter', in order to save the Emperor the trouble to read the book. The earliest Latin letter of dedication, written by Aulus Hirtius, the author of the eighth book of Caesar's *De bello gallico*, on the other hand, ends on *Vale* but has no opening formula, merely the vocative "Balbe".[22] Openings may well have been lost in our manuscripts; on the other hand, corrections may unduly normalize. Thus sometimes *vale* is added, unnecessarily, at the end of the dedicatory letter belonging to Avianus' *Fables* (early 5th century), which lacks a formal opening as well.[23]

A collection of letters can, of course, also be dedicated by a letter (just as a collection of poems may be dedicated by its opening poem). Such is the case with Pliny's *Epistles*, dedicated to his friend Septicius Clarus, praetorian prefect under Hadrian.[24] On the other hand, Seneca's letters are all written to Lucilius, but not one book is dedicated to him. Every letter has an addressee, but some longer letters, texts which stand on their own, *are* also dedicated in a certain sense: epistolary treatises addressed to one

[22] Archimedes in his *quadratura parabolae* has both χαίρειν and ἔρρωσο, and similarly Servius *De centum metris*: "clarissimo Albino Servius grammaticus. Tibi hunc libellum, praetextatorum decus, Albine, devovi ... Vale". The elder Seneca addressed each book of his *Controversies* to his sons, and they all begin with *Seneca Novato Senecae Melae filiis salutem*, but none of them has a concluding formula. Scrib. Larg. *Praef.*: "Scribonius Largus Callisto suo s.", Sol. *Praef*:. "Solinus Advento salutem", Plin. *nat. praef.* 1: "... Libros Naturalis Historiae ... natos apud me proxima fetura licentiore epistula narrare constitui tibi, iucundissime Imperator; sit enim haec tui praefatio ... (33) Quia occupationibus tuis publico bono parcendum erat, quid singulis contineretur libris, huic epistulae subiunxi", Hirt. *Gall.* 8.1: "Coactus assiduis tuis vocibus, Balbe, cum cotidiana mea recusatio non difficultatis excusationem, sed inertiae videretur deprecationem habere, rem difficillimam suscepi ... Vale".

[23] Avian. *fab. praef.*: "Dubitanti mihi, Theodosi optime, quonam litterarum titulo nostri nominis memoriam mandaremus, fabularum textus occurrit ...", Baehrens *PLM* V p. 35 *in app*:. vale *vulgo*: om. *codd.*

[24] Plin. *epist.* 1.1: "C. Plinius Septicio <Claro> suo s. Frequenter hortatus es, ut epistulas, si quas paulo curatius scripsissem, colligerem publicaremque. Collegi ...Vale". Sidonius' dedication of the first volume of his letters to his friend Constantius is virtually a pastiche of this letter.

person, such as the letters of Epicurus, to Herodotus on Physics and to Pythocles on Meteora, and similar technical treatises. Here also belong the long verse-epistles of Horace on poetry, *Epistles* II 1 and II 2 to Augustus and Florus, and especially of course, the *Epistula ad Pisones*, all of them with epistolary characteristics.[25] If we do accept these epistolary treatises, these single letters, as dedications, arguing that they combine address to a specific person with the wish for larger circulation, that would imply that in this case the whole text can be seen as dedication, that the dedication is not *paratexte*, nor part of the *texte*, but nothing but text.

The earliest letters to introduce collections of *poetry* are those in Statius' *Silvae*, and Martial's *Epigrams*, much later. Those of Statius especially, had a great vogue in late antiquity with poets like Ausonius, Sidonius, Venantius Fortunatus and Ennodius, and thus influenced renaissance prefaces.[26]

## Dedications and addressees

Let us now survey a number of dedications and make some observations: in the *appendix* I have collected and tried to group according to 'genre' (not in a technical sense of the word) a fair number of dedications.[27] As we see, dedication had its beginnings in hellenistic literature, and did become an important factor in the Greco-Roman world of the first century BC and later. The main reason for its popularity is the Roman system of patronage, which includes the Emperor and the court as patrons.

A first observation is that dedication is especially popular in didactical and technical literature. Thence the frequency of words for explaining and teaching such as δεικνύειν, used by Archimedes, for instance, or *docere*.[28] Up to the second century AD didactic poetry is more prominent, whereas in the second century and later technical prose takes over. Here we find many works which few classicists ever read nowadays, but which were very popular as long as ancient knowledge was still topical. A common *topos* in those dedications, but also in the dedications of

[25] Cf. *epist*. 2.1.1-4, 1.2.1, *ars* 5-6, 24.

[26] See Pavlovskis, 'From Statius to Ennodius' and below; and on renaissance prefaces, Verbeke, *"Ad musicae patronos"*, I, 18 ff. and below.

[27] The reader should keep in mind the reservations I made in the introductory paragraph.

[28] Archim. *Arenarius* 1.3: "ἐγὼ δὲ πειρασοῦμαί τοι δεικνύειν".

rhetorical and philosophical work, is that the dedicatee is eager to learn: 'I have written this book because you want to know everything' says Lucius Ampelius to his dedicatee Macrinus (perhaps the man who became emperor in 217), and according to Vegetius the emperor should know everything, and he hastens to add that, in fact, the emperor already *does* know it all.[29]

Some kinds of text do not lend themselves well to dedication: drama is the genre of showing, and although Quintilian speaks of prefaces in which Seneca and Pomponius discussed dramatic technique, I do not see that dedication could have played a part here.[30] Didactic poetry lends itself more easily to dedication than epic, but some epics do start by addressing the emperor. However, in this paper I will sidestep the intricacies of Silver epic and the dedicatory quality of their *prooemia* which praise the emperor and at the same time refuse to write a poem on him (*recusatio*).[31]

Who dedicates to whom and why? Given the underlying thought that literature makes one famous, there are roughly speaking two groups: one circle of peers, aristocrats, gentlemen, such as the Ciceronian circle where dedication is an industry, with people asking for and receiving books, as a tribute to their learning, or proof that they are one of the boys. Or also that of Sidonius and his friends in the fifth century, who are dedicating extremely elaborate and far-fetched literature to each other, in an attempt to keep the barbarians at bay, at least psychologically.[32] Most authors of

[29] Ampel. *Prol*:. "Lucius Ampelius Macrino suo salutem. Volenti tibi omnia nosse scripsi hunc librum memorialem, ut noris quid sit mundus....", Veg. *mil. Praef*:. "... neque quemquam magis decet vel meliora scire vel plura quam principem ... non quo tibi, imperator invicte, ista videantur incognita ...".

[30] Quint. *inst*. 8.3.31. What kind of prefaces they were is debated. Spalding's old commentary on Quintilian leaves it open (on the stage or in "editions"), Janson, *Latin prose prefaces*, p. 111 concludes that they were "epistolary prefaces in prose (or possibly in verse)", Elaine Fantham (*Roman Literary Culture. From Cicero to Apuleius* (Baltimore-London: Johns Hopkins Press 1999), p. 149) claims that they were "spoken introductions to recitations of their plays", see also Nauta, *Poetry for patrons*, p. 282 with n. 91.

[31] For a recent discussion, see Ruurd R. Nauta, 'The *recusatio* in Flavian poetry', in Ruurd R. Nauta, Harm-Jan van Dam, Johannes J.L. Smolenaars (eds.), *Flavian poetry* (Leiden: Brill, 2006), pp. 21-40. Note that invocation of/ dedication to the emperor and dedication to someone else occur in one and the same poem, Vergil's *Georgics*. The letter which Statius wrote about his *Thebaid* may have been a dedicatory one, see Stat. *silv*. 4. *praef*. 17-8.

[32] See Ralph W. Mathisen, *Roman aristocrats in barbarian Gaul. Strategies for survival in an age of transition* (Austin: Univ. of Texas Press, 1993), pp. 105-118: "The pursuit of literary studies as a unifying element".

technical prose are aristocrats. The other group is that of clients and patrons — although the word *cliens*, is hardly ever used; the terminology is always that of friendship. Patrons are aristocrats, kings and emperors, but it is good to realize that the poets themselves are rarely poor (Phaedrus is an exception): the Augustan poets are all of equestrian status, and Statius and Martial were not at all poor.[33] The highest goal was, of course, to reach the Emperor, who was in a different range from both client-authors and aristocrats, and writers sometimes thank their patron for his brokerage, as Scribonius Largus does.[34] It is remarkable that, though the Golden Age of Patronage is, of course, the time of Augustus and Maecenas, we do find quite a number of dedications to Emperors who are less popular with historiographers, such as Tiberius and Commodus.[35] There is one other large category: modern books, especially scholarly ones, are sometimes dedicated by sons and daughters to their father. This is relatively rare in antiquity, whereas the reverse is frequent: Cicero dedicated *De officiis* to his son Marcus, Plutarch an essay on the *Timaeus* to his two sons, the elder Seneca and Artemidorus addressed several books to their sons, as we shall see, and Sidonius the eighth book of his Letters, to mention just a few.[36]

Dedications of prose-works are sometimes repeated over and over: in each preface, the elder Seneca presents an other famous orator from the past to his sons. In a similar but less sophisticated way Columella, writing on agriculture, addresses his neighbour and dedicatee Publius Silvinus in every new book, from the second book onwards by just mentioning his name in each first sentence without ever using new dedicatory

[33] See e.g. Nauta, *Poetry for patrons*, especially pp. 1-34, also Peter White, 'Positions for poets in early imperial Rome', in Barbara K. Gold (ed.), *Literary and artistic patronage in ancient Rome* (Austin: Univ. of Texas Press, 1982), pp. 50-66.

[34] Scrib. 12: "... non es passus cessare tuae erga me pietatis officium tradendo scripta mea latina medicinalia deo nostro Caesari, quorum potestatem tibi feceram" (so Scribonius had already given a hint to the dedicatee, Callistus). On brokerage (as for instance in Stat. *silv. praef.* 5. 7-12 and *silv.* 5.1): Nauta, *Poetry for patrons*, pp. 21-22, 67, 193-194, 342-348, 364.

[35] To Tiberius: Valerius Maximus, Velleius Paterculus, Germanicus' *Aratea*, to Commodus: Oppian's *Halieutica*, Pollux'*Onomasticon*, Phrynichus' *Sophistikè paraskeué* (only in epitome, but see note 3). For the proverbial Augustan age of patronage cf. the poem written by Robert Frost for the inauguration of J.F. Kennedy on 20.I.1961, entitled *Dedication*: "... The glory of a next Augustan age... / A golden age of poetry and power / Of which this noonday's the beginning hour".

[36] Perhaps Livy dedicated one or more philosophical works to his son, see Quint. *inst.* 10.1.39 and Sen. *epist.* 100.9.

topoi — except for book X, the poem on gardening, in which he addresses his friend both in the prose-preface and in its first hexameter.[37] In this last respect he is a trendsetter: he is imitated by the late agricultural writer Palladius who dedicated *De insitione*, the fourteenth and last book, in verse, of his prose-work on farming to a certain Pasiphilus both in the preface and in the first line of the poem. This technique of the prose dedication followed by a verse dedication is typical of Ausonius and Sidonius, and this in its turn could well be a major influence on the renaissance practice of ever-expanding prefaces and combinations of letter and poem.[38]

Other authors are less profuse: Quintilian addresses Vitorius Marcellus in three prefaces out of twelve books, but also at the end of the whole work: "this was, Marcellus Vitorius, what I had to say about ...". This kind of repetition of the dedication in an epilogue occurs elsewhere too: Phaedrus, having dedicated his 3rd book of fables to Eutychus, comes back to him in its last poem, *Ad Eutychum*, and there explicitly asks for a reward, saying 'and make it snappy, please, for I could be dead otherwise', thus revealing his low social status.[39] Propertius does this more subtly: his first poem, about Cynthia, is addressed to Tullus; the epigram on which the book ends is a *sphragis*, a seal or signature, in which the author tells something about himself. In this sense, the *sphragis* may be considered as the counterpart to the dedication: the poet opens with

[37] Colum. 1 *praef.*: "... Quas ego causas, Publi Silvine,...", 2 *praef*:. "Quaeris ex me, Publi Silvine, quod ego sine cunctatione non recuso docere, cur priore libro ...", 3 *praef*:. "Hactenus arvorum cultus, ut ait praestantissimus poeta. Nihil enim prohibet nos, P. Silvine, ...", 4 *praef.:* "Cum de vineis conserendis librum a me scriptum, Publi Silvine" etc., 10 *praef.*: "Faenoris tui, Silvine, quod stipulanti spoponderam tibi, reliquam pensiunculam percipe ..." (beginning of the poem) "Hortorum quoque te cultus, Silvine, docebo". Repeated dedication also: Vegetius to Theodosius I: each of his four books on the military, and the end of 1, 3 and 4; Firmicus Maternus: almost all books of his *Mathesis* to his Friend Lollianus Mavortius, also the end of books 6-8.

[38] Pallad. 14,1: "Pasiphile, ornatus fidei, cui iure fatemur", cf. Auson. *Bissula* (Green 130-1), with a dedication in prose and one in poetry to his friend Paulus, followed by one to the general reader, similarly his *Cento* (Green 132-4). The 'double letter', poetry and prose, is a characteristic of Ausonius' letters, cf. Pavlovskis, 'From Statius to Ennodius', pp. 545 ff., also Sidon. *carm.* 15, 22 and below. In Verbeke, *"Ad musicae patronos"*, there are 132 preliminary Latin letters, mainly of dedication, and 50 Latin poems (sometimes more than one poem per book).

[39] Quint. *inst.* 1 *prooem.* 6: "Quod opus, Marcelle Vitori, tibi dicamus", 4 *prooem* 1, 6 *prooem.* 1, 12.11.31: "Haec erant, Marcelle Vitori,...". On Phaedrus, see note 9 and 3. *Epil.* 8 ff.: "Brevitatis nostrae praemium ut reddas peto, / quod es pollicitus; exhibe vocis fidem, / Nam vita morti propior est cotidie; / et hoc minus redibit ad me muneris, / quo plus consumet temporis dilatio"; see also n. 37 and Graefenhain, *De more*, pp. 37-38.

his patron, but he ends with himself. Propertius, however, combines the *sphragis* with the concluding dedication, for this poem, like the first one, is addressed to his patron Tullus. The most sophisticated repetition of naming the dedicatee at the end is that in Horace's *Odes*, where Maecenas, addressed in 1.1, is *not* named in 3.30, the last poem of the volume, which is, again, a *sphragis*, but where the *metre* of 1.1 is repeated for the first and only time.[40]

Finally, consecutive books of a work may be dedicated to different persons: Varro, over eighty years of age, promised three books on agriculture to his wife Fundania, but after the first he changed his mind and addressed the second to an otherwise unknown cattle-farmer Turranius Niger, and the third to a Pinnius.[41] Multiple dedication could be advantageous to poor or ambitious men, as the example of Phrynichus shows.[42] However, sometimes it rather seems to suggest bad planning, as in the case of the famous Dreambook by Artemidorus: the first and second book are dedicated to Cassius Maximus (perhaps the sophist Maximus of Tyre), in the preface to the third book the author explains to Cassius that he had thought to have fulfilled his wishes (!) in two books, but then discovered there was more to be said; this (short) third book however, which is again dedicated to him, fills all the gaps. Then, in the fourth book, Artemidorus addresses his son, saying that people tell him his book is incomplete and shallow; therefore he composed this addition especially for his son. At the end of this book he writes: "son, this is all there is to say. Now I add another book" (!). And this fifth book is, again, for his son.

## Themes and *topoi*

In dedications the author may tell something about the genesis of his work and explain what it is all about and how it should be read. This is prefatory rather than dedicatory material. Apart from that, in dedications we meet with various *topoi* about the relationship between dedicator and

[40] Prop. 1.1.9 and 1.22.1-2, Hor. *carm* 1.1.1 and 3.30. On the *sphragis*, see Nisbet-Hubbard on Horace *carm*. 2.20, pp. 335-336.

[41] Varro *rust*. 1: "Otium si essem consecutus, Fundania, commodius tibi haec scriberem, quae nunc ... senex ... Quocirca scribam tibi tres libros", 2 *praef*:. "tibi, Niger Turrani noster ... de re pecuaria breviter ac summatim percurram", 3 1.1 "Pinni... (3.1.10): "haec ad te misi".

[42] See note 3. Photius mentions ten different dedicatees for the 37 books.

dedicatee and about the contents. A prominent theme is self-disparagement by the author, frequently by playing down the importance of the book. Since Catullus' dedicatory poem to Nepos, literary works are coyly designated as 'a booklet' (*libellus*), 'trifles' (*nugae*). The word *libellus* returns for instance in Phaedrus and Luxorius, and no poet has it more often than Martial; in one of the first presentation-poems of book 4 he flaunts his imitation of Catullus.[43] Vegetius and Palladius even call their large prose-treatises short *libelli*, in imitation of the elder Pliny, as I suspect, who explicitly quotes Catullus and refers to his own massive encyclopaedia as *nugae* — surely tongue in cheek.[44] In Ausonius the word *libellus* occurs over 20 times, and in the dedication of his *Eclogae*, he quotes Catullus' opening literally (one of the few identified quotations in Latin literature), capping it immediately by qualifying his own book as an ugly rough *libellus*.[45] Most critics agree that Catullus' dedicatory poem for Cornelius Nepos cannot have introduced all of his poetry as we know it, for that would have made a bulky book indeed by ancient standards; but even if this poem originally was the dedication of a slim volume, a real *libellus*, it is clear that we must not believe the poet's self-disparagement: the confident prayer for immortality of the last lines alone is enough to prove that. Indeed, we do not take any of these authors at their word in their pseudo-modesty and self-humiliation. Statius in his prefaces claims to be afraid that critics will condemn his poetry as unimportant, for the poems *are* trifles, the work of a hasty hack. However, in his first preface he puts himself on a par with Homer and Vergil, who also composed *lusus*, trifles. Moreover, in his fourth preface he states that this

[43] Catull. 1.1-4: "... libellum/ ... namque tu solebas / meas esse aliquid putare nugas, ... 10 plus uno maneat perenne saeclo", Phaedr. 4 *praef.* 14: "(Ad Particulonem) quartum libellum cum vacabit perleges", Mart. 4.10: "Dum novus est nec adhuc rasa mihi fronte libellus,/ pagina dum tangi non bene sicca timet, / i, puer, et caro perfer leve munus amico / qui meruit nugas primus habere meas", Statius *Silvae* 1 *Praef.*: "Diu multumque dubitavi, Stella (see Cicero in n. 15), ... an hos libellos, qui mihi subito calore et quadam festinandi voluptate fluxerunt... dimitterem", Luxorius *Ad Faustum* 10 (*PLM* 4, 441 Baehrens), Sidon. *epist.* 9.16.1.

[44] Pallad. 14.3: "bis septem parvos, opus agricolare, libellos", Veget. *praef.* 1: "parvo libello, quicquid de maximis rebus semperque necessariis requirendum credis, invenias", 1.28, cf. Servius *De centum metris praef.*, Plin. *nat. praef. 1*: "namque tu solebas nugas esse aliquid meas putare, ut obiter emolliam Catullum conterraneum meum (agnoscis et hoc castrense verbum): ille enim, ut scis, permutatis prioribus syllabis duriusculum se fecit quam volebat existimari a Veraniolis suis et Fabullis", *praef.* 12: "... libellos...", see also n. 46.

[45] Auson. *ecl.* 1.1-5: "Cui dono lepidum novum libellum?', / Veronensis ait poeta quondam / inventoque dedit statim Nepoti. / At nos inlepidum, rudem libellum, / burras, quisquilias ineptiasque, / credemus gremio cui fovendum?".

book counts more poems than earlier books, in order to teach his unfair critics a lesson. The word *ludere*, to write unimportant things, also occurs in the dedication of the Pseudo-Vergilian *Culex* to Octavius / Octavian / Augustus, and a general attitude of humility towards the rich patron or Emperor is common: the author of *Ciris*, addressed to Messalla, adduces his youth and inexperience as an excuse for his poor poetry, nevertheless the result of endless, even nightly, labour. Again, the elder Pliny, scholar, statesman and friend of the emperor calls himself mediocre — surely insincerely.[46]

Another dedicatory theme is that of inspiration, frequent in poetry: the old view that the Muses and Apollo or other gods of poetry inspire the poet remains in existence: after his dedication to Octavian, the author of the *Culex* claims that Apollo will inspire him.[47] Manilius goes somewhat further: in dedicating his astronomical poem to the Emperor Tiberius he also claims that Tiberius gave him the necessary strength; then he goes on to address Mercury for inspiration.[48] Another direction

[46] Stat. *silv.* 1 *praef.* 8-9 (Courtney): "nec quisquam est inlustrium poetarum qui non aliquid operibus suis stilo remissiore praeluserit", 3 *praef.* 1-4: "Tibi certe, Polli dulcissime ... non habeo diu probandam libellorum istorum temeritatem, cum scias multos ex illis in sinu tuo subito natos", 4 *Praef.* 24-7: "quare ergo plura in quarto Silvarum quam in prioribus? ne se putent aliquid egisse, qui reprehenderunt ut audio, quod hoc stili genus edidissem", *Culex* 1: "Lusimus, Octavi, gracili modulante Thalia", 3: "lusimus", *Ciris* 36 ff.: "tale te vellem, iuvenum doctissime, ... intexere chartis, / ... Sed quoniam ad tantas nunc primum nascimur artes, / nunc primum teneros firmamus robore nervos, / haec tamen interea quae possumus, in quibus aevi / prima rudimenta et iuvenes exegimus annos, / accipe dona meo multum vigilata labore/ promissa". The author is an insignificant person with a small gift and his words can never match his patron's deeds: *Pan. Mess.* 1 ff.: "Te, Messalla, canam, quamquam me cognita virtus / Terret: ut infirmae nequeant subsistere vires, / Incipiam tamen. At meritas si carmina laudes / Deficiant, humilis tantis sim conditor actis, / Nec tua praeter te chartis intexere quisquam / Facta queat, dictis ut non maiora supersint. / Est nobis voluisse satis, nec munera parva / Respueris". See Plin. *nat. praef.* 12: "levioris operae hos tibi dedicavi libellos. nam nec ingenii sunt capaces, quod alioqui in nobis perquam mediocre erat". On *ludere*, see e.g. Walter Wimmel, *Kallimachos in Rom* (Wiesbaden, 1960), pp. 295 296, on various prefatory topoi of incompetence Janson, *Latin prose prefaces*, pp. 124 ff., 145-146 (on diminutives), on Statius' self-disparagement in prefaces e.g. Harm-Jan van Dam, *Statius Silvae Book II. A Commentary* (Leiden: Brill, 1984), p. 53; on the epic ambitions of the *Silvae*, see Bruce Gibson in Nauta-van Dam-Smolenaars, *Flavian poetry*, pp. 163 ff.

[47] The poem *Aetna* is not dedicated, but does claim Apollo as an inspirator: 4 ff. *Culex* 12 ff.: "Latonae magnique Iovis decus, aurea proles,/ Phoebus erit nostri princeps et carminis auctor".

[48] Manilius *Astronomica* 7 ff.: "hunc mihi tu, Caesar, patriae princepsque paterque, qui regis augustis parentem legibus orbem / concessumque patri mundum deus ipse mereris, / das animum viresque facis ad tanta canenda....", 30: "tu princeps auctorque sacri, Cyllenie, tanti ...".

was taken by Germanicus in his *Aratea*, his translation of the Greek *Phainomena* by Aratus, which the prince dedicated to his adoptive father Tiberius. Aratus began his poem with the words "Let us begin with Zeus", one of the most popular quotations of antiquity (even in the New Testament: *Acts* 17:28). Statius alludes to these words when in the preface of his fourth book of *Silvae* he states that he never began any work without invoking the divinity of the Emperor. Germanicus may well be the source of this conceit, for he boldly states: "Aratus began with Zeus, but I adore *you*, father, you are my beginning, your divinity will inspire and help me". In a similar way Ovid, in the first book of his *Fasti*, presents his dedicatee Germanicus as his Apollo (the God of Clarus), his divine inspiration.[49]

This brings us to a last item, or rather, a complex of factors, that is the relation of dedication to publication. As we saw, one signal that a work is dedicated is a request for criticism; moreover, dedicating means relinquishing all your rights — that what we would call 'copyright', which did not exist in antiquity. The words of 'sending' and 'giving' which we have seen mean that, in offering a manuscript, the author also gives the dedicatee the right to put his work into circulation. For anyone had the right to multiply a text, and authors were careful to ensure that incorrect texts or texts they did not want to divulge were corrected or taken back. Thus Cicero repeatedly asked his friend Atticus to make corrections in books, in his own and other people's copies, and to make it known that the text was changed, with various results: some of them have entered our manuscript tradition, others have disappeared.[50] Apollonius of Perge in his

[49] Statius *silv. 4 praef.*: "reor equidem aliter quam invocato numine maximi imperatoris nullum opusculum meum coepisse", Germ. 1 ff.: "Ab Iove principium magno deduxit Aratus, / carminis at nobis, genitor, tu maximus auctor, / te veneror, tibi sacra fero doctique laboris / primitias. probat ipse deum rectorque satorque ... pax tua tuque adsis nato numenque secundes", Ov. *fast*. 1.1 ff.: "excipe pacato, Caesar Germanice, voltu / hoc opus et timidae derige navis iter, / ... devoto numine dexter ades./ ... adnue conanti per laudes ire tuorum / deque meo pavidos excute corde metus./ da mihi te placidum, dederis in carmina vires / ingenium voltu statque caditque tuo. / pagina iudicium docti subitura movetur / principis, ut Clario missa legenda deo", Tib. 2.1.35: "Huc ades aspiraque mihi" (= Messalla), Val. Max. 1.1: "Te igitur huic coepto... certissima salus patriae, Caesar, invoco", Lact. *inst praef.*: "opus nunc nominis tui auspicio incohamus, Constantine imperator maxime"; see also n. 56.

[50] In *Att*. 12.6a.3 (SB 243) Cicero asked Atticus to change "Eupolis" into "Aristophanes" in *Orator* 29, in his own and other peoples' copies, and this was done; similarly his wish (*Att*. 13.2.3 = 251,3) that *inhibere* were changed back into *sustinere* in *Academica* 2.94 was fulfilled, but his mistake in *pro Ligario* 33, where Corfidius' presence is mentioned although he was already dead, lives on in our texts in spite of his request to Atticus to delete the name (13.44.3 = SB 336,3).

*Conics* already complained that "... it happened that some persons also, among those whom I have met, have got the first and second books before they were corrected". In other words, books could be distributed by a book-seller / publisher, when the author had given him his master copy, but they could also be dedicated to a friend or patron instead, who would show the work to his friends and multiply it, in order to give away copies — if he liked it. Publishing by way of patrons or friends, such as Cicero's friend Atticus, is the older method. Cicero often sent manuscripts to Atticus, and in his letters he made it clear whether it was to be reproduced as such and brought into circulation, or whether he wished to have a look at it first.[51] When the patron brought the book into circulation by copying and handing out manuscripts, he included the letter of presentation or dedicatory poem, for all the world to see. This is true of the letters preceding Statius' *Silvae*: the first addressing his friend Stella is incomplete, but the letter preceding the second book, to Atedius Melior, ends on a telling phrase: if Melior dislikes the poetry, nobody will read it. Ausonius in the introduction to his *Cento* closely imitates it. That is to say publication of the work depends on, or rather, amounts to, circulation of copies of this one copy which is dedicated to Melior. By taking care of this, Melior changes the dedication of one copy into a dedication of the work as a whole; in Genette's terms: what was *dédicacer* becomes *dédier*, just as the poet had intended all along.[52]

Sometimes a poet asked his patron or friend for correction before publication, something we can only know if the request lives on in our textual tradition: thus Martial's book six opens with a poem requesting Julius Martialis to correct the epigrams with his fine ear before the book is ready

[51] Cic. *Att.* 13.21a.1 (SB 327): "scripsi enim ad librarios ut fieret tuis, si tu velles, describendi potestas. Ea vero continebis quoad ipse te videam; quod diligentissime facere soles cum a me tibi dictum est", 13.22.3 (SB 329): "scripta nostra nusquam malo esse quam apud te, sed ea tum foras dari cum utrique nostrum videbitur", *Att.* 15.1a.2 (SB 378): "Brutus noster misit ad me orationem suam habitam in contione Capitolina petivitque a me ut eam ne ambitiose corrigerem ante quam ederet".

[52] Statius *silv. praef.* 2: "Haec qualiacumque sunt, Melior carissime, si tibi non displicuerint, a te publicum accipiant; si minus, ad me revertantur", Plin. *epist.* 9.25.3, Balbus *praef.* "et si meretur publica conversatione sufferre universorum oculos, a te potissimum incipiat", Auson. *praefatio* 4.17: "ignoscenda teget, probata tradet", *cento nuptialis* 48-50: "... sin aliter, aere dirutum facies ut cumulo carminis in fiscum suum redacto redeant versus unde venerunt, Vale", Sidon. *carm.* 3.7: "si probat, emittat, si damnat carmina celet", *epist.* 5.17.11: "si placet, edentes fovete, si displicet, delentes ignoscitote", Nauta, *Poetry for patrons*, pp. 125, 279, 281-284, van Dam, *Statius*, p. 53.

to be read by Domitian.[53] It is possible that he did correct the poems, and that we are reading the result, but in other cases it is clear that we cannot take these requests at face-value, for example when there would be no time for it before what we know to be the moment of publishing. So this request is in most cases fictional and just part of the standard vocabulary of modesty.[54] Authors did not really think that their fine dedication copy, trimmed and rubricated, would be returned to them by a displeased patron; and they could also use the topos that the patron had pressed them for a book, or asked for information. Apart from the examples above, there is Quintilian's letter to the bookseller Trypho, who is asked to provide a perfect edition of the *Institutio oratoria*. Actually, this seems to be an anomaly for it is made clear in this letter, and in the book itself, that the *Institutio oratoria* is dedicated to Vitorius Marcellus and not to the addressee of the letter; although the letter contains several dedicatory topoi of modesty. Here we have a case where an opening letter does *not* represent a dedication, and we should expect that Quintilian had not wished to include it.[55] However, Sidonius may imitate Quintilian by dividing dedication and edition between two persons, which would suggest that in the fifth century already the letter to Trypho was included in Quintilian's text.[56] The reverse may be true for Cicero's *Academica* which

[53] Mart. 6.1: "Sextus mittitur hic tibi libellus, / in primis mihi care Martialis: / quem si terseris aure diligenti, / audebit minus anxius tremensque / magnas Caesaris in manus venire".

[54] See Nauta, *Poetry for patrons*, pp. 123-128, who shows that Martial's requests for correction in 5.80 and 12 *praef.* 22-6 are fictional. For other requests for correction, see for instance Iustin. *praef.* 5: "ad te non cognoscendi magis quam emendandi causa transmisi", Sidon. *epist.* 1.1: "sed scilicet tibi parui tuaeque examinationi has non recensendas (hoc enim parum est) sed defaecandas, ut aiunt, limandasque commisi".

[55] See note 15, Quint. *inst. ep. ad Trypho* I: "Efflagitasti cotidiano convicio ut libros quos ad Marcellum meum de institutione oratoria scripseram iam emittere inciperem. Nam ipse eos nondum opinabar satis maturuisse...", III: "Sed si tantopere efflagitantur quam tu adfirmas, permittamus vela ventis et oram solventibus bene precemur. Multum autem in tua quoque fide ac diligentia positum est, ut in manus hominum quam emendatissimi veniant".

[56] Sidonius dedicated the first book of his letters to his friend Constantius in 469. Only when he published his collected letters in 7 books, in 477, did he dedicate the whole work to his friend, by including a final letter (7.18) beginning with: "a te principium, tibi desinet" (a quotation from Verg. *buc.* 8.11, see also n. 49). Book 8 begins with a dedication to Petronius who 'commanded' Sidonius to publish more letters: "... etiam scrinia Averna petis eventilari... morem geremus iniunctis". In its last letter, however, 8.16, Sidonius explains that Petronius did the correction of this book, but that Sidonius dedicates it to Constantius all the same: "... perveniretque in manus vestras volumen istud alieno periculo, obsequio meo". At the end of book 9 Sidonius repeats that the first eight books were for Constantius: *epist.* 9.16.1: "ceteris octo... quos ad Constantium scripsi".

he wanted to dedicate to Varro, but there is no letter attached to the work. A dedicatory letter of sorts which we *do* know is found in Cicero's *Ad Familiares* and has a different manuscript tradition. The story of the *Academica* is intricate (we have two different versions of it, both incomplete, one of the rare examples when an earlier version was not suppressed), and this letter seems unfit for dedication, but perhaps the 'real' letter of dedication has just disappeared from the manuscript tradition. Or perhaps in this rare case the fact that Varro is a speaker in the dialogue suffices, without any of our three necessary devices for dedicating.[57] Flavius Josephus in the preface of his *Contra Apionem* only speaks *of*, not *to* Epaphroditus; nevertheless we do assume that the treatise is dedicated to him.

There are other instances of complicated or less clear-cut dedication: poems within in a book of lyric poetry or epigrams or poetic epistles may be addressed to someone, and these poems are, or were, dedicated to their addressee; but the book as a whole is a different matter: there can be only one dedication of it, otherwise different versions of texts would be circulating. Thus the poems were 'published', since the author had given them to their addressees, but an unknown percentage of these single poems was republished as part of a book. Single poems could still be copied if their dedicatees wished them to be, but in collecting his poems and dedicating them to a single patron, the poet hopes and expects that this new text will be authoritative. The dedicatee must take care of that, and giving a copy to all the addressees will help. This is roughly how it worked for the Augustan poets, and also for Statius. Martial who composed many, short poems, is original. Throughout his books of epigrams around 45 presentation poems are scattered, that is to say poems which refer to the gift of a book. This has sometimes been supposed to mean that Martial dedicated 45 smaller books (*libelli*) to different patrons, later to collect those into 14 books of epigrams. However, recently it has been shown that Martial dedicated only books of collected poetry, always by a prefatory letter or poem to one special person; and that he dedicated

[57] Cicero planned, hesitated and endlessly asked Atticus for advice whether or not to dedicate something to Varro, for which he chose his revised version of the *Academica*, see *Att*. 13.12.3 (SB 320), 13.13-14.1 (SB 321), 13.14-15.1 (322), 13.16.1 (323), 13.18 (325)13.19.3-5 (326), 13.21a.1 (327), 13.22.1 (329), 13.23.2 (331), 13.24.1 (332), 13.25.3 (333), 13.35-36.2 (334), 13.44.2 (336). That Cicero is speaking of dedication is clear, especially from 320 and 325: "libros ad Varronem". Apart from that he tries very much to make Atticus responsible for the book in some way or another. The letter to Varro accompanying the four books *Academica* is *Fam*. 9.8 (SB 254).

the same book to other people as well, who might read 'their' dedication poem somewhere in the book.[58] So Martial's epigrams are a case of 'multiple dedication' scattered throughout the books. We may compare other forms of original or anomalous dedication, such as the technique of the prose dedication followed by a verse dedication in later Latin, which we have seen earlier, or Claudian's way of introducing his occasional poems addressed to the high and mighty: most of his (hexameter) poems have poetical introductions in a different metre, which in a few cases represent dedications.[59] All these variations, which tend to give the dedication more importance and multiply it, may also point a way to renaissance practices of variation on and expansion of ancient examples. The rest of this book will show how authors and musicians used or ignored antiquity.

FACULTEIT DER LETTEREN
VU University Amsterdam
NL – 1081 HV Amsterdam
hj.van.dam@let.vu.nl

[58] See Nauta, *Poetry for patrons*, pp. 279 ff.

[59] The prefaces of *III Cons. Honorii* and *Cons. Malli Theodosii* both by implication; the second book of *De raptu Proserpinae* is explicitly dedicated by its elegiac preface to Florentinus *praefectus urbi* in 396.

## Appendix
## Dedications in Classical Texts

**Didactic poetry:** Nicander *Alexipharmaka*, *Theriaka*, Lucretius *De rerum natura*, Germanicus *Aratea*, Vergilius *Georgica*, Horatius *Ad Pisones*, Ovidius *Fasti*, Manilius *Astronomica*, Columella *De re rustica* 10, Palladius *De insitione*, Oppianus *Halieutica*

**Technical prose:** Apollonius *Conica*, Archimedes *Arenarius*, *De quadratura parabolae*, Parthenius *Erotika Pathemata*, Varro *De lingua latina*, Varro *De re rustica* (1-3, 4 ff.), Vitruvius *De architectura*, Scribonius Largus *Compositiones*, Columella *De re rustica*, Onasander *Strategikos*, Plinius *Naturalis Historia*, Balbus *Militaria*, Polyaenus *Strategemata*, Galenus *several "unpublished" treatises*, Artemidorus *Oneirokritika*, Apollodorus of Damascus *Poliorcetica*, L. Ampelius *Liber memorialis*, Pollux *Onomasticon*, Solinus *De mirabilibus mundi*, Censorinus *De die natali*, Nonius Marcellus *De compendiosa doctrina*, Vegetius *Epitome rei militaris*, Donatus *Commentary on Vergil*, Palladius *Opus agriculturae*, Servius *De centum metris*, Caelius Aurelianus *De morbis acutis*, Hesychius *Lexicon*

**Rhetoric:** *Rhetorica ad Herennium*, Cicero *De oratore*, *Brutus*, *Orator*, Dionysius Halic. *De compositione verborum*, Apollonius of Pergamon *Techne*, Valerius Maximus *Dicta et facta memorabilia*, Seneca *Controversiae* (9 books), Tacitus *Dialogus de oratoribus*, Longinus *Peri Hupsous*, Quintilianus *Institutio oratoria*, Iulius Paris *Excerpt from Valerius Maximus*

**Philosophy:** Epicurus *Ad Herodotum*, *Ad Pythoclen*, Cicero *Academica* (?), *De officiis*, *De finibus bonorum ac malorum*, *Paradoxa Stoicorum*, *Topica*, *Laelius*, *Cato maior*, Seneca *All dialogues*, Arrianus *Enchiridion Epicteti*, Lactantius *De mortibus persecutorum*, *Epitoma Divinarum institutionum*, Tertullianus *De fuga in persecutione*, Augustinus *Many treatises*

**Lyric poetry:** Catullus, Propertius I-II, Tibullus, Hor. *Iambi*, *Sermones*, *Epistulae*, *Carmina*, Anonymus *Ciris*, *Culex*, *Panegyricus Messallae*, *Laus Pisonis*, *Elegiae in Maecenatem*, Statius *Silvae* 1, 2, 3, 4, 5.1, Martialis 1, 2, 8, 9, 12 (letters), 3, 5, 6, 10, 11 (poems), and several other poems, Optatianus *De figuris* (Constantine), Ausonius *various poems and letters*, Claudianus *De raptu Proserpinae II* (*Cons. Mallii Theodori*, *3rd cons. Honorii*), Sidonius Apollinaris *Many poems and letters*, Luxorius

**Epic:** Lucanus, Valerius Flaccus, Statius

**Miscellaneous:** Isocrates *Nicocles*, *Euagoras*, Hirtius *De Bello gallico VIII*, Velleius Paterculus *Historia romana*, Phaedrus *Fables*, Avianus *Fables*, Josephus *Contra Apionem*, *Jewish Archaeology*, Lucas *Gospel*, *Acts*, Plinius *Epistulae*, Justinus *Excerpt from Pomp. Trogus*, Plutarchus *Peri philadelphias*, *Explicatio Timaei*, *al*., Lucianus *Various essays*, Philostratus *Vitae sophistarum*, *Scriptores Historiae Augustae* 13 of 21 Lives

# RECIPROCAL AUTHORISATION: THE FUNCTION OF DEDICATIONS AND DEDICATORY PREFACES IN THE 15TH- AND 16TH-CENTURY 'ARTES ANTIQUITATIS'

Karl A.E. Enenkel

This inquiry focuses on a group of texts which have hardly been studied in the last two hundred years: the dedications of early modern Latin treatises on the culture of Roman antiquity and on Roman archaeology. This lacuna may be partly due to the fact that modern scholarship has unjustly neglected the study of archaeology and Roman cultural history during the early modern period. The *Ars antiquitatis*, however, represents one of the most intriguing and rapid developments in humanist scholarship during the 15th and 16th centuries; it was an impressive effort to achieve a new understanding of antiquity and its literature, which was considered the source of knowledge par excellence. In the course of a wider research on the typologies of formal organisation of knowledge in the early modern printed book, which I initiated together with my colleague Wolfgang Neuber,[1] it turned out that the *Artes antiquitatis* form a very fruitful group of texts for questions regarding the paratextual organisation of knowledge.[2] The fact that we have here a new and booming field of scholarship implies that there was a special need of legitimisation, organisation and administration of knowledge and, therefore, of various representational means.

In my view, the dedication should be considered as one of these representational means which legitimize, organize and administrate knowledge (*Wissensverwaltung*). This is somewhat different from what had been done up to that point. I will come back to this after briefly introducing

[1] Karl A.E. Enenkel – Wolfgang Neuber (eds.), *Cognition and the Book. Typologies of Formal Organisation of Knowledge in the Printed Book of the Early Modern Period*, Intersections, 4 (Leiden-Boston: Brill, 2005).

[2] Karl A.E. Enenkel, '*Ars Antiquitatis*: Erkenntnissteuerung und Wissensverwaltung in Werken zur römischen Kulturgeschichte (ca. 1500-1750)', in Enenkel – Neuber, *Cognition and the Book*, pp. 51-123. For bibliographical details, see *ibid.*, pp. 120-123; for the present state of research regarding the early modern study of Roman archaeology and Roman cultural history, see *ibid.*, p. 52, note 2.

the texts I will focus on. I have chosen for this contribution ten dedications, which accompany the landmarks of the new scholarly enterprise from 1446 to 1612, starting with Biondo's *Roma instaurata* and ending with Thomas Dempster's reworked edition of Rosinus's *Romanae antiquitates*. The effort to achieve a new understanding of antiquity and its literature advanced swiftly and the dedications I have chosen reflect some significant developments along the way. Biondo is generally regarded as the founding father of the new field of study. In the first decades of the 16th century, knowledge increased substantially, especially under popes Leo X and Clement VII. Andrea Fulvio set a new standard with his *Antiquitates* published in 1527.[3] In the decade from 1548 to 1558 the *Ars antiquitatis* developed more rapidly, starting with the discovery of the *Fasti consulares* in 1548. The important consequence of this discovery was that it had become possible now to link the material remains of antiquity in a substantial way to the literary tradition of Roman historiography. This brought forward a new quality of understanding and interpreting Roman history. Rosinus's *Romanae antiquitates* of 1583 already represents a retrospective summary of the new field of study. The notion 'Ars antiquitatis' was in fact coined by his friend Thomas Freigius.[4] Rosinus collected in his compendium the results of the research done predominantly in the middle of the 16th century. Dempster's edition of Rosinus's work represents a new phase of authorisation of knowledge, a phase of profound controlling of that knowledge, through the collecting and checking of the literary sources anew. The texts I will examine here are thus:

1. Flavio Biondo's dedication of his *Roma instaurata* to Pope Eugenius IV from 1446.[5]
2. the same author's dedication of the *Roma triumphans* to Pope Pius II from 1459/1460.[6]

[3] *Antiquitates urbis* (s.l. [Rome], 1527).

[4] 'Letter to the Reader' ('[...] Freigius benevolo lectori S.'), in Ioannes Rosinus, *Romanae Antiquitates* [...]. *Ex variis scriptoribus summa fide singularique diligentia collecti* [...] (Basel: heirs of P. Perna, 1583), f. <A3> v. Cf. Enenkel, '*Ars antiquitatis*', p. 51.

[5] Flavio Biondo, *Romae instauratae li. III* (Basel: J. Froben, 1559). I have used here the edition by Cesare D'Onofrio in *Visitiamo Roma nel Quattrocento. La città degli Umanisti*, Collana di studi e testi per la storia della città di Roma, 9 (Rome: Romana Società Editrice, 1989), pp. 99-100.

[6] Flavio Biondo, *De Roma triumphante libri decem. Diligentissime castigati et ita suo nitori restituti, ut in iis plus quam duo mille errores corrigantur* [...] (Brescia: Angelus Britannicus, 1503), f. a r.

3. Andrea Fulvio's dedication of his *Romanae antiquitates* to Pope Clement VII from 1526.[7]
4. Georg Fabricius's dedication of his *Roma* to the patrician Wolfgang Werther from 1550.[8]
5. Carlo Sigonio's dedication of the *Fasti consulares* to Ercole II d'Este, duke of Ferrara, dated 1550.[9]
6. the same author's dedication of the commentary on the same work, to the doge of Venice, Lorenzo Priuli, from 1556.[10]
7. Paolo Manuzio's dedication of his *Antiquitates*, part I, *De legibus* to Cardinal Ippolito d'Este, from 1557.[11]
8. Onofrio Panvinio's dedication of his commentary on Roman history to the Emperor Ferdinand I, from 1558.[12]
9. Johannes Rosinus' dedication of his *Antiquitates Romanae* to the sons of the duke of Saxony, Wilhelm Friederich and Johann, from 1580.[13]
10. Thomas Dempster's dedication of his new edition of the same work to James I, king of England.[14]

These dedications all accompanied the officially authorised editions; all of them were printed, including those of Biondo whose works naturally

[7] *Antiquitates urbis* (Rome: [M. Silber], [1527]), ff. A IIr – A IIIv.

[8] Georgius Fabricius, *Roma* (Basel: J. Oporinus, 1550).

[9] Carlo Sigonio, *Fasti Consulares ac triumphi acti a Romulo rege usque ad Ti. Caesarem. Eiusdem in fastos et triumphos, id est in universam Romanam historiam commentarius. Eiusdem De nominibus Romanorum liber* (Modena, 1550).

[10] Carlo Sigonio, *Fasti Consulares ac triumphi acti a Romulo rege usque ad Ti. Caesarem. Eiusdem in fastos et triumphos, id est in universam Romanam historiam commentarius. Eiusdem De nominibus Romanorum liber* (Venice: P. Manutius, 1556), ff. a2r-<a3>r.

[11] Paolo Manuzio, *Antiquitatum Romanarum liber de legibus* (Venice: Aldus Manutius, 1557). I have used here the edition Cologne: J. Gymnicus, 1582, ff. A2r-A3v.

[12] Onofrio Panvinio, *Reipublicae Romanae Commentariorum li. III* (Venice: Vincentius Valgrisius, 1558), ff. a2r-<a6>r. For Panvinio, cf. Jean-Louis Ferrary, *Onofrio Panvinio et les Antiquités Romaines*, Collection de l'Ecole Française de Rome, 214 (Rome: Ecole Française de Rome, 1996).

[13] As quoted above, ff. A2r-<A3>v.

[14] Ioannes Rosinus, *Antiquitatum Romanarum Corpus absolutissimum, in quo praeter ea quae Ioannes Rosinus delineaverat, infinita supplentur, mutantur, adduntur. Ex criticis, et omnibus utriusque linguae auctoribus collectum: poetis, oratoribus, historicis, iurisconsultis, qui laudati, explicati correctique Thoma Dempster a Muresk, I.C. Scoto, auctore* [...] (Paris: J. Le Bouc, 1613). I have used here the edition Ioannes Rosinus, *Antiquitatum Romanarum Corpus absolutissimum. Cum notis doctissimis ac locupletissimis Thomae Dempsteri I.C.* [...] *Cum indice locupletissimo rerum ac verborum [...] accurante Cornelio Screvelio* (Utrecht: W. vande Water, 1701), ff. **2v-**3r.

appeared first in manuscript form. In these editions, the dedications take a prominent place, marked by their position (first pages) and by several typographic devices, including lavish title inscriptions in different sizes of *antiqua* capitals (more than once imitating the letter types of ancient Roman inscriptions) and separate paging or the use of (sometimes lavish) initials. Thus, the formal presentation alone makes it difficult for the dedications to be overlooked. This has, nevertheless, been exactly the case in modern scholarship. Apparently the readers of the 19th and the better part of the 20th century did not expect that the dedications could tell us anything worthwhile about the way in which the works in question should be read, used and interpreted. I think that we are dealing here with a remarkable discontinuity: whereas the authors of the texts and their early modern publishers considered the dedications so important that they had them printed in prominent position and embellished them with a whole arsenal of typographical devices, modern readers considered them so insignificant as to ignore them completely.

During the 19th and most of the 20th century, readers generally regarded the dedication as a kind of obsolete historical relic — an unpleasant text consisting of awful topics and arguments, and as a rhetorical exercise predominantly directed to flattering. Dedications are a way of communication despised by 'modern', 'enlightened', 'democratic' and, recently even, politically correct readers.

In 1987, Gerard Genette published a wonderful eye-opener of a book, *Paratexts*, in which he drew for the first time substantial attention to the *Beiwerk des Buches*.[15] A drawback of this pioneering work, however, is that it focuses predominantly on modern literature. This also counts for his chapter on the dedication.[16] In Genette's view, the dedication has become a separate text and a text of its own right in the 17th and 18th century, after having surpassed the dedicatory preface of antiquity and the middle ages. In defining the separate dedication from the 17th century to the present day, Genette referred in principal to texts in which the topic is treated as a literary play with an almost immediate focus on the general reader. Genette is much less interested in the historical contexts of dedications and in the historical dedicatee, in the *konkrete Wirklichkeitsbezug* of the dedication. I think, however, that with respect to early modern

[15] Originally in French: *Seuils* (Paris, 1987); revised and augmented edition in German *Paratexte. Das Buch vom Beiwerk des Buches* (Frankfurt – New York: Campus-Verlag, 1992).

[16] *Ibid.*, 5th chapter.

dedications, the *konkrete Wirklichkeitsbezug* and the historical dedicatee play an essential role. In my view, the *konkrete Wirklichkeitsbezug* and the historical dedicatee are fundamental for the mediation of the text, especially for the *Wissensverwaltung*. This will become apparent in my discussion of the examples that follow.

Focusing on the *konkrete Wirklichkeitsbezug* and the *Wissensverwaltung*, I will try to understand how the dedications functioned in the interaction between the author, the dedicatee, and the general reader. I will look closer here at the role of the dedicatee and ask what his function was in the transmission of knowledge, and also what his relation was to the general reader. In doing so, I will question Genette's view of the alleged separation of the dedication from the main text in the 17$^{th}$ century.

For me, it is hard to believe the clear-cut line of development offered by Genette. First of all, the separate dedicatory letter does occur sometimes even in Roman antiquity.[17] In the 15$^{th}$ and 16$^{th}$ centuries, however, there exists *a massive amount of separate dedicatory letters*. My small corpus of texts fits well within this picture; in all cases we are dealing with separate dedications: 9 of the 10 examples stem from the period before 1600, from 1446-1580. Thus, the separation of the dedicatory letter, if there is such a thing as a linear development, must have taken place at least two centuries earlier. But what does this split imply in terms of content and argument? Does it imply a certain specialisation, in the sense that henceforth the dedication would deal predominantly with the relationship between the author and the dedicatee and with the symbolic act of the dedication, whereas the preface ('praefatio'; 'prooemium') or the 'To the Reader' ('Ad lectorem') would discuss issues related to the content, reading, reception and use of the work in question?

With respect to the function of the dedicatee, one aspect seems crucial to me. Whatever the division of tasks between the dedication and the preface may be, one thing is certain: the dedication locates the text primarily in the system of the social and political hierarchy, thus in a system of power. My question will be: what does this imply with regard to the reading and in what way does it guide the reader's perception of the text? It is noteworthy that the most important *Artes antiquitatis* are in the majority of the cases dedicated to persons who rank extremely high in the hierarchy of power: to Popes (Biondo: Eugen IV and Pius II; Andrea Fulvio:

[17] For this cf. Tore Janson, *Latin Prose Prefaces. Studies in literary conventions*, Studia Latina Stockholmiensia, 13 (Stockholm: Almqvist och Wiksell, 1964).

Clement VII), Cardinals (Manuzio: Ippolito d'Este), Dukes (Sigonio: Ercole II of Ferrara), the Venetian doge (Sigonio: Andrea Priuli), a king (Dempster: James I of England) and even to the Roman Emperor (Panvino: Ferdinand I).

Before going into specific arguments regarding the location of the text within the hierarchy of power, a most important issue not mentioned by Genette deserves attention. In the world of the humanist manuscript book of the 14th and 15th centuries, *the dedication functions in fact as the official act of publication*. A work without a dedication is in fact synonymous with an unpublished work. It effectively does not count. Transferred to the present situation it would mean that an author had not succeeded in finding a publisher. This peculiar feature of the dedication of the printed book was taken over, along with many other features, from the manuscript book. Already from this one aspect, we can see how important the role of the dedicatee was in the transmission of knowledge. The questions 'Who may speak?' and 'Who is an author?' are in early modern times essentially connected with the dedicatee. As Biondo in his dedication of the *Roma triumphans* to Pope Pius II explicitly states: It is the dedicatee who provides the author with authority. If a princely dedicatee approves of a work, the general readership will accept it.[18] Consequently, without the approval of a dedicatee, a work will not be accepted by the general readership. Thus, *without a dedicatee, a work does not have any auctoritas; without auctoritas there is no authorship.*

From Paolo Manuzio's dedication to Ippolito d'Este, in which he describes the history of his studies in the *Ars antiquitatis*, the crucial role of the dedicatee as the authorizer of the author clearly appears. Manuzio states that he could work on this topic *only because* he was supported by high patrons, the Cardinals Bembo and Maffei. After they died (1547) — apparently almost 'selbstverständlich' — he had to abandon his studies, which were then interrupted for several years. Only after he found Cardinal Ippolito d'Este in 1556 was Manuzio able to proceed with his project. Why so? One may suppose that the humanist was financially dependent on the cardinals for his studies. Interestingly enough, this cannot have been the reason: Manuzio was the heir of an extremely rich and influential publishing house. The reason is that because he lacked an authorizer of his studies for a couple of years, he apparently felt that he

[18] Biondo, *De Roma triumphante*, f. a r.: "Quod princeps probat, gratum habet, caeteri etiam laudent, cupiant, tueantur".

could not publish his research and, therefore, lost his inspiration. In 1556, however, Manuzio was so glad to have found an *auctoritas* for his authorship that he almost immediately published the two books *De legibus*, although this was only a fragment of the *Romanae antiquitates* he had planned (ca. 20%). Thus again: no author without a dedicatee as an authorizer.

Until well into the 16th century the dedication is an indispensable part of any literary or scientific work. This specific function of the dedication, as the primary certification of the act of publishing, was gradually taken over strangely enough by a typographical device, the development of the title page in the course of the 16th century.[19]

Given the crucial role of the dedicatee, in my opinion, it does not make much sense to dismiss the dedications as empty rhetoric or flattering. The description of the dedicatee, for example, by a *laus patroni* or by mentioning certain virtues, should be considered in the first place not just as asking for money or gratifications, *but as an act of self-definition by the author*. It is important for an author to have a *praiseworthy* dedicatee. Lacking one, the work may be of questionable quality. If one analyses our ten dedications, one cannot say that they consist of an orgy of flattery. On the contrary, about 70% of the total amount of the text does not deal with the dedicatee at all, but with central questions concerning the position of the field of study, the contents of the work and the method of research, or the special qualifications of the author. Moreover, if the dedicatee is praised, the arguments that prevail are chosen specifically with an eye toward the self-definition of the author or the authorisation of the dedicatee, and by this, of course, of the authorisation of the author. A few examples will suffice. In Biondo's dedication of the *Roma triumphans* there is considerable praise of Pope Pius II. But, the praise is directed exclusively to Pius's abilities as an intellectual, as a writer and rhetorician. This is not just because Pius *was* a writer, but because it is especially this aspect which increases his auctoritas in judging the work of Biondo. 'Thus if you accept and approve my work', Biondo says, 'it is certain that all the others will approve and praise it, since it is approved and praised by such an eloquent pope'.[20] As it happens, Pius II in fact

[19] For the development of the title page in the *Artes antiquitatis*, cf. Enenkel, '*Ars antiquitatis*', pp. 53-85; for the early stages of the title page in general, cf. Margaret M. Smith, *The Title Page. Its Early Development 1460-1510* (London: British Library, 2000).

[20] Biondo, *De Roma triumphante*, f. a r.: "Si itaque meum opus accipis et probare videris, abesse non poterit quin a tam eloquente laudatum summo pontifice laudandum quoque caeteri omnes existiment".

despised Biondo's Latin style, but nevertheless accepted the *Roma triumphans*.

In their dedications, Sigonio praised the intellectual capacities of the doge Lorenzo Priuli, Panvinio those of the Emperor Ferdinand, and Dempster those of King James I of England. The arguments are all composed in a similar way. According to Sigonio, Priuli is deeply attached to the *studia bonarum artium* and to antiquity — the knowledge of antiquity is in fact depicted as the very source of his virtue. Moreover, in this field, the Doge has become an omniscient specialist ('cui omnia notissima sunt').[21] This is of course flattery, but at the same time it is the best authorisation an author can dream of — to be approved by a dedicatee who is such a good specialist. One must understand Dempster's praise of James I, who was of course an intellectual, in the same sense. First, Dempster emphasises in his dedication that James was himself an author, for instance of the *True Law of true Monarchies* of 1598. The second argument seems pure exaggeration. According to Dempster, the intellectual heroes of antiquity — Pythagoras, Plato, Socrates, Hortensius and Demosthenes — if they were alive nowadays, would have been taught by James.[22] There is no authorisation, therefore, which surpasses the approval of such a wise and eloquent dedicatee.

In analysing these ten dedications, I discovered a certain ratio between the quantity of the praise and the actual relationship of the author with the dedicatee. The praise is stronger when the actual relationship between the author and dedicatee is weaker. It is hardly coincidental that in all four cases mentioned here, the bonds between the author and the dedicatee are very loose. The impoverished Scottish nobleman Thomas Dempster did not know James I personally nor was he invited or encouraged to dedicate the treatise to him; likewise, Sigonio by then had no bonds with Priuli. In fact, he had dedicated his work some years earlier to the Duke of Ferrara, Ercole II d'Este (1550).[23] Neither did Biondo have a close relationship with Pius II. In fact, he wrote his work almost entirely under Pius' predecessor Nicolaus V, and without doubt had planned originally to dedicate it to this pope. But Nicolaus V died before Biondo finished the work. *Mutatis mutandis* the same is true for Panvinio: he had no bonds with Emperor Ferdinand I, who neither invited nor encouraged the

[21] Sigonio, *Fasti Consulares* (ed. 1556), f. a2r.

[22] Rosinus, *Antiquitatum Romanarum*, f. **2v: "A te sentire Pythagoras, explicare Plato, dividere Socrates, vernare Hortensius, irasci Demosthenes didicissent".

[23] Sigonio, *Fasti Consulares* (ed. 1550).

historian to dedicate the work to him. On the other hand, if there does exist a clear relationship between the author and the dedicatee, as is the case with Biondo and Eugenius IV, Fabricius and Werther, Manuzio and Ippolito d'Este, Sigonio and Ercole II d'Este, the praise of the dedicatee receives less emphasis. One can understand the sense of this inverse ratio. If an actual relationship does *not* exist, it must be created and constituted precisely in the dedication. Such a relationship, therefore, is absolutely indispensable for an effective transmission of the text to the general reader.

Let's turn now to the issue of the specialisation of the dedication. The letter of dedication is neither an invention of the 17th century nor is there a clear and linear development towards it. The letter of dedication is sometimes accompanied by a preface to the general reader; but this is no general rule. Biondo's *Roma triumphans* has a general preface next to the letter of dedication, his *Roma instaurata* has none; Panvino's *Fasti et triumphi* from 1557 have both, Manuzio's *De legibus*, published in the same year, has only the letter of dedication. There is no clear distinction of the functions, as Genette supposed. Topics concerning the field of knowledge, the special sense and usefulness of the work, the qualification of the author, etc. are discussed in the letters of dedication as well, in a number of cases in the letters of dedication only. This means that the letter of dedication functioned also as the principal guide to the reader. In fact, almost every sentence is meant for the dedicatee and for the general reader as well.

Two examples may serve to illustrate this. Firstly, it is a recurring argument in the dedications that the work presented is written in a way that facilitates its use by the dedicatee: that it is written in a concise style, formulated in a clear way, and above all that it is short. This is important for the dedicatees, who are often politicians and busy clergymen, readers who do not have time to study a piece of prose for many hours. The argument of the brevity and conciseness clearly emphasises the personal attachment of the author to the dedicatee, since the author claims to have taken into account the personal needs of the dedicatee when composing the work. Now the same argument also makes sense with respect to the general reader, albeit in a different way. Of course, the reader knows that the work was not written for him personally and of course he is not necessarily a busy politician; but, even if he is a scholar who has at his disposal a considerable amount of *otium*, he will be glad as well if the work is concise, clearly formulated and not exuberantly long. The second example: Biondo's dedication of the *Roma instaurata* to Eugenius IV starts seemingly with pure *Wissensverwaltung*. Explaining the reasons why he wrote this work, Biondo states that he considered it a shame that nowadays nobody, not even an intellectual, is able to identify the archaeological monuments of Rome.[24] This is directed toward the general reader in a sense of identifying a *gap in knowledge*. In the preface of each scholarly work one can read such an argument. For the dedicatee Eugenius IV, however, it had a special meaning: Eugenius directed the last years of his papacy to a fundamental restoration of papal power by reconstituting the pope as the lord of Rome. A loss of the identity of Rome, as Biondo described it, was a fundamental loss of Eugenius's political identity as well.[25]

This double function of the dedication is, in my opinion, a crucial feature. It also bears on the important fact that the *Artes antiquitatis* are dedicated to the highest representatives of the political hierarchy. This is no coincidental constellation and it is also not determined simply by materialistic motives (i.e. the more powerful the dedicatee, that larger the potential financial reward). In the case of very high dedicatees there is always the danger that they might refuse the present or that they might answer in a humiliating way. In my view, the most important reason is the specific connection of the *Altertumswissenschaft* with the top of the political hierarchy. The effect of legitimisation was reciprocal: on the one hand, authorisation by the most powerful legitimised the scholarly work; on the other hand, the *Artes antiquitatis* legitimised the political hierarchy by connecting it with antiquity.

This feature can be clearly demonstrated by the dedication of his *Reipublicae Romanae commentarii* by Onofrio Panvinio to the Roman emperor Ferdinand I. The main reasons for his dedication, states Panvinio, were first the fact that the Roman emperor is the person who would provide the greatest splendour and prestige to the work; second, that the emperor is the only person to whom a work on Roman antiquity really belongs, since he is the legitimate heir of the Roman Empire of Antiquity.[26] For Ferdinand, the dedication functioned as an assertion of his magnificent position, all the more so because it was offered by Panvinio as a present on the occasion of his coronation as Roman Emperor

[24] Biondo in d'Onofrio, *Visitiamo Roma nel Quattrocento*, p. 99.
[25] Cf. *ibid*., p. 100.
[26] Panvinio, *Reipublicae Romanae*, f. a4v.

in 1558.[27] Since the Habsburgs traced their pedigree back to Aeneas, the founding father of the Romans, the dedication of a work on Roman culture functioned as an assertion of their family identity as well as a legitimisation of their political position as well. For the general reader, in terms of *Wissensverwaltung*, the argument functioned as an 'Aufwertung' for the field of knowledge in question. He gets the message that this field of knowledge is so important that it even affects the centre of the earthly power, the Roman Empire. Thus, it has the highest status one can imagine. Needless to say, this provides the reader with a very strong motivation.

The same process can also be detected with respect to dedicatees who have a somewhat lower position than the Roman Emperor. As Sigonio puts it, the doge Priuli has reached the highest office only by imitating the virtue of the ancient Romans.[28] With this argument, Sigonio connects the doge to Roman history and culture. When he dedicates the *Fasti consulares* to him, he in fact hands over to him the legitimate power of the Roman imperium. He constitutes Priuli as one of those almost superhuman Roman politicians who appear on the *Fasti consulares*: champions of virtue like Cato the Elder and the Camilli. In his summary of the career of Priuli, Sigonio assimilates the offices of the Venetian Republic to those of the Roman Republic: Priuli has become a senator, like the Roman senators, provincial governor, like the Roman praetores, and in the end a doge, like a Roman consul.[29]

The connection of the field of knowledge to political power functions also in the case of a Protestant dedicatee, as is the case for Rosinus's dedication of his *Romanae antiquitates* to the Lutheran Princes, Friedrich Wilhelm and Johann von Sachsen. Rosinus says that he composed the work for the sake of the duchy of Saxony, his patria. As he states, the mental structure and the civilisation of the Sachsen State depend essentially on the *Altertumswissenschaft*.[30] As Rosinus puts it, the intellectual foundation of the state is constituted by jurists, theologians, rhetoricians and historians. Their knowledge is fundamentally based on the knowledge of the *Altertumswissenschaft*. Only the *Altertumswissenschaft* enables them to understand the Roman Law, the legal basis of the Sachsen State,

[27] Cf. *ibid.*, f. <a5r>-v.

[28] Sigonio, *Fasti Consulares* (ed. 1556), f. a2v.

[29] *Ibid.*

[30] *Romanae Antiquitates* [...]. *Ex variis scriptoribus summa fide singularique diligentia collecti* [...] (Basel: heirs of P. Perna, 1583), f. A2v.

the Bible and the church fathers, the basis of Protestant religion, etc.[31] The transmission of the necessary knowledge takes place in Protestant gymnasia and universities. When Rosinus composed the *Romanae antiquitates*, he held the office of vice-rector at the Lutheran gymnasium in Regensburg. Rosinus's extended argument is directed not only to the dedicatee, but also provides a clear guidance for the general reader, who would with greatest likelihood be a young Protestant attending a gymnasium or a university. This means that the reader is explicitly invited to assimilate the *Romanae antiquitates* with an eye toward his future profession, be it theologian, lawyer, politician or humanist writer in the service of a prince or a community.

A most striking connection of the *Altertumswissenschaft* to political power takes place in Biondo's dedications. In the dedication of the *Roma instaurata* he locates the description of Rome's archeological remains in the framework of a whole programme for the political restoration of the papacy in Rome. Moreover, he associates it with a programme of architectural restoration of the antique city which he ascribes to Eugenius IV. Here he offers a remarkable indication to the reader: he should understand the text itself as a reconstruction of the ancient city of Rome. Interestingly enough, the actual description of the buildings is rather rudimentary. Therefore, this was obviously not the restoration Biondo had in mind. Biondo's restoration is more about the true identification and localisation of the antique buildings, which really had become a mess in the course of the Middle Ages. Besides, Eugenius's programme of architectural restoration differed somewhat from Biondo's. Whereas the cultural historian and archaeologist Biondo points to the whole city with a special emphasis on the antique buildings, Eugenius's attention was directed almost exclusively to the churches and to the quarter directly connected to the Vatican, the Leonine city.

In the dedication of the *Roma triumphans* to Pope Pius II, Biondo advances an even more striking argument. His systematic description of Roman culture should be read as a mental preparation for Pius's main project, the crusade against the Turks.[32] Biondo formulates it as clearly as can be: the participants in Pius's crusade — the French, Italians, Germans and Spaniards — should learn from the *Roma triumphans* the

[31] *Ibid.*

[32] Biondo, *De Roma triumphante*, f. a r.

'priscorum virtutis imitatio'.[33] Thus, the *Altertumswissenschaft* functioned as a manual for the participants in a holy war. Biondo unfolds before the eyes of the reader the imaginary scene of Pius II reading the *Roma triumphans* while his soldiers celebrate their triumph after the conquest of Jerusalem. In the dedication to Pius, the *Altertumswissenschaft* is also presented as an ideological weapon in the framework of the political restoration of papal power. In addition, in the case of Biondo's *Roma triumphans*, the *Altertumswissenschaft* provides identity, but this time not only for the papal state, but for all Christianity in opposition to the 'otherness' of the Ottoman empire. Because of our historical distance we may be tempted to think that Biondo brought forward these thoughts only in order to flatter Pius II. In the *Roma triumphans*, however, Biondo has also added a preface to the general reader[34] which enables us to make a comparison. In this preface, Biondo explicitly states that the general reader should understand the cultural history of Rome as a mirror of virtue ('speculum virtutis'): as a 'speculum, exemplar, imaginem, doctrinam omnis virtutis et bene, sancte ac foeliciter vivendi rationis'.[35] Thus, the argument of the dedication turns out to be a 'Leseanleitung' for the general reader. Here, once again, it appears that the dedicatee is not just an indispensable part of the message to the general reader, but actually its most important mediator.[36]

Griekse en Latijnse Talen en Culturen
Doelensteeg 16
Universiteit Leiden
NL – 2311 VL Leiden
k.a.e.enenkel@let.leidenuniv.nl

[33] *Ibid.*
[34] *Ibid.*, f. av-a iiv.
[35] *Ibid.*, f. a iir.
[36] For the correction of my English I want to express my gratitude to Todd Richardson and William McCuaig.

# *"ERGO CAPE ET CANTA SANCTOS QUOS FECIMUS HYMNOS"* PRELIMINARIES IN SIXTEENTH-CENTURY MOTET EDITIONS BY COMPOSERS FROM THE LOW COUNTRIES

Demmy Verbeke

Scholarly interest in so-called "paratexts" (texts which accompany other texts and influence their use and understanding) has gradually grown after the publication of influential studies by Jacques Derrida[1] and Gérard Genette.[2] Various scholars soon became aware of the fact that books published in the Early Modern Period are of specific relevance for the study of these paratexts, because their form and effect changed significantly owing to the alterations in the production and distribution of books after the invention of the printing press.[3] This statement is true for all sorts of publications from the Renaissance, and so also for Renaissance editions of music which regularly contain, besides the music itself, preliminary texts. Nonetheless, it was not until the publication of Raimund Redeker's *Lateinische Widmungsvorreden zu Mess- und Motettendrucken*[4] that the world of musicologists paid sufficient attention to this important group of texts. Redeker's example was followed by Dagmar Schnell in 2002.[5] Both studies discuss a relatively large selection of editions dealing with music, dating from the first half of the sixteenth (Redeker) and the first

* I wish to thank my friend and colleague Charles Fantazzi for correcting my English.

[1] *Hors livre. Préfaces*, published in *La Dissémination* (Paris: Éditions du Seuil, 1972).

[2] *Palimpsestes. La littérature au second degré* (Paris: Éditions du Seuil, 1982) and especially *Seuils* (Paris: Éditions du Seuil, 1987).

[3] See — among others — Michel Jeanneret, 'Présentation', in André Gendre – Michel Jeanneret (eds.), *Prologues au XVIe siècle*, special volume of *Versants. Revue Suisse des littératures romanes*, 15 (1989), 3-5; Arnaud Tripet, *Montaigne et l'art du prologue au XVIe siècle*, Études montaignistes, 9 (Paris: Champion, 1992), p. V and Deborah N. Losse, *Sampling the Book. Renaissance Prologues and the French* Conteurs (London-Toronto: Associated University Presses, 1994), p. 13.

[4] Raimund Redeker, *Lateinische Widmungsvorreden zu Meß- und Motettendrucken der ersten Hälfte des 16. Jahrhunderts* (Eisenach: Wagner, 1995).

[5] Dagmar Schnell, *In lucem edidit. Der deutsche Notendruck der ersten Hälfte des 17. Jahrhunderts als Kommunikationsmedium. Dargestellt an den Vorreden* (PhD diss. Berlin, 2002). A commercial version of this dissertation appeared in Osnabrück (Der Andere Verlag) in 2003.

half of the seventeenth century (Schnell). In order to lay the foundations for further musicological study of preliminary texts, this paper discusses their presence and language in a specific corpus of publications of polyphonic music of the second half of the sixteenth century, thus bridging the gap between the studies of Redeker and Schnell.

For this purpose, a corpus of editions was selected and studied in detail. The corpus consists of all motet editions by composers from the Low Countries in the second half of the sixteenth century which are considered to be *Einzeldrucke* (i.e. motet editions which are devoted to one single composer). These limitations resulted in a collection of in total 261 editions, including 160 *editiones principes* and 101 reprints.[6] I focus on printed liminaria of a literary nature, consisting of dedication letters, poems and notices to the reader, which contain the most relevant information for the interpretation of the music they accompany. This implies that I do not discuss other paratexts (such as title pages, indices, approbations or privilegia), nor elements which form part of a specific copy such as ex-libris inscriptions, handwritten dedications, manuscript marginalia and the like.

After a short presentation of the studied corpus, I will elaborate on the following questions: Are there preliminary texts in the editions belonging to the corpus? If so, in which language are these preliminary texts written and why did the author choose that specific language? What happens with the preliminaries if the volume is reprinted? Is there a preferred form of preliminary text? And, finally, who writes the dedication for a motet edition in this period?

## The corpus

The corpus under discussion has a specific relevance for a number of reasons.[7] In the sixteenth century the genre of the Latin motet, a primarily

[6] The complete list of studied editions is presented in Demmy Verbeke, *"Ad musicae patronos" – Latijnse dedicaties en inleidende teksten in motettenbundels van componisten uit de Nederlanden (ca. 1550 – ca. 1600)*, 4 vols. (PhD diss. Katholieke Universiteit Leuven, 2005; fulltext version available at http://hdl.handle.net/1979/160), IV, 1-41. The said dissertation contains, among other things, a critical edition, with Dutch translation and extensive notes, of all Latin preliminary texts in the corpus under discussion.

[7] See also Nele Gabriëls – Demmy Verbeke, 'The Latin dedications of the motet editions of the Franco-Flemish polyphonists from the second half of the sixteenth century as musical and literary sources', published in *Lias*, 29 (2002), 153-156 and (slightly altered) *Acta Musicologica*, LXXV-1 (2003), 134-135.

religious composition setting to music a sacred, often biblical text, won a privileged position within the genre hierarchy alongside the polyphonic mass. Furthermore, composers from the Low Countries, who were active as singers and chapel-masters both at home and abroad and whose works were dispersed by the most renowned music printers of Europe, were the authoritative representatives. The ever-growing success of printed editions of music, the democratisation of the market for music and an overwhelming musical production provided a shift by 1530/1540 from anthologies collecting the works of various polyphonists towards more and more editions devoted to one single genre and one single composer. These *Einzeldrucke* originated most of the time in a different way than the anthologies. The initiative to print the edition mostly came from the composer himself, and the composer was more and more involved in the different aspects of the production process. The preliminary texts in the editions from the second half of the century therefore offer us more direct information on the composer, his patrons, his contacts with printers, and so on.

To study the use of preliminaries in this demarcated corpus, I first had to determine whether the editions which corresponded to the defined terms contained preliminary texts or not.[8] A complication, which will come as no surprise to the musicologists studying music from this period, is that almost all of these editions are not a publication of one book (as is the case, for example, of a collection of poems or a historical work), but the publication of a number of part-books which together form the edition. My research has shown that the preliminary material in the different part-books is for the most part identical, but it does happen that some part-books contain preliminary texts, and others not. An example is the *Liber quintus cantionum sacrarum* of Pierre de Manchicourt from 1554 (M272).[9] The dedication letter in this collection only appears in the part-book of the tenor. In other cases, different preliminaries appear in the

[8] This part of the research was conducted in collaboration with Nele Gabriëls. The collections we are dealing with are only partially available in modern editions, in which normally little or no attention is paid to possible preliminaries. Therefore, it was necessary to trace all of the 261 editions and to try to determine, through the use of catalogues, contacts with library staff and, most of all, collation of as many copies as possible, whether they contain preliminaries or not and if so, which preliminaries appear.

[9] I refer to the editions with their RISM-number, i.e. the number attributed to them in *Einzeldrucke vor 1800*, Répertoire international des sources musicales – Internationales Quellenlexikon der Musik – International Inventory of Musical Sources (Kassel-Basel-Tours-London, 1971; henceforth: RISM). Bibliographical details of all editions discussed in this paper are found in appendix.

different part-books, e.g. in the *Novae cantiones sacrae* of Jean de Castro from 1588 (C1478). All part-books contain an identical dedicatory poem, but tenor and bassus also offer a laudatory poem written by Jean Polit, while the superius, altus and quinta pars offer an additional poem by the composer himself. Because the liminary material in the different part-books is not necessarily identical, it was obligatory (as far as possible) not only to trace and check an original copy of an edition, but also to trace and check as many different part-books as was possible.

Another complication is that one obviously can only work with the material that still exists today. I was able, for instance, to study the *Liber primus Rinaldi del Mel motettorum* (M2193) and the *Liber tertius Rinaldi del Mel motectorum* (M2194), but a *Liber secundus* is presumed lost. The loss of certain collections can exceptionally be compensated by older secondary literature. This is the case for a volume of Philippus de Monte, entitled *Sacrarum cantionum cum quinque vocibus… liber sextus*, printed in 1584. A unique copy of this edition was preserved in the academic library in Gdańsk (Danzig), but was destroyed during the Second World War. I was still able to incorporate this volume, because Georges Van Doorslaer already published a transcription of the dedication letter in his *La vie et les oeuvres de Philippe de Monte*.[10] Of quite a number of other editions, not all of the part-books have survived and therefore it remains impossible to be certain about the presence of preliminary material in the edition as a whole. An example is the *Modulorum quatuor, quinque et sex vocum liber primus* (R1300) of Jean Richafort. The preserved part-books of contratenor, bassus and superius contain no preliminary texts. But it is possible that liminaria only appear in the tenor. Since we only possess two pages of the tenor (namely pages 17 and 18), I cannot determine with certainty whether this collection contained preliminaries or not.

## Presence and language preliminaries

When we look at the entire corpus of 261 motet editions, we come to the conclusion that almost 40% (being 104 editions) do not contain any preliminary material:

[10] Georges Van Doorslaer, *La vie et les oeuvres de Philippe de Monte* (Hildesheim-New York, 1980 = Bruxelles, 1921), pp. 265-266.

| **entire corpus (first editions + reprints)** | **261 editions (160 + 101)** | **100%** |
|---|---|---|
| no literary preliminaries | 104 | 39,8% |
| with literary preliminary texts | 157 | 60,2% |

This is quite a remarkable result, because most existing secondary literature claims that dedications and other preliminaries were an almost indispensable feature of publications in this period.[11] However, this conclusion was primarily based on the study of publications of a philological or bellettristic nature and takes too little account of publications of a different sort (such as editions of music, almanacs, legal works, ...).[12]

When we focus on first editions, the number of publications without preliminaries drops significantly, but still one quarter of them appear without a dedication or another text.

Sometimes we can conjecture a reason for the absence of preliminaries, for instance in the case of Jacobus Vaet's *Modulationes quinque vocum... Liber primus* and *Modulationes quinque vocum... Liber secundus*. In the year 1562, Vaet published two motet editions with Gardano in Venice, the first one with a dedication letter, a poem to the reader and a poem addressing the critics; the second one without preliminaries. Because both editions were printed in the same year by the same printer and because of the title of the publications, I believe that they were considered to be sort of one edition in two volumes. In that respect, it makes sense that volume one (V26) contains the preliminary texts to the whole edition and that volume two (V27) does not have preliminaries.

[11] See, for instance, Karl Schottenloher, *Die Widmungsvorrede im Buch des 16. Jahrhunderts*, Reformationsgeschichtliche Studien und Texte, 76/77 (Münster: Aschendorff, 1953); Sabine Vogel, *Kulturtransfer in der frühen Neuzeit. Die Vorworte der Lyoner Drucke des 16. Jahrhunderts*, Spätmittelalter und Reformation. Neue Reihe, 12 (Tübingen: Mohr Siebeck, 1999), p. 7; and Schnell, *In lucem edidit*, p. 8. See also the satirical *Somme Dédicatoire* of Antoine Furetière in *Le Roman Bourgeois. Ouvrage Comique* (Paris: Jannet, 1854), I, 5 (p. 317).

[12] Prof. Hubert Meeus (University of Antwerp) cited (in a personal conversation) a number of characteristics of publications of the sixteenth century without preliminaries: 1) books with a specified public so that printer or publisher see no reason for advertising or explanation 2) pamphlets or other ephemeral printings 3) books which are not considered to be controversial or innovative.

In the 157 editions which do contain liminary texts (as we just saw, about 60% of the entire corpus), the use of Latin is overwhelming:

EDITIONS WITH LITERARY PRELIMINARIES

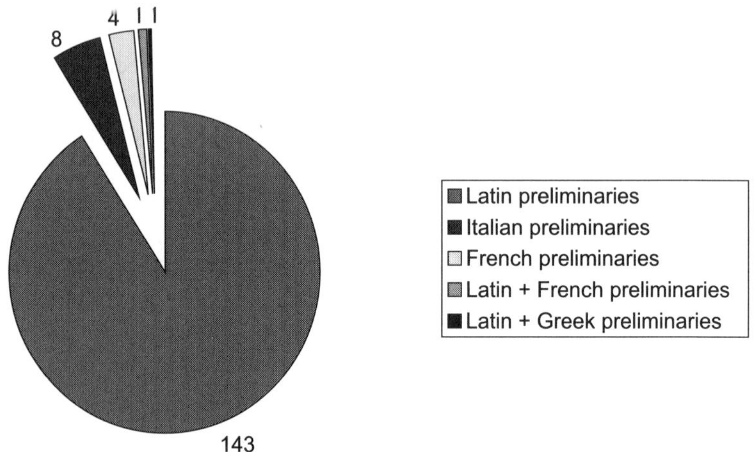


In more than 90% of the cases, there is at least one Latin paratext involved. A French or Italian preliminary text, without a Latin one, appears in only 12 editions of the 157 with preliminaries belonging to our corpus.

The dominance of Latin is of course connected with the fact that Latin still was the *lingua franca* in the cultural world in this period. Generally speaking, the authors also chose Latin because a dedication was a formal occasion and because it was almost mandatory in the sixteenth century that a public letter addressed to a person of higher rank was written in Latin.

But an example taken from the dedication letters in editions of Orlandus Lassus also proves that the content of the volume influenced the choice for the language of the dedication. Orlandus Lassus signed a large number of dedications in different languages, but of special relevance in this context are his seven dedication letters addressed to the same patron, Wilhelm of Bavaria[13]:

[13] I only count the original dedication letters, personally signed by Orlandus Lassus, not including identical reprints of these letters.

| | author of dedication letter | dedicatee(s) | language of dedication letter |
|---|---|---|---|
| *Neue teütsche Liedlein mit fünff stimmen* (L814) | Orlandus Lassus | Wilhelm of Bavaria | German |
| *Moduli quinis vocibus nunquam hactenus editi* (L843) | Orlandus Lassus | Wilhelm of Bavaria | Latin |
| *Fasciculus aliquot cantionum sacrarum quinque vocum* (L851) | Orlandus Lassus | Wilhelm of Bavaria | Latin |
| *Patrocinium musices... prima pars* (L857) | Orlandus Lassus | Wilhelm of Bavaria | Latin |
| *Liber mottetarum, trium vocum* (L878) | Orlandus Lassus | Wilhelm, Ferdinand and Ernst of Bavaria | Latin |
| *Novae aliquot... ad duas voces cantiones* (L902) | Orlandus Lassus | Wilhelm of Bavaria | Latin |
| *Libro de villanelle, moresche, et altre canzoni, a 4, 5, 6 et 8 voci* (L930) | Orlandus Lassus | Wilhelm of Bavaria | Italian |

As the table shows, five of the seven dedication letters are written in Latin, one is written in German, and one is written in Italian. When we have a closer look into the reasons why he uses different languages for dedication letters to the same person, it becomes clear that his choice is connected with the contents of the publication.[14] A collection of German songs has a German dedication, five motet collections with compositions on Latin texts have a Latin dedication and a collection with *villanelle, moresche* and other songs on Italian texts are preceded by an Italian dedication. The language of the dedication letter is thus connected with the contents of the publication, and not so much with the dedicatee. It is therefore obvious that dedication letters to motet editions, with compositions on Latin texts, will predominantly have a Latin dedication letter.

[14] There is one semi-exception to this general rule. The motet edition L843, which appeared in Paris when the composer was there himself, does offer (as do the other motet editions) a Latin dedication letter, but also a French laudatory poem on Wilhelm and his wife, which is also signed by the composer.

## The case of reprints

It is relevant to consider what happens with paratexts in reprints, especially because no less than 101 editions of the 261 editions which belong to the studied corpus are reprints as far as the music is concerned.[15]

My research shows that the use of preliminaries in reprints is normally quite straightforward: a vast majority of the reprints contain identical liminary material compared to the original edition (that is, if the original had no preliminaries, the reprint has none either; if the original edition had one or more preliminaries, the reprint has the same preliminaries). If the reprint does not repeat the preliminary texts which appeared in the original, they are normally left out and the reprint appears without preliminaries.

There is one big exception to this general rule, namely reprints of the work of Orlandus Lassus. In editions of Lassus, which are considered to be reprints as far as the music is concerned, the liminary material of the original is quite regularly altered, which makes the study of these reprints a complex and unpredictable undertaking. There are, for instance, reprints which appear with a new dedication letter, in which the reason for reprinting the edition is explained. Sometimes, the dedication letter of the original is reprinted, but a second letter is added with a similar explanation.

An interesting example is Lassus' *Fasciculus aliquot cantionum sacrarum, quinque vocum, nunc primum in lucem editus* (L851), published by Adam Berg in Munich in 1572. This is not, as the title page suggests, a collection "primum in lucem editus", but a reprint of the *Moduli quinis vocibus* (L843), published the year before by Le Roy and Ballard at the time that the composer himself was in Paris. In his dedication letter to the Munich republication, Lassus explains that he himself has taken the initiative for the reprint, because he noticed that the first publication of this music was not available in Germany. And since he had dedicated the first version to Wilhelm, he decided to dedicate this reprint to the same person:

> *Illustrissimo atque excellentissimo Principi Guilielmo Comiti Palatino Rheni, utriusque Bavariae Duci, etc. Domino suo clementiss*[*imo*]
> Illustrissime atque excellentissime Princeps, libros eos quos anno elapso Lutetiae Parisiorum typis excudendos dederam, in hisce partibus plane ignotos, neque ullum eorum exemplar, praeter paucula illa, quae ipse ego mecum inde attuli, ad nos perlatum esse video. Cum igitur Germanos singulari prope

[15] In order to determine which editions are reprints as far as the music is concerned, I relied on the information given in RISM and Horst Leuchtmann – Bernhold Schmid, *Orlando di Lasso. Supplement. Seine Werke in zeitgenössischen Drucken*, 3 vols. (Kassel-Basel-London-New York-Prag: Bärenreiter, 2001).

animi affectu in me esse multis iam argumentis abunde cognoverim, facere non potui quin hanc meam qualemcunque operam praelo denuo subiicerem eosque illius redderem participes, idque sub Illustriss[imae] T[uae] Cel[situdinis] nomine maxime, cuius honori prior quoque aeditio consecrata erat. Eidem ut me pro summa ipsius in me benevolentia commendatissimum esse certus sum, ita nihil unquam eorum quae efficere in eius gratiam potero, omittam. Illustriss[imae] T[uae] Cel[situdini] addictissimus Orlandus di Lassus.

*To the illustrious and elevated prince Wilhelm, paltsgrave at the Rhine, Duke of both Bavarias, etc. his most clement Lord*
Illustrious and elevated prince, I see that the books that I had published in Paris last year are almost unknown in these parts and that no copy has reached us except for the very few that I myself brought from there. Since I was fully aware through many indications that the Germans are almost exceptionally favourably-disposed towards me, I could not but trust this little work of mine, whatever its worth, to the press again and share it with them, and this specifically under the name of Your illustrious Excellency, to whose honour the previous edition was also dedicated. As I very well know due to your great kindness towards me, that you are very well-disposed towards me, I shall leave nothing undone to manifest my gratitude to you.
Orlandus Lassus, very dedicated to Your illustrious Excellence.

Another example of what happens in reprints of Lassus' music suggests that paratexts were sometimes used to "falsify" an edition. An example is the dedication letter of the *Sacrae cantiones quinque vocum*, first published in 1562. This edition is within the limits of our corpus the most popular edition, since it went through not less than fourteen reprints.[16]

All of these reprints, except for two which have no preliminaries, repeat the dedication letter and the poem of the original edition. But the date and place of the dedication letter is changed in the different versions. All editions which are printed at Nuremberg preserve the date of the original "Nuremberg, June 1 1562"; but the reprints published in Venice alter the original, first into "Nuremberg, November 1 1562" and later into "Venice, November 1 1562". I suspect that the original date was changed first to create the impression that it was a first edition. Later reprints in Venice afterwards also changed the place in order to complete the illusion.

## Use of different forms of paratexts

Looking into the preliminaries published in the motet editions belonging to the corpus, I have ascertained that different sorts of paratexts are used.

[16] Table (see p. 58) adapted from Leuchtmann – Schmid, *Orlando di Lasso. Supplement*, I, p. 92.

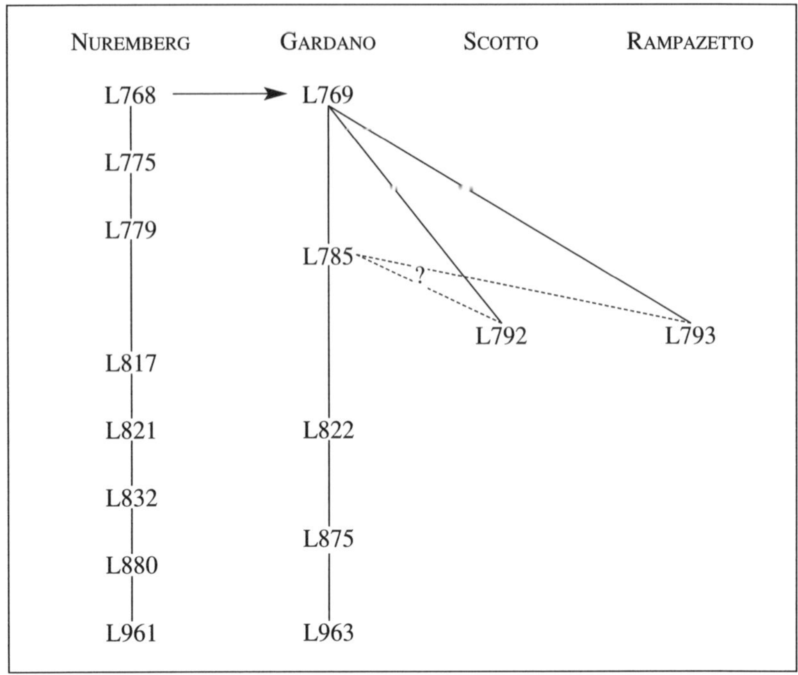


There are dedication letters, dedicatory formulas or poems, notices to the reader, poems praising the art of music, poems praising the composer and poems addressing the critics. Drawing up a list of the different sorts[17], it becomes immediately clear that a prose dedication letter is the most usual and most important paratext in the studied corpus. In more than half of the cases where at least one paratext is part of the edition, it is a dedication letter and only a dedication letter. When there is more then one preliminary text, it is almost always a prose dedication letter in combination with one or more poems. In less than ten percent of the editions in question, there is no dedication letter. This does not always imply that there is no dedication: the letter can be, although rarely, replaced by a dedicatory poem or a dedicatory formula. Of the 157 editions belonging to the corpus which contain preliminary texts, 151 contain at least one text with a clear dedicatory function (letter, poem or formula). The remaining six only have a poem praising the composer or a foreword addressed to the general public.

[17] A complete overview of all the different paratexts and their combination in the studied corpus is listed in Verbeke, *"Ad musicae patronos"*, I, 35-36.

## Authors of the dedication letters

Finally, I come to the question of authorship of the dedication. In other words, who is responsible for the 151 editions in the corpus which are dedicated to a specific person or group of people? Looking into the matter, we obtain the following numerical results:

| **Dedication (letter, poem or formula)** | TOTAL **151** |
|---|---|
| written by the composer | 126 |
| written by the printer(s) and/or bookseller | 12 |
| written by the posthumous curator of the works of the composer | 5 |
| written by another person | 8 |

It is obvious that only on rare occasions composers are not responsible for the dedication themselves. This is an important difference with the editions of music in the first half of the sixteenth century, because these were mostly anthologies dedicated by the printer or the compiler.

In the corpus under discussion, it is in the first place the composer himself who chooses a specific dedicatee, writes (or perhaps more correctly: signs) the dedication and most probably also collects the reward for the dedication.

The table also shows that in five of the cases where the composer does not write the dedication himself, he had a good reason not to do so, namely because he was dead at the time of publication. The person who dedicates the volume in place of the deceased composer each time stresses that he/she was responsible for the collection and publication of the volume, and put a lot of effort into it. Implicitly, this is a message for the dedicatee that the edition is also partly the work of the editor and that he/she for that reason is also entitled to the acknowledgment that the composer might have received for the dedication were he still alive.

A revealing example of this strategy is the publication of the *Cantiones aliquot musicae* (D1729), composed by Michael Desbuissons and printed in Munich by Adam Berg in 1573. The title page already mentions the fact that this is a publication of Desbuissons' work, collected and edited after his death by Johann Faber: "Cantiones aliquot musicae, quae (*sic*) vulgo muteta vocant, quatuor, quinque et sex vocum, authore M[agistro] Michaële Carle Desbuissons, Flandro Insulano, serenissimi Archiducis Austriae Ferdinandi cantore musico. Post obitum authoris collecta ac edita per Ioannem Fabrum, eiusdem illustrissimi Principis cantorem". There are two Latin preliminary texts in this edition: a dedication letter, written by Johann Faber and addressed to Ferdinand of Austria; and a laudatory poem by the Dutch humanist Gerard de Roo. Johann Faber mentions in his dedication how much effort he put into the collection of these works and why he wanted to dedicate this volume to Ferdinand. The poem of De Roo not only sings the praise of the composer, but also of the editor of his work:

> *In musicas cantiones M*[*agistri*] *Michaelis Carle Desbuissons p*[*iae*] *m*[*emoriae*] *olim collegae atque amici pientissimi beneque meriti, decasti<c>hon Gerardi de Roo, Batavi*

Pieria quondam non ultimus arte Michaël
   ingenii nobis haec monimenta dedit.
Qui primae postquam decessit flore iuventae,
   iactura tanti Musica moesta viri,
"Ecquis erit," dixit, "qui doctae munera venae
   non sinet immundo pressa iacere situ?"
Audiit haec Faber et studio congesta fideli
   edidit a Domini funere rapta sui.
Quisquis es Aoniis operatus rite Deabus,
   his fruere et foelix semper utrique fave.

> Michael, an important person in the art of music, gave us this monument of his talent once. After he passed away in the bloom of his youth, Music mourned the loss of such a man. "Will there be anyone who will ensure that the fruits of such a great talent do not lie in squalid neglect?", she asked. Faber heard this, collected the works with faithful zeal en published what he could save after the death of their author. You, whoever you are, who faithfully honour the gods of Aonia (i.e. the Muses), enjoy these works and show your favour to both of them (i.e. Desbuissons and Faber).

Another example of the "claims" of the posthumous editor of musical works is the dedication letter in the *Sacrarum cantionum... liber primus* (R737) of Jacob Regnart, published in Frankfurt in 1605. This is the only letter in the entire corpus which is signed by a woman. Anna Regnardin, as she calls herself, reminds the dedicatee that she has been left behind with six children after the death of her husband, who served the family of the dedicatee for many years. She explicitly asks him to support her in her time of need:

> Consideranti autem mihi, cuius auspiciis eae tutissime prodire possent, Ser[eni]tas V[estr]a occurrit, ob plurimas causas, praecipue vero, quod ipse maritus meus nobilissimae et clarissimae Domui Austriacae pene a pueris inter musicos servierit,... e vita migravit, me vidua, moerore atque tristitia plena, cum sex liberis relicta. Hosce igitur qualescunque mariti mei ad Dei gloriam susceptos labores atque conatus Ser[enita]ti V[estr]ae qua possum animi demissione offero, dedico atque consecro, humillimeque oro et supplico, ut me afflictam viduam liberosque orphanos pro innata Domus Austriacae in omnes clementia et benignitate, suo patrocinio atque defensione conservet, foveat ac tueatur.
>
> Considering under whose protection these songs might appear safely, I thought of Your Highness for many reasons, but especially because my husband himself served, almost from childhood onwards, the very noble and famous house of Austria as a musician ... He passed away and left me behind as a widow, full of sorrow and grief, with six children. So, with the largest humility of spirit possible, I offer, dedicate and devote these works and efforts, whatever their value, of my husband, undertaken for the glory of God, to Your Highness. I humbly beg you that, by virtue of the innate clemency and kindness of the house of Austria towards all, you may safeguard, support and protect me and my orphans with your patronage and protection.

Archival material proves that her request did not fall on deaf ears: Anna did receive financial compensation for her loss and for the dedication of her deceased husband's work.

## Conclusion

In order to determine the presence of preliminaries in (a group of) editions of music from the sixteenth century, it is important to check the editions as a whole, that is to say, all available part-books. The same remark holds for reprints: it is wrong to assume that a reprint will merely repeat the preliminaries of the original edition.

A motet edition written by a composer from the Low Countries from the second half of the sixteenth century appears in approximately 60% of the cases with at least one literary preliminary text. The vast majority of these texts is written in Latin, which partly is determined by the content of the publication: a motet edition containing compositions on Latin texts is normally preceded by a Latin paratext.

When an edition contains a preliminary text, it is in the first place a Latin dedication letter, sometimes in combination with a Latin text of a different sort. Most of these dedication letters are signed by the composer himself. Rarely, a dedicatory poem or formula replaces the prose dedication letter and only by exception is a motet edition published with preliminaries but no dedication.

CENTRE FOR THE STUDY OF THE RENAISSANCE
University of Warwick
UK – Coventry CV4 7AL
D.R.Verbeke@warwick.ac.uk

## APPENDIX OF QUOTED EDITIONS

C1478 Jean de Castro, *Novae cantiones sacrae quae vulgo motetta vocantur cum quinque, sex et octo vocibus, auctore Ioanne a Castro Eburone, serenissimi Ioannis Guilielmi, Iuliae, Cliviae, Montium, etc. Ducis, musices Praefecto* (Douai: Jean Bogard, 1588)

D1729 Michael Desbuissons, *Cantiones aliquot musicae, quae* (sic) *vulgo muteta vocant, quatuor, quinque et sex vocum, authore m*[*agistro*] *Michaële Carle Desbuissons, Flandro Insulano, serenissimi Archiducis Austriae Ferdinandi cantore musico. Post obitum authoris collecta ac edita per Ioannem Fabrum, eiusdem illustrissimi Principis cantorem* (Munich: Adam Berg, 1573)

L768 Orlandus Lassus, *Sacrae cantiones quinque vocum, tum viva voce, tum omnis generis instrumentis cantatu commodissimae, iam primum in lucem editae, authore Orlando di Lassus* (Nuremberg: Johann Berg – Ulrich Neuber, 1562)

L769 Orlandus Lassus, *Orlandi Lassi sacrea* [sic] *cantiones (vulgo motecta appellatae) quinque vocum, tum viva voce, tum omnis generis instrumentis cantatu commodissimae, liber primus* (Venice: Antonio Gardano, 1562)

L775 Orlandus Lassus, *Sacrae cantiones quinque vocum, tum viva voce, tum omnis generis instrumentis cantatu commodissimae, iam primum in lucem editae, authore Orlando di Lassus* (Nuremberg: Johann Berg – Ulrich Neuber, 1563)

L779 Orlandus Lassus, *Sacrae cantiones quinque vocum, tum viva voce, tum omnis generis instrumentis cantatu commodissimae, iam primum in lucem editae, authore Orlando di Lassus* (Nuremberg: Johann Berg – Ulrich Neuber, 1564)

L785 Orlandus Lassus, *Orlandi Lassi sacrae cantiones (vulgo motecta appellatae) quinque vocum, tum viva voce, tum omnis generis instrumentis cantatu commodissimae, liber primus* (Venice: Antonio Gardano, 1565)

L792 Orlandus Lassus, *Orlandi Lassi sacrae cantiones vulgo motecta appellatae quinque vocum, tum viva voce, tum omnis generis instrumentis cantatu commodissimae, liber primus* (Venice: Girolamo Scotto, 1566)

L793 Orlandus Lassus, *Orlandi Lassi sacrae cantiones (vulgo motecta appellatae) quinque vocum, tum viva voce, tum omnis generis instrumentis cantatu commodissimae, liber primus* (Venice: Francesco Rampazzetto, 1566)

L814 Orlandus Lassus, *Newe Teütsche Liedlein mit Fünff Stimmen welche ganz lieblich zu zinge und auff allerlen Instrumenten zugebrauchen. Von Orlando di Lasso F. Bay. Cappellmeister componirt und von im selbst corrigirt unnd inn druck verfertigt worden* (Munich: Adam Berg, 1567)

L817 Orlandus Lassus, *Sacrae cantiones quinque vocum, tum viva voce, tum omnis generis instrumentis cantatu commodissimae, authore Orlando di Lassus* (Nuremberg: Theodor Gerlach (in officina Johann Berg †), 1568)

L821 Orlando di Lasso, *Sacrae cantiones quinque vocum, tum viva voce, tum omnis generis instrumentis cantatu commodissimae, authore Orlando di Lassus* (Nuremberg: Ulrich Neuber, 1569)

L822 Orlandus Lassus, *Orlandi Lassi sacrae cantiones (vulgo motecta appellatae) quinque vocum, tum viva voce, tum omnis generis instrumentis cantatu commodissimae, liber primus* (Venice: Antonio Gardano, 1569)

L832 Orlandus Lassus, *Viginti quinque sacrae cantiones, quinque vocum, tum viva voce, tum omnis generis instrumentis cantatu commodissimae, authore Orlando di Lassus* (Nuremberg: Theodor Gerlach (in officina Johann Berg †), 1570)

L843 Orlandus Lassus, *Moduli quinis vocibus nunquam hactenus editi Monachii Boioariae compositi, Orlando Lasso auctore* (Paris: Adrian Le Roy – Robert Ballard, 1571)

L851 Orlandus Lassus, *Fasciculus aliquot cantionum sacrarum, quinque vocum, nunc primum in lucem editus, Orlando di Lasso authore, illustrissimi Bavariae Ducis Alberti musici chori magistro* (Munich: Adam Berg, 1572)

L857 Orlandus Lassus, *Patrocinium Musices Orlandi de Lasso, illustrissimi Ducis Bavariae, chori magistri, cantionum, quas mutetas vocant, opus novum. Prima Pars. Illustrissimi Principis D*[*omini*] *Guilhelmi Comitis Palatini Rheni, utriusque Bavariae Ducis liberalitate in lucem editum* (Munich: Adam Berg, 1573)

L875 Orlandus Lassus, *Orlandi Lassi sacrae cantiones (vulgo motecta appellatae) quinque vocum, tum viva voce, tum omnis generis instrumentis cantatu commodissimae, liber primus* (Venice: sons of Antonio Gardano, 1574)

L878 Orlandus Lassus, *Orlandi de Lasso illustrissimi Bavariae Ducis Alberti chori magistri, liber mottetarum, trium vocum, quae cum vivae voci, tum omnis generis instrumentis musicis commodissime applicari possunt, summa diligentia compositae, correctae et nunc primum in lucem aeditae* (Munich: Adam Berg, 1575)

L880 Orlandus Lassus, *Orlandi Lassi sacrae cantiones, vulgo motecta appellatae, quinque vocum, tum viva voce, tum omnis generis instrumentis cantatu commodissimae* (Nuremberg: Theodor Gerlach, 1575)

L902 Orlandus Lassus, *Novae aliquot et antehac non ita usitatae ad duas voces cantiones suavissimae, omnibus musicis summe utiles necnon tyronibus quam eius artis peritioribus summopere inservientes, authore Orlando di Lasso, illustrissimi Bavariae Ducis Alberti musici chori magistro, summa diligentia compositae, correctae et nunc primum in lucem aeditae* (Munich: Adam Berg, 1577)

L930 Orlandus Lassus, *Libro de villanelle, moresche, et altre canzoni a 4, 5, 6 & 8 voci di Orlando di Lasso* (Paris: Adrian Le Roy – Robert Ballard, 1581)

L961 Orlandus Lassus, *Orlandi Lassi sacrae cantiones, vulgo motecta appellatae, quinque vocum, tum viva voce, tum omnis generis instrumentis cantatu commodissimae* (Nuremberg: Katharina Gerlach, 1586)

L963 Orlandus Lassus, *Orlandi Lassi sacrae cantiones (vulgo motecta appellatae) quinque vocum, tum viva voce, tum omnis generis instrumentis cantatu commodissimae, liber primus* (Venice: Angelo Gardano, 1586)

M272 Pierre de Manchicourt, *Liber quintus cantionum sacrarum vulgo mo<te>ta vocant, quinque et sex vocum a D*[*omino*] *magistro Petro Manchicurtio Betunio insignis ecclesiae Tornacensis phonasco nunc primum in lucem aeditus* (Louvain: Pierre Phalèse, 1554)

M2193 Rinaldo del Mel, *Liber primus Rinaldi del Mel mottettorum quae partim quaternis, partim quinis, partim senis ac unum septenis, alterum vero octonis vocibus concinuntur* (Venice: Angelo Gardano, 1581)

M2194 =1585/4 Rinaldo del Mel, *Liber tertius Rinaldi del Mel motectorum partim quinis, partim senis vocibus concinuntur* (Venice: Angelo Gardano, 1585)

R737 Jacob Regnart, *Iacobi Regnardi, S*[*acrae*] *Caes*[*areae*] *Maiest*[*atis*] *musici vice-magistri, sacrarum cantionum IV, V, VI, VII, VIII, X et XII vocum, pro certis quibusdam diebus dominicis sanctorumque festivitatibus concinnatarum et tam viva voce, quam omni instrumentorum genere decantandarum, liber primus, nunc primum in lucem editus* (Frankfurt: Wolfgang Richter by commission of Nicolaus Stein, 1605)

R1300 Jean Richafort, *Modulorum quatuor, quinque et sex vocum, liber primus* (Paris: Adrian Le Roy – Robert Ballard, 1556)

V26 Jacobus Vaet, *Iacobi Vaet Flandri modulationes quinque vocum (vulgo motecta) nuncupatae, serenissimi Bohemiae Regis musicarum modulaminum rectoris celeberrimi, liber primus* (Venice: Antonio Gardano, 1562)

V27 Jacobus Vaet, *Iacobi Vaet Flandri modulationes quinque vocum (vulgo motecta) nuncupatae, serenissimi Bohemiae Regis musicarum modulaminum rectoris celeberrimi, liber secundus* (Venice: Antonio Gardano, 1562)

# READING (BETWEEN) THE LINES: WHAT DEDICATIONS CAN TELL US

NELE GABRIËLS

As source material, the dedication encloses multiple layers of meaning. This equally applies to the dedicatory texts included in the motet prints of the second half of the sixteenth century. Revealing the various meanings of these texts in connection to the music and music history was one of the musicological goals at the outset of the research project concerning *The Latin dedications of the motet editions by the Franco-Flemish polyphonists from the second half of the sixteenth century as musical and literary sources.*[1] A thorough reading of the dedications can expand knowledge of musical and socio-musical history, for it has the potential to shed light (1) on the human network built up around the printed book (the role of the composer, printer, author, dedicatee; who chose the music, wrote the liminary texts or chose the dedicatee?); (2) on specifics about the composer's biography and that of others; (3) on contemporary views on religion, culture and music; (4) on the status of the composer, both as a group within society and as an individual in the world of patrons; and (5) on the functioning of a printed dedication in society, on the social context of music patronage and on the music market in which the composer was working. Besides, the question arises as to the possibility of a connection between the liminary texts and the musical content of the respective prints. During the second half of the sixteenth century the motet was one of the freest musical genres in which composers could experiment with new musical means. The texts to be set to music, the disposition of the voices, the compositional style and the musical themes (e.g. through the use of a *soggetto cavato dalle vocali*) were all elements that could be chosen in order to satisfy the musical taste and/or the practical conditions of the dedicatee. Here, the question to be asked to the printed music book

[1] For a project description see Nele Gabriëls – Demmy Verbeke, 'The Latin Dedications of the Motet Editions of the Franco-Flemish Polyphonists from the Second Half of the Sixteenth Century as Musical and Literary Sources', *Lias*, 29 (2002), 153-156.

is one of specificity: what makes this particular edition unique and what links it directly to its dedicatee.

The latter issue naturally implies the scrutiny of each of the 261 music editions in the corpus at hand. Such an endeavour is not within the scope of this exposé. Here, the most persistent question that occurred when studying the dedications (including some texts of editions not incorporated in the corpus but related to it) is dealt with, punctuated with examples: what do the dedications actually tell us?

## Reading the lines: the facts in the texts[2]

Telling the story of many a composer's life would not have been possible without the information provided by liminary texts. A striking example is the editions of Rinaldo del Mel, discussed elsewhere in these proceedings.[3] Likewise, most facts presently known about Arnoldus Flander are deduced from his 1595 *Sacrae cantiones* for four voices.[4] At the time monk and organist in Tolmezzo — as stated on the title page — Flander got acquainted eight years earlier with Felix Bidernuccio, the dedicatee of the edition, who most likely offered the composer a helping hand to obtain this position.

Some liminaries present small pieces of the biographical puzzle, offering new information or confirming other sources. Jacobus Flori and Balduin

[2] Unless stated otherwise, Demmy Verbeke, *"Ad musicae patronos" – Latijnse dedicaties en inleidende teksten in motettenbundels van componisten uit de Nederlanden (ca. 1550 – ca. 1600)*, 4 vols (PhD diss. Katholieke Universiteit Leuven, 2005; full text available at http://hdl.handle.net/1979/160) was consulted concerning the liminary texts as well as for a transcription of the titles of the editions discussed. The Latin citations are taken from vol. III of this dissertation, which presents all liminaries of the motet prints of Franco-Flemish polyphonists (1550-1600) in a critical edition and Dutch translation (translations in vol. II). For paraphrased liminaries without quotation in this article, reference to the relevant pages in Verbeke will be given. I thank Verbeke for his permission to use his typescript.

[3] See Emilie Corswarem's contribution to this volume.

[4] *Sacrae cantiones Arnoldi Flandri eremitae organistae Tulmetini, quatuor vocibus decantandae, liber primus* (Venice: Angelo Gardano, 1595; RISM A 2477 [i.e. the number attributed to musical sources by the *Répertoire international des sources musicales*, Series A/I (Kassel-Basel: Bärenreiter, 1971-2003) and Series B/I (Munch: Herle Verlag, 1960); henceforth: RISM]): 'Quare, cum meo quodam felici fato contigerit, ut tuam, Felix praestantissime, amicitiam consecutus, qua nihil mihi in vita optabilius accidit, te auctore atque adeo adiutore sedem in his locis ponerem liberiusque et arbitratu meo Musis vacarem, ... Eas comitate illa tua singulari, qua te omnes in caelum ferunt, accipere et benevolentiam, qua me octo ab hinc annis complexus es humanissime, mihi, obsecro te, eandem in perpetuum praestare ne graveris.'

Hoyoul both claim to have studied with Orlando di Lasso in Munich.[5] In the case of Flori, this allegiance is also apparent from his tricinium *Fratres sobrii estote* of which the melodic material is clearly related to Lasso's four-voice setting published by Pierre Phalèse in the *Liber secundus sacrarum cantionum quatuor vocum*.[6] For other composers too, the liminaries or title of the printed music book functioned as a place to advertise their professional background, referring to their teacher, patron, employment or previous achievements. Adrianus Petit Coclico, self-claimed pupil of Josquin Desprez, also recounts his peregrinations following his departure from his homeland due to his protestant leanings.[7]

Some of the data in the liminaries has blatantly been overlooked by scholars. The late example of Ferdinando di Lasso's *Apparatus musicus* comes to mind, with a dedicatory letter to Maximilian of Bavaria revealing the composer not to be Orlando di Lasso's son, as generally assumed in musicological literature, but his grandson.[8] This recognition

[5] Jacobus Flori, *Modulorum aliquot tam sacrorum quam prophanorum cum tribus vocibus, et tum musicis instrumentis, tum vocibus concinnentium accommodatorum, liber unus* (Louvain: Petrus Phalesius, 1573; RISM F 1185); complete edition in *Jacobus Flori: Motetten en Nederlandse polyfone liederen/Motets and Dutch Polyphonic Songs (Leuven, 1573)*, eds. Nele Gabriëls *et al*., Monumenta Flandriae Musica, 11 (Leuven-Neerpelt: Alamire Uitgeverij, 2006); liminaries on pp. 3-4: '[...] idque sub eo praeceptore, qui citra controversiam omnium superiorum aetatum Musicorum facile princeps haberi possit, Orlando di Lasso, Musicae harmoniae apud illustrissimum Bavarie Ducem praefecto et doctore.' Balduin Hoyoul, *Sacrae cantiones quinque, sex, septem, octo, novem et decem vocum, quae cum vivae voci, tum omnis generis instrumentis musicis commodissime applicari possunt* (Nuremberg: Katharina Gerlach, 1587; RISM H 7593): 'Nam et ipsius Celsitudo musicam non modo fovit, cantores et instrumentistas (ut vocant) aluit, verum etiam me puerum fere ad dominum Orlandum (nostro seculo praestantissimum musicum) misit sumptusque liberaliter subministravit, ut ab illo peritissimo artifice componendi artem addiscerem.'

[6] Louvain: Petrus Phalesius, 1569 (RISM 1569[8]).

[7] Adrianus Petit Coclico, *Musica reservata. Consolationes piae ex psalmis Davidicis, ornatae suavissimis concentibus musicis, a peritissimo musico Adriano Petit Coclico, discipulo Iosquini de Pratis* (Nuremberg: Johann Berg – Ulrich Neuber, 1552; RISM C 3258): 'Inter caetera autem mala huius postremae aetatis et senectae mundi, etiam hoc se profert, quod artes bonae et earum cultores negliguntur et contemnuntur. Cuius ego rei magna cum iactura mea periculum feci, cum propter nomen Christi et religionis verae confessionem ab infidelibus patria eiectus et omnibus bonis spoliatus, me conferrem ad musicam, quae mihi sola adhuc ex naufragio (ut ita dicam) relicta erat et quam a praestantissimo artifice Iosquino de Pratis videlicet, cuius me discipulum esse profiteor, hauseram ....'

[8] Ferdinando di Lasso, *Apparatus musicus vocum octo varias easque sacras et divinis officiis aptas complectens odas* (Munich: Nikolaus Henricus, 1622; RISM L754): 'Quare statim ... sacravi ingenioli mei has, quantulascunque primulas lucubrationes, avi, patris, patruique mei vestigia premens, quibus *Serenissima Domus Bavarica* non vacivissimas, & benevolentissimas tantum aures, sed manus insuper liberalissimas praebuit.' See Nele Gabriëls, 'Expanding the Lasso Dynasty: Ferdinand (II) di Lasso', *Tijdschrift van de Koninklijke Vereniging voor Nederlandse Muziekgeschiedenis*, 56 (2006), 17-23.

of Ferdinand (II) di Lasso as a composer of his own merits instigates the demand for a reconsideration of the repertoire previously assigned to his father Ferdinand (I) Lassus.

Dedications often bear witness of historic events — being offered on the occasion of coronations, consecrations etc. — while some even hint at the specifics about a composer's daily-life. Johannes Lefebure's letter dedicating the 1596 hymn book to cardinal Andreas of Austria, governor of Tyrol and Alsace, offers such a glimpse.[9] Here, Lefebure reveals the reason for the publication of this particular repertoire. During the many travels with the cardinal, the chapel had to carry around 'a heavy burden of books' in order to sing the divine office on feast-days as was customary at the dedicatee's court. The (printed) choirbook at hand would lighten the burden for a copy of it could now easily be available for the singers at the residences where the court was staying. Note how this primarily liturgical function is reflected in the choirbook format of the edition. The chapel master's tasks are expanded upon by Jacobus Vaet in the letter to Maximilian II preceding his first book of five-voice motets.[10] As the three basic duties, the composer mentions leading the choir, providing the schoolboys' musical education and composing new music. Since the musical proficiency of the chapel singers was high, leading the choir needed little effort except for establishing the musical integration of the inexperienced singers with those more skilled. Instructing the youth in music was much more time-consuming, which — taken together with other smaller issues arising — left Vaet insufficient time to fulfil his third major task, composing. Hence the master decided to make good use of his limited time and to compose music in honour of God and the house of Austria.

The information provided by Lefebure and Vaet is rather exceptional within the corpus at hand: dedications by and large refer to events related

[9] Jan Lefebure, *Devoti ac sacri per totum annum hymni ... quatuor solum vocum iuxta choralem tantum Romanum, pie & religiose accomodati, item, quatuor antiphonae de B. Maria virgine, quinque vocum* (Konstanz: Leonhard Straub, 1596; RISM L 1435): 'Ne ergo in itinere suscipiendo magna veluti librorum sarcinula ubique onerari cogamur, opere praecium fore existimavi, si horum Hymnorum aliquot exemplaria imprimerentur, ut pro loci et residentiae necessitate in promptu essent.' Thanks to Jeanine De Landtsheer for help with the translation of these liminaries transcribed by Verbeke, as well as of those of RISM B 3469, S 395, S 398 and several others not included in this article.

[10] Jacobus Vaet, *Modulationes quinque vocum (vulgo motecta) nuncupatae ... liber primus* (Venice: Antonio Gardano, 1562; RISM V 26): 'et ut multae mihi fuerint curae in hac mea provincia sustinendae, tres tamen praecipue fuerunt: cura musici concentus regendi, cura rudis iuventutis recte in eo studio instituendae et cura etiam novae et ad tempus accommodate musices componendae.'

to the addressee of the text. Examples are numerous. Pierre Bonhomme's letter prefacing his *Melodiae sacrae* from 1603 recounts Ferdinand of Bavaria's visit to Liege not long before the publication of this edition, while Giovanni de Macque offers his 1596 motetbook to Francisco Maria Tarugi on the occasion of his appointment to the cardinalate for which Tarugi was called to Rome.[11] Pierre de Manchicourt's letter to Antoine Perrenot de Granvelle, dated 1553 and printed in his fifth motetbook from 1554, mentions a 'recent' meeting of many officials in Brussels.[12] The dedication itself suggests the composer here refers to Granvelle's instalment as Secretary of State to Charles V in 1550.

With the inclusion of the dedicatory motet *O decus o patriae lux* in honour of the dedicatee at the start of the publication, Manchicourt subscribes to the tradition of musical *Fürstenlob*. In this respect, one must note the three motetbooks by Johannes de Cleve, which feature no less than thirteen laudatory motets, mostly to members of the Habsburg dynasty.[13] A particular typographical case is Martin Peu d'Argent's compositions for the birth of Karl Friedrich (1555-1575), son of Wilhelm of Cleve and heir to the ducal title, as printed in his *Liber secundus sacrarum cantionum quinque vocum quae vulgo moteta vocantur.*[14] *Misericordia est Iesu Christi* and *Dux optatus adest* occupy the third-to-last and penultimate position

[11] Pierre Bonhomme, *Melodiae sacrae, quas vulgo motectas appellant, iam noviter quinis, senis, octonis et novenis suavissimis vocibus concinnatae* (Frankfurt: Wolfgang Richter – Nicolas Stein, 1603; RISM B 3469): 'cum deditissimos tibi Leodienses tua Serenissima nuper praesentia recreares, sapientissimisque consiliis illustrares.' Giovanni de Macque, *Motectorum quinque, sex et octo vocum, liber primus* (Rome: Nicolo Mutii, 1596; RISM M 91): 'Quum primum te amplissima ista Purpuratorum Patrum dignitate auctum fuisse Neapoli nunciatum est, tanto sum gaudio affectus et laetitia perfusus, verbis vix explicare ut queam.'

[12] Pierre de Manchicourt, *Liber quintus cantionum sacrarum vulgo mo<te>ta vocant, quinque et sex vocum* (Louvain: Petrus Phalesius, 1554; RISM M 272): 'Quod profecto tu etiam in tot clariss[imorum] et illustriss[imorum] virorum coetu nuper Bruxellis satis superque testatum esse voluisti, dum in tanto dignitatis culmine constitutus me non solum veterem commilitonem et agnoscere et nuncupare dignatus es.'

[13] Johannes de Cleve, *Cantiones sacrae, quae vulgo muteta vocantur, quatuor, quinque et sex vocum, ... Liber Primus* (Augsburg: Philipp Ulhard, 1559; RISM C 3203); *Cantiones sacrae, quae vulgo muteta vocantur, quatuor, quinque et sex vocum ... Liber secundus* (Augsburg: Philipp Ulhard, 1559; RISM C 3204); *Cantiones seu harmoniae sacrae (quas vulgo moteta vocant) quattuor, quinque, sex, septem, octo et decem vocum* (Augsburg: Philipp Ulhard – Andreas Reinheckel, 1579/80; RISM C 3205). For a discussion of de Cleve's motet oeuvre see Nele Gabriëls, 'Johannes de Cleve (1529-1582) and His Laudatory Motets for the Habsburg House: The Odd Man Out?' (with full work list) (forthcoming).

[14] Düsseldorf: Jacob Baethen (by order of the heirs of Arnold Birckmann), 1555 (RISM M 782).

in the book, preceded by the motet *Terram nunc pede* (2a pars: *En foecunda Aquila*) for the birth of Maria Leonora (ducal daughter) and followed by *Ego sum qui sum* setting an antiphon for Matins on Easter Sunday. The motet texts for Karl Friedrich are notated as chronograms: the capitalised letters (excluding the D) add up to the number 1555 (see illustration 1). This device to commemorate the year of birth seems to be reserved exclusively for the heir to the ducal title as it is not applied to *Terram nunc pede*. The inclusion of these compositions together with the lack of a dedication to the collection, suggest the book was considered as a unity with Peu d'Argent's first five-voice motetbook, printed in the same year and dedicated to Wilhelm of Cleve.[15] While the *liber primus* is adorned with no fewer than six liminary texts — an extensive dedication letter supplemented by a dedicatory poem, an *Ad Zoilum* and a lengthy poem in praise of music, all enveloped by two odes to the composer — the second book only contains Heinrich Zilmann of Düren's verses on *musica sit natura homini indita*. It can be read as complementary to the thorough, humanistic liminaries of the first book — praising music and defending it from unjust critique — in which one of the only missing elements is the reference to the harmony of the spheres.

On the whole, information on music in the dedications — be it aesthetics, theory or the compositions in the edition at hand — is very limited. Most commonly, a (topical) praise of music offers an insight into the contemporary view on music, as in Peu d'Argent's *Liber primus*. Both the composer's dedicatory letter as well as the ode to music by Paulus Chimarrhaeus provide an exceptionally lengthy example of *laudatio musices* (at which many liminaries hint only briefly), honouring the art for its effect on both humans and gods.[16] Especially Chimarrhaeus expands upon the topic. Peu d'Argent exemplifies the importance of music in both Greek history and the catholic faith, the latter of which considers music — leader of the human affects — as 'the most closely connected to the Word of God'.[17] This leads to a defence of music by means of its praise, against the ignorant critics who accuse music of arousing licentiousness

[15] Martin Peu d'Argent, *Liber primus sacrarum cantionum quinque vocum quae vulgo moteta vocantur* (Düsseldorf: Jacob Baethen (by order of the heirs of Arnold Birckmann), 1555; RISM M 781).

[16] See Verbeke, *'Ad musicae patronos'*, III, 110-117 for an edition of the liminaries in RISM M 781.

[17] 'Nihil enim verbo Dei statuerunt esse coniunctius, quam musicam, dominam et gubernatricem humanorum affectuum.'

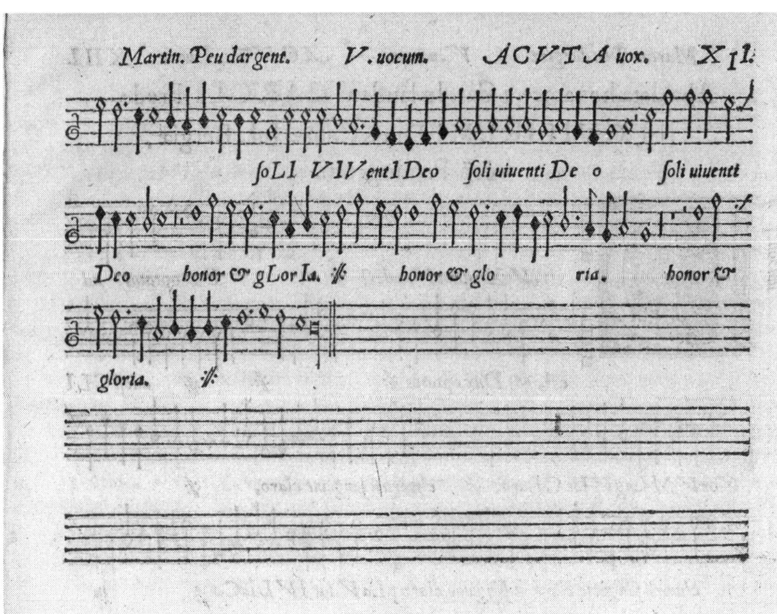


Martin Peu d'Argent, *Misericordia est Iesu Christi*
(RISM M782, Acuta vox, ff. 11v-12); by permission of the British Library.

and fail to notice the difference between the cause (music) and abuse of this cause. Music is deemed a gift from God. In the current period this is noticeable more than ever: the composer refers to the refined standard, even perfection of the music of his days, which outshines that of all previous times.

Mattheus Le Maistre too elaborates upon music's importance for and effect on the human spirit in his writing to August of Saxony in 1570.[18] He balances profane (generating pleasure, discipline and moderation of affects) and Christian (serving theology, dispelling the evil spirit and grief, offering a foretaste of celestial life) reasons for which (the) God(s) created music.

In the same year, Alexander Utendal refers to Glareanus' theory of the modes as well as to Gioseffo Zarlino in his letter *Ad lectores*. The composer extensively refutes the adherents to the eight-mode system and presents his book as a means by which he wishes to stimulate German musicians to read the Swiss theorist's work.[19] Five years earlier, Homerus Herpol (once private pupil of Glareanus) had explained his former teacher's theory in more detail in the *Novum et insigne opus musicum*.[20] The lengthy first (cf. infra) dedicatory letter is addressed to Otto Truchsess von Waldburg, bishop of Augsburg and recipient of Glareanus' *Dodecachordon*. It presents

[18] Mattheus Le Maistre, *Liber primus sacrarum cantionum (quas vulgo moteta vocant) ab illustrissimi Principis, Ducis ac Electoris Saxoniae, etc. ... quinque vocibus compositarum* (Dresden: Gimel Bergen, 1570; RISM L 1844); liminaries edited in Verbeke, *'Ad musicae patronos'*, III, 100-102.

[19] Alexander Utendal, *Septem psalmi poenitentiales, adiunctis ex prophetarum scriptis orationibus eiusdem argumenti quinque, ad dodecachordi modos duodecim, hac quidem aetate doctiorum quorundam musicorum opera ab obscuritate vindicatos, nihilominus quamplurimis adhuc incognitos, aptissima tam vivae voci, quam diversis musicorum instrumentorum generibus harmonia accommodati* (Nuremberg: Theodor Gerlach, 1570; RISM U 119): 'Abunde ergo dico, meis votis satisfactum esse tunc putabo, si aliquando hoc meo conatu, ad exemplum clarissimi Zerlini [sic], qui iam id, quod tantopere expecto, foelicissimo opere praestitit, Germanos quoque (qui hac aetate nulli etiam nationi ingenii foelicitate, luculentissimis suis omnium disciplinarum undique indies prodeuntibus in lucem voluminibus, se cedere manifesto ostendunt) hisce meis lucubratiunculis ad Glareani lectionem invitare queam.' See Verbeke, *'Ad musicae patronos'*, III, 154-156 for the complete liminaries and Ignace Bossuyt, 'Die 'Psalmi poenitentiales' (1570) des Alexander Utendal. Ein künstlerisches Gegenstück der Busspsalmen von O. Lassus und eine praktische Anwendung von Glareans Theorie der zwölf Modi', *Archiv für Musikwissenschaft*, 38 (1981), 279-295 for a discussion of this motetbook in the light of Glareanus's modal theory.

[20] Homerus Herpol, *Novum et insigne opus musicum, in quo textus Evangeliorum totius anni, vero ritui Ecclesiae correspondens, quinque vocum modulamine... exprimitur* (Nuremberg: Ulrich Neuber & heirs of Johann Berg, 1565; RISM H 5187). See Verbeke, *'Ad musicae patronos'*, III, 33-41 for an edition of the complete liminaries to this edition.

the music as a practical illustration of the theory discussed for those who cannot read Greek or Latin. Besides, it elucidates the collection's structure, consisting of four *dodecades* — each ordered in a different way — with five compositions in the five most commonly used modes interspersed between the second and third *dodecade*.

Herpol and Utendal are two of the very few composers who deal with the musical content of their motet publications more extensively than by merely referring to the religious nature of the texts or the number of voices used. One other composer doing so is Franciscus Sales who, at the end of the century, drew attention to the possible performance of his *Missa Exultandi tempus est* as a dialogue between voices and the organ as indicated in the music notation itself.[21] Overall, however, the motets published were only rarely subject of the liminary texts. This is surprising as a large majority of the liminaries under consideration were written — or at least signed — by the composers and not by editors, printers or theologians as was the case in earlier sixteenth century printed sources. As is clear from Raimund Redecker's study,[22] those earlier sources demonstrate the importance of liminaries as a vehicle to advocate and explain both the upcoming art of printing as well as the new religion prophesised by followers of Luther, Melanchton, etc. It seems composers of the later sixteenth century were working in a different market place, promoting their patrons rather than their own art. This leads to the question as to how the dedication actually functioned within society. Thereto, one can turn to the dedications themselves, as they bear witness both explicitly and implicitly of this functioning.

## Reading between the lines: the functioning of the dedication

The printed music book is situated in the midst of the triangle formed by composer, patron/dedicatee and buying public.[23] It functions on the interface

[21] Franciscus Sales, *Patrocinium musices. In natalem domini Iesu Christi … mutetum quinque vocum & Missa ad eius imitationem composita* (Munich: Adam Berg, 1598; RISM S 398): '[…] quae instar Dialogi, in Choro, et Organo, mutuis intervallis (quod interposita signa satis superque demonstrant) decantari potest.'

[22] Raimund Redeker, *Lateinische Widmungsvorreden zu Meß- und Motettendrucken der ersten Hälfte des 16. Jahrhunderts*, Schriften zur Musikwissenschaft aus Münster, 6 (Eisenach: Wagner, 1995).

[23] The theory of patronage c. 1600 is especially dealt with by Claudio Annibaldi in various articles, including 'Towards a Theory of Musical Patronage in the Renaissance and

of the public and the private domain: public as it is a 'publication' for everyone to buy, read and use, and private as the book is most often dedicated by one individual to another and as the dedication is the expression of a private though generally professional relation (or wished-for relation).

For the patron, the 'public' of the triangle just mentioned is the 'world' towards whom he ought to symbolise his social rank. Music then — both in its sounding and in its printed form — is a means to represent and reinforce power and wealth to the world and, in the case of the printed book, to the (potential) buyers. This happens by exhibiting good taste, a refined and noble mind, and generosity. From the composer's point of view, the public is the hidden cause of his need for protection: it is potentially hostile to his work and can make or break his name. Thus, the patron needs the composer as he is a possible originator of a much sought-after instrument (i.e. music) to represent his rank, while the composer depends on the goodwill and generosity of the patron to make a living. Against this background, the dedication of a music book naturally can be seen as a 'gift' (the necessary tool for the patron) to compensate for benefactions (employment or remuneration) received by the composer.

It is important, however, to realise the particular importance of the public of buyers ('the world') for this 'private' relation between patron and artist. It is especially the existence of a public that reads the music book's printed dedication, which forms a trump card in the hands of the composer: the public is the actual cause of the patron's need for the composer. As a result, the composer can use this public as a witness of a private yet professional relation with his patron. The public then serves as a counter-balance against the uncertainty of an asymmetrical patron-client relation: the buyers are bystanders to the declaration of this relation. Moreover, the lavish praise of the dedicatee in many of the letters — presenting an undoubtedly idealised image of the person and his (or her) deeds — functions in the area of tension between image and reality. It evokes the idea of a truthful representation of the ruler in order to honour this ruler as well as to accomplish the assimilation of image and

the Baroque', *Recercare*, 10 (1998), 173-182 and 'Introduzione', in *La musica e il mondo. Mecenatismo e committenza musicale in Italia tra Quatro e Settecento*, ed. Claudio Annibaldi (Bologna: Società editrice il Mulino, 1993), pp. 9-45. On this topic specifically related to later sixteenth-century music prints, see also Nele Gabriëls, 'Dedicating Music: The Case of Philippus de Monte's Motets in print', in *Yearbook of the Alamire Foundation*, 8 (forthcoming).

reality in the tradition of the *Fürstenspiegel*.[24] By publicly mirroring the addressee's personality in an idealised way in the dedication, that patron (ideally) will need to live up to this image in order to keep the reputation which that dedication brought him. The buyers hence play a very important role as witnesses to the glorious presentation of the dedicatee as well as to the affirmation of the patron-client relation in general. Thus, the public nature of the printed music book forms a quintessential characteristic of the act of dedicating these books.[25]

To what extent were the composers conscious of the place occupied by the published dedication within the system of patronage when dedicating their music? Examination of the letters shows them to have been fairly well aware.

Composers — or editors — frequently make explicit the incentive for dedicating their work. Time and again, they subscribe to an age-old tradition, as articulated amongst others by Franciscus Sales in his 1593 dedication to Wolfgang Rumpf.[26] With regard to the composer's need for authoritative protection against the potentially hostile public, examples abound as well: one of the most common topical elements in the dedications is the plea for acceptance and approval of the 'gift', which thus will benefit from the protection offered by the dedicatee's name. Matthias Werrecore for example, declares that, when people will see that the dedicatee Antonius Marinus Pansanus often enjoys this music to take his mind off various worries, they too will take these partbooks in hand.[27] Andreas Pevernage states that for the forebears too — be it men of learning,

[24] The image of the mirror is touched upon by Claudia Brink in her study *Arte et Marte. Kriegskunst und Kunstliebe im Herrscherbild des 15. und 16. Jahrhunderts in Italien*, Kunstwissenschaftliche Studien, 91 (Munich: Deutscher Kunstverlag, 2000), pp. 194-195.

[25] For an interesting point of comparison, see Thomas Schmidt-Beste's article on dedications of manuscripts in this volume.

[26] Franciscus Sales, *Sacrarum cantionum, omnis generis instrumentis musicis et vivae voci accomodatarum* [sic], *hactenus non editarum, liber primus* (Prague: Georg Nigrin, 1593; RISM S 394): 'Cum sacros hosce cantus ... ad divinarum laudum incrementum in lucem edere constituissem, illust[rissi]me Domine, eisque Moecenatem more iam recepto quaererem, prima omnium illust[rissi]ma D[ominatio] Tua animo se obtulit meo.'

[27] Matthias Werrecore, *Cantuum quinque vocum (quos motetta vocant) Hermanni Matthiae Werrecoren*[*sis*] *musici excelentissimi, liber primus* (Milan: Franciscus – Simon Moschenius, 1555; RISM M 1407): 'Quamobrem fore confido ut te nonnunquam, sepositis paulisper gravioribus curis, animum his nostris levare non pigeat: ita enim mihi non minimus laudis ac ornamenti cumulus accesserit, si in quam plurimorum manibus hi nostri libri aliqua cum laude versentur. Id autem proculdubio fiet, nam quod te facere homines animadvertent, id sibi quoque faciendum summa cum dignitate existimabunt.'

philosophers, writers or musicians — protection against unjust criticism was the reason to dedicate their work: hence the justifiable establishment of this tradition.[28]

The liminaries equally demonstrate an awareness on the composers' behalf of the possibilities to spread the name and fame of the dedicatee by means of a dedication. Thus, Martin Peu d'Argent explicitly states that he published and dedicated his music to add to the dedicatee's fame.[29] A far more striking example is Lasso's *Moduli quinis vocibus*,[30] dedicated by the composer himself to Wilhelm of Bavaria during a sojourn in Paris. The dedication is an ingenious move for both dedicatee and composer and has a multi-layered implication. On the one hand, it entails a clever form of political propaganda for the Wittelsbach court in a foreign country. Maybe this dedication was a prerequisite for Lasso's travel to Paris? Even if Lasso himself chose to dedicate the book to Wilhelm, it will still have functioned in such a promotional way. On the other hand, it equally entails publicity for the composer. The dedication might also have been a confirmation of Lasso's pledge to stay in the service of the Bavarian dukes: in the light of the rumours about his wish to take service with the French king Charles IX, the standard closing assertion that this print is a sign of the author's devotion to the dedicatee takes on an extra meaning.[31]

[28] Andreas Pevernage, *Cantiones aliquot sacrae sex, septem et octo vocum, quibus addita sunt elogia nonnulla versibus latinis expressa, tam viva voce, quam omnis generis instrumentis cantatu commodissimae* (Douai: Jean Bogard, 1578; RISM P 1669): 'Optima ratione a maioribus institutum et a viris philosophis observatum semper fuit, reverendiss[ime] Praesul, ut cuiuscunque argumenti opera ederentur, ea non nisi sub alicuius viri Principis nomine in publicum prodirent. Sic etenim iniquas invidorum calumnias et insanam sycophantarum rabiem posse comprimi, sic dignitatem eruditorum, authoritatem philosophorum, innocentiam scriptorum defendi, ipsamque sacrosanctam musices, hoc est totius philosophiae, maiestatem integram, intactam et illibatam conservari posse recte arbitrabantur.'

[29] Peu d'Argent, *Liber primus*: 'aliquid etiam illustrissimo tuo nomini laudis et honoris accederet, dum divulgabitur, quam benigne, humaniter prolixeque non hanc solum artem, sed caeteras omnes earumque professores foveas ac defendas.'

[30] Orlando di Lasso, *Moduli quinis vocibus nunquam hactenus editi Monachii Boioariae compositi* (Paris: Adrian Le Roy – Robert Ballard, 1571; RISM L 843). See Verbeke, *'Ad musicae patronos'*, III, 69 for a transcription of this dedication. Note how a few months later, Le Roy and Ballard dedicated RISM L 845 to Charles IX as well as RISM L 847 by means of a letter written by Jacques Gohory (cf. infra).

[31] On the circumstances for Lasso's Paris travel, see Horst Leuchtmann, *Orlando di Lasso. Sein Leben. Versuch einer Bestandsaufnahme der biografischen Einzelheiten* (Wiesbaden: Breitkopf und Härtel, 1976), pp. 157 and 166-167.

That the public also simultaneously protects the composer against the whimsicality of his patron is aptly put into words by Philippus de Monte. In his fourth motetbook for five voices, he writes to Cardinal Flavio Orsini in Rome: 'I wanted to give a distinct proof to all once more, of my continuous and never interrupted — but rather increased — devotion or reverence, and with a certain new judicial document confirm my old property by means of this edition of musical songs which by myself are dedicated to the honoured name of your illustrious lordship'.[32] De Monte openly equates the book and its dedication to a judicial document of his relation with the dedicatee. As a result, the public is implicitly called upon as witnesses to the dedicatory act.

Still, it goes without saying that more tangible motives, such as financial aid and (finding or ensuring) employment, inspired many a dedication, even if these are not generally mentioned. It is tempting to link, for example, Orlando di Lasso's dedication to Eitelfriedrich IV of Hohenzollern-Hechingen of his 1585 *Cantica sacra* to his son Ferdinand's appointment as chapel master at the Hechingen court the very same year.[33] The tone of the letter strengthens this supposition, with its extensive praise of the addressee's generosity towards musicians and its explicit mention of large stipends conferred upon the court musicians.[34] Some exceptions prove the rule, however, and make explicit the pecuniary facets of the dedicatory act. Thus, in his 1594 dedication to bishop Stanislas Pavlov of Olmucz, Francisus Sales declares his first book of music for the mass propers in choirbook format — the *Missarum solenniorum* edited in 1589 in Adam Berg's prestigious series *Patrocinium musices* — to have been a real financial drain on both himself and the printer.[35] It is

[32] Philippus de Monte, *Libro quarto de motetti* (Venice: sons of Antonio Gardano, 1575; RISM M 3314): 'volui denuo fidem cunctis facere continuatae et nunquam interruptae devotionis vel observantiae meae, sed potius adauctae, atque novo quodam iuris documento corroborare veterem meam possessionem hac editione cantionum musicarum honorato nomini illustrissimae D[ominationis] V[estrae] a me consecratarum.'

[33] Orlando di Lasso, *Cantica sacra, recens numeris et modulis ornata, nec ullibi antea typis evulgata, sex et octo vocibus* (Munich: Adam Berg, 1585; RISM L 796).

[34] 'Tu enim maximis opibus circumfluens, ex diversis orbis terrarum provinciis evocatos musicos et benignissime complecteris et stipendiis in aula tua alis, usque adeo lautis et liberalibus, ut paucis admodum totius Romani Imperii cedas principibus, multos vero etiam longissime superes.'

[35] Franciscus Sales, *Patrocinium musices. Missarum solenniorum, tam sanctorum quam festorum officia labentis anni, in catholicae ecclesiae usum, harmonice contra punctum ac suavissime concinnata …primus tomus* (Munich: Adam Berg, 1589; RISM S 392); idem, *Officiorum Missalium, quibus Introitus, Alleluia et Communiones de omnibus omnium*

the reason why this collection appears as a set of partbooks. Most astoundingly, Sales also mentions the earlier book's dedicatee, archbishop of Salzburg Wolfgang Dietrich (of Raitenau), which results in a taunt rather than a compliment to the latter. More than twenty years earlier, the French poet Jacques Gohory had been even more direct when he terminated his dedicatory letter to Lasso's second motetbook for five voices in Paris to Charles IX of France with a reference to a previous dedication to the king which had not been rewarded, 'not even with a copper coin'.[36]

One may wonder how a dedication came about, especially when there was no direct patron–client relation between the dedicatee and the composer of the edition. This aspect is hardly ever explicitly dealt with in the liminaries studied for this research. Homer Herpol lifts a corner of the veil in his double dedication to the above mentioned *Novum et insigne opus musicum*,[37] firstly dedicated with a letter to the bishop of Augsburg, Otto Truchsess von Waldburg, and secondly with another letter to Johann Egolf of Knöringen, canon in Augsburg and scholasticus in Würzburg. The second letter — quite clearly a print of an actual private letter to the canon, which was sent along with the music to be delivered to the printer — details the lobbying undertaken by Johann Egolf. Herpol relates how the canon had contacted Georg Roggenbach, jurist in Nuremberg, who had succeeded in convincing Johann Berg to print the music. Presumably this had happened before Berg's death in August 1563. Johann Egolf then had advised the composer to send the corrected music as soon as possible, which was done together with this letter in which Herpol also verifies that Berg will send him some copies when the book will be printed. The matter of dedication had not really been decided upon when this letter was written. Hence the composer asks Johann Egolf to put in a good

*sanctorum, per totum anni circulum, diebus festis & solennibus quinque & sex vocum continentur, liber secundus* (Prague: Georg Nigrinus, 1594; RISM S 395): 'Atque cum ante annos aliquot, officiorum Missarum solenniorum tomum primum in magno folio, mea et Typographi ingenti iactura ediderim, ac Reverendissimo et Illustrissimo Principi D[omino] D[omino] Wolff[gango] Theodorico … dedicaverim; Secundum eorundem divinorum officiorum totum minori hac forma excusum, Reverendissimae et Illustrissimae Celsitudini tuae … humiliter offero.'

[36] Orlando di Lasso, *Secundus liber modulorum, quinis vocibus constantium* (Paris: Adrian Le Roy — Robert Ballard, 1571; RISM L 847). 'Haec ego, Rex magnificentissime, qui tibi quondam vellus Iasonis aureum egregia pictura insigne ne teruncio quidem aereo remuneratum dicavi, quique francicam T[iti] Livii historiam (quae inchoata pendet) aliaque ingenii monumenta (si faveas iubeasque) maiestati tuae primo quoque tempore consecrabo.'

[37] Cf. footnote 20.

word for him with Otto Truchsess, that is: if the canon agrees with this choice of dedicatee.[38]

Intermediaries like Johann Egolf in the case of Herpol were surely no exception. However, these generally are only mentioned in the dedication itself as in Jacobus de Kerle's letter addressed to the new Pope Sixtus V in his 1585 motetbook *Selectiorum aliquot modulorum*,[39] where the papal nuncio and bishop of San Severo, Germanico Malaspina, is mentioned as Kerle's 'advisor' concerning this edition. In Herpol's case, the inclusion of verses honouring Johann Egolf as well as the explicit dedication to the Augsburg canon of a poem in praise of music and Herpol, can jeopardise the precarious balance between the primary and the secondary recipient of the dedication.

At this point, the question arises as to how composers viewed themselves or musicians in general. As said before, dedications of course were also a form of publicity for the composer himself: his name was connected to that of high-ranking officials whose fame radiated on the artist. It must be pointed out how self-conscious some composers were, especially towards the later sixteenth and early seventeenth century. The late example of Lambert de Sayve's *Sacrae symphoniae* from 1612, dedicated to the new emperor Matthias, is an obvious one, even though the dedication itself is rather traditional.[40] Besides the (rather commonly included) laudatory poem to the composer, it also features a portrait of the composer appearing on the exact place where often the dedicatee's coat of arms was printed, as well as a motet (*Quod nova nupta cupis*) written for his own (second) marriage. Philippus de Monte is an earlier example of a self-confident composer. In his 1596 dedication to Thomas Mermann (physician at the Munich court), he explicitly claimed not to need protection by the addressee's power, nor recommendation by his learning

[38] Verbeke offers a similar interpretation; see *'Ad musicae patronos'*, II, 126-127.

[39] Jacobus de Kerle, *Selectiorum aliquot modulorum, qui in sacris templis, ad celebrandas divinas laudes, partim quatuor, partim quinque et octo vocibus, decantari solent. Nunc primum in lucem editi* (Prague: Georg Nigrin, 1585; RISM K 455): 'eos typis excudendos Tuaeque Sanctitati vel eo nomine libentius consecrandos esse duxi, quod ab illustriss[imo] reverendissimoque Episcopo S[ancti] Severi, Domino Germanico Marchione Malaspina, Tuae Sanctitatis ad Sac[ram] Caes[aream] Maiestatem Nuncio, cum potestate Legati de latere, etc. tam benigne tamque amanter fuerim in hoc proposito meo confirmatus.'

[40] Lambert de Sayve, *Sacrae symphoniae, quas vulgo motetas appellant, tam de totius anni festis solennibus, quam de tempore, 4. 5. 6. 7. 8. 9. 10. 11. 12. 13. 15. & 16. tam vocibus quam instrumentis accommodatae* (Klosterbruck: Johannes Fidler, 1612; RISM S 1126).

because of 'the applause and the approval that the other songs that I have edited far and wide have brought'.[41] It is the expression of a composer's self-awareness and consciousness that could probably hardly have been imagined earlier in the century, leaving out of consideration Lasso's mature career. Just one year earlier, in 1595, Philippe Rogier claimed to be true to the age-old tradition of publishing with the intention of reaching immortality of one's name. According to the composer, dedicating the edition — to Alberto Acquaviva, Duke of Atri and possibly son of Giovanni Girolamo — enhanced this purpose.[42]

It is my conviction that composers were attentive to the new possibilities of music printing and that they became ever more conscious of the power of this medium. Reading the dedications, one doesn't only come across extra bits and pieces of biographical and historical information. When reading between the lines, the liminary texts on the whole allow insight in the functioning of the dedicatory act, its aims and effect. While taking care not to over-interpret the words, one shouldn't be hesitant to interpret them either, for we can be certain that in the sixteenth century, just as now, one could read the lines but also read between the lines.

Onderzoekseenheid Musicologie
Katholieke Universiteit Leuven
Blijde-Inkomststraat 21
B – 3000 Leuven
Nele.Gabriels@arts.kuleuven.be

[41] Philippus de Monte, *Sacrarum cantionum cum quatuor vocibus,... liber primus* (Venice: Angelo Gardano, 1596; RISM M 3325): 'Verum consideranti mihi plausum et approbationem quam reliquae cantiones a me editae passim tulerunt, neque novum patrocinium ab Auctoritate tua, neque novam laudem ab amaenissimo ingenio tuo hac dedicatione aucupor.'

[42] Philippe Rogier, *Sacrarum modulationum, quas vulgo motecta appellant, quae quaternis, quinis, senis et octonis vocibus concinuntur, liber primus* (Naples: "ex typographia Stelliolae", 1595; RISM R 1936): 'Natura comparatum est, ut homo, qui animo constat immortali, quoad eius fieri potest, immortalitati nomen commendet suum. Id cum praecipua quadam ratione scriptis facile comparari possit; qui in aliquo versantur disciplinarum genere, totam operam in eo ponunt suam, ut quicquid scribunt aut excogitant novi, eo spectare videatur; ac ne ulla unquam oblivione hominum deleatur, alicuius principis viri clarissimo nomine illustratum emittunt.'

# DEDICATING MUSIC MANUSCRIPTS: ON FUNCTION AND FORM OF PARATEXTS IN FIFTEENTH- AND SIXTEENTH-CENTURY SOURCES

THOMAS SCHMIDT-BESTE

One reads a great deal about dedications in the printed book — and this volume is indeed given over almost exclusively to the study of printed music and printed literature as well. On the other hand, one reads very little about dedications in manuscripts — for the simple fact that few exist. This lack has attracted surprisingly little attention in the literature on the history of the book. When describing the 'Printing Press as an Agent of Change' (Elizabeth Eisenstein),[1] much is made of the way in which — at first — printing imitated manuscript production, and much is made of the new modes of production, presentation and distribution; in terms of "packaging", it is the title page that receives accolades as the new defining element of the printed book, the element that sets it apart from the manuscript because it "explains" things which hitherto required no explanation.[2] This paper will argue that dedications actually serve a similarly important function in clarifying what distinguishes a printed book functionally from a manuscript. Furthermore, for reasons that will

[1] Elizabeth Eisenstein, *The printing press as an agent of change. Communications and cultural transformations in early modern Europe*, 2 vols (Cambridge: Cambridge University Press, 1979); abridged edition in one volume published as *The printing revolution in Early Modern Europe* (Cambridge: Cambridge University Press, 1983).

[2] 'Most studies of printing have, quite rightly, singled out the regular provision of title pages as the most significant new feature associated with the printed book format.' Eisenstein, *The printing press*, I, 106. See also the excellent study by Margaret M. Smith, *The title-page. Its early development, 1460-1510*, (London-New Castle, Del.: British Library-Oak Knoll Press, 2000), pp. 25-34: 'With a few notable exceptions that will concern us later, manuscripts were not provided with title-pages' (p. 25). The standard work on dedications in music prints of the sixteenth century is Raimund Redeker, *Lateinische Widmungsvorreden zu Meß- und Motettendrucken der ersten Hälfte des 16. Jahrhunderts*, Schriften zur Musikwissenschaft aus Münster, 6 (Eisenach: Wagner, 1995). However, aside from limiting himself to motet and mass prints and from failing to present the full text of the dedicatory texts he is examining (which severely limits the usefulness of his book), Redeker takes little notice of the current scholarship on paratexts. In his chapter on the thematic context of dedications (pp. 7-49), he concentrates on the function of the dedicatory letter as an essentially humanistic device of panegyric.

become clear below, musical sources (i.e. sources that are primarily devoted to notated music, whether monophonic or polyphonic) played a special role in this development — or, at the very least, they throw the functional distinction which I postulate into higher relief than sources of verbal text.

Dedications are paratexts. The French literary theorist Gérard Genette coined this extremely useful term in 1987 to encompass all elements that "surround and extend" the text as such (analogous to the meaning of the Greek preposition "para-": "about", "alongside"): 'the paratext is what enables a text to become a book and to be offered as such to its readers and, more generally, to the public. More than a boundary or a sealed border, the paratext is, rather, a *threshold*, or [...] a "vestibule" that offers the world at large the possibility of either stepping inside or turning back.'[3] Genette first defines "peritexts" as elements that determine the book as a material object and situate it in time and place, and ascribes these elements to the publisher: font, format, material, binding, cover, imprint, title page, table of contents, index, colophon. "Paratexts" proper, for Genette, are authorial: the name of the author himself, the title, the dedication, the inscription (defined by Genette as that dedication which is not printed, but "inscribed" by the author or a later owner to the person to whom the book is presented), the epigraph, prefaces and postfaces (be they original, added later or by somebody else), intertitles and notes. Genette also defines "epitexts" (i.e. reception documents such as reviews), but these are of less interest in this context. It is immediately obvious that not all of Genette's categories apply easily to fifteenth- and sixteenth-century sources, and his distinction between publisher and author is partly artificial in early prints and even more questionable in manuscripts; but he does provide literary scholarship with an extremely useful tool to classify and contemplate the texts "alongside" the text as well as their potential uses. Indeed, a comparison of manuscripts and the earliest prints in terms of how and to what extent they contain (or do not contain) paratexts tells us a great deal about how these sources "work" in their respective social contexts.

As all other peritexts and paratexts, dedications are defined by content, mode of presentation and — most importantly of all — function. Who is supposed to read the dedication, who is the addressee, the "implied reader"?

[3] Gérard Genette, *Paratexts. Tresholds of Interpretation*, transl. Jane E. Lewin (Cambridge: Cambridge University Press, 1997), pp. 1-2; original: *Seuils* [= Tresholds] (Paris: Seuil, 1987).

There is of course the obvious answer to this question: the dedication — most often in form of a stylised letter — is directed towards the dedicatee. However, as is well known, the matter is more complicated: the process of communication involved in the dedication of a written or printed source is by no means a one-way — or even a two-way — street, and one could even argue that the dedicatee is not the real implied reader at all. To be sure, the primary function of a dedication is to establish a relationship between the two parties most directly involved: dedicator and dedicatee. Both parties expect to gain from this relationship. The dedicator wants to attract the favourable attention of the dedicatee, possibly with the hope of financial remuneration; or the dedication is the result of such gain already achieved. There is also the "public relation" value of being associated with a person of high rank or social status, with the possible benefit of achieving a higher standing in one's own professional context or in society at large. The dedicatee receives a boost to his or her self-esteem, and possibly also to his or her reputation as a patron of the arts or of scholarship. In his/her own eyes, this gain — however immaterial — justifies the financial outlay.

But beyond the purely financial transaction which allowed the production of the book to happen in the first place, all these "added values" require the presence of a third party: a gain in "standing" or "reputation" can only work in the desired manner if there is a "public", an "audience". And it is really this public which is the actual "implied reader", not the notional recipient or dedicatee. The latter did not need to see the book to find out about the dedication which would have been arranged beforehand, nor would he (or she) be likely to have read the text of the dedicatory letter for the first time when receiving the finished book. It is the public which needs to see and read the dedication — otherwise, there is no gain in status for either dedicator or dedicatee. The dedication — as all other paratexts — explains to the readers "what the book is". It conveys information which those directly involved in the production process would have known anyway.[4] Without the publicity achieved through the prominent placement of a dedication at the beginning of a source, the whole process would become pointless.[5] In a sense, a dedication is a game

[4] Redeker also points to the very public nature of the dedicatory letter which transcends the private dialogue of a "real" letter. See *Lateinische Widmungsvorreden*, pp. 12-13.

[5] See Carl Schottenloher, *Die Widmungsvorrede im Buch des 16. Jahrhunderts*, Reformationsgeschichtliche Studien und Texte, 76/77 (Münster: Aschendorff, 1953), pp. 1-4.

— a game which does not necessarily look for a winner, but which requires three players (or maybe more accurately, two players and a group of spectators).

This, of course, is not a new insight, but it helps to be reminded of it in order to understand the fundamental difference between print dedications and manuscript dedications that is the topic of this paper. This difference does not essentially concern the identity (or indeed existence) of a dedicator and a dedicatee, although their relationship will usually be a different one in prints and in manuscripts; rather, it concerns the "implied public" to whom the dedication is factually, if not notionally, addressed. This public, for printed sources, is made up of the persons who buy the book. It is, in terms of marketing, a "target group"; the presentation and the contents of a book must be geared towards this target group by the author, editor and publisher. In our case, this target group are the potential buyers of polyphonic music. This group is not limitless since it is restricted to those individuals who could read mensural music (or music of any kind); in the sixteenth century, it can be narrowed down to the professional musical institutions plus the musically literate higher bourgeoisie and nobility.[6] But even in the context of this clearly controllable market, print runs that range anywhere from an estimated 300 to 500 with Petrucci in the early sixteenth century[7] up to 1,000 towards mid-century (when single-impression printing made polyphonic music quicker and easier to produce and thus more affordable)[8] make this a rather large and potentially diverse group. This public is, to a certain degree, anonymous: at least in theory, anybody can buy a book. There is also a fairly clear demarcation between the production side (sponsor/patron/commissioner, author, editor,

[6] See for example Stanley Boorman, 'Early Music Printing: Working for a Specialized Market', in *Print and Culture in the Renaissance. Essays on the Advent of Printing in Europe*, eds. G. P. Tyson – S. S. Wagonheim (Newark-London-Toronto: University of Delaware Press-Associated University Presses, 1986); repr. in Stanley Boorman, *Studies in the Printing, Publishing and Performance of Music in the 16th Century* (Aldershot: Ashgate, 2005), pp. 222-245 (pp. 228-230).

[7] See Stanley Boorman, *Ottaviano Petrucci, Catalogue Raisonné* (Oxford: Oxford University Press, 2006), pp. 360-366.

[8] Mary S. Lewis estimates the average output of the Venetian music printer Antonio Gardano at c. 500 to 1000, possibly sometimes more, sometimes less; see Mary S. Lewis, *Antonio Gardano, Venetian Music Printer, 1538-1569. A Descriptive Bibliography and Historical Study*, vol. 1 (New York-London: Garland, 1988), pp. 84-89. Daniel Heartz arrives at similar figures for the Parisian printer and publisher Pierre Attaingnant; see Daniel Heartz, *Pierre Attaingnant, Royal Printer of Music: A Historical Study and Bibliographical Catalogue* (Berkeley-Los Angeles: University of California Press, 1969), p. 122.

publisher, printer, bookseller) and the consumption side (dedicatee, buyer, owner, musician, listener). The only potentially overlapping element between the two camps is indeed the dedicatee who is likely to be involved in the production (as a sponsor or patron) and in the consumption of the book.

In any case, the dedicator — in the context of musical prints most often the composer, but possibly also the sponsor, compiler or editor — has no immediate control over his target group. Even if the buyer is known, the book can be passed along. The works contained therein are performed by an indeterminate number of singers and listened to by an even larger, even more indeterminate number of listeners. Hence, the consumer of a print — the "implied reader" of the print dedication — is to a certain degree an "outsider", somebody who will be interested in music, but does not necessarily know much (or anything) about the composer, the dedicatee and their mutual relationship. Therefore, any information that the producer(s) deem(s) necessary or desirable for the recipient to have must be made explicit in the printed paratexts, either on the title page or indeed in the dedication or preface: the nature of the repertoire; the identity, rank and status of the composer, editor, publisher and printer (all of whom may be different persons or the same person, and any of whom, with the possible exception of the printer, may be the dedicator); the identity, rank and status of the dedicatee; the special relationship between the two as it is or as the dedicator wishes it to be; the specific reason, if there is one, for dedicating the specific object; etc. Print dedications, for this very reason, tend to be wordy, sometimes occupying two pages and more.

Hence, it does not come as a surprise that a number of even the earliest prints of polyphonic music contain substantial paratexts, often including a lengthy dedication or a preface. The first such publication of all, Ottaviano Petrucci's *Harmonice Musices Odhecaton A*, features not one, but two dedicatory letters: one by Petrucci to the dedicatee and patron, the Venetian nobleman Girolamo Donato, the other by a certain Bartolomeo Budrio — the person who apparently initiated the whole enterprise of polyphonic music printing — likewise to Donato.[9] The two earliest German prints devoted exclusively to polyphonic music are also provided with paratexts beyond the title page: Gregor Mewes' print of Obrecht's

[9] See Bonnie Blackburn, 'Lorenzo de' Medici, A Lost Isaac Manuscript, and the Venetian Ambassador', in *Musica Franca: Essays in Honor of Frank D'Accone*, eds. I. Alm – A. McLamore – C. Reardon (Stuyvesant, N.Y.: Pendragon Press, 1996), pp. 19-44; repr. in Bonnie Blackburn, *Composition, Printing and Performance. Studies in Renaissance Music* (Aldershot: Ashgate, 2000); see also Boorman, *Ottaviano Petrucci*, p. xx.

masses (*Concentus harmonici quattuor missarum, peritissimi musicorum Jacobi Obrecht*, Basel [1507]) contains a humanistically-inspired preface *ad lectores*,[10] and Erhard Oeglin's *Melopoiae sive harmoniae tetracenticae* of the same year, although not dedicated to a specific person but rather to the *musiphili* (the music-lovers), literally brims with paratexts. Most of these are from the pen of the patron and initiator of the "humanistic ode project", Conrad Celtis[11] (and thus once more not by the composer, Petrus Tritonius): two prefatory poems *ad musiphilos*, elegiac couplets accompanying the frontispiece depicting Apollo with the lyre, and a poem addressed to the Augsburg musician 'Iordanus'.[12] This set of paratexts — in a print whose function appears to be more that of a humanistic manifesto than that of a music print in the narrow sense[13] — is rounded off with a congratulatory Sapphic ode by the humanist Benedictus Chelidonius (or Benedikt Schwalbe) from Nuremberg. Andrea Antico's folio choirbook print *Liber Quindecim Missarum* (Rome, 1516) likewise contains a dedication by the editor to Pope Leo X. Admittedly, many other prints of the early years did not contain dedications or paratexts of any kind, especially the simple German song prints[14] or Petrucci's efforts subsequent to the *Odhecaton A*. Nevertheless, their number rises in the following decades, and dedications become the norm. This, in turn, is of course very helpful to today's scholars — rarely are we left in the dark about dates, context and function of a given print, and in not a few cases, all the information we have about a composer is what we read in the dedication or dedications of his printed work or works.

[10] See Birgit Lodes, 'An anderem Ort, auf andere Art: Petruccis und Mewes' Obrecht-Drucke', *Basler Jahrbuch für historische Musikpraxis*, 25 (2001), 85-111.

[11] Schottenloher emphasises Celtis' role as the pioneer of the dedicatory preface in German humanism in general: 'Wie auf so vielen Gebieten des humanistischen Geisteslebens in Deutschland hat auch für die Widmungsvorrede der 'Erzhumanist' Konrad Celtis Weisung und Richtung gegeben.' Schottenloher, *Die Widmungsvorrede*, p. 3.

[12] See Giuseppe Vecchi, 'Dalle "Melopoiae sive harmoniae tetracentiae" oraziane di Tritonio (1507) alle "Gemine undeviginti odarum Horatii melodiae" (1552)', *Accademia delle scienze dell'istituto di Bologna, Classe di scienze morali*, *Memorie*, 8 (Bologna: Accad., 1960), 99-124.

[13] This is corroborated by the fact that, in the same year, Oeglin published a "practical edition" of the same pieces, the *Harmoniae Petri Tritonii*, without the frontispiece and the poems, and in much smaller format, but with a much more accurate musical text — obviously directed at the singers and not at the scholars. See Vecchi, 'Dalle "Melopoiae"', p. 108.

[14] See Nicole Schwindt, 'Zwischen Musikhandschrift und Notendruck: Paratexte in den ersten deutschen Liederbüchern', in *Die Pluralisierung des Paratextes. Formen, Funktionen und Theorie eines Phänomens frühneuzeitlicher Kommunikation*, eds. H. Vögel – F. von Ammon (Münster: LIT Verlag, in press).

The "implied public" for a manuscript source, on the other hand, is quite different from that of a print. Manuscripts were not sold on an open market — they were unique objects which were produced and changed hands (if they changed hands at all) within a small, controlled, closed environment. As Margaret Smith writes:

> Its producer, the scribe, made one manuscript, usually on commission, for a known purchaser. Once it was finished it would be bound up, or at least it would pass into the ownership and care of the purchaser. There was no need to store or to market it. The purchaser, having commissioned the book, had no immediate need of a protective leaf, or of an identifying label, because he knew its textual content.[15]

Manuscripts almost invariably simply begin, without a title page, without a preface, without a dedication, often even without a table of contents; in short, without any explanation at all as to contents, function and person or persons involved. The simple reason for that is that the person or persons involved did not need any such explanations: everybody involved in the production and/or consumption of a manuscript was an insider, did not have to be told in writing. If manuscripts changed hands at all, they were given directly from one person or institution to another. For all practical purposes, there is no anonymous "public" in manuscript culture, no demarcation line between producer and consumer.

As far as dedications are concerned: if any proof were needed that dedications required that third party to "work", this proof is found in their almost complete absence in manuscripts[16] (except sometimes in those books produced in multiple copies by professional *scriptoria* as a "precursor" to the market-driven print culture). Of course, there was in many cases a sponsor, a patron, an addressee to whom the codex was dedicated or at least destined — but as we will see, the means of communication tended to be much less explicit, much more subtle than in the printed book. There were no spectators; hence there was no game on, no advertisement or self-promotion necessary, no added value or gain in prestige or status to be had through the explication of a "special relationship" between dedicator and dedicatee. Such games, if they were played at all, were played in private, and everybody knew the rules. If anything,

[15] Smith, *The title-page*, p. 27.

[16] 'Wie die Handschriftenzeit des Mittelalters trotz einiger Beispiele aus dem Altertum die Widmungsvorrede kaum kannte, so wandte sie auch der Frühdruck nur selten an.' Schottenloher, *Die Widmungsvorrede*, p. 1.

the scribe added a brief incipit on the first notated page to allow the owner to identify the contents at a glance, and a *colophon* or *explicit* at the very end, identifying the author of the text, the copyist, the date of copying and maybe a brief comment on the purpose of the book — rarely indeed the person who had sponsored it and/or was to receive it.[17]

For music manuscripts, this applies to an even greater extent than for literary manuscripts, simply because their context of production and use was even more restricted and "non-public". Texts like the Bible, university texts (especially in law and theology), literary texts and — increasingly in the fifteenth century — the classics of Latin antiquity and humanist texts enjoyed wide circulation and engendered a regular book industry, with stationers, professional *scriptoria* and "editions" or "publications" in multiple copies almost in the modern sense;[18] for example, the Brethren of the Common Life (or *devotio moderna*) in the Low Countries maintained thriving *scriptoria* throughout the fifteenth century.[19] Manuscripts of polyphonic music, on the other hand, are invariably *unica*, tied to a specific person, place, time and context.[20] This has partly to do with the ephemeral nature of the polyphonic repertoire (very little polyphonic music was transmitted for more than a generation after its composition), partly again with the limited number of persons who might possibly be

[17] See Smith, *The title-page*, pp. 27-31; Bernhard Bischoff, *Paläographie des römischen Altertums und des abendländischen Mittelalters*, Grundlagen der Germanistik, 24 (Berlin: Erich Schmidt, 1979), pp. 61-63; in greater detail Wilhelm Wattenbach, *Das Schriftwesen im Mittelalter*, 3rd ed. (Leipzig: Hirzel, 1896; repr. Graz: Akademische Druck- und Verlagsanstalt, 1958), pp. 491-534.

[18] See, for example, Graham Pollard, 'The *pecia* system in the medieval universities', and A. I. Doyle – M. B. Parkes, 'The production of copies of the *Canterbury Tales* and the *Confessio Amantis* in the early fifteenth century', both in *Medieval Scribes, Manuscripts & Libraries. Essays presented to N. R. Ker*, eds. M. B. Parkes – A. G. Watson (London: Scholar Press, 1978), pp. 145-161 and 163-210; also the essays by C. Paul Christianson ('Evidence for the study of London's late medieval manuscript-book trade'), A. I. Doyle ('Publication by members of the religious orders') and Anne Hudson ('Lollard book production'), in *Book production and publishing in Britain 1375-1475*, eds. J. Griffiths – D. Pascall (Cambridge: Cambridge University Press, 1989), pp. 87-108, 109-123 and 125-142; Liselotte E. Saurma-Jeltsch, *Spätformen mittelalterlicher Buchherstellung. Bilderhandschriften aus der Werkstatt Diebold Laubers in Hagenau*, 2 vols (Wiesbaden: Reichert Verlag, 2001), I, 85-88 ('Die Standardisierung der Schreibarbeit') and 167ff. ('Ausprägung und Herkunft des Werkstattstils').

[19] See Regnerus Richardus Post, *The Modern Devotion. Confrontation with Reformation and Humanism*, Studies in Medieval and Reformation Thought, 3 (Leiden: Brill, 1968), pp. 304-308, 346-349.

[20] See Andrew Wathey, 'The production of books of liturgical polyphony', in *Book production and publishing in Britain 1375-1475*, pp. 143-161.

interested in it — i.e. persons who could read and perform music. Also, manuscripts of polyphonic music are very often not produced "in one piece" as a book, but are collections of fascicles or gatherings, not rarely by various scribes, bound together only at a later point in time. By their very nature, such codices bear no dedication since they were not originally conceived as a unit. To be sure, manuscripts of polyphonic music are not unique in this regard, but the share of such collections is much higher than in other genres because of the uniqueness of their contents and their limitation to a small group of users and a specific place or function.

Finally, the specific knowledge required to notate polyphonic music normally did not permit the "outsourcing" of the production to a *scriptorium* – because none existed that could supply these specialised skills. Hence, these sources were normally produced in-house — by the singer(s) or institution which needed or wanted them. Even in the one known case of what could be called a *scriptorium* of polyphonic music — the Alamire workshop active in the context of the Habsburg-Burgundian court from about 1495 to about 1535 — the method and pace of production differs markedly from the big text *scriptoria*.[21] There was no systematic, much less speculative production "for a market" in this workshop; on the contrary, the work was apparently done ad hoc, with considerable breaks of activity (if the extant sources are any indication) and comparatively little effort to present a unified external appearance or a unified musical repertoire (except for some staples, such as the masses by Pierre de La Rue). Instead, external and internal characteristics were tailor-made to fit a specific purpose, commission and/or dedicatee. The quality and characteristics of the script vary as much as the size of the codices and the effort spent on decoration. The large number of different scribes who were active in the workshop from time to time — according to Flynn Warmington, up to twenty — argues for the same scenario.[22] Alamire, who copied very little himself, was active as a manager rather than as the chief scribe, and drew on such personnel capable of writing polyphonic music (in all likelihood, singers from the Burgundian court chapel) as and when necessary

[21] See Martin Staehelin, 'Alamire und die Skriptoriums-Tradition', in *The Burgundian-Habsburg Court Complex of Music Manuscripts (1500-1535) and the Workshop of Petrus Alamire*, eds. B. Bouckaert – E. Schreurs, Yearbook of the Alamire Foundation, 5 (Leuven-Neerpelt: Alamire, 2003), pp. 31-35.

[22] Flynn Warmington – Jacobijn Kiel, 'A Survey of Scribal Hands in the Manuscripts', in *The Treasury of Petrus Alamire. Music and Art in Flemish Court Manuscripts 1500-1535*, ed. H. Kellman (Ghent: Ludion, 1999), pp. 41-52.

and available. There was no such thing as a professional scribe of polyphonic music at the time (in the sense of a person who was employed solely for that purpose), and the rate of production of the Alamire workshop (less than two per year even if one counts all the fragments as once having been complete manuscripts) is much lower than that of a true professional text scriptorium.[23] Thus, even the Alamire codices, while part of a larger group, are *unica* in many ways as well.

Manuscripts with monophonic music are, as a rule, more "organised" and unified in their contents; this applies in particular to books with liturgical chant. While these, again, contain no dedications because they were almost invariably specific to the institution for which they were produced and either copied in-house or specifically commissioned, they do regularly contain incipits and colophons stating the name of the scribe and the year of copying. The fact that even these basic pieces of information are missing from most manuscripts of polyphonic music is of course a source of unending frustration to scholars who have to infer the persons involved, the place and the date indirectly or from secondary sources. If one is very lucky, at least the original owner (or one of the later owners) has put down his name and maybe a bit of additional information, as in the annotation to Pompeius Occo's book of music for the rite of the *Heilige Stede* in Amsterdam (Brussels, Koninklijke Bibliotheek van België / Bibliothèque royale de Belgique, MS IV.922) from 1537, documenting the loan of this book to the *Heilige Stede*.[24] This, however, was entered years after the production of the manuscript itself which again forms part of the output of the Alamire workshop; possible dates for the compilation of the particular source range from 1516 to 1534.[25]

Broadly speaking, music manuscripts (as far as extant today) fall into three categories: personal collections, institutional collections and presentation sources or gifts. Private collections, by their very nature, did not

[23] See Thomas Schmidt-Beste, 'Über Quantität und Qualität von Musikhandschriften des 16. Jahrhunderts', in *Die Münchner Hofkapelle des 16. Jahrhunderts im europäischen Kontext*, eds. Theodor Göllner – Bernhold Schmid, Bayerische Akademie der Wissenschaften, Philosophisch-Historische Klasse. Abhandlungen Neue Folge, 128 (Munich: Verlag der Bayerischen Akademie der Wissenschaften, 2006), pp. 191-211.

[24] 'Anno salutis humanae MDXXXVII Calendis Decembris / Pompeius Occo Frisius et Sibrandus filius libri huius usum / huius sacelli, qui Sacer Locus apellatur, esse voluerunt, proprie/tatem tamen sibi posterisque suis in perpetuum reservantes'. *Occo Codex ... Facsimile Edition*, ed. Bernard Huys (Amsterdam/Utrecht: Vereniging voor Nederlandse Muziekgeschiedenis, 1979), p. xi.

[25] See *The Treasury of Petrus Alamire*, pp. 76-77.

require paratexts, much less dedications. Quite a number of these sources are extant from the late fifteenth and sixteenth centuries. Some were copied by the collectors themselves such as the *Liederbücher* by Hartmann Schedel,[26] Fridolin Sicher,[27] Aegidius Tschudi[28] and others; some were produced on commission by a copyist for the collector, such as the aforementioned *Occo Codex* or the set of partbooks copied in 1542 for the Bruges merchant Zeghere van Male[29]; and some were compiled from many individual gatherings and fascicles for and/or by a collector, such as the *Apel Codex* (copied c. 1490-1504)[30] or the *Magister Nicolaus Leopold Codex* (copied c. 1466-1511).[31] There is no "public" for these sources, implied or otherwise, except for the hypothetical friend or visitor to whom the owner might show his book; here, dedications would serve no purpose whatsoever and consequently do not exist. Again, the exception proves the rule: a few of the more elaborate music books do contain paratexts whose purpose, however, seems to be to embellish rather than to impart information. One example of this is the so-called *Chansonnier Cordiforme* produced for Jean de Montchenu before 1477, which opens with a frontispiece depicting Amor and Fortuna, including a four-line allegorical Italian poem.[32]

The second category is that of the *Gebrauchshandschriften* — books produced by a courtly and/or sacred institution for the use of precisely that same institution, either in a sacred (liturgical music for the *cappella*) or in a courtly context (chansons and other secular genres). Most musical manuscripts from the fourteenth to sixteenth centuries fall in this category.

[26] Munich, Bayerische Staatsbibliothek, Cgm. 810; see Martin Kirnbauer, *Hartmann Schedel und sein "Liederbuch". Studien zu einer spätmittelalterlichen Musikhandschrift (Bayerische Staatsbibliothek München, Cgm 810) und ihrem Kontext* (Frankfurt e.a.: Peter Lang, 2001).

[27] St. Gallen, Stiftsbibliothek, Cod. Sang. 461; see *The songbook of Fridolin Sicher*, Facsmile ed. D. Fallows (Peer: Alamire, 1996).

[28] St. Gallen, Stiftsbibliothek, Cod. Sang. 463; see Donald Glenn Loach, 'Aegidius Tschudi's songbook (St. Gall MS 463)' (PhD diss. University of California, Berkeley, 1969).

[29] Cambrai, Médiathèque Municipale, Mss. 125-128.

[30] Leipzig, Universitätsbibliothek, MS 1494; see *Der Mensuralkodex des Nikolaus Apel (MS. 1494 der Universitätsbibliothek Leipzig)*, eds. R. Gerber – L. Finscher – W. Dömling, 3 vols, Das Erbe deutscher Musik, 32-34 (Kassel e.a.: Bärenreiter, 1956-1975).

[31] Munich, Bayerische Staatsbibliothek, Mus. Ms. 3154; see *Der Kodex des Magister Nicolaus Leopold. Staatsbibliothek München Mus. ms. 3154*, ed. T. L. Noblitt, 4 vols, Das Erbe deutscher Musik, 80-83 (Kassel e.a.: Bärenreiter, 1987-1996).

[32] Paris, Bibliothèque Nationale, MS Rothschild 2973; see *Chansonnier de Jean de Montchenu*, eds. D. Fallows – G. Thibault (Paris: Société Française de Musicologie, 1991).

These sources — some simple, some elaborate — also exist in a closed context: that of the institution. Functionally and often actually, the *Gebrauchshandschrift* did not change hands; there was no dedicator or dedicatee; all the actors and contexts were known to everybody involved; the repertoire was either predetermined by liturgical or ceremonial requirements or was selected by the patron/employer or the chapel members; and the scribes were either employed by the institution, pressed into service ad hoc if there were no professional music scribes available, or commissioned. Hence all the information usually imparted in print prefaces is superfluous. A potential "public" could conceivably have entered the picture in the form of the patron/employer — who at least notionally could be seen as the dedicatee of the sources — or possibly, in liturgical contexts, the congregation. But even if one accepts this concept of a limited public, the process of communication is entirely different from that of print publications. If at all, the congregation would not read from the book, but see it from afar as an object of beauty and reverence, similar to the celebrant's vestments, the altar decorations and the fittings of the building in general, designed to inspire awe and impress the visitor both with the glory of the Creator and the financial capabilities of the patron. In this context, the most effective peritext would concern size and visual adornment — which is indeed the defining characteristic of the large choirbooks since the late fifteenth century. These visual peritexts are situated where they could actually be seen during the service while the music was performed: in the form of miniatures, calligraphic initials or adorned borders on the opening with the music itself. Frontispieces, title pages and verbal paratexts, on the other hand, would only have been visible to the "insiders": the singers. Again, they are lacking almost without exception because they are superfluous for this particular category of readers.

There are some rare cases in which short paratexts exist even in this type of source, without apparent function, seemingly on a whim: some scribes, editors or composers were sufficiently proud of their achievement that they "dedicated" their work to the institution in which they were employed — or directly to their employer. One example of such a person is Federico Mario Perugino, chant scribe for Pope Paul III and the Papal Chapel from 1538 to 1547.[33] In two of the three extant manuscripts he copied for his employer (an *Antiphonarium de sanctis* of

[33] See Mitchell P. Brauner, 'The Parvus Manuscripts: A Study of Vatican Polyphony, ca. 1535 to 1580' (PhD diss. Brandeis University, 1982), p. 4.

1538[34] and an *Antiphonarium de tempore* of 1545[35]) — he adorns the colophon on the last page of each of the two codices with a short poem in elegiac couplets (see Appendices 6 and 7). These are not dedications in the proper sense of the word, but they serve a related function: the author of the poem — whether Perugino himself or another chapel member — can be assumed to speak for the Papal Chapel as an institution. In Capp. Sist. 11, he addresses himself explicitly to the reader (*lector*), extolling the virtues of the pontiff who has brought about and maintained peace; moreover, Paul has not only commissioned the two books in question, but has also provided the funds necessary for their lavish production from his own purse (*aere suo*). The laudatory language and content are entirely typical for sixteenth-century humanist-inspired dedications, and the practice of adorning the explicit or colophon with a short poem is a time-honoured medieval tradition[36]. But the question remains: who could have seen it to whom this beneficence would actually have been news? Where is the "public relations" value of an inscription hidden away in the back of such a codex that was not only used exclusively by the Papal singers but whose content could only have been seen by them as the lectern on the singers' balcony in the Sistine Chapel faces *away* from the congregation? For once, the process of communication is here indeed limited to the dedicator (the Papal Chapel as an institution) and the dedicatee (Pope Paul III, who is known to have taken a vivid interest in the workings of his private chapel and to whose papacy a vast number of new manuscripts can be dated).[37] It is, in this context, probably not even important if the pope ever actually saw the dedication; it is a gesture through which the Papal Chapel affirmed its close relationship with the pontiff.

But similar gestures are rare in the extant body of music manuscripts destined for institutional use; indeed, I could trace no instances at all before the 1520s. A few more dedications can be found in the polyphonic codices of the Bavarian court chapel in Munich, significantly, another institution with a high degree of self-confidence, indeed self-importance. Ludwig Senfl's pair of motet codices (Munich, Bayerische Staatsbibliothek, MS 12 and 10), probably copied in the mid-1520s, proudly announce the

[34] Biblioteca Apostolica Vaticana, MS Capp. Sist. 11.

[35] Biblioteca Apostolica Vaticana, MS Capp. Sist. 9.

[36] Wattenbach, *Das Schriftwesen im Mittelalter*, pp. 491ff.

[37] See Klaus Pietschmann, *Kirchenmusik zwischen Tradition und Reform. Die päpstliche Sängerkapelle und ihr Repertoire im Pontifikat Papst Pauls III. (1534-1549)* (Città del Vaticano: Biblioteca Apostolica Vaticana, 2007).

fact that they were commissioned by Duke Wilhelm IV, composed by none other than the court composer Senfl and prepared with utmost diligence and obedience — *summis et studia et obedientia* (see Appendix 3 for the text of MS 10).[38] The text of MS 10 obviously fulfils the double function of title page and dedication, opening the manuscript on fol. 1r and beginning by naming the musical contents of the book.[39] This can be interpreted as a gesture both of subservience and of assertion by Senfl to his new ruler in a period when the Bavarian court chapel was profiting from the disbandment of Emperor Maximilian I's chapel (which had brought Senfl and others to Munich in the first place) and was about to evolve into one of the foremost musical institutions in central Europe, not least through Senfl's own efforts. The two books of motets were copied shortly after Senfl's arrival and are the earliest codices of the Bavarian court chapel containing primarily contemporary repertoire of a chapel member and not older works (by Isaac, Josquin, La Rue, Brumel and others). It is extremely telling that precisely these two books — which first document Senfl as the central figure of the musical scene at the Bavarian court — also appear to be the first instances in polyphonic music manuscripts where the composer — and not the scribe, the institution, the publisher or the patron — dedicates the book, in a conscious act of personal self-affirmation. This act appears to be so blatantly addressed at an "audience" that Bente even speculated about the two manuscripts having been prepared with printed publication in mind.[40]

[38] Martin Bente, *Neue Wege der Quellenkritik und die Biographie Ludwig Senfls. Ein Beitrag zur Musikgeschichte des Reformationszeitalters* (Wiesbaden: Breitkopf & Härtel, 1968), pp. 63-70; *Bayerische Staatsbibliothek: Katalog der Musikhandschriften 1: Chorbücher und Handschriften in chorbuchartiger Notierung*, Kataloge Bayerischer Musiksammlungen, 5/1, eds. M. Bente – M. L. Göllner – H. Hell – B. Wackernagel (Munich: Henle, 1989), pp. 71-72. Bente assumed that the scribe who copied the bulk of the two codices (his 'Schreiber A II') was Lucas Wagenrieder, a colleague of Senfl's in the chapel (Bente, *Neue Wege der Quellenkritik*, pp. 214-215; *Katalog der Musikhandschriften*, 35*-36*, 39*). New research by Joshua Rifkin and David Fallows, however, has found that the scribe was in fact Bernhart Rem of Augsburg — apparently, the codices (or large parts thereof) were not produced in Munich at all, but on commission in the nearby Imperial city. See Joshua Rifkin, 'Jean Michel and "Lucas Wagenrieder". Some New Findings', *Tijdschrift van de Vereniging voor Nederlandse Muziekgeschiedenis*, 55 (2005), 113-152; David Fallows, 'The Copyist Formerly Known as Wagenrieder', in *Die Münchner Hofkapelle des 16. Jahrhunderts im europäischen Kontext* (forthcoming).

[39] In MS 12, the dedicatory inscription is on fol. 55r — at the beginning of a new fascicle by a different scribe (Bente's scribe A II = Bernhart Rem); it was apparently conceived as a separate unit and combined with the first fascicle at a later date.

[40] Bente, *Neue Wege der Quellenkritik*, pp. 65, 68-69.

Written much in the same spirit, but even more elaborate is the dedicatory text of Senfl's *Opus musicum*: his revision and completion of Heinrich Isaac's *Choralis Constantinus* proper cycles in four volumes, completed in and dated 1531.[41] Both halves (consisting of two volumes each) are prefaced by a full-page text praising both Isaac's and Senfl's contribution to the compositional effort as well as Emperor Maximilian's and again Duke Wilhelm's munificence in sponsoring the whole enterprise (one of the two — very similar — texts is reproduced as Appendix 5). Once more, there is nothing whatsoever unusual about content and wording — but also once more, everybody who was in any position to see these books would have known all that the text contains, and the effort seems wasted in a manuscript source for internal use only. The likelihood that these codices would have been shown to visitors is very slim indeed, as they were held in the chapel and not in the court.[42] They are handsome books, certainly, but not the kind of hugely elaborate presentation codices that were the showpieces of many court libraries.

Again, the text itself offers at least a partial clue: the collection is called *opus musicum*, a 'musical work'. One should resist the temptation to read too much into this term — this is not the emphatic concept that the nineteenth century had of the "work" and the "genius" who created it. Nevertheless, it is not a common term for music in the first half of the sixteenth century. Analogous to Nicolaus Listenius' famous 'opus perfectum et absolutum',[43] it signifies a composition (or group of compositions) that is finished, polished, written down and ready for circulation in written form, thus reproducible and transcending the ephemeral nature of performed music — music as text instead of music as act.[44] The dedicatory text reaffirms this essence of the *opus musicum* through its focus — again — on the composer, the *auctor*; first Isaac, then Senfl. It is surely no accident that

[41] Munich, Bayerische Staatsbibliothek, Mus. Ms. 35, 36, 37, 38; see *Katalog der Musikhandschriften*, 145-57; Bente, *Neue Wege der Quellenkritik*, pp. 73-145.

[42] *Katalog der Musikhandschriften*, 12*-13*, 54-59.

[43] '[MUSICA] POETICA que neque rei cognitione, neque solo exercitio contenta, sed aliquid post laborem relinquit operis, veluti cum a quopiam Musica, aut musicum carmen conscribitur, cuius finis est opus consummatum & effectum. Consistit enim in faciendo sive fabricando, hoc est, in labore tali, qui post se etiam, artifice mortuo, opus perfectum & absolutum relinquat, Unde Poeticus musicus, qui in negotio aliquid relinquendo versatur.' Nicolaus Listenius, *Musica* (Wittenberg: Rhau, 1537), fol. a3v.

[44] See Heinz von Loesch, 'Musica — Musica practica — Musica poetica', in *Deutsche Musiktheorie des 15. bis 17. Jahrhunderts*, Geschichte der Musiktheorie, 8/i (Darmstadt: Wissenschaftliche Buchgesellschaft, 2003), pp. 99-264 (pp. 121-125).

dedications like this one (more frequently in print than in manuscript, to be sure) coincide with the "appearance" of the composer as a professional designation (none other than Isaac himself is one of the first musicians to be employed specifically by Maximilian I as a 'componist') and as a central topic in musical writings.[45] In a sense, without the dedication, the repertoire contained in the manuscripts Munich 35-38 would be no more than an enormous cycle of mass propers for use in the liturgy of the Bavarian court, arranged and written down like many other liturgical cycles in composed polyphony during that period (often even transmitted anonymously). Only the verbal explanation makes it unequivocally and emphatically clear that this is indeed an *opus musicum* by two of the greatest *auctores* of their time. This was apparently important enough to Senfl (who, as the compiler of the collection, is doubtlessly the *auctor* of the dedication as well) to insert the text even where few people would be likely to ever see it. Indeed, it is not implausible that the text was prepared already with the print publication of the *Choralis Constantinus* cycle in mind (which would have been the consummation of the *opus* idea), a publication which Hans Ott had already announced in the foreword to his *Novum et insigne opus musicum* in 1537.[46] This would also explain the strong emphasis on the role of Wilhelm and the Bavarian court in the dedication, as if Senfl was hoping that the duke would sponsor this publication.[47] In the event, the cycle did not appear in print until 1550/55, in a different form (including the parts of the cycle specific to Constance cathedral which had not been present in the *opus musicum*) and with a completely different set of dedicatory paratexts which make no mention of the Bavarian court at all.

This brings us to the last type of manuscripts: presentation sources. This is the one category of handwritten sources where one would most

[45] See Rob C. Wegman, 'From Maker to Composer: Improvisation and Musical Authorship in the Low Countries, 1450-1500', *Journal of the American Musicological Society*, 49 (1996), 409-479. In the records of the Imperial Court Chapel, Isaac is named specifically as 'Hainrich Isaac, componist' (and not as 'cantor', 'capellanus' or 'musicus' as would have been far more common); see Martin Staehelin, *Die Messen Heinrich Isaacs*, Publikationen der Schweizerischen Musikforschenden Gesellschaft, Serie II, vol. 28, I-III (Bern-Stuttgart: Haupt, 1977-78), II, 66-67.

[46] Bente, *Neue Wege der Quellenkritik*, pp. 154-159. See also Ludwig Finscher, 'Liturgische Gebrauchsmusik', in *Die Musik des 15. und 16. Jahrhunderts*, Neues Handbuch der Musikwissenschaft, 3 (Laaber: Laaber Verlag, 1989), pp. 371-433 (p. 430).

[47] The idea that Munich 35-38 might have been intended as a kind of *Stichvorlage* for Ott's planned publication of the *Choralis Constantinus* equally goes back to Bente (*ibid.*), although he does not use the presence of the dedication as part of his argument. This was suggested to me by David Fallows in private conversation; I am most grateful to him for this.

likely expect dedicatory texts: they did change hands; they were commissioned by and given to heads of states or other important figures; they were objects of high monetary value and often quite stunning beauty of which both dedicator and dedicatee had every reason to be proud; they were often held in the *camera*, not in the *cappella*, and were shown to visiting dignitaries instead of being put to any sort of practical use, hence they did achieve a sort of "publicity" in the sense described above; they, in short, fulfil every textual and contextual condition of a written-out dedication.

At least a few of these presentation manuscripts do not disappoint in having exactly the kind of dedicatory text one might hope for. The earliest such instance is as spectacular as it is exceptional: it is the codex Modena, Biblioteca Estense α.F.9.9.[48] The small oblong book (c. 16.6 × 11 cm) is an anthology of Italian *strambotti*, copied in 1496 in Padua. Possibly inspired by the humanist circles of the university, the patron and dedicator — a certain 'Iohannes' who is only identified as the *Pierides magister* (the 'master of the muses') — endowed his small treasure with no less than seven paratexts (see Appendix 1): an inscription, a lengthy quotation on the power of music from Isidor of Seville's *Sententiae de musica*, an Italian sonnet echoing Isidor's text, an aphorism from Pliny's *Natural History*, another (anonymous) aphorism on the power of music, the dedication proper (to a certain 'Francesco de Fa'), again in the form of a sonnet, and a final inscription panel which specifies Padua as the place of copying and the date as the fourth day before the Nones of October in the year of the 1314th olimpiad, counted from the beginning of time (which is 3761 BC after the Jewish calendar), i.e. 4 October 1496.[49] All this is typical of the mannered humanist learning that also characterised early humanist printed books from the same period — but the private character of the manuscript is emphasised by the fact that the two main participants are only named in passing, almost enigmatically. The dedicator and patron is only 'Iohannes', the recipient 'Francesco de Fa (?)'.[50] Where a print dedication, more often than not, would have specified full

[48] *Modena, Biblioteca Estense e Universitaria, MS alpha F.9.9*, ed. F. A. D'Accone, Renaissance Music in Facsimile, 13 (New York-London: Garland, 1987).

[49] Knud Jeppesen, *La Frottola* II. *Zur Bibliographie der handschriftlichen musikalischen Überlieferung des weltlichen italienischen Lieds um 1500*, Acta Jutlandica, XLI/1 (Aarhus-København: Wilhelm Hansen, 1969), pp. 76-79.

[50] It is unclear whether 'de Fa' is actually a proper name or an abbreviation, possibly of a toponym ('de Faenza'?); see Giuseppina La Face Bianconi, *Gli strambotti del codice estense α.F.9.9*, Studi e testi per la storia della musica, 8 (Firenze: Leo S. Olschki, 1990), p. 12; Jeppesen, *La Frottola*, p. 78.

name, rank, provenance and relationship between the two principals (after all, the readership/audience would want to know these things, and the principals would wanted them to be known) the handwritten source once again presupposes inside knowledge of those involved. As the dedicatory sonnet states, Iohannes presents the small book to Francesco specifically for his personal use (*sapi ben che 'n quel to solo harai l'uso per te*), to return to its source — probably Iohannes' library — after Francesco's death. Beyond the two protagonists, only the small circle of friends alluded to in the first inscription (*pro nostro amicorumque solatio*) would have had access and presumably sung from it.[51] The non-initiated are purposefully left in the dark.

A much more public — and correspondingly more famous and flamboyant — example of manuscript dedication once again originated in Munich, namely the so-called *Prachthandschriften* or luxury codices, one containing Lasso's *Penitential Psalms* and the other motets by Cipriano de Rore, together representing the two most famous composers of the Munich court chapel in the middle of the sixteenth century.[52] Copied by the court scribe Jean Pollet, they contain lavish miniatures by the court painter Hans Mielich — among them portraits of count Albrecht, his wife Anna and their respective courts as well as portraits of Lasso, Rore, the court chapel and of course Mielich himself.[53] The humanist scholar Samuel Quickelberg (or Quicchelberg) added copious commentaries in separate volumes. Last but not least, the back page of the Lasso volume and the front page of the Rore volume again display a lengthy dedication to Albrecht. Appendix 8 reproduces that from the Lasso volume — on the page, the composer himself is depicted to the left of the inscription and Mielich to the right.[54] All this, of course, is pure display and, in terms of imparting information, actually quite redundant: neither the dedication nor anything else tells any of the persons involved anything they did not know or had not seen. Nor does the dedication, in this case, place particular emphasis on the musical works contained in the codex — or really,

[51] See La Face Bianconi, *Gli strambotti*, pp. 13-14.

[52] Munich, Bayerische Staatsbibliothek, Mus. Ms. A (Lasso, *Penitential Psalms*) and Mus. Ms. B (Rore, Motets); *Katalog der Musikhandschriften*, 54-58.

[53] See Nicole Schwindt, 'Hans Mielichs bildliche Darstellung der Münchner Hofkapelle', *Acta Musicologica*, 68 (1996), 48-85.

[54] See *Orlando di Lasso. Prachthandschriften und Quellenüberlieferung*, eds. H. Leuchtmann – H. Schaefer, Bayerische Staatsbibliothek: Ausstellungskataloge, 62 (Tutzing: Schneider, 1994).

on the composer himself. The first person named in the text is Duke Albrecht; Lasso and Mielich are mentioned later on as the most excellent representatives of their art, but their importance is only emphasised in relationship to the glory and munificence of the ruler. Mention of the compositions is only made in passing — 'amongst many other things, Lasso also composed the psalms found here'. The function of this dedication is that of representation and particularly that of *memoria*, to let both visiting contemporaries and later generations know what the court looked like and what it was capable of, in terms of artistry, scholarship, musicianship and sheer financial prowess. Significantly, these manuscripts were not kept in the chapel with the other choirbooks, but in the ducal chamber.[55] The dedication itself is an artificial gesture as dedicator and dedicatee are really one and the same: Albrecht himself.

Other, more straightforward manuscripts do follow the "normal" rules of dedicator and dedicatee. One example is the exemplar of Elzéar Genet's (*alias* Carpentras) *Lamentations of Jeremiah* which the composer had specially produced to be presented to his patron and employer, Pope Clement VII, in 1525 (Appendix 4).[56] Here, we have the typical, humanistically-inspired constellation often found in prints as well: a coat of arms of the dedicatee, an inscription naming the involved parties and specifying their mutual relationship (Clement of course, as the pontiff, and Carpentras as the former *magister capellae*), and a laudatory poem in classical metre (in this case, elegiac couplets). Also not unexpectedly, the text is a mixture of subservience and assertion.

Dedications like these, however, are not the rule even in presentation manuscripts. In the majority of the cases where a presentation manuscript did change hands — that is, where it was produced or commissioned by one institution or individual and given to another — all participants were well-acquainted with one another. The purpose of the gift was to give or receive a favour — be it monetary, dynastic or just to obtain or retain good graces — and was clear to all parties. In particular, it was clear to the implied public: the courtly, civic or institutional environment. All persons who would ever be able to see such a presentation manuscript, and to whom it ever had to mean something, were members of an in-group, a closed or at the very least very circumscribed circle. The dedicatory ritual or game, therefore, could be played without an explicitly formulated

[55] *Katalog der Musikhandschriften*, 12*.
[56] Biblioteca Apostolica Vaticana, MS Capp. Sist. 163.

text. This applies even to the lavish manuscripts of the Alamire workshop which were commissioned by the Habsburg-Burgundian court in Mechelen as presentation gifts. These books travelled long distances — to Spain, Italy, Germany and England — and were given to the great political rulers of the time.[57] They were copied on the finest parchment and lavishly decorated — but again, not a single one contains a dedication or even an inscription, an incipit or a colophon. The high and mighty of Europe were apparently a sufficiently close-knit group to require no such explanation: Henry VIII, Leo X, Frederick the Wise and Philip the Fair knew what they had in front of him and from whom it came without having to have it spelled out for them.

Hence, the much more frequent method of dedicating a presentation manuscript of polyphonic music — and the much more frustrating way to modern scholars — was not explicit but implicit, aimed precisely at this kind of "in-group". Both donor and dedicatee are indicated through a variety of means which would have been meaningful only to the initiated; again, a game is played, but a game whose rules were known to only a few. Within that context, the degree to which a dedication is concealed varies greatly. Sometimes a dedicatory inscription is hidden in a banner or somewhere within the manuscript, as in Johannes Tinctoris' chansonnier for Beatrice of Aragon in Naples[58] where the nineteenth of fifty-seven pieces — Tinctoris' own *O virgo miserere mei* — bears the inscription *Beatissime virgini domine Beatrici de Aragonia*. Another fairly blatant method is the use of heraldry: in many manuscripts, the coats of arms of the donor and/or the dedicatee are displayed prominently, usually on the first opening of the book. An example for this from the Alamire sources is the manuscript London, British Library, MS Royal 8.g.vii:[59] the first opening displays the heraldic emblems of King Henry VIII of England combined with those of his first wife, Catherine of Aragon — it is thus quite clear that the manuscript was prepared for that couple. However, any further information that could have been gleaned from a dedicatory text — most importantly, date and occasion — are not forthcoming.

[57] For a description of the corpus, with approximate dates of copying and destination, see *The Treasury of Petrus Alamire*.

[58] New Haven, School of Music Library, MS 91; Facsimile and edition in *The Mellon Chansonnier*, eds. L. Perkins – H. Garey, 2 vols (New Haven-London: Yale University Press, 1979).

[59] *London, British Library, Royal 8 G.vii*, ed. H. Kellman, Renaissance Music in Facsimile, 9 (New York-London: Garland, 1987).

Of course, it would have had to be compiled during the time of their marriage, but that lasted from 1509 to 1532; modern scholarship has suggested the date of the manuscript to range anywhere from 1513 to 1525.[60]

Even more difficult to put into the right context today is pictorial evidence: many presentation manuscripts contain portraits, either next to the heraldic imagery or separate from them, often themselves forming part of the large illuminated initials on the first opening. Again in the Alamire corpus, the manuscript Jena, Thüringer Universitäts- und Landesbibliothek, MS 3, contains a portrait of the recipient of the manuscript: Frederick the Wise, the elector of Saxony. He is rather clearly identified by his regalia and his motto *Tant que je puis* on a banner above it.[61] In this case, we are lucky because the motto is present and the pictorial evidence is equally clear through the use of regalia. More often than not, however, one is confronted with portraits that presumably represent *some* actual person but provide little or no clue as to who that person is. The lack of explicit text sometimes makes this type of pictorial evidence hard to pinpoint even where we do know what persons are meant. In Jena, Thüringer Universitäts- und Landesbibliothek, MS 4, for example, no less than fifteen portraits are found: of members of the English crown as well as of various branches of the Habsburgs plus several popes — but not that of Frederick the Wise who ended up with the book.[62] Here again, we are lacking the inside knowledge that would have tied all this information together in a meaningful and unequivocal fashion. Information — or non-information — such as this has resulted in a great deal of speculation among musicologists and others dealing with similar sources. The proportion of manuscript sources of polyphonic music from the fifteenth and sixteenth centuries in which even the most basic information about place, time and people involved is lacking or ambiguous remains worryingly high, higher than in any other type of manuscript.

To make matters even more confusing, some manuscripts changed dedicatee, either during the course of production or later on. To remain in the Alamire context: it was apparently only decided at the last moment that the codex Brussels, Koninklijke Bibliotheek van België / Bibliothèque royale de Belgique, MS 15075 was to be presented to John II of Portugal and his wife Catherine of Austria — the relevant miniatures appear

[60] *The Treasury of Petrus Alamire*, p. 111.

[61] A reproduction of the page is in *The Treasury of Petrus Alamire*, p. 89.

[62] *The Treasury of Petrus Alamire*, pp. 90-93.

to be added a long time after the codex itself was copied.[63] Another example is famous *Chigi Codex* (Biblioteca Apostolica Vaticana, MS Chigi C.VIII.234) where the original miniatures and coats of arms relating to the first owner, Philippe Bouton, were painted over with those of the later owners, the Cordova family of Spain.[64]

Finally, even in cases where there is no "hard evidence" — textual or pictorial — at all, attempts have been made to infer a "hidden dedication" through the repertoire contained in what appear to be presentation manuscripts. As hardly any of them were destined for actual liturgical use, the donor was — at least in theory — free to select and arrange the pieces to suit the dedicatory purpose. Some manuscripts where the repertoire corroborates other evidence show that this is not a far-fetched assumption. In the Habsburg-Burgundian manuscript Brussels, Koninklijke Bibliotheek van België / Bibliothèque royale de Belgique, MS 9126, for Philip the Fair and Juana of Castile, not only a great deal of heraldic evidence points towards the two dedicatees, but also the title of Josquin's *Hercules Dux Ferrariae* mass which appears changed to *Philippus Rex Castiliae*.[65] Similar strategies are found in many other sources; but wherever such corroborating evidence is lacking, the identification of dedicator and dedicatee purely through repertoire is by necessity speculative. Examples of this approach abound.

Moreover, the implicit or semi-explicit dedications described above almost invariably identify the destination of the manuscript, not its origin: only in those cases where the source was commissioned for a certain person or institution by that same person or institution (such as the two chansonniers which Marguerite of Austria had commissioned for herself from the Alamire scribes) can the donor or sponsor of the manuscript also be identified. More frequently, the dedicator remains in the dark. In the case of the Alamire manuscripts, we are fortunate enough to know that they originated in the context of Marguerite of Austria's Habsburg-Burgundian court in Mechelen, but in many other cases this information is lacking. A famous case where this has led to wrong conclusions is the so-called *Medici Codex* (Florence, Biblioteca Medicea-Laurenziana, Acquisti e doni 666), copied in 1518.[66] The information about the dedicatee and the

[63] *The Treasury of Petrus Alamire*, pp. 74-75.

[64] *The Treasury of Petrus Alamire*, pp. 125-127.

[65] *Choirbook for Philip the Fair and Juana of Castile, c. 1504-6. Brussel, Koninklijke Bibliotheek MS. 9126*, Facsimile ed. F. Fitch (Peer: Alamire, 2000).

[66] Edition, Commentary and Facsimile in *The Medici Codex of 1518. A Choirbook of Motets Dedicated to Lorenzo de' Medici, Duke of Urbino*, ed. Edward E. Lowinsky,

occasion is unequivocal, with a dedicatory poem in elegiac couplets and the acrostic 'VIVAT SEMPER INVICTUS LAURENTIUS MEDICES DVX VRBINI' in the table of contents (Appendix 2): Duke Lorenzo II de Medici married Madeleine de la Tour de l'Auvergne on 2 May 1518. However, there is no apparent information about the dedicator. The original editor of the manuscript, Edward Lowinsky, argued in favour of a French provenance, on the basis of a French script, predominantly French repertoire and the close links between the French court and the Medici family.[67] However, Joshua Rifkin, Jeffrey Dean and others were able to show that, on the contrary, the manuscript was commissioned by Lorenzo's uncle, Pope Leo X, and produced at the Papal court.[68] Again, repertoire provides a partial clue — next to music by the many French composers favoured by Leo X, there are a number of pieces by musicians active at the Papal court. But the decisive argument is external: the main scribe of the *Medici Codex* — whose name we do not know — also copied manuscripts for the Papal Chapel and was quite possibly employed at that institution.

An even less clear-cut case is that of the so-called *Rusconi Codex* (Bologna, Civico museo bibliografico musicale, MS Q19), dated 1518.[69] Neither dedicator nor dedicatee is made explicit — the only clue is a silhouette of a stag under a tree and the inscription 'D. P.'. On the basis of repertoire, watermarks and scribal characteristics, no less than three hypotheses have been put forward. Lowinsky again favours a connection to the French Court, with 'Diane de Poitiers' as dedicatee;[70] Rainer Heyink proposes a dedication of the codex to the Gonzaga court, specifically to 'Divus Pirro [Gonzaga]' in Mantua;[71] Robert Nosow links it to the cathedral of Padua with 'Dominus Petrus [Renaldus]' as the compiler and most frequently represented composer.[72] The discussion is far from

3 vols, Monuments of Renaissance Music, 3-5 (Chicago-London: Chicago University Press, 1968).

67 *The Medici Codex of 1518*, 3, Commentary, pp. 28-36.

68 See Thomas Schmidt-Beste, 'Medici-Codex', in *Die Musik in Geschichte und Gegenwart*, 2nd edition ed. L. Finscher, Sachteil vol. 5 (Kassel-Stuttgart: Bärenreiter-Metzler, 1996), cols. 1745-1747.

69 *Bologna, Civico museo bibliografico musicale, MS. Q19: The Rusconi codex*, ed. J. A. Owens, Renaissance Music in Facsimile, 1 (New York-London: Garland, 1988).

70 *The Medici Codex of 1518*, 3, Commentary, pp. 52-60.

71 Rainer Heyink, *Der Gonzaga-Kodex Bologna Q19. Geschichte und Repertoire einer Musikhandschrift des 16. Jahrhunderts*, Beiträge zur Geschichte der Kirchenmusik, 1 (Paderborn: Schöningh, 1994), pp. 31-36.

72 Robert Nosow, 'The Dating, and Provenance of Bologna, Civico Museo Bibliografico Musicale, MS Q 19', *Journal of Musicology*, 9 (1991), 91-108.

over (except that it is now commonly accepted that the characteristics of script, material and repertoire place the source in Northern Italy); but it is clear that the information contained in the manuscript as such is far from sufficient to allow any outsider (and that includes modern-day musicologists) to draw unequivocal conclusions.

This essay has been more about paratexts which do not exist than about those which do. Nevertheless, I think that their lack tells us at least as much about the production, function and indeed the very nature of manuscripts containing polyphonic music than their presence would have done, and the very few examples that I was able to give are each telling in the way in which they contravene the conventions of non-dedication. A next step would be a comparison with dedications in text manuscripts — which likewise have not nearly been studied in such depth as their printed siblings have been. In any case, I hope to have made clear the very basic distinctions between a print dedication and a manuscript dedication — the former by nature explicit, informative, "public" — the latter implicit, elliptical, "private". This intimacy makes the study of manuscripts certainly more intriguing, but it can also make it infinitely more frustrating.

School of Music
Bangor University
UK – Bangor, Gwynedd LL57 2DG
mus205@bangor.ac.uk

## APPENDIX
## DEDICATIONS AND INSCRIPTIONS IN MUSIC MANUSCRIPTS OF THE SIXTEENTH CENTURY

All transcriptions were made from the original sources. Original spelling and punctuation have been retained except for the standardisation of "u" and "v" according to modern Latin spelling and the conversion of square capital script in inscriptions to modern uppercase/lowercase. Abbreviations have been tacitly resolved for better legibility.

### 1. Modena, Biblioteca Estense, MS α.F.9.9 [1496][73]

*1v*
Pro nostro amicorumque solatio

*2v*
Quid possit Musica.
Itaque sine musica nulla disciplina potest esse perfecta. Nichil enim est sine illa. Nam et ipse mundus quadam armonia sonorum fertur esse compositus. Et celum ipsum sub armoniae modulatione revolvi. Musica vero movet affectus. provocat in diuersum habitum sensus. In proeliis quoque tubae concentus pugnantes accendit et quanto vehementior fuerit clangor. tanto fit ad certamen animus fortior. Siquidem et remiges cantus hortatur. Ad tolerandos quoque labores musica animum mulcet. et singulorum operum fatigationem modulatio vocis solatur. Excitatos quoque animos musica sedat. sicut de david [*sic*] legitur qui a spiritu inmundo saulem arte modulationis eripuit. Ipsas quoque bestias nec non et serpentes volucres atque delphinos. ad auditum suae modulationis musica provocat. Sed et quicquid loquimur vel intrinsecus venarum pulsibus commovemur per musicos rithmos. armoniae virtutibus probatur esse sociatum. Haec Sanctus Isidorus hispalensis episcopus libro etymologiarum [3, 17].

*3r*
Quid possit musica
Grande e la forçia e grandi son li effetti
    Che in se ritien la musica soave
    Che sanza questa mai alcun non have
    L'altre sorelle con gli soi sogetti
Questa e quella che move i nostri affetti
    In habito diversi con sue chiave
    Et fanne prompti alle fatiche grave
    Sança altra stima e sança altri sospetti

[73] Transcriptions after La Face Bianconi, *Gli strambotti*, pp. 8-9 and 12-13.

Cum sta armonia il ciel vasse girrando
E'l mondo anchor di questa fo composto
Saul si sanò pur armonizando
Gli serpi con gli uceli e'l delphin posto
In un e l'altro mar lontan passando
Vengono al son di questa tosto tosto

*6r*
Harmonica ratio rerum naturam sibi ipsam congruere cogit. Plinius. Ultimum II [2, 248]

*6v*
Quantam igitur prae se dignitatem ferat musica satis ea docet ratio quod deos habeat auctores

*7r*
Pierides Magister Iohannes ad Franciscum de Fa [?] Alumnus salutem
Perche non fosti a reverirne lento
Né al sacro nostro fonte in fargli honore
Anci tu prompto (ancor sul primo errore)
Volesti al culto nostro esser intento
Eccoti, açiò restar debbi contento
Del gravoso pensiero e del sudore,
Dei passi sparsi el tempo e tutte l'hore
Spendesti in visitarne a pioggia e vento
Questo sacrato libro or piglierai
Con le temprate note in verdi colli
E tra rivere nel tuo nome ordito
Ma sapi ben chen quel tu solo harai
L'uso per te e poscia in ciel tu volli
Libero tornarassi onde fo uscito

*7v*
Patavii IIII nonas octobres a prima elementorum concordia olimpiade MCCCXIIII.

2. Florence, Biblioteca Medicea-Laurenziana, Nuovi acquisti 666 (*Medici Codex*), fol. Iv-1r [1518]

Perge liber propera ventoque citatior omni
Ad faustum fausto sidere tende ducem
Excipiet manibus laetis vultuque sereno
Gaudebitque tuo munere posse frui
Quum te respiciet letus tecumque loquetur
Tum iubeo ut domini sis memor ipse tui

Canon In primis litteris scriptum est de te

VIVAT SEMPER INVICTUS LAURENTIUS MEDICES DVX VRBINI

3. Munich, Bayerische Staatsbibliothek, Mus. Ms. 10, fol. 1r [1520s]

Quinque Salutationes Domini nostri Hiesu Christi. Ex illustrissimi principis & Domini. Domini Vuilhelmi Comitis Palatini Rheni. Utriusque Bavariae Ducis, &c. Comissione, A Ludovico Sennphlio, Eiusdem Illustri Domini Musico Intonatore humilimo excusae Dicataeque. Summis et studio et obedientia.

4. Biblioteca Apostolica Vaticana, MS Capp. Sist. 163, fol. 2v [1525]

Ad sanctissimum maximumque pontificem Clementem VII. Elziarii Geneti nomine vulgo nuncupato Carpentras Capelle Pontificie olim Magistri epigramma.
Que fuerant olim decimi pergrata Leonis
Lamenta atque tuis auribus alme parens
Corrupta haec vester vix agnoscebat alumnus
Carpentras. Qui operis musicus author erat
Quocirca illa suis non solum cantibus idem
Restituit, multo sed meliora dedit.
An meliora autem dederit subitura veretur
Iudicium docti pagina pontificis.
Qualecunque manet donum pater alme serena
Fronte cape, et famuli sis memor usque tui.

5. Munich, Bayerische Staatsbibliothek (D-Mbs), Mus. Ms. 38, fol. 1r [1531]

EN Opus Musicum festorum dierum hyemalium, cuius cantum choralem gravis vox habet a laudatissimo musicae artis auctore Domino Henrico Yzac. Divi Maximiliani Caesaris a lucubrationibus Musices, foeliciter et magno nisu coeptum, sed cogentibus alio fatis, imperfectum maxima ex parte relictum, postea a gratissimo ipsius discipulo Domino Ludovico Sennfflio, eiusdem Caesarea [*sic*] maiestatis iuditio in defuncti praeceptoris locum adoptato, nunc vero apud Illustrissimum Boiorum Principem Gulielmum, Comitem Rheni Palatinum, utriusque Boiariae ducem et Patrem patriae optime meritum, Musico intonatore facile celeberrimo, magna cura ac vigiliis singulari arte et industria ad extremam (quod dicitur) manum Musis omnibus faventibus perductum, Optimoque Principi Gulielmo, incomparabili Musarum Mecoenati, iure optimo sacrum et dicatum, Anno a Christo nato M.D.XXXI.

6. Biblioteca Apostolica Vaticana, MS Capp. Sist. 11, fol. 97v [1539]

Ad Lectorem
Si te forte movent Lector speciesque decorque
Scire quis hunc librum iusserit aere suo
Exscribi, et pingi, minima haec, ne noscere cures
Orsa sed ingentis maxima cerne animi.

Italiae pacem sanctissima foedera Regum
In Turcas classem, iustaque bella feros
Et Vaticana moles, et suspice Templa
Qui facit aeterna haec: haecque caduca iubet.
Sedente PAVLO III. Pontifice Maximo Optimo / Kalendis Aprilis M.D.xxxix. Completum. / Federicus Marius Perusinus scribebat.

7. Biblioteca Apostolica Vaticana, MS Capp. Sist. 9, fol. 110v [1545]

Liminibus Iani clausis clementia Pauli
Pontificis iussit thura cremanda Iovi.
Praebeat ut castis faciles concentibus aures
Dum veniam placido poscimus ore Deum,
Idque ut commodius fieri per secula possit
Hunc scribi Librum iussit: et aere suo.
Sedente Paulo Tertio Pontifice Maximo Optimo / Anno xi. Sedente Octobri M.D.xlv. / Federicus Marius Perusinus scribebat.

8. Munich, Bayerische Staatsbibliothek, Mus. Ms. A [Lassus *Prachtkodex*], p. 1 [1560s]

Deo Optimo Maximo Sacrum. Aeternaeque memoriae illustrissimi principis Alberti Bavariae ducis, qui dum a gubernanda amplissima regione sua, et sacro imperio consiliis indefesse iuvando interdum respiraret, quo erat erga omnia liberalissima studia, tum vero maxime erga musicam et picturam animo, benigne admodum apud se fovebat audiebatque, celeberrimum per Europam musicum Orlandum de Lassus, multorum ibi cantionum et horum quoque psalmorum compositorem. Et Iohannis Muelichii Monachiensis pictoris biblicarum imaginum praesentium unici collectoris architecti et inventoris operibus contemplandis, memorandisque sacris historiis, tum his, tum aliis omnibus, illustrissimo exemplo divine penitus vacabat. Tomus primus hoc loco absolvitur.

# *"TO THE BENEVOLENT READER..."* DEDICATIONS ATTACHED TO EDITIONS OF NEO-LATIN PLAYS IN THE NETHERLANDS OF THE 16TH AND THE 17TH CENTURY – FORMS, FUNCTIONS AND RELIGIOUS STANDPOINTS*

JAN BLOEMENDAL

## Introduction

Theatre is a specific medium. This also holds true for the sixteenth and seventeenth centuries. Most of the plays written are meant to be staged at a particular event, at a particular place for a particular audience. In the sixteenth century Latin comedies were staged by Latin schoolmasters and their pupils for their fellow pupils and others, e.g. parents and the city council. By writing these plays the *rectores* imitated the comedies of the Roman playwrights Plautus and Terence, but they often used biblical subjects instead of the pagan and morally damaging themes they saw in their Roman models. In this period the Low Countries were involved in religious quarrels that ended in a recatholisation of the Southern Provinces and a further Reformation of the Northern regions, especially because of the migration of intellectuals and artisans from Flanders and Brabant and from the German countries.[1] The biblical plays of this period often implicitly reflect these two reformations.

In the seventeenth century the writing of drama for educational purposes continued, but there was a paradigm shift. While in the sixteenth century most of the drama performed and written were comedies meant to be read and staged at the Latin schools, in the seventeenth century tragedy in the style of the Roman philosopher and tragedian Seneca prevailed.

* This paper is written as a corollary to the Vidi-project 'Latin and Vernacular Cultures. Theatre and Public Opinion in the Netherlands (ca. 1510-1625)', subsidized by the Netherlands Organisation for Scientific Research (NWO), dossiernr. 276-49-001. It is meant to be a first introduction in the field of the dedications of early modern Latin plays. I wish to thank Gerard Huijing for correcting my English.

[1] See Nicoline Van der Sijs, *Taal als mensenwerk: het ontstaan van het ABN* (Den Haag: Sdu uitgevers, 2004), pp. 46-48.

This tragedy was generally meant to be read and performed in a university setting. The writers of tragedies also chose biblical and religious topics that in their own way reflected the developments of their times.

When the plays were performed, some of them were printed. In that case the authors often added a dedicatory letter to a specific person or a preface to a 'general' or 'benevolent reader'.[2] This raises interesting questions on the choice of the dedicatees and the contents of the dedicatory letters and the prefaces. These could be written by the authors themselves, but also added by the printers, which generates new questions.[3] A third kind of questions can be put regarding genre. Did the different genres, comedy and tragedy, and the different purposes require their own dedicatees and their own contents?[4]

## Dedications and prefaces

Usually a distinction is made between dedications to a specific person or body and a preface to the general reader. The letter of dedication[5] addresses somebody and in him or in it the general reader, so it is more of a momentary nature than the preface to the 'benevolent reader' that is more 'timeless'.[6] For the contents of dedications and prefaces to early modern drama this distinction does not matter as much as one would expect. In the dedicatory letter, too, the author can make general remarks. A specific difference is of course that a letter is often marked as such, by an opening formula, the name of the addressee, the use of vocatives and verb forms in the second person, and an ending formula, and the preface does not necessarily have these features.

[2] I leave aside the prefaces and dedications to editions of Plautus and Terence, although it would have been interesting to include them in this survey.

[3] The dedications and prefaces that were added to the compilation works that the printers Brylinger and Oporinus published in 1540 and 1547 are a special case. *Comoediae et tragoediae ex Novo et Veteri Testamento desumptae*... (Basle: Nicolaus Brylinger, 1540) and *Dramata sacra. Comoediae et tragoediae aliquot e Veteri Testamento desumptae*... (Basle: Joannes Oporinus, 1547). See below, pp. 124-125.

[4] In passing it will also be addressed if the theory on paratexts by Genette are applicable to this material. Gérard Genette, *Seuils* (Paris: Seuil, 1987) = Gérard Genette, *Paratexts. Thresholds of Interpretation*, tr. Jane E. Lewin (Cambridge: Cambridge U.P., 1997).

[5] All dedications added to the drama's of my corpus have the form of a letter in prose.

[6] Genette, *Seuils*, pp. 182-183; Genette, *Paratexts*, pp. 196-197, states that a preface concentrates on 'comment' (how) and a dedication on 'pourquoi' (why).

Also Georgius Macropedius' preface/dedication to *Aluta* (1535) may warn us to be cautious with the distinction. Its heading is: 'Ad pueros bonarum litterarum studiosos', which more or less holds the middle between addressing specific dedicatees and a more general reader. In the preface/dedication itself the 'studiosi adulescentes', who in the first place are his own pupils, are addressed. Among other things their enthusiasm (*vestris studiis*) made him publish his play, as Macropedius says. At the end of the letter he also adds some formulary matter.[7]

Both in comedy and in tragedy the addition of dedicatory letters implied some support or patronage from the dedicatee, whether in friendship — actually existing or hoped for — or in money or *in natura*. The dedication for friendship was ranked higher than a dedication for patronage.[8] Of course in the preliminaries themselves the authors do not mention it explicitly, since this was considered unworthy. But the dedicatees understood the hint, at least some of them gave something. The authors of tragedies might get a substantial amount for their dedications.[9] The writers of comedies, however, could not expect such a reward. They often hoped for financial or moral support from the city council and, when staging the play, for a reward of wine or beer for themselves and the schoolboys who staged the plays.[10] When Macropedius dedicated his

[7] If the *adulescentes* (addressed by 'vos') will like this farce, he will publish some more plays for them to go and see. The end is clearly that of a letter: 'Valete et Macropedium vestrum non secus atque soletis observate aut, si id insolentius videtur, amate!' (Farewell and honour your Macropedius just as you did so far, or, unless this sounds overexaggerated, love him!), Georgius Macropedius, *Aluta*, ed. Jan Bloemendal and Jan W. Steenbeek (Voorthuizen: Florivallis, 1997²), p. 40.

[8] One has to bear in mind that friendship had different connotations than the modern concept: it meant mutual support (as 'social capital') instead of affectionate feelings, see, e.g., Luc Kooijmans, *Vriendschap en de kunst van het overleven in de zeventiende en achttiende eeuw* (Amsterdam: Bert Bakker, 1997), pp. 14-18; Saskia Stegeman, *Patronage en dienstverlening. Het netwerk van Theodorus Janssonius van Almeloveen (1657-1712) in de Republiek der Letteren* (PhD diss. Nijmegen, 1996), pp. 113-121.

[9] It is known, e.g., that Daniel Heinsius (1580-1655) received 200 guilders from the States of Holland and Western Friesland for his tragedy on William of Orange, the *Auriacus* (1602), see Jan Bloemendal, 'Daniel Heinsius, *Auriacus, sive Libertas saucia (1602)*. Editie met vertaling, inleiding en commentaar (...)', 2 vols. (PhD diss. Utrecht; Voorthuizen: Florivallis, 1997). Gerardus Johannes Vossius (1577-1649), too, e.g., was rewarded for the dedication of the *Poeticae institutiones* (1647) to the States-General, see Gerardus Johannes Vossius, *Poeticarum institutionum libri III*, ed. Jan Bloemendal (Stuttgart: Frommann Holzboog, forthcoming).

[10] When such a reward was not given, the author might express disappointment, as Crocus did when he had his *Ioseph* staged in 1535: 'Dimetri' 4-8 'nec tamen / Ingrata, vini cantharo / Dignata poetam patria est / Nec actione ephebulos / Cunctis probatos plurimum'

*Aluta* to the 'studiosi adulescentes', he could only hope to win their respect or affection.

The authors did not publish everything they wrote. It is among other things this reason that led them to state that friends made them publish their texts, or the success of the staging of plays composed by themselves or by others. Although this may be a commonplace of the humanists' modesty, it will not have been completely disingenuous. They often made such statements in a dedicatory letter or in a preface. In these preliminaries they often call their pieces *munuscula*, small gifts hardly worth mentioning, thus disparaging themselves. This was also a *topos*, but as most *topoi*, it is not without reason: comedy was considered a minor genre, as opposed to the 'lofty' tragedy, so when the author planned to publish such a comedy, he felt obliged to justify this and to show himself aware of its lowly character.[11]

## Dedications

The dedication or 'Widmungsvorrede' is as old as the hills.[12] In Antiquity it could occur in the work itself or — especially in Hellenistic literature —

(the ungrateful city did not deign the poet worthy of a jug of wine nor the boys that were so praised by all because of their performance).

[11] On this different 'level' of tragedy and comedy with regard to characters and style, see, e.g., the summary given by Gerardus Johannes Vossius, *Poeticarum institutionum libri III* (Amsterdam: Louis Elzevier, 1647), 2.22.4, 2.24.8 and 2.25.3.

[12] On the dedication in antiquity, see the contribution of Harm-Jan van Dam to this volume and, i.a., for antiquity: Tore Janson, *Latin Prose Prefaces: Studies in Literary Conventions*, Acta Universitatis Stockholmiensis, Studia Latina Stockholmiensia, 13 (Stockholm: Almqvist and Wicksel, 1964). For early modern times, see Wolfgang Leiner, *Der Widmungsbrief in der französischen Literatur (1580-1715)* (Heidelberg: s.n., 1964); U. Maché, 'Author and Patron: On the Function of Dedications in Seventeenth-Century German Literature', in James A. Parente, Jr. – Richard Erich Schade – George C. Schoolfield (eds.), *Literary Culture in the Holy Roman Empire, 1555-1720* (Chapel Hill, London: University of South Carolina Press, 1991), pp. 195-205; Johannes Ruppert, *Quaestiones ad historiam dedicationis librorum pertinentes* (Leipzig: Robert Noske, 1911); Karl Schottenloher, *Die Widmungsvorrede im Buch des 16. Jahrhunderts*, Reformationsgeschichtliche Studien und Texte, 76/77 (Münster: Aschendorffsche Verlagsbuchhandlung, 1953); Saskia Stegemann, *Patronage en dienstverlening*, pp. 187-194; Piet J. Verkruijsse, 'Holland "gedediceerd": Boekopdrachten in Holland in de 17e eeuw', *Holland*, 23 (1991), 225-242 [also www.dbnl.nl]; Genette, *Seuils*; idem, *Paratexts*; Jan Bloemendal, 'Schrijvers, drukkers en gededicaceerden in het Latijnstalige toneel', in Tom Deneire – Demmy Verbeke – Dirk Sacré (eds.), *De verhoudingen tussen auteur, drukker en gededicaceerde bij Neolatijnse publicaties. Acta selecta van de studiedag voor Neolatijn te Antwerpen,*

as a separate letter. The invention and use of the printing press, especially after the invention of movable type, made the distribution of books possible on a larger scale. This made it the more attractive to add a dedicatory letter. The dedicatee saw his name capitalized in a book, immediately after the title page. In their dedicatory letters the authors could express their gratitude for support they had had from the dedicatee, win his friendship or continue the existing relationship, gain some money, and state their points more explicitly or justify their choices of subject matter or of the way they treated it. As a paratext these dedications introduced the readers to the play and sometimes directed their interpretations of it.[13] Moreover some of the preliminary matter of comedies informed about the staging and production of plays, the author and his views, and the dedicatee. The playwrights themselves wrote most of the dedications, but in some cases the printer who collected some plays written by more than one author wrote the dedicatory letter or had it written, and at least once the author wrote a preface under the name of the printer.[14] The length of the dedications might vary from half a page to thirteen pages.

The practice of dedicating works also roused criticism. Erasmus who barefacedly wrote dedications himself attacked the habit of insincere ones in his paradoxical *Praise of Folly*. Folly praises herself and then she says:

> Yet in general I think I show a good deal more discretion than the general run of gentry and scholars, whose distorted sense of modesty leads them to make a practice of bribing some sycophantic speaker or babbling poet hired for a fee so that they can listen to him praising their merits, purely fictitious though they are. The bashful listener spreads his tail-feathers like a peacock and carries his head high, while the brazen flatterer rates this worthless individual with the gods and sets him up as the perfect model of all the virtues — though the man himself knows he is nowhere near that; 'infinity doubled' would not be too far away. Thus the wretched crow is

*Museum Plantin-Moretus, 17 december 2004* (Leuven, 2005 [2006]). Published online on http://www.arts.kuleuven.be/sph/acta.htm.

[13] Here the distinction has been made between the inscription of a copy (dédicacer) and the dedication of a text (dédier), cf. Génette, *Seuils*, p. 110 and pp. 127-128; *Paratexts*, p. 117 and pp. 136-137, but I deal with the latter type of dedication only.

[14] Schonaeus, 'Typographus candido lectori S.' to the *Terentius Christianus, seu Comoediae sacrae sex* (1594), see Hans van de Venne, 'Cornelius Schonaeus Goudanus (1540-1611). Brieven' (PhD diss. Katholieke Universiteit Leuven; Voorthuizen: Florivallis, 2001), pp. 172-176. This raises the question of the importance of the (actual) writer compared to the person who is made or makes himself responsible for the text. In other words: to whom must this dedication be ascribed and who 'owns' it?

decked out in borrowed plumage, the 'Ethiopian washed white', an 'elephant created out of a gnat'.[15]

## General background

In the Latin schools the schoolmasters taught Latin language as a preparation for the university.[16] In the first decades of the sixteenth century the medieval schools in the Netherlands were reformed, under the influence of Erasmian humanism and reformatory tendencies. One of the consequences of this educational reform was the return to the sources, *ad fontes*. Knowledge of pagan literature (*litterae prophanae*) was deemed indispensable for the study of theology concerned with language and exegesis. Also Christian sources, the Old and New Testament, and the Fathers of the Church, were read in their original language or in Latin. The Brethren of the Common Life, adhering to the Modern Devotion, also played their role in the reformatory tendencies. These Brethren focussed on practicing Christianity in everyday life.

The purport of the educational reform was the return to classical languages, especially to Latin, and through the language to erudition, as propagated by, e.g., Erasmus (1466/69-1536) and Johannes Ludovicus Vives (1492-1540).[17] But the final aim of the Northern humanists was not the knowledge of Latin (and to a lesser extent of Greek), but intellectual education and piety, according to the Socratic *adagium* that knowledge must lead to good conduct. The Amsterdam rector Petrus Apherdianus (*ca* 1520-1583?) put it thus in 1560: 'All misery in a human life is the result of ignorance and lack of knowledge'.[18] In this ideal of education, comedy could take its role, as Macropedius stated in the dedication of his farce-play *Aluta* to the inquisitive young people mentioned above:

[15] Erasmus, *Praise of Folly and Letter to Martin Dorp 1515*. Trans. Betty Radice, intr. A.H.T. Levi (Harmondsworth: Penguin Books, 1982 = 1971), pp. 65-66. Cf. also Henry Benjamin Wheatley, *The Dedication of Books to Patron and Friend. A Chapter in Literary History* (London: Elliot Stock, 1887), pp. 9-10.

[16] A recent survey is offered by Jan Bloemendal, *Spiegel van het dagelijks leven? Latijnse school en toneel in de noordelijke Nederlanden in de zestiende en de zeventiende eeuw*, Zeven Provinciën Reeks, 22 (Hilversum: Verloren, 2003).

[17] See, e.g., Jan Bloemendal, 'Humanistische onderwijsvernieuwing en Latijns toneel in de noordelijke Nederlanden: Murmellius en Crocus', *Historisch tijdschrift Holland*, 32 (2005), 134-147, esp. pp. 139-140.

[18] 'Omnia mala quibus vita humana est obnoxia ex sola ignorantia proficiscuntur', Apherdianus, *Institutio puerum*, f. 2r, quoted from Petrus N.M. Bot, *Humanisme en onderwijs in Nederland* (PhD diss. Nijmegen; Utrecht: Spectrum, 1954), p. 21.

> What would be more useful for the knowledge of young pupils, what would contribute more to the literary education of the pupils of the fourth and third class, wherefrom could the advanced pupils gain more profit than from a serious comedy?[19]

This quotation moreover makes clear that the humanists were not only keen on spreading knowledge, but also looked at didactics and the educational climate. They contributed to this climate by having their pupils stage comedies in Latin, so that the schoolboys would learn better Latin and could improve their mastery of public speaking. Also it was a means of public relations for the school, and last but not least the headmasters gave moral lessons in the plays they wrote themselves.

University drama was more sophisticated. It often treated 'lofty' and more cruel subjects and it staged lofty characters like kings or princes and their deeds, as was deemed to fit the tragic genre. So Daniel Heinsius wrote tragedies on the assassination of William of Orange (*Auriacus, sive Libertas saucia*, William of Orange or the Wounding of Liberty, 1602) and the Massacre of the innocent children (*Herodes infanticida*, 1632). Hugo Grotius (1583-1645) published biblical drama's on the fall of man (*Adamus exul*, 1601), the Passion (*Christus patiens*, 1608) and Joseph (*Sophompaneas*, 1635). Although these topics had already been treated in school dramas, tragedy elaborated them to a far greater extent, or went off in directions all of its own. E.g., the theme of Joseph was the subject of a drama by Cornelius Crocus (*ca* 1500-1555), who treated the patriarch as an example of virtuous, chaste conduct for daily life, while Grotius presented him as an ideal, merciful, prince.

## The dedicatees

The choice of the persons to whom the playwrights dedicated their dramas may tell us something about the 'Sitz im Leben' of the authors. One of the prolific playwrights of the sixteenth century, Georgius Macropedius

[19] 'Quid enim plus pueris ad eruditionem, plus adolescentibus ad honesta studia, plus provectioribus, immo omnibus in commune ad virtutem conducat quam docta comoedia?' Macropedius, *Aluta*, ed. Bloemendal and Steenbeek, pp. 38-39. On Macropedius see Henk Giebels & Frans Slits, *Georgius Macropedius 1487-1558. Leven en werken van een Brabantse humanist* (Tilburg: Stichting Zuidelijk Historisch Contact Tilburg, 2005). The only introduction in English is by Thomas W. Best, *Macropedius*, Twaine's World Author Series, 218 (New York: Twaine Publishers, [1972]).

(1487-1558), chose either former pupils or magistrates of the city where he worked most of the time, Utrecht. As a Brother of the Common Life he chose to be not very outspoken and preferred 'safe' persons to address his works to. He wrote short, almost obligatory dedications in which he in most cases defended himself against possible criticism and stated that this comedy was a 'small gift' to thank the dedicatee. Also 'safe', at least in 1536, was the choice that Cornelius Crocus (ca. 1500-1550) made in dedicating his Joseph-play to his friend and colleague Maarten Dircksz. Nieuveen.[20] Yet it was a statement, for together they strove to sustain the Roman Catholic Church and testified against their colleague of Hebrew and Greek, Mr. Wouter Deelen.[21] Defensive, too, was the dedicatory preface to the 'inquisitive young people' or the 'benevolent reader', that Macropedius and Christianus Ischyrius (d. after 1536) wrote. The Louvain teacher Hadrianus Barlandus (1486-1538) dedicated his collection of *Dialogi* (1524) to his pupil Charles de Croÿ, who by then was commendatory abbot of Aumont and would soon become bishop of Tournai.[22] The Roman Catholic schoolmaster Cornelius Laurimanus (*ca* 1520-1573) dedicated his plays in 1562 and 1565 to Boudewijn Adriaen van Crayenstein from IJsselstein, a small town in the neighbourhood of Utrecht, and to the 'domproost' and archdeacon Cornelis van Mierop.[23] The Roman Catholic Church still had its prominent position — the Utrecht iconoclasm was not to begin until 1566 — so he could still be sure it would do him no harm.

Quite another choice is made by Gulielmus Gnapheus (1493-1568) in the dedication of his *Acolastus* (1529), the tremendously successful play on the Prodigal Son, a prominent protestant theme on grace and mercy.[24]

[20] On Crocus see Albertus Josefus Kölker, *Alardus Aemstelredamus en Cornelius Crocus, twee Amsterdamsche priester-humanisten: hun leven, werken en theologische opvattingen: Bijdrage tot de kennis van het Humanisme in Noord-Nederland in de eerste helft van de zestiende eeuw* (PhD diss. Nijmegen; Nijmegen: Dekker & Van de Vegt, 1963).

[21] On this see Kölker, *Alardus en Crocus*, pp. 198-202; Johannes Franciscus Maria Sterck, *Onder Amsterdamsche Humanisten: hun opkomst en bloei in de 16e eeuwsche stad* (Hilversum: Paul Brand, [1934]), pp. 91-107.

[22] See Étienne Daxhelet, *Adrien Barlandus, humaniste belge (1486-1538). Sa Vie — Son Œuvre — Sa Personnalité*, Humanistica Lovaniensia, 6 (Louvain: Librairie Universitaire, 1938), pp. 18-19 and 158.

[23] On this Utrecht Latin poet, successor of Macropedius at the Hieronymusschool, see Abraham Jacob van der Aa, *Biographisch woordenboek der Nederlanden* (Haarlem: Van Brederode, [1878]), 11, 211-212.

[24] On Gnapheus, see Johannes Trapman, G.J. Graafland, 'Gnapheus', *Biografisch Lexicon voor de Geschiedenis van het Nederlandse Protestantisme*, 4 (1998), 142-144. One

He dedicated it to his friend Ioannes Sartorius, whom the Roman Catholic mainstream considered a heretic.[25] After moving to the German countries Gnapheus adopted the local customs and dedicated his next two plays, *Morosophus* (The Wise Fool, 1541) and *Hypocrisis* (1544) to the archbishop of Magdeburg and Mainz, margrave Albrecht of Brandenburg (1490-1545) and the Alsatian philologist and physician Jodocus Willichius (1501-1552). He chose the margrave as a dedicatee for his *Morosophus* to ensure, as he himself states, the orthodoxy of the play. This was not so strange, since the play mocked some astronomers, perhaps notably Copernicus, and theologians, so it was conceivable that there some doubts might rise about the position of the play and its author.[26]

Seventy years after the first edition of *Acolastus* things had changed considerably. Caspar Ens or Casparius (1569-1642) dedicated his *Princeps Auriacus, sive Libertas defensa* (The Prince of Orange or the Defence of Liberty, 1599) to the ministers of the Reformed Church of Holland and he could do so without any trouble.[27] In the seventies and eighties of the sixteenth century the Haarlem rector Cornelius Schonaeus (1540-1611) dedicated his many plays to Roman Catholic friends and patrons, and the town councils of Haarlem and of his native town Gouda. His position was special in the sense that he was not compelled to leave his post after his home town took the side of the Reformation, but could maintain his position although he did not renounce his Roman Catholic faith. For the moment the conclusion may be that the *rectores* chose the dedicatees constrained by circumstances, because they wished to choose those people to dedicate their works to by whom they would not be compromised.

In (university) tragedy things were different. The loftier genre required loftier dedicatees, or rather the loftiness of the genre made it possible to

must, however, be careful in determining the denomination of a play, see Jacobus Bernardus Drewes, 'Het interpreteren van godsdienstige spelen van zinne', *Jaarboek de Fonteine*, 29 (1978-1979), 5-124.

[25] On Sartorius, see Sterck, *Onder Amsterdamsche humanisten*, pp. 91-107; Johannes Trapman, 'Ioannes Sartorius (ca. 1500-1557), gymnasiarch te Amsterdam en Noordwijk, als Erasmiaan en Spiritualist', *Nederlands Archief voor Kerkgeschiedenis*, 70 (1990), 30-51. The circumstance that Sartorius was the dedicatee did not stop the play from becoming extremely popular both among protestant and Roman Catholic humanists.

[26] This is one of the few examples that the dedicatee added more or less his *auctoritas* to the orthodox character of the play. Nicolaus Copernicus (1473-1543) wrote down his ideas in *De revolutionibus orbium caelestium* (Nuremberg: Johannes Petreius, 1543), two years after the publication of *Morosophus*, so his theories were known beforehand.

[27] Caspar Ens, *Princeps Auriacus (1599) (De prins van Oranje)*, ed. Jan Bloemendal and Jan Wieger Steenbeek (Voorthuizen: Florivallis, 1999).

choose these loftier persons to dedicate a work to. So Heinsius dedicated his plays to the States of Holland and Western Friesland (*Auriacus*) and to the courtier Sir Constantine Huygens (1596-1687) (*Herodes infanticida*), Grotius to Henry II of Bourbon, Prince of Condé (1588-1646) (*Adamus exul*), the French envoy in the Dutch Republic, the knight and counsellor Pierre Jeannin (1540-1622) (*Christus patiens*), and Gerardus Johannes Vossius, professor of the Amsterdam Athenaeum illustre (*Sophompaneas*). Nicolaus Vernulaeus (1583-1648) dedicated his *Fritlandus* (1637) to Petrus Roose (1585/6-1673), His Majesty's counsellor in Spain and Belgium and added a preface 'Ad Lectorem'.[28] He offered his other plays also to counsellors, provosts and the like. Jacobus Cornelius Lummenaeus a Marca (1570-1629) dedicated his *Bustum Sodomae* (The Destruction of Sodom, 1615) to the abbot of Laet Antonius of Winghe, his *Carcer Babylonius* (1610) to archduke Albrecht and other plays to other ecclesiastical chancellors and to cardinal Carolus Borromaeus (1538-1584). It is striking that tragedies are dedicated to persons of high rank, but not of the highest rank: kings and emperors are not addressed. In these matters the Dutch Republic had more or less a special position in Europe because in the Northern Netherlands sovereign and nobility had a less dominant influence on society as patrons of arts and sciences than in other countries. For playwrights in the Southern Provinces, who could choose the Spanish king, this Majesty might have been too high and too remote: no dedication is directed to him.

## The content of dedications

In their dedications, as we already have seen, the playwrights made remarks on the staging of their plays. The authors often stated that they had their play printed as a result of the success of the performance, or that they were stimulated by the success of their earlier play or plays, which gives us some insight into the impact the plays had. Mentioning the success had also apologetic reasons, for besides this the authors defended the value of comedy, that still had to win its place in the curriculum, witness what Macropedius had said in the dedication of his *Aluta*. But in other dedications he stated almost nothing substantial, referring only to the gratitude

[28] See Jean-Marie Rousseau (ed.) and Henri Plard (intr. and trans.), *Un 'Wallenstein' néo-latin: 'Le duc de Friedland', 'Fritlandus. Tragoedia' (1637) par Nicolaus Vernulaeus (Nicolas de Vernulz)* (Brussels: University Press, 1989), pp. 10-13 and 14-15.

owed to him and to his inability to pay in money, so that this *munus literarium* (gift of literature) must suffice.[29]

The dedicators also tell us something about the aims they had in writing and staging their dramas. Gnapheus in his *Acolastus* relates that his goal is to preach the Gospel and in this way to propagate Christian faith and piety (*pietatis respectus*), and to bring people to their senses. In the prologue of the play, the same Gnapheus hastens to say that this is a new play, but that it is not drenched in Lutheranism:

> Dear gentlemen, please do not let the surprise you feel at the appearance of a play with a new title lead you to suppose that we are going to present a new story. We are not unaware of the hatred which people feel towards the very word 'new'. Well, let us assure you that in this work there is not even a suspicion of new doctrine.[30]

Concurrently the Louvain humanist Levinus Brechtus stated in the Preface to his *Euripus*, a kind of 'Elckerlyc-play', dedicated to George of Austria, bishop of Liège, that his aim was to show the schoolboys the vanity of human life:

> We took the subject matter from the heart of human life, and its primary aim is that youth, that is mostly blind and vacillating, may look carefully at its instability, vanity and horridness as in a mirror, after inspection it may acknowledge and abhor, once recognised learn to condemn, and in hate take pains to abandon and ceaselessly deplore them.[31]

Although Crocus with his *Ioseph* (1536) is reacting to the Anabaptist riots of Amsterdam 1534-1535, when Anabaptists wanted to found the Kingdom

[29] This allusion to the author's poverty may be an implicit reference to a possible financial reward.

[30] 'Vos nulla captet, obsecro, admiratio, / Quod hic uidetis, optimi uiri, nouos. / In apparatu scaenico titulos, nouam / Qui nos daturos esse fabulam arguant. / Haud me latet, quanto odio uocabulum / Noui laboret, uerum enimuero hic nouis?/ De dogmatis ne mû quidem (…).' Gulielmus Gnapheus, *Acolastus*, 1-7; see Gulielmus Gnapheus, *Acolastus: a Latin Play of the Sixteenth Century*, ed. W.E.D. Atkinson, University of Western Ontario Studies in the Humanities, 3 (Thesis Ontario; London, Ontario: University of Western Ontario, 1964), p. 91. Cf. Genette, *Seuils*, p. 186; *Paratexts*, p. 200 on the themes of 'novelty' and 'tradition' in the dedications and prefaces as arguments to read the text.

[31] 'Est enim quod hic tractamus argumentum e media hominum vita desumptum, huc potissimum spectans, ut iuventus caeca plerunque et lubrica, inconstantiam suam, vanitatem, foeditatem, velut in speculo diligenter inspiciat, inspectam agnoscat et exhorreat, agnitam damnare discat et odisse, damnatam atque exosam relinquere studeat et perpetuo deplorare.' Laevinus Brecht, *Euripus*, in Fidel Rädle, *Lateinische Ordensdramen des XVI. Jahrhunderts mit deutschen Übersetzungen*, Ausgaben deutscher Literatur des XV. bis XVIII. Jahrhunderts, 82. Reihe Drama, 6 (Berlin, etc.: De Gruyter, 1979), p. 6.

of God on earth, he, too, gives general reasons for writing his *comoedia sacra*: he wants to educate the youngsters towards the wisdom of God and to direct them to His kingdom. One is led to think that he mentions the Kingdom of God in heaven to counterbalance implicitly the Anabaptists' ideas of founding the Kingdom of God on earth.[32]

Before the new and old religions actually clashed — the Lutherans and the like on one side, and Roman Catholics on the other — the coming events had already cast their shadows. The Utrecht rector Laurimanus could write in 1565 in the dedicatory letter to his play *Miles Christianus* (Christian Soldier):[33]

> I am plodding along in the dust of my schoolwork and barely, no, not even barely dare I raise my head in public, although almost everything is in turmoil by the false and schismatic doctrines.[34]

Laurimanus even suggests a solution for the troubles of the time, that we may find a bit naïve, but some of his contemporaries will have embraced the remedy, that we may summarize as 'back to basics':

> This is my doctrine that my play everywhere preaches and teaches simplicity of mind, peace, concord, clemency and unanimity. (...) Let us return to that form the church had at its birth, when there was more faith in life than in quarrels or in the stating of many rules.[35]

The early church did not quarrel:

> For in the young church they humbled themselves to the extent that they recognised that they, with Paul, knew nothing save Jesus Christ and his crucifixion. [1 Corinthians 2:2]. For this is the nucleus of our doctrine, this its head, this its source, that we, people crucified by the world, should imitate him who is crucified, not in eminent speech but in showing the fruits of the Spirit: love, joy, peace, endurance, benevolence, patience, gentleness,

[32] He also directs the interpretation of the play by stressing this wisdom and by linking pagan wisdom to christian revelation, see Emily Kearns, 'Pagan Wisdom, Christian Revelation: Two Latin Biblical Plays', *Humanistica Lovaniensia*, 36 (1987), 212-238.

[33] After St. Paul's letter to the Ephesians, ch. 6. Cf. Erasmus, *Enchiridion militis christiani* (1501).

[34] 'Nos autem in scholastico puluere desudantes vix ac ne vix quidem caput efferre in publicum audemus, quantumlibet adulterinis ac schismaticis pene omnia perturbata sint doctrinis', Corn. Laurimanus, *Miles Christianus, comoedia sacra* (Antwerpen: Gulielmus Silvius, 1565), p. A2v.

[35] 'At ea est nostra doctrina, ut animorum simplicitatem, pacem, concordiam, mansuetudinem, unanimitatem ubique praedicet ac doceat (...). Redeamus ad primam illam nascentis ecclesiae formam, ubi fides magis erat in vita, quam in disceptationibus et articulorum multiplici professione', *ibidem*, p. A3r.

> goodness, faith, meekness, temperance, moderation and chastity.[36] [Galatians 2:22-23]

Laurimanus puts it even more briefly, stating that the two main principles of the Bible are the love of God and the love of one's neighbour, the 'summary of the law',[37] thus implicitly criticizing the 'heretics' with their schisms:

> For all of Scripture, whether we would look at the Old or the New Testament, can be principally reduced to two main chapters so to speak, i.e. that we love and obey God and that we treat our neighbours just like ourselves and love them with all our hearts.[38]

This is the aim that Laurimanus sets himself in writing and staging this *Miles Christianus*: the spectators should learn that they ought to confess Christ not in their words, but in their acts and way of life.

Cornelius Schonaeus, a Roman Catholic rector who wrote and published his plays some decades later, referred to events that already have taken place, at least partly: the devastation of the Roman Catholic church and the destruction of its buildings.[39] For instance in the dedication of his *Saulus conversus* (1570) to his friend the prelate Philips of Hogesteijn he tells us that with this play he aims at the spreading of Catholicism: Gods grace has converted those who like Saul in their blind zeal and unwittingly have committed crimes against the church. For those who persevere in their error one can only hope that they will repent. These *pia vota* of Schonaeus were uttered in vain, for only a few years later the Haarlem convents were destroyed. In 1572 he dedicated his *Naaman* to

[36] 'Nam huc illi tum in primaeua Ecclesia sese deijciebant, vt nihil se scire cum Paulo intelligerent, nisi Iesum Christum et ipsum crucifixum. Haec enim est doctrinae nostrae summa, hoc caput, hic fons: quem crucifixum scimus, eum vt crucifixi mundo sequamur, non in eminentia sermonis, sed in ostensione spiritus, cuius opera sunt charitas, gaudium, pax, patientia, benignitas, longanimitas, mansuetudo, fides, modestia, continentia, castitas', *ibidem*, p. A3v.

[37] Matthew 22:37-40, Mark 12:30-31 and Luke 10:27; cf. Deuteronomy 6:5 and Leviticus 19:18.

[38] 'Omnis siquidem scriptura, siue nouum siue vetus testamentum spectemus, potissimum ad duo tanquam primaria capita referri potest, nempe vt dilectionem atque obedientiam habeamus erga Deum, ac deinde vt proximos non aliter ac nosmetipsos omni cura et studio amemus et obseruemus', *ibidem*, p. A3v.

[39] Now a vast biography is available, Hans van de Venne, *Cornelius Schonaeus Goudanus (1540-1611): 1. Leven en werk van de Christelijke Terentius: Nieuwe bijdragen tot de geschiedenis van de Latijnse scholen van Gouda, 's-Gravenhage en Haarlem*, Haerlem Reeks 15.1 (Voorthuizen: Florivallis, 2001). Van de Venne also edited the letters, including the dedicatory ones, in an unpublished thesis.

Cornelis van der Myle and to the Magistrate and town council of Gouda. Here, too, he alludes to good administration and makes remarks against the heresy Lutheranism is to him.

Twenty-five years later the same Schonaeus is far more cautious. When writing a preface to his edition of six plays, the *Terentius Christianus* (1595) to the 'Benevolent Reader', he only hints at bringing youth to the fear of God and to good manners and Christian behaviour. Perhaps he implies that Christian behaviour is synonymous with Roman Catholic, but any overt reference to his own faith or any mentioning of a heresy would by then be inappropriate and even dangerous.

One of the reasons for dedicating a play was, just as in antiquity, the possibility that the dedicatee might correct it, as Gnapheus hints at in the dedication to his *Acolastus*, in which he is deliberately ambiguous, referring to both the play and the protagonist:

> (...) my dear Sartorius, here is my Acolastus (for so I have named him), come to you for disciplining (...).[40]

In tragedy, things were a bit different, given the changing circumstances. Heinsius defended in the dedication of his *Auriacus* the writing of a tragedy and expanded on the loftiness of the genre, referring to among others Sophocles who wrote tragedy when he was a leader of the Athenian state, and its educational value by linking tragedy to philosophy. Moreover, he gives account for the choice of subject: he chose to write a drama on the political and religious murder of William of Orange (1533-1584) out of gratitude to the States who were hospitable to him when he had to flee from Flanders and sheltered him in their Leiden Academy.[41] In this manner he relates tragedy to politics, to religion and to the university. He achieves this by dedicating his work to the States of Holland and West-Friesland. These were *political* bodies, that were so to say the heirs of the 'Father of the Fatherland', killed in 1584 because of religious reasons. Consequently, its members saw themselves as the founding fathers, together with William, of the University of Leiden. This dedication must have been a sort of application for a grant: he received an amount of

[40] '(...) sub tuam, mi Sartori, ferulam hic noster Acolastus, sic enim illi nomen fecimus, uenit.' Gnapheus, *Acolastus*, ed. Atkinson, p. 85, 87.

[41] When he was three years of age, his parents fled from Ghent to the Northern Netherlands and eventually settled in the town of Leiden. He studied law at the University of Franeker and *artes* at Leiden University. See for this and the following Heinsius, *Auriacus*, ed. Bloemendal.

fl. 200 for this dedication. He also added a dedicatory letter in Greek to his teacher Josephus Justus Scaliger (1540-1609), whom he asked to correct the work, like Gnapheus addressed his teacher Sartorius. With this he probably wished to maintain the good contacts with his admired professor. More specifically, he wanted to impress him and the curators of the university of Leiden in order to obtain an appointment, as he actually did: he became lecturer and soon full professor. Finally in a preface to the 'Benevolent Reader' he excused himself for not adding some notes on Greek and Roman tragedy, for the division in scenes, for some metrical questions, and for observing the unities of place and time that were required by Aristotle in his *Poetics*.[42] Heinsius states that he had introduced prince Frederick Henry (1584-1647) in his tragedy and left prince Maurice (1567-1625) out since the latter had not been in Delft during the assassination. So in the first dedication he implicitly asks for money, in the second for friendship and a job and in the third literary justifications prevail. In the dedication to the States Heinsius does refer to the religious troubles that took place eighteen years before, but not that much as one would expect in the case of a tragedy that could be seen as having for a subject a protestant martyr, and he keeps silent about the situation in his own days on the threshold of the Twelve Years' Truce (1609-1621) with its debates and struggles between Remonstrants and Contra-Remonstrants.

Grotius, in the dedication of his *Adamus exul* to Henry II of Bourbon, written in the same years as Heinsius's first tragedy, goes similar ways. He links tragedy to philosophy, especially metaphysics (God, angels and the like), physics (the creation of the world) and ethics,[43] and to geography and astronomy.[44] He does not mention the situation in his own times either, nor does he in the dedication to his *Sophompaneas* (1535), but this does not imply that the situation is completely absent. Joseph is an example of mercy, an example for the States General of the Republic, which makes Grotius, then an exile, less perturbed, confident about a return to his country.

A striking metaphor to connect tragedy with politics, religion and morality is used by Nicolaus Vernulaeus in the dedication of his *Fritlandus*

[42] This led to some problems, since he also wanted to introduce Prince Maurice who had not been in Delft on the day of assassination. So the wish to observe historical reality and the aim of observing the unities of time and place were incompatible.

[43] In these matters Grotius adheres to the Stoic division of philosophy.

[44] See Grotius, *Sacra in quibus Adamus exul*, ed. B.L. Meulenbroek et al., Dichtwerken, 1.1.A/B, 2 vols (Assen: Van Gorcum, 1970-1971).

(1637), a play about the count who conspired against emperor Ferdinand II of Austria three years before: the eponymous hero 'is now coming from the theatre to the dedicatee', as Vernulaeus states.[45] According to Vernulaeus the story of Frietland is a warning against ambition and rebellion. These are acts that will be punished by God. He keeps the implications for his own country implicit, but of course this will play a role on the background in this letter to Petrus Roose, 'Catholicae Maiestati in Hispania et Belgio a consiliis'. This dedication is followed by another paratext, 'Ad Lectorem', which is a 'tragoediae argumentum'. In this Vernulaeus summarizes the play, but here too he gives the story a religious explanation: 'Heaven did not want the House of Austria to be annihilated by such an abominable crime'.[46]

## Dedications in collections of dramas

The collections of dramas that were published by Brylinger and Oporinus (Basle, 1540 and 1547) have a special position. Nicolaus Brylinger or Breyling collected ten biblical plays among which seven plays written by authors from the Netherlands, three by Macropedius, Gnapheus' *Acolastus*, Crocus' *Ioseph*, Nicolaus Bartholomaeus' *Christus xylonicus*, and Jacobus Zovitius' *Ovis perdita* (The lost sheep). He did not add a dedication to his collection. Instead, he added a short preface to the 'candidus lector' who in the letter itself is addressed as 'adulescens ingeniose' and 'lector Christiane' to whom he recommends his work, a 'new Terence', born 'not in Rome, but in the Christian schools'. Therefore and because of the 'holiness of its sacred subject' it should be in the library of every school, in the theatres and in the libraries of kings and other rulers. The address ends with the wish that many more playwrights may arise. This preface clearly is meant as an 'advertising text' to promote the sale of this booklet.

The printer Joannes Oporinus (1507-1568) added a dedicatory letter addressed to the sons of the banker Hieronymus Sailer, probably written by himself, to his two volume collection of school plays in which he adopted Crocus' *Ioseph* and Zovitius' *Ruth* but that he for the other part

[45] Vernulaeus, *Fritlandus*, ed. Rousseau and Plard, p. 10: 'Ecce Fritlandus, vir amplissime, e theatro ad te iam venit'; cf. what Gnapheus had done in his dedication.

[46] 'Coelum tum abominando scelere exstingui Austriacam Gentem non voluit', Vernulaeus, *Fritlandus*, ed. Rousseau and Plard, p. 14.

filled with plays written by Augsburger humanists. He stresses the use of knowledge and erudition for a happy and morally good life — a *topos* among the sixteenth century humanists — especially for those who are destined to obtain high positions in the state. They have to take their responsibilities for the state and the church, like the two Sailer boys. The dedication of these dramas is meant — so Oporinus says — to contribute to their education and moral behaviour. This dedication to the sons of a banker implies that the author expects a generous grant from the father for the edition of the plays. With the sons, the general reader, especially the headmasters and other teachers of the Latin schools and the pupils, will have been addressed and made aware that the biblical comedies collected in these two volumes will contribute to a better society, which is a perfect reason to buy them. This dedicatory letter of Oporinus is more sophisticated than the preface by Brylinger. One is led to think, also by the similarity in the titles, that Oporinus wanted to imitate and surpass his predecessor.

## Final remarks

The choice of the dedicatees and the content of the dedication letter vary according to the circumstances, viz. the writer and what he aimed to achieve; moreover, it also depends on the situation in the Northern Netherlands which was special because a predominant role of the monarch or nobility for supporting the arts and sciences was absent. It is evident that in these Northern Provinces until circa 1566, the year of the iconoclasms, the Roman Catholic authors were more overt in their particular faith than the Protestant. Afterwards, this changed. In the early years, until the fifties of the sixteenth century, one of the often recurring topics is the defence of writing, reading and staging comedies, while in the beginning of the seventeenth century dedications to tragedies take on that role of defence. Gnapheus in 1529 even wondered why the art of writing comedies was neglected, which led Macropedius to a response in the Preface to his *Aluta* and *Rebelles* edited in 1535, but written already in the second decade of the sixteenth century.[47] The authors' main goal in writing comedies is to

[47] Gnapheus, Dedication to *Acolastus*: 'Cum sint, mi Sartori, hoc nostro tam docto saeculo viri egregie docti, qui omne disciplinarum genus tractent, versent et excolant, demiror poesim comicam sic iacere neglectam, sic porro intactam relinqui, tanquam res sit

encourage the schoolboys to practice their creed in daily life. If there is a reference to the religious quarrels of the time, mostly the riots are hinted at, not the tenets of faith, not, e.g., the much disputed topic of transubstantiation. This is a bit surprising. Since the biblical humanists did not have the opportunity to discuss these topics in the plays, one might think they would do so in these preliminaries. For they really were involved in these highly debated issues and kept abreast of them, especially when their creed was at stake. But probably they avoided mentioning those topics of Christian doctrine because of their wish to return to the simplicity of the early church which in their opinion was still undivided. Moreover, they wanted to be read at as many schools as possible, be it Protestant or Roman Catholic. The dedicatee might be more or even less immortalized by the dedication, and the dedicator could win some fame by his play, albeit not immortal fame because of the baseness of the genre. For tragedy things were a bit different, but the highest authorities such as kings and princes were even in this lofty genre seldom the dedicatees.

Plays were meant to be staged at a particular event, at a particular place for a particular audience by particular players. By having their plays printed the schoolmasters made these particularities general. For in the early modern era, as we should bear in mind, 'eeuwig gaat voor ogenblik', 'eternity prevails over matters temporal'[48] and according to the schoolmasters good conduct led to eternal life.[49] For these and other reasons they wrote their plays and had them printed, published, and dedicated.

HUYGENS INSTITUTE
P.O. Box 90754
NL – 2509 LT Den Haag

DEPARTMENT OF LATIN
University of Amsterdam
Spuistraat 134
NL – 1012 VB Amsterdam
j.bloemendal@uva.nl

inimitabilis et cui opera parum utiliter collocetur.' Macropedius, Preface to *Aluta* and *Rebelles*: 'Miratur quidam et ipse profecto doleo inter tot saeculi nostri viros doctissimos nullos Menandros, nullos Terentios reperiri, sed hoc scribendi genus paene ab ipsis Terentii aut certe Lucilii temporibus oblitteratum esse et antiquatum, quod tamen prae ceteris scriptorum generibus pluris merito foret aestimandum.'

[48] Vondel, 'Kinder-lijk'.

[49] The reformers' two major questions were: How can man be saved? What is the evidence and what are the proofs or consequences of salvation, both temporarily and eternally? Therefore the reformatory humanists' approach was first of all practical, moral and ethical, and only secondarily theological, see William Echard Keeney, *The Development of Dutch Anabaptist Thought and Practice 1539-1564* (Nieuwkoop: De Graaf, 1968), p. 22.

# *"AEQUABIT LAUDES NULLA CAMENA TUAS"* POETRY AND MUSIC IN LATIN LAUDATORY MOTETS*

Victoria Panagl

'No Muse is able to praise you in an adequate way.' This sentence — a pentameter in the original Latin — is the cantus firmus and the motto of a laudatory motet dealing with dedicatory topoi, Orlando di Lasso's *Si qua tibi obtulerint.*[1] The cantus firmus, which deals with a literary commonplace, states two things: it praises the addressee as a person whose glory is so great that even the Muses, the "best artists", cannot find the right words for praise, and simultaneously says that the poet is attempting to praise the addressee in a very skillful way. In some respect, the message between the lines is that since laudatory poetry and laudatory motets sought to praise the addressees adequately, the authors of the texts strove to write poems of good quality.

We should ask first of all: what is a laudatory motet? There are some characteristic features for laudatory motets of the fifteenth and especially the sixteenth century. They are always written in praise of, or dedicated to a specific person and/or a specific occasion, and usually we can identify at least the person or the occasion in the text.[2] During the Renaissance, many laudatory motets were written in praise of emperors, noblemen or patrons, celebrating official and private occasions. Such ceremonies were

* Cordial thanks to Robert Lindell and especially to Nele Gabriëls for proofreading this paper.

[1] Orlando di Lasso, *Il primo libro de mottetti a cinque et a sei voci* (Antwerp: de Laet, 1556). Modern edition: *Orlando di Lasso, The Complete Motets 1. Il primo libro de mottetti a cinque et a sei voci (Antwerp 1556)*, ed. James Erb, Recent Researches in the Music of the Renaissance, 114 (Middleton, Wisconsin: A-R Editions, 1998).

[2] Of course some motets do not reveal anything about the addressee or the occasion. However, necessary information might then be obtained from descriptions, letters, literary or other archival documents. Franz Körndle, for example, was able to show through documents from the Geheimes Hausarchiv, Munich, that Orlando di Lasso's laudatory motet *Ergo rex vivat* was not composed for Emperor Rudolf II but for Philip II. Körndle also showed that the text of Lasso's *Huc ades o Erneste* is based on two originally separate poems; cf. Franz Körndle, 'Orlando di Lasso's "Fireworks" Music', *Early Music*, 32 (2004), 97-116. It is clear that one could also find additional information on other (official) laudatory motets within documents that have not been examined so far.

of great importance for the rulers, witness the extant descriptions of those festivities, which tell us about their splendor. Often great artists created the overall concepts and details for these ceremonies, and composers wrote musical compositions, so-called *Staatsmotetten*, which reflected the ruler's magnificence, power and esthetic sense. It was Albert Dunning who started a systematic collection of such motets composed in Italy, France, England, the Netherlands and the Habsburg territories.[3] Laudatory motets can be seen as an important type of *Staatsmotette* though naturally not every *Staatsmotette* is a laudatory motet.[4] On the other hand, one must realize that during the sixteenth century the number of motets for the *bourgeoisie* increased. Thus, a lot of laudatory motets were not written in praise of statesmen or rulers but rather celebrated people of lesser standing. Evidently, such pieces can hardly be classified as *Staatsmotetten.*

The texts of these motets are in Latin, and, a few exceptions notwithstanding, the compositions are based on Neo-Latin poems, mainly elegiac couplets, sometimes also hexameters or other meters. From these texts we can get information about persons, occasions, historical details, relations between persons, etc. Thus, it is not surprising that nowadays these texts are read as historical and sociological sources that inform us about the culture of the Renaissance or about specific persons.

So far we can conclude that a laudatory motet is primarily determined by its text. This leads us to the question as to whether we do justice to these texts by judging them solely on historical, sociological and esthetic aspects. What about the literary background? Are there lines of tradition to ancient or medieval poetry? These questions have generally been neglected, and laudatory motets have sometimes been classified as occasional pieces without any literary ambition or tradition. However, as I have demonstrated in my dissertation about Latin laudatory motets for members of the Habsburg family, a philological analysis of the poems can

[3] Albert Dunning, *Die Staatsmotette 1480-1555* (Utrecht: Oosthoek, 1970).

[4] See for example Dunning, *Staatsmotette*, p. XV. Dunning says a large number of compositions cannot be classified as *Staatsmotetten* even though they fulfilled political functions, such as sacred motets like the *Te Deum*. If we think of the famous motet collection by Petrus Ioanellus (*Thesauri musici* (Venice: Gardano, 1568); I will discuss two examples from this collection later on), we can see that the *Tomus Quintus et ultimus*, containing only laudatory motets, concludes with a *Te Deum* by Jacobus Vaet. The inscription says '*Pro omnibus Festiuitatibus*' and we can assume that this *Te Deum* — although a sacred composition — may have had a similar function as the laudatory motets, the *Staatsmotetten* in this collection.

shed light on some more details of the text and indeed, on the whole composition.[5]

Originally, the texts of the laudatory motets for the Habsburg family were liturgical or paraliturgical; the first non-liturgical laudatory motets for the Habsburg family were composed around 1530, by, for example, Nicolas Gombert and Adriaan Willaert.[6] This development — from paraliturgical to secular — seems to be typical for laudatory motets of the fifteenth and sixteenth century in general, and not only for those honoring the Habsburg family (as we can see from Dunning's findings).[7] Moreover, many of the early motets that Dunning mentions are not based on Neo-Latin poetry but prose.

After about 1530, the laudatory motet seems to develop its characteristic features mentioned above: the texts are Neo-Latin poems celebrating persons and/or occasions or dedicated to specific persons and are written in a humanistic tradition, with many allusions to classical Latin literature. Humanistic poets allude to classical poetry in order to continue the literary tradition on which their poetry was based and to which they subscribed, and to achieve a level of recognition comparable to ancient Latin poets such as Virgil and Horace. Quoting phrases or words from

[5] Victoria Panagl, *Lateinische Huldigungsmotetten für Angehörige des Hauses Habsburg: Vertonte Gelegenheitsdichtung im Rahmen neulateinischer Herrscherpanegyrik* (Frankfurt/Main: Peter Lang, 2004). This research topic was suggested to me by Univ.-Prof. Franz Römer and Prof. Elisabeth Klecker (Universität Wien, Institut für Klass. Phil., Mittel- und Neulatein) who started a project with the goal of collecting and analyzing the large number of literary works written for members of the Habsburg family.

[6] Laudatory motets for the Habsburg family by Gombert are: *Dicite in magni* for the birth of Philip, son of Charles V, in 1527, and *Felix Austriae domus* for the coronation of Ferdinand I in 1531. *Veni electa mea* for the wedding of Charles V and Isabella in 1526 in Sevilla is another example of the fact that not every *Staatsmotette* is a laudatory motet. *Qui colis Ausoniam* was written for Pope Clemens VII and Emperor Charles V in 1533. Cf. Michael Zywietz, 'Gombert', in *Die Musik in Geschichte und Gegenwart*, second rev. ed. Ludwig Finscher, 27 vols. (Kassel: Bärenreiter – Stuttgart: Metzler, 1994-2007), VII (2002), 1294-1305; idem, 'Karl V. – Der Kaiser und die Musik: Neue Wege der Relation von Text und Musik im Motettenschaffen seines Kapellmeisters Nicolas Gombert' (unpublished habil. Universität Münster, 1999); Dunning, *Staatsmotette*, pp. 143-150 and 339; Panagl, *Huldigungsmotetten*, pp. 85-91 and 100-102. Adriaan Willaert wrote several laudatory motets, listed in Dunning, *Staatsmotette*, p. 345. Explicitly in praise of the Habsburg family: *Haud aliter pugnans* in honor of Ferdinand I which Dunning, *Staatsmotette*, discusses on pp. 282-288; cf. Panagl, *Huldigungsmotetten*, pp. 92-94.

[7] See also Louise Cuyler, 'The Imperial Motet: Barometer of Relations between Church and State', in *The Pursuit of Holiness in the late Medieval and Renaissance Religion. Paper from the U. of Michigan Conference*, eds. Charles Trinkhaus – Heiko A. Oberman (Leiden: Brill, 1974), pp. 483-496.

ancient literature was a literary technique by means of which Neo-Latin poets could both upgrade their literary products as well as praise their patrons in a more subtle way. This can also be gleaned from the texts of laudatory motets.

Several examples of laudatory motets demonstrate how allusions or quotations can remind the reader or the listener of specific passages of ancient Latin literature. One of the first laudatory motets for the Habsburg family setting a newly-written humanistic text is the anonymous motet *Martia terque quater*.[8] It celebrates Charles V upon his arrival in Augsburg in 1530, after his coronation as Holy Roman Emperor in Italy. The second distich — *Aurea qui terris revehat regnata parente / secula Saturno Carolus ecce venit*[9] — forms a central part of the poem: Charles brings back the Golden ages, an ideal time when joy and peace are ubiquitous. However, there is more praise and a deeper sense in these words.[10] The text alludes to Virgil, who with these words prophesized the ages of Augustus, the Roman Emperor who was celebrated by Virgil as the ideal Emperor bringing peace and a new Golden age and reigning an Imperium with no end (see *Aeneis* 6, 792-794: *Augustus Caesar, divi genus, aurea condet / saecula qui rursus Latio regnata per arva / Saturno quondam*[11]). Charles V, characterized as the ideal Emperor Augustus, is thus proclaimed to be as ideal as Augustus who ruled the *Imperium Romanum* that is continued in the Habsburg territories. It is precisely the allusion to Virgil that gives the text this deeper level of meaning. Naturally, allusions and quotations are not only present in motets honoring the Habsburg family. Many other texts of laudatory motets quote passages from ancient literature. They display a wide variety of commonplaces and ways of making allusions, although not every motet (be it for the Habsburg family or others) is of the same quality.

[8] Cf. *Imperiale Musik von Schloß Ambras*, ed. Walter Salmen (Innsbruck: Helbling, 1992); Walter Salmen, 'Eine Begrüßungsmotette für Karl V. — betrachtet im Kontext imperialen Musizierens', in *Musik als Text. Bericht über den internationalen Kongress der Gesellschaft für Musikforschung Freibug im Breisgau 1993*, eds. Hermann Danuser — Tobias Plebuch, 2 vols (Kassel: Bärenreiter, 1998), I, 224-225; Panagl, *Huldigungsmotetten*, pp. 95-100.

[9] 'Charles, who brings back the golden ages, reigned by father Saturn, look, he is coming.'

[10] Cf. Panagl, *Huldigungsmotetten*, pp. 95-100.

[11] 'Augustus Caesar, son of a god, who will again establish a golden age in Latium amid fields once ruled by Saturn'; English translation from *Virgil. Eclogues, Georgics, Aeneid*, Engl. transl. by H. Rushton Fairclough, second edition rev. by G.P. Goold (Cambridge e.a.: Harvard University Press, 1999), p. 589.

As far as the musical settings of these texts are concerned, it is difficult to talk about specific characteristic features. Laudatory motets are largely written in the same style and develop in the same way as the other motets of the sixteenth century: since ca. the middle of the sixteenth century, the music emphasizes the text and underlines specific passages.

In what follows, some examples will provide an insight into these works of art. The focus is not directly on dedicatory motets although such pieces seem to fulfill a similar function as dedicatory poems or prefaces with all their topoi.[12] Instead, we will concentrate on a special group of laudatory motets which praise the addressees in a very specific way and which will lead us back to our starting point: the relationship between the composer/ the poet, the addressee and the laudatory motet itself as a work of art — a work of the Muses. In some respect, these compositions reveal why poems and laudatory motets were written for or given/dedicated to a specific person. On the other hand, within the scope of literary tradition, they inform the patron about the benefit of patronage for himself. They also show how the texts refer to a literary tradition and how text and music can interact.

Jacob Regnart[13] (ca. 1540/45-1599) was a musician and composer at the Habsburg court under the Emperors Maximilian II and Rudolf II. He wrote the following motet, published in the *Novi Thesauri musici, liber quintus et ultimus*, 1568, in praise of Johannes Trautson.[14]

Quod mitis sapiens nulli virtute secundus,
    Trautsoni, et Lyciae Palladis arte grauis,
Hactenus egregio celebreris carmine vatum,
    Hoc meruit famae gloria magna tuae.
Quae sic compleuit magnis virtutibus orbem,
    Vt sis Eois notus et Hesperiis.
Dumque Medusei labentur flumina riui
    Musarum viues viua corona nouem.

[12] For the Habsburg family see Panagl, *Huldigungsmotetten*, pp. 439-440.

[13] Cf. Michael Zywietz, 'Regnart 2. Jacob', in *Die Musik in Geschichte und Gegenwart*, XIII, 1439-1443; Walter Pass, 'Regnart', in *The New Grove Dictionary of Music and Musicians*, ed. Stanley Sadie, 29 vols (London: Macmillan, 2001; henceforth: NGroveD), XXI, 118-121; Walter Pass, 'Jacob Regnart und seine lateinischen Motetten' (PhD diss. Universität Wien, 1967).

[14] [*Novi atque catholici thesauri musici*] *Liber Quintus et ultimus*... (Venice: Gardano, 1568; RISM 1568[6] [i.e. the number attributed to musical sources by the *Répertoire international des sources musicales*; henceforth: RISM]). Cf. *Novi Thesauri Musici a Petro Ioanello collecti, Volumen V*, ed. Albert Dunning, Corpus mensurabilis musicae, 64, 1.2 (American Institute of Musicology, 1974). The transcriptions of the motets follow the orthography of the *Liber Quintus*..., 1568. Only *Hesperiis* is capitalized here; the punctuation is modernized.

> 'Because you are benevolent, wise and second in valor to no one else, Trautson, and you are skilled with the art of Lycian Pallas, you are celebrated by the poets with an excellent poem, this is the reward of the great glory of your fame. Your fame has filled the world with great virtues, so that you are known to East and West. And as long as the waters of Medusa's river are flowing, you will live as the vivid crown of the nine Muses.'

The function of the motet is clear: the fame and the glory of the statesman Johannes Trautson shall be praised. Born in Tirol around 1507, Trautson received a humanistic education and had many functions at the Habsburg court, where he served the Emperors Charles V, Ferdinand I and Rudolf II (with whom he went to Prague). He was one of the closest and most trusted advisors to these Emperors, to whom he was *Geheimer Rat* or Privy Counselor, a position of high responsibility, for forty-nine years. He died on December 29th 1589 in Prague.[15]

In Regnart's motet, Trautson is called benevolent, wise and full of virtue in general, and he is said to be *Palladis arte gravis*, so that such 'great glory and fame' must be celebrated by poets. The poetry itself is called *egregius*, 'excellent', so that one can imagine such writings as a product of good quality and as an attempt to praise the great addressee in an adequate way. When the poet calls Trautson a person full of virtue (*nulli virtute secundus*), he uses words that resemble those of Virgil's *Aeneis* 11, 441: *Turnus ego, haud ulli veterum virtute secundus*. These words come from an epic text and the author may have wanted to upgrade his poem with epic words, which of course can also be found in other poetry.[16] Another laudatory motet using them is Orlando di Lasso's epithalamium *Quo properas facunde nepos Atlantis*.[17]

The next question to be asked is: what does *Palladis arte gravis* mean?[18] While Pallas Athena, the goddess of wisdom, is associated with

[15] Cf. Franz Hadriga, *Die Trautson, Paladine Habsburgs* (Graz-Wien-Köln: Styria, 1996), pp. 51-62.

[16] Cf. Sil. 7, 55; or during the Middle ages e.g. Theodulf., *carm.*, 76, 5; Ermold., *Ludow.*, 3, 153.

[17] Epithalamium for Albrecht V of Bavaria and Anna (daughter of Emperor Ferdinand I). At the end of this motet, Albrecht is celebrated by saying: *Albertus vivat nulli virtute secundus / Bavariae et nostri gloria duxque chori* ('Albert, second to no one else in valor, shall live, the glory and leader of Bavaria and of our chorus'). *Facunde nepos Atlantis* is a metonymy for the god Mercurius/Hermes taken from Hor., *carm.*, 1, 10, an Ode to Mercurius.

[18] We can find the words *Palladis arte* at different places in ancient literature: for example Verg., *Aen.*, 2, 13-16: *Fracti bello fatisque repulsi / ductores Danaum tot iam labentibus annis / instar montis equom divina Palladis arte / aedificant*... ('Broken in war

war and battles, she is also art-loving and art-protecting and therefore the goddess of fine arts. Thus, Trautson is characterized in the same way as Pallas Athena: as full of virtue in state and war but also as art-loving, qualities characteristic of the perfect statesman at that time. It does not matter that Pallas Athena is a female god; this form of praise does not seem to be unusual in those days. The Habsburg Archduke Ferdinand, for example, is said to be Pallas Athena himself in Andrea Gabrieli's motet *Lucida ceu fulvo* (he is strong in war but also a patron of art).[19] We can think here of the famous words *Arte et Marte*, which say that an excellent ruler or statesman must unite the virtues of war and of art (*Arte et Marte* can also be found as a motto on emblems, for example).[20]

Pallas Athena has an epithet in our text, *Lycia*, which is not typical for her. *Lycius* is the epithet for Apollo (*Lycius deus* is his metonymy, see for example Propertius 3, 1, 38; Statius, *Theb.*, 10, 344), the god associated with the nine Muses and prophecy. Why did the poet choose this unusual epithet for Athena? Maybe the use of Apollo's epithet emphasizes the art-loving and art-protecting side of Pallas Athena — and, at the same time, the art-loving qualities of Johannes Trautson who is compared to the goddess.

The third distich describes the great fame of Trautson, which is spread around the whole world: the pentameter *ut sis Eois notus et Hesperiis* reveals the large extension of Trautson's glory. Of course this is not to be taken literally, as it is a topos in classical literature where it can be found since Homer's Odyssey: all people, all countries, all periods celebrate a person. During the Middle Ages, 'the whole world is praising a person' was an equally famous commonplace in Latin literature.[21]

and thwarted by the fates, the Danaan chiefs, now that so many years were gliding by, build by Pallas' divine art a horse of mountainous bulk...' English translation: *Virgil*, transl. by Fairclough / rev. by Goold, p. 317) and Ov., *Ars*, 1, 691-2: *quid facis, Aeacide? Non sunt tua munera lanae / tu titulos alia Palladis arte petas* ('What dost thou, Aeacides? Wools are not thy business; by another art of Pallas do thou seek fame.' English translation: *Ovid, The Art of Love, and other Poems*, with an Engl. transl. by J.H. Mozley, second ed. rev. by G.P. Goold (Cambridge e.a.: Harvard University Press, 1985), p. 61).

[19] For the source and modern edition of this motet see note 14.

[20] Cf. *Emblemata. Handbuch zur Sinnbildkunst des XVI. und XVII. Jahrhunderts*, eds. Arthur Henkel – Albrecht Schöne (Stuttgart: Metzler, 1967), p. 1739.

[21] Cf. e.g. Ernst Robert Curtius, *Europäische Literatur und lateinisches Mittelalter* (Bern: Francke, 1948), pp. 166-169. The first time in classical Latin literature that the words *notus Eois et Hesperiis* are used together is Ov., *am.*, 1, 15, 29-30: *Gallus et Hesperiis et Gallus notus Eois / et sua cum Gallo nota Lycoris erit* ('Gallus shall be known to Hesperia's sons, and Gallus to the sons of Eos, and known with Gallus shall his own

The last distich is very important for the interpretation of the whole text. The poem ends with a wish or prophecy for Trautson: as long as the rivers flow — a poetic metaphor for eternity — Trautson will live. We know passages from classical Latin literature — e.g. from Virgil and Ovid[22] — which say that one shall live or one's glory shall remain as long as rivers flow or as long as there are stars in the heaven etc. Thus, in this case Trautson shall live eternally. However, in this particular text a very specific river is mentioned, the river of Medusa. The adjective *Medusaeus* was used for the first time by Ovid: in his famous *Metamorphoses*, where he mentions the *fons Medusaeus* (a spring of Medusa; *met.* 5, 312). This is nothing other than the Hippocrene, i.e. the river of the Muses at Mount Helicon, where the Muses lived and where inspiration for poets originated. Hence, we can conclude that in this case 'as long as the river of Medusa flows' means that as long as poets write, as long as poetry is read and as long as poetry exists, Trautson — celebrated by poets — will live. Here we find the literary commonplace of 'immortality through poetry'[23] and see that *vives* does not only mean Trautson's life on earth but also his immortality, since he is praised by poetry. Needless to say that, with these words, the poet emphasizes the importance and glory of Trautson. On the other hand, however, he also underlines the importance of being praised in poetry or — in this case — laudatory motets. This reminds us of Horace, *carm.*, 4, 8, where the author says that, while he could dedicate/give things of material value to his addressee Censorinus,

Lycoris be.' English translation: *Ovid. Heroides and Amores*, with Engl. transl. by Grant Showerman, second ed. rev. by G.P. Goold (Cambridge e.a.: Harvard University Press, 1986), p. 379). The context of these words is the following: Gallus, a Latin poet, is known (and will be immortal) because of his poetry and with him Lycoris, about whom he writes in his poems. Maybe our poet had this passage in mind when he wrote the motet text and wanted to say that the great fame of Trautson is spread around the world and known from East to West also by poetry. It might in some respect be a humanistic play with the context of Ovid's passage, but as the line of thought 'one is known from East to West' is very common in general, I do not wish to overemphasize this. See also for example a dedicatory poem by Jean Pollet dealing with this topos in vv. 15f.: Demmy Verbeke, 'Jean Pollet's Poem *Ad librum Orlandi Lassi* (1562) reconsidered', *Lias*, 31 (2004), 107-118, esp. p. 111. This poem is also published in Verbeke's dissertation: *"Ad musicae patronos" – Latijnse dedicaties en inleidende teksten in motettenbundels van componisten uit de Nederlanden (ca. 1550 – ca. 1600)*, 4 vols. (PhD diss. Katholieke Universiteit Leuven, 2005; fulltext version available at http://hdl.handle.net/1979/160), III, 57. See also the last line of Jacob Vaet's motet *Aurea nunc tandem* honoring Emperor Maximilian II: *(cum sis) / notus et Eois victor et Hesperiis* (cf. Panagl, *Huldigungsmotetten*, p. 201-203).

[22] Cf. Verg., *Aen.*, 1, 607-610; *ecl.* 5, 76-78; Ov., *am.*, 1, 15, 9ff. etc.

[23] Cf. Curtius, *Europäische Literatur*, pp. 471-472.

he rather offers poetry, which is of great (or even much greater) value too since it praises the addressee, makes him celebrated and immortal.

In the last line of the text, there is a play on words: *vives viva*. Trautson is addressed as 'vivid crown of the nine Muses' — what does the poet mean by this? Once again this goes together with the art-loving side of Trautson. *Corona Musarum* could be interpreted as *decus* ('ornament', 'pride') *Musarum*. *Viva corona* then would imply that Trautson is both the vivid pride of the Muses as well as their vivid 'reward', the vivid laurels. Thus, Trautson seems to be praised as a Maecenas or patron, which implies not only great praise for him as art-loving but also the expectation and the hope that Trautson supports the Muses — the artists.[24]

Thus, to summarize the poem's line of thought, Trautson — praised as an art-loving statesman — shall support the poets/artists, and will therefore be praised and become immortal by their poetry.

A motet by Jacob Vaet,[25] also printed in the *Liber Quintus et ultimus* from 1568, deals with the same topos.

Anteuenis virides raris qui dotibus annos
    Laudibus et sortem quamlibet eximiam,
Bauarici dux magne soli, post fata superstes
    Effugiat Stygias vis tua fama domos?
Respice fatorum domitrices, respice Musas,
    Tutor et illarum ductor et esse velis,
Vt celebris patulum virtus tua compleat orbem;
    Sola dabit domitrix Musa potentis herae.

[24] Trautson is honored as *patronus* and Maecenas in an Elegia funebris as well: *Luctus Caesareae Scholae Provincialium Inferioris Austriae in luctuosam... Domini Ioannis Trautsonii... mortem a Rectore eiusdem Scholae Huberto Luetano Noviomago et quibusdam alumnis positus* (Vienna: Formica, 1590): *mente patris quoties memori considero laudes / Et Moecenatis gesta revolvo mei / Gaudia concipio...//... qui fuerit summa mihi cum pietate patronus* ('whenever I think about the merits of the father (i.e. Trautson) and whenever I reconsider the deeds of my Maecenas, I get a lot of pleasure...// ... (he) who was a patron for me with highest piety'). Cf. also another poem in this collection: Martinus Pachalius Silesius, *Elegia funebris: ingenio clarum, summo de sanguine natum / Magnanimum fortem, turba novena dolet / Ingemit amissum cygnea voce patronum* ('the nine Muses grieve for him, who was of great wit, of splendid descent, magnanimous and brave, they sigh over the bereavement of the patron in their swan song').

[25] Cf. Michael Zywietz, 'Vaet', in *Die Musik in Geschichte und Gegenwart*, XVI, 1259-1261; Milton Steinhardt, 'Vaet', in *NGroveD*, XXVI, 196-197; idem, *Jacobus Vaet an his Motets* (East Lansing/MI, 1951), pp. 22f. The transcription of the text follows again the original (see note 14); only in v. 4 the word *Stigias* is standardized to *Stygias* and in v. 8 *musa* to *Musa*, the punctuation is modernized.

> 'You, who by your rare gifts excel your youth and by your glory excel whatever great fate has been bestowed on you, great Duke of the Bavarian soil, you wish that your fame, living on after your death, flees from the reign where the river Styx flows? Show concern for those who subdue fate, show concern for the Muses, and you should want to be their protector and leader so that your celebrated virtue fills the wide-spreading world; only the Muse, who subdues the mighty mistress, will give.'

In this case the author of the text is known to be the poet Charles Utenhove, born in Ghent in 1536 and a close friend of Orlando di Lasso.[26] The inscription above the poem in Utenhove's *Xenia… liber I* of 1568[27] suggests that the text might have been set to music by Orlando di Lasso, though no such motet has been traced so far. It was Jacob Vaet, *Kapellmeister* at the court of Emperor Maximilian II, who set the poem to music. The text celebrates Duke Albrecht of Bavaria and is an acrostic on the name ALBERTVS. In the *Xenia*, the poem is dated 1566, so we can assume that Vaet composed the motet between 1566 and 1568.

Albrecht is praised for having many gifts, virtues and merits, even though he is still young. Thus, he seems to be more famous than one would expect considering his young age.[28] Utenhove then asks if Albrecht wants his great fame to remain after his death;[29] here, the words *post fata superstes* are of special interest. They allude to Ovid, *Amores*, 3, 15, 20 — *post mea mansurum fata superstes opus* — where Ovid says that, although he himself will die one day, his poetic works will live on forever, and of course, united with his poetry, so will his name. Utenhove thus refers to the previously mentioned long tradition of the literary topos 'poetry can give immortality'.

The poet advises Albrecht what to do in order to become immortal: he should concern himself with those who subdue fate by supporting immortality, i.e. the nine Muses, who of course stand for poetry. Utenhove maybe uses the word *respicere* not incidentally. He might have had a

[26] Paul Bergmans, 'Deux amis de Roland de Lassus: les humanistes Charles Utenhove et Paul Melissus Schede', *Academie royale de Belgique, Bulletins de la Classe des Beaux-arts*, 15 (1933), 101-112; Willem Janssen, *Charles Utenhove: sa vie et son œuvre (1536-1600)* (Maastricht: Van Aelst, 1939).

[27] *Caroli Utenhovii Xenia seu Ad illustrium aliquot Europae hominum nomina, Allusionum… liber I* (Basel, c. 1568), p. 44.

[28] Of course this emphasizes the praise for the addressee and is not to be taken literally only.

[29] *Stygias domos* is a poetical metonymy for the underworld (cf. Lucan. 6, 514; Mart. 6, 18, 2; 12, 52, 12; Ps. Sen., *Herc. O.*, 1870 etc.; once again we can think also of Hor., *carm.*, 4, 8, 25), where the river Styx is flowing and where all mortal beings are dead.

classical text in mind, for Juvenal, a Latin poet at the time of Emperor Trajan, writes (*sat.* 7, 1-3): *Et spes et ratio studiorum in Caesare tantum; / solus enim tristes hac tempestate Camenas / respexit.*[30] In this passage, Juvenal is dealing with the prospects for poets of patronage by the emperor; according to Ferguson, *respicere* is the same here as 'show respect for' (a word often used of the gods).[31] Just as Emperor Trajan was Juvenal's only hope, Utenhove too hopes that Albrecht will take notice of and show respect and concern for the Muses and the artists.

Furthermore Albrecht should become their 'leader and protector': he should be an *Apollon Musagetes*, a leader of the Muses.[32] This of course implies praise for the addressee as he is honored as Phoebus/Apollo. It also insinuates that he must protect the Muses and therefore the poets, and be their patron and Maecenas. The 'reward' will be great, though, namely immortality.

The last distich once more states why Albrecht should do this, and it underlines yet again that only by poetry the fame of Albrecht's virtue, which was praised as being genuinely extraordinary, can be spread around the whole world. The Muse once again is mentioned as the only one who subdues the 'mighty mistress'; but who is this 'mighty mistress'? *Hera*[33] — 'mistress' — stands for *era* which was used for goddesses. In the classical poem *Epicedium Drusi* (the *Consolatio ad Liviam*, ascribed to Ovid),[34] *Fortuna*, goddess of fate, is mentioned as *potens era* (line 376).[35] Fortuna can end your life if she wishes to do so. Thus, Utenhove says that,

[30] 'The hopes and incentives of literature depend upon Caesar (i.e. Trajan) alone. He's the only one these days to have given a second glance to the despondent Camenae (i.e. the Muses)'. English translation: *Iuvenal and Persius*, ed. and transl. by Susanna Morton Braund (Cambridge e.a.: Harvard University Press, 2004), p. 299. Another laudatory motet that may allude to this passage is Orlando di Lasso's *Heroum soboles* for Emperor Charles V (*solus es afflicto Musarum tempore alumnus / qui colis et facili largiris munera dextra*).

[31] *Juvenal, The Satires*, ed. with introd. John Ferguson (New York: St. Martin's Press, 1979), p. 218.

[32] Cf. O. Höfer, 'Musagetes', in *Lexikon der griechischen und römischen Mythologie*, ed. W. H. Roscher (Leipzig: Teubner, 1884-1937; reprint Hildesheim: Olms, 1965), II, 2, 3233f.

[33] It is definitely not the Greek goddess Hera who is mentioned here, as Steinhardt, *Vaet and his Motets*, p. 23, seems to believe.

[34] *The Pseudo-Ovidian Ad Liviam De morte Drusi* (*Consolatio ad Liviam, Epicedium Drusi*), *a critical text with introduction and commentary*, ed. by Henk Schoonhoven (Groningen: Forsten, 1992).

[35] (Ps. Ov.) *Epiced. Drusi* (*Consolatio ad Liviam*), 371: *Fortuna arbitriis tempus dispensat iniquis*; 375-376: *regna deae immitis parce irritare querendo / sollicitare animos parce potentis erae*. Cf. also Plaut., *Merc.*, 842: *divom atque hominum quae spectatrix atque era eadem es hominibus*.

while people are mortal and subject to Fortuna's arbitrariness, the Muse/ the poets can defeat Fortuna's power and can give immortality to those who are praised by their poetry or laudatory motets.

At this point, let us consider the musical settings, the musical interpretation of these poems.[36] The musical settings of both texts start homophonically, which is rather unusual for the motet repertoire at that time. However, as both texts start with the praise of the addressee's person, it is not difficult to imagine that the composer wanted these praising words to be heard more clearly than they would be if the motet started polyphonically. Neither composer underlined the name of the praised persons with a homophonic setting, though in other laudatory motets names were sometimes underlined by such texture.[37]

Vaet seems to underline the words *post fata superstes* somewhat (which allude to Ovid) by combining at least 4 of the 6 voices. The text continues by saying that fame can flee from the *Stygias domos*, and it is clearly audible how it escapes: Vaet repeats *effugiat* (*Stygias*) several times and sets the word to an ascending melismatic melody. Thus, just as fame is ascending from the underworld and flees, so is the music ascending. Notice how Vaet gives a lot of space to the setting of *effugiat*: twenty-five out of the fifty-seven measures of the first part of the motet. *Respice* — a signal-word indicating that the addressee should take care of the Muses/the poets and also the composers — is also set homophonically at the beginning of the secunda pars of the motet. Another passage to which Vaet seems to add weight is *ut celebris patulum virtus tua compleat orbem*: the setting is divided into two choirs, with first the three low voices entering and then the three high voices.

Regnart's setting of the other poem reveals another way of underlining a (central) passage of the text. In the secunda pars of his motet, the words *dumque Medusaei* refer — as discussed earlier — to the Hippocrene, and the poet implies that Trautson will live as long as poetry exists. While Regnart sets these words using various combinations of voices (similar to Vaet), he also uses a lot of sixth chords so that the listener may pay more attention to this passage. The setting of the following word *labentur* (*flumina*) reminds one of Vaet's music for *effugiat*: imitation, melismatic melodies and short note values are the characteristic features

[36] Both motets are edited by Dunning in Corpus mensurabilis musicae 64, 2 (see note 14).

[37] Cf. for example in Johannes de Cleve's *Principis Ausoniae* for Emperor Ferdinand I or Orlando di Lasso's *Pacis amans* for Emperor Maximilian II; see Panagl, *Huldigungsmotetten*, pp. 171-172 and 193.

here, which musically imitate the flowing of the rivers. One central passage seems to be *Musarum vives*: the return to a homophonic setting suggests that Regnart wanted to emphasize these words.

We have seen that both poems deal with the same literary commonplace but each in its own way. The music directs the audience's attention to specific passages of the text, though naturally it depended on the composer's choices how this was done and for which passage.

Before we conclude, I would like to emphasize that the commonplace 'poetry creates immortality' can also be found in various other laudatory motets, such as Jacob Vaet's *Si qua fides vatum* for Emperor Ferdinand I.[38] A particularly interesting example to be mentioned here is a motet by Gabriele Martinengo,[39] who wanted to succeed Jacob Vaet as *Kapellmeister* at the imperial court and who used this topos very cleverly. Martinengo composed five Latin motets and one Italian piece and sent them — a beautiful manuscript collection[40] — to the court. The last Latin motet, addressed to the dedicatee Maximilian II himself, is a dialogue between Apollo and the nine Muses. In it, Apollo complains that he and the Muses must sing about Emperor Maximilian II even though that is nearly impossible as the importance and splendor of Maximilian cannot be praised in an adequate way: even the Muses and Apollo are unable to do so.[41] In the end they praise the emperor and say that he will be known in the whole world thanks to their poem, their song: *nostro carmine*

[38] This motet can be found in Vaet's motet collection *Modulationes quinque vocum... liber primus* (Venice: Gardano, 1562) and in the collection *Thesauri musici tomus quartus...* (Nuremberg: Montanus & Neuber, 1564; RISM 1564[4]); cf. *Jacobus Vaet, Sämtliche Werke, Band 2, Motetten*, ed. Milton Steinhardt, Denkmäler der Tonkunst in Österreich, 100 (Graz e.a.: Akad. Druck- und Verlagsanstalt, 1962). In Vaet's motet-edition the composition fulfils the function of a dedication, cf. Panagl, *Huldigungsmotetten*, pp. 184-185.

[39] Cf. Daniele V. Filippi, 'Martinengo', in *Die Musik in Geschichte und Gegenwart*, XI, 1187 1188; Denis Arnold – Tiziana Morsanuto, 'Martinengo', in *NGroveD*, XV, 916.

[40] The manuscript can be found at the Österreichische Nationalbibliothek, shelfmark Mus.-Hs. 18.951. Cf. Walter Pass, *Musik und Musiker am Hof Maximilians II.* (Tutzing: Schneider, 1980), esp. pp. 408-415. Robert Lindell, 'Die Neubesetzung der Hofkapellmeisterstelle am Kaiserhof in den Jahren 1567-1568: Palestrina oder Monte?', *Studien zur Musikwissenschaft*, 36 (1985), 35-52 (esp. pp. 39-42). Lindell states that this manuscript collection was sent to the court in the hope of employment there.

[41] This line of thought, this literary topos is comparable to our starting point, Lasso's Cantus firmus *Aequabit laudes nulla Camena tuas*. The text of Martinengo's motet is divided in the chorus of Apollo (A) and of the Muses (M): (A) *Grande onus, o Musae, nostro dignumque labore / impositum nobis*. (M) *Diis leue pondus erit.* / (A) *Quin graue.* (M) *Diuinis num uero uiribus impar?* / (A) *Maxima sunt magni facta canenda Ducis*. For the whole text see Panagl, *Huldigungsmotetten*, pp. 283-284.

*clarus eris* ('because of our poem you will be known'). This seems a particularly appropriate conclusion for Martinengo's presentation of his work: the best artists themselves (Apollo and the Muses) sing a song for Maximilian, "using" Martinengo's composition. Thus, the composer concludes by recommending himself as a musician who proclaims Maximilian's glory and who makes the Emperor known and immortal. There could not be any better reason for Maximilian to employ such a composer, whose compositions proclaim his glory; Martinengo uses the literary commonplace very cleverly. By doing so, Martinengo also indicates why he dedicates his manuscript to Maximilian, and by consequence, no other dedication was necessary.[42]

It has been shown once again that the poetry on which Latin laudatory motets are based often has its roots in classical poetry and must be read within the literary tradition. The literary/dedicatory topos that a patron is famous and will live on if he is praised by poetry can also be found in Latin laudatory motets, where it is used in skilful ways; one single word can remind the reader/listener of a special context. Considering the fact that laudatory motets deal with this topos, one should be more cautious about judging them only as works that have been written and without any ambitions. In order to judge such dedicatory and laudatory motets the historical, sociological, musical and literary aspects should be recognized. It is important to acknowledge that the texts are in many cases literary products of a long tradition with its many commonplaces. If we want to do justice to the laudatory motet, we must not neglect its poetry: it is the foundation on which the whole motet is built. The motets discussed in this article tell us that they want to be seen also as little ornaments and monuments — for the author, for the collection containing the motet and for the person to whom the motet is dedicated.

Kommission zu Herausgabe der lateinischen Kirchenväter (CSEL)
Österreichische Akademie der Wissenschaften
Sonnefelsgasse 19
A – 1010 Wien
victoria.panagl@oeaw.ac.at

[42] Only three voice-parts of this composition have survived so that a satisfactory musical analysis is hardly possible.

# CONSTRUCTING THE IMAGE OF A HUMANIST SCHOLAR. LATIN DEDICATIONS IN HUNGARY AND THE USE OF ADAGES (1460-1525)

FARKAS GÁBOR KISS

Humanist dedication was an ambivalent and delicate matter, as Peter Schaeffer pointed out: "Within the curious dialectic of humility and self-confidence, the exigency of belittling his own literary merit while also advertising his achievement, the author or editor had to find precisely the right tone to play with the received conventions, so as to state explicitly on one side of the apparent contradiction without sounding so convincing as not to leave room for an implicit understanding of the other."[1] The author of the work, the dedicatee, and the author of the dedication (if he was different from the author) all participated in this complex interplay and there were several means to bring the complex image of the "learned but humble" author to the notice of the dedicatee. Very often, the authors of dedications used a linguistic tension: the text, which expressed humility and self-depreciation on the surface, was formulated in a highly sophisticated and stylised language, that was meant to transmit the opposite message: high education, cultural independence and readiness to serve at the same time. This tension is more palpable in dedications than in missive letters, since letters could hide under the false pretence of unintended publication, while dedications could not.[2]

In the following, I would like to examine one of the rhetorical strategies which provided the author with the desired eloquence: the use of adages and proverbs in dedications. Adages and proverbs were particularly suitable for the purpose of creating a double image of the author. This becomes obvious if we quote one of the many definitions that Erasmus gives of the paroemia: "Proverbium est sermo rem manifestam

[1] Peter Schaeffer, 'Humanism on Display: The Epistles Dedicatory of Georg von Logau', *Sixteenth Century Journal*, 17 (1986), 215-223 (p. 217).

[2] About letters, see the studies of Karl Enenkel and Warren V. Boutcher in *Self-Presentation and Social Identification: The Rhetoric of Letter Writing in Early Modern Times*, eds. Toon van Houdt, Jan Papy, Gilbert Tournoy, Constant Matheeussen, Supplementa Humanistica Lovaniensia, 18 (Leuven: Leuven University Press, 2002).

obscuritate tegens."[3] Thus, with the help of proverbs, the dedicator could easily achieve his goal, since covering obvious intentions with obscurity is an elegant mode of self-expression. My source material was the corpus of humanistic dedications of Hungarian authors which appeared down to the fatal battle of Mohács (1526); I also take into account those works of Italian humanists dedicated to Hungarians which had a major influence in Hungary.[4]

It is obvious that we cannot expect too much sincerity from these dedicatons; still, one wonders how mechanical this practice was and how much we can deduce about the education of the author and the dedicatee on the basis of these texts. It is an important question in Hungarian humanism, since, generally, our information about humanists and humanism is scarce. The history of Hungarian humanism is a fragmentary one: its greatest light, the poet Janus Pannonius died in 1472, and John of Zredna (Vitéz), his mentor and uncle, the first Hungarian humanist and author of a collection of political epistles, followed him soon after in the same year. Almost nothing remains from the literary output of subsequent years, down to around 1500, with the sole exception of the epistolary volume of Peter of Várad (Váradi), archbishop of Kalocsa. After the early blossoming of the poetry of Janus, it seems, everything had to be started up again, but the second wave of humanism was already connected to the contemporary revival of *litterae humanae* at the University of Vienna, and later at the University of Cracow. To understand the mechanisms of patronage and dedication in this region, it is important to give an outline of the social background of this second humanism. Civic or lay humanism was practically nonexistent until the reformation. In the absence of a strong bourgeoisie, humanism could develop only in religious and political centres until the reformation. Despite the efforts of

[3] Desiderius Erasmus, 'Adagiorum chilias prima', in *Opera omnia*, ordo II., t. I., eds. M. L. van Poll-van de Lisdonk, M. Mann Phillips, Chr. Robinson (Amsterdam: North Holland, 1993), pp. 45-46.

[4] One can find an almost complete catalogue of these rare editions and their library locations in *Régi Magyar Könyvtár* III [*Old Hungarian Library*], ed. by Károly Szabó and Árpád Hellebrant, and supplemented up to the present, which contains a description of books published abroad by Hungarian authors, but not in Hungarian. I cannot deal here with the dedications of Italian humanists to King Matthias. About these see Klára Pajorin, 'Humanista irodalmi müvek Mátyás király dicsöítésére' ['Humanist literature in praise of King Matthias'], in *Emlékkönyv Mátyás király halálának 500. évfordulójára* [*Studies in memory of the 500*th *anniversary of the death of King Matthias*], ed. Gyula Rázsó (Budapest: Zrínyi, 1990), pp. 333-361.

Emperor Sigismund and King Matthias, there was no university in the Kingdom of Hungary and a printing press was established only in 1528, after two unsuccessful ventures in the 1470s. Most of the clergy was educated at the local *studia generalia*, but large numbers of students went to study to the neighbouring universities of Cracow and Vienna for a semester or a year, and few of them received a degree there. After returning to the country, they constituted the middle layer of literate clergy, while the higher clergy was educated in the fashionable schools of Italy for several years, often after receiving a degree in Cracow or Vienna. Naturally, nepotism was as important in Hungary at the turn of the 15th and 16th century, as anywhere else in Europe, so the lucky students who had the greatest chance to imbibe humanism in Padua, Bologna or Rome, were usually supported by their wealthy uncles: bishops or archbishops.[5]

As noted by Peter Schaeffer, the heyday of book dedications is the 16th century.[6] We hardly have any humanist dedications by Hungarian authors from the 15th century. The only exception might be the prefatory letter of Paul of Iwanich, who edited the epistles of John Vitéz, bishop of Várad (Oradea/Grosswardein) in 1451. Although the aim of the edition with commentary of the letters of his bishop was probably to offer a humanistic model of letter writing to the Hungarian royal chancery, the editor lacked humanist language competence, as can be seen from the diction of his dedicatory letter.[7] Janus Pannonius appended *prooimia* to

[5] Gerézdi Rabán, 'A krakkói egyetem és a magyar müvelödés' ['The Cracow university and Hungarian culture'], in id., *Janus Pannoniustól Balassi Bálintig* [*From Janus Pannonius to Bálint Balassi*] (Budapest: Akadémiai, 1968), pp. 267-274. About the overlap of political and religious elites see András Kubinyi, 'Az egyház szerepe az országos politikában és a honvédelemben a középkor végén' ['The role of the Church in national politics and defense at the end of the Middle Ages'], in id., *Föpapok, egyházi intézmények és vallásosság a középkori Magyarországon* [*High priests, church institutions and religion in medieval Hungary*] (Budapest: METEM, 1999), pp. 87-99 (pp. 91-93).

[6] Karl Schottenloher, *Die Widmungsvorrede im Buch des 16. Jahrhunderts* (München: Aschendorf, 1953) and Schaeffer, 'Humanism on Display', p. 215.

[7] Iohannis Vitéz de Zredna, *Opera quae supersunt*, ed. Iván Boronkai (Budapest: Akadémiai, 1980), pp. 27-28. E.g. 'cave sis, ne conditionis indicte prevaricator existas', 'postremo avisatus esto'. About Paul of Iwanich (Ivanić) see József Huszti, 'Magyar humanista mint török tudós V. Miklós pápa udvarában' ['A Hungarian humanist as a scholar of Turkish in the court of Pope Nicholas V'], *Századok*, 61 (1927), 344-350 and Florio Banfi, 'Pier Paolo Vergerio il Vecchio in Ungheria', *Archivio di scienze, lettere ed arti della società italo-ungherese Mattia Corvino*, 2 (1940), p. 30. A reevaluation of the letter collection of Vitéz, emphasising the role of his medieval heritage: Pajorin Klára, 'Vitéz János retorikai müveltsége' ['The rhetoric culture of John Vitéz'], *Irodalomtörténeti Közlemények*, 108 (2004), p. 540.

two of his panegyrics (those in praise of Guarino Veronese and Giacomo Antonio Marcello), following the model given by Claudianus, but these can hardly be called dedications. We can observe a preliminary form of dedication in a letter to Galeotto Marzio, to which he attached a translation from the sixth book of the Iliad. But long prefatory letters and dedications became voguish only around 1500, with verbal references to the dedications of the antiquity, not only to Catullus, but to Martial, Statius and Pliny as well. As Paul of Krosno, a well-known Polish humanist writes to Gabriel Perényi, his temporary Hungarian patron in 1509:

> It was the most praiseworthy and proper custom of age-old antiquity, which I was required to observe, that if our forefathers extracted and excerpted any studious fruit from the sweet little springs of their Muses, as from some repository cells, with their continual and uninterrupted study, they customarily dedicated it by name to some king, leader, senate, or to someone, who had great merits in literature [...] They knew, that the common folk, and other mortals of inferior rank will like and cherish and be delighted by those things, which are praised, approved and chosen by kings, leaders, aristocrats, and similar people. Therefore this custom greatly appealed to me, who am just a wretched little man, unpolished by the pickaxe of Latin eloquence, born and raised in a far corner of Barbary.[8]

Thus, the work could gain popularity through the patron, but very soon it turned out that the credence easily given to such works bearing a famous name on the title page, could also have its drawbacks. As Johannes Cuspinian in a 1511 Vienna edition of Florus says, printers tend to use the dedication so as to put the name of a famous scholar on the book, which would trumpet around the world, that the text is corrected, although the

[8] 'Laudatissima et probatissima apud canam illam antiquitatem Gabriel Perenaee d[omi]ne, et Patrone mihi nimiopere obseruande fuerat consuetudo, ut si quidquam uigiliarum lucubrationumque ex suauissimis Musarum fonticulis ueluti promptuariis quibusdam cellulis iugi et perpeti studio maiores nostri hausissent, excerpsissentque, id cuipiam Regi, duci, senatui, uel de re litteraria bene merito inscribere, nuncupatimque dicare consueuisse, eorumque sidere et auspicio e scriniolis exlatebrare, et in lucem emittere. Sperabant enim eorum magnificentia et claritudine studiis laboribusque suis ingentem et gratiam et authoritatem se conciliaturos, nec inconsulto id quidem: Norant namque quae reges, duces, primores et id genus homines laudarent, probarent, amarent, ea plebeculae, et caeteris inferioris conditionis mortalibus fore grata, iucunda, oblectatoriaque, quae mihi homunculo ruditatis pleno, nulloque latialis eloquii dolatorio polito in extremaque barbaria progenito nutritoque mirum in modum placuit.' About Paul of Krosno and Gabriel Perényi see Albert Gorzkowski, *Paweł z Krosna. Humanistyczne peregrynacje krakowskiego profesora* [*Paul of Krosno. The humanist peregrination of a Cracovian professor*] (Cracow: Księgarna Akademicka, 2000), pp. 106-120.

famous scholar hasn't even looked through the first two or three pages, and sometimes even the entire dedication is falsified.[9]

However, in most cases, due to the reasons mentioned above, Hungarian humanists did not belong to the group of those famous scholars, under whose names printers would have issued bogus editions. In most publications between the years 1500 and 1520, the aim of the author of the dedication is simply to prove that he has spent his period of scholarship abroad well. Printing short texts with a dedicatory letter to the patron at home (usually an archbishop or a bishop) was something similar to what is called today a progress report in scientific projects. We find such statements in the Isocrates translation of Michael Chesserius (Mihály Kesserü, bishop of Bosnia) in 1507/8, in the panegyric poem of Valentinus Cybeleius (Hagymási), written in 1512 to his patron, George Szathmári (bishop of Pécs): both of them studied in Bologna, Chesserius under Beroaldo, and Cybeleius under Giovanni Battista Pio.[10] Two students in Rome, Ignatius of Besse and Clemens, bishop of Szörény, published two orations of their teacher, Iulius Simon Siculus, with the titles *Oratio de inventione artium liberalium* (1516) and *Divus Gerardus episcopus et martyr* (1519), respectively, both of which were directed to Cardinal Thomas Bakócz, archbishop of Esztergom, the most powerful man of Hungary in those days.[11] As can

[9] 'Mos enim est Bibliopolarum hodie, ut si quid opus sumpserit aere imprimendum ac inuulgandum, docti alicuius petant epistolium, in frontispitioque ac liminari pagina affigant, Quo opus emendatum ueluti buccina per praeconem proclametur. Licet uel duas uel tres tantum operis uiderint Chartas uiri illi, quandoque nullas: satis esse arbitrantes si speciosa quaedam epistola opus ipsum ceu antesignani milites exercitum antecedat: quae uerba habeat selecta, parum quidem uera, sed pulchre ementita, quibus emptores fallant: mercesque suas uendibiliores faciant. Saepe etiam plagiarii isti, docti uiri titulo, epistolam comminiscuntur, ut lectores decipiant mediocriter eruditos, libros ut facilius uendant. Sic olim Crispi Salustii opuscula quaedam a Pomponio Laeto correcta ementiebantur. Sic nuper Florum hunc nostrum a Beroaldo castigatum quidam falso publicarunt.' Lucius Florus, *Libri historiarum quatuor*, ed. Joannes Cuspinianus (Vienna: Joannes Winterburger, 1511). The edition is dedicated by Cuspinian to Joachim Vadianus and Joannes Marius (Mair). Also quoted by Hans Ankwicz-Kleehoven, *Der Wiener Humanist Johannes Cuspinian* (Graz-Köln: Böhlau, 1959), p. 99.

[10] About the contacts of Hungarian humanists with Bologna see Rabán Gerézdi, 'A levélíró Váradi Péter' ['Peter of Várad, epistolographer'], and 'Aldus Manutius magyar barátai' ['Hungarian friends of Aldus Manutius'], in *Janus Pannoniustól Balassi Bálintig* (Budapest: Akadémiai, 1968), pp. 75-142; pp. 204-266; and Mária Révész, *Romulus Amasaeus, Egy bolognai humanista magyar összeköttetései a XVI. század elején* [*Romulus Amasaeus: A humanist from Bologna and his Hungarian contacts*] (Szeged: Ferenc József Tudományegyetem, 1933).

[11] Gedeon Borsa, 'Az 1519. évben nyomtatott Gellért-legenda' ['The legend of St Gerard printed in 1519'], *Magyar Könyvszemle*, 96 (1980), 376-384. About Bakócz see Vilmos Fraknói, *Erdödi Bakócz Tamás* (Budapest: Magyar Történelmi Társulat, 1889).

be seen, these students studied in Italy, which was on one hand farther from Hungary, than Vienna or Cracow, so it was more difficult to control the students' behaviour, and on the other hand the living and education costs were higher than in the neighbouring countries, which might be a reason why students were required to publish such 'progress reports'.[12]

However, teachers could contact the patrons directly, as well, and this occured even more often. At the end of the 15th century, the Ferrara school of Guarino lost some of its old fame, and Northern students longing to study humanities preferred to attend the school of Beroaldo in Bologna. A telling testimony of the changing rank of schools is a letter of Vincentius Lang to Konrad Celtis from 1500, in which he describes his journey to Italy. Vincentius mentions that he visited Aldus Manutius, Georgius Valla, M. Antonius Sabellicus in Venice, Calfurnio and Bartholomaeus Prosper in Padova, Battista Guarino in Ferrara and Lucius Bellantius in Siena (Ficino died before he arrived in Florence), but the Bologna school receives the greatest praise, since the city is "most famous in our century in literature, and the most abundant spring of all of Italy in several and very illustrious sciences", and he came to this school, "where his ship stopped in the safest port, with clasping and firm anchors", to listen to the lectures of Beroaldo, Codro and others.[13]

There is a well-known story about Beroaldo; he dedicated his famous edition of the *Golden Ass* of Apuleius to Peter of Várad, archbishop of Kalocsa, and the dedicatee promised to return his ass laiden with gold.[14]

[12] Johann Eck mentions in one of his letters that he went to study in Bologna at great expense ('magnis et impendiis et molestiis Bononiam'). Cf. *Disputatio Joan. Eckij Theologi Viennae Pannoniae habita…* (Augsburg: Miller, 1517), f. A2v. A detailed list of travel and study expenses in Bologna survives from Heinrich von Rosenberg (Jindřich z Rožmberka), 1511, according to which the trip of the young Czech aristocrat cost as much as 248 golden ducats! See Bohumil Ryba, 'Filip Beroaldus a čeští humaništé' ['Filippo Beroaldo and the Czech humanists'], in *Zpráva o činnosti městského musea v Č. Budějovicích za léta 1932 a 1933* (České Budějovice: Karel Fiala, 1934), pp. 1-39 (pp. 35-36).

[13] *Der Briefwechsel des Konrad Celtis*, ed. Hans Rupprich (München: C. H. Beck, 1934), pp. 435-443. 'Petivimus tandem per togatam Galliam Bononiam, rerum litterariarum nostro saeculo urbem clarissimam totiusque Italiae in variis disciplinis et quidem illustrissimis fontem uberrimum.' 'Hic tandem navis tanquam in portum tutissimum uncosis et firmis anchoris infixis stabilita est. Hic audivimus Anthonium Codrum, virum et Graece et Latine magna eruditione legentem; Philippum Beroaldum in philosophia [morali], in oratoria et poetica interpretem fidelissimum et lectorem eloquentissimum, qui et soluta oratione et carmine scripsit complurima…' Celtis himself also visited Beroaldo during his Italian trip: see *Der Briefwechsel*, p. 601.

[14] Unfortunately, a comprehensive history of Beroaldo's school and its contacts with the Czech, German and Hungarian students has not been written yet. The story appears in

Although they might have known each other from the time when Peter Váradi studied in Bologna from 1465,[15] this familiar tie between the archbishop and the humanist was due rather to the Hungarian students present in the school of Beroaldo. He dedicated his edition of the *Tusculanae disputationes* to Philip Csulai Móré, who was his student already for six years in 1496, the *Polyhistor* of Solinus to Michael Chesserius (his student between 1496-1503) in 1502, and his commentary on the *Symbola pythagorea* to Tamás Bakócz, archbishop of Esztergom in 1503, precisely when two nephews of the archbishop were studying in his school. [16] What else can these dedicatory letters tell us beyond the institution of patronage and the history of schooling? On one hand, we can call attention to the mechanical process of writing book dedications: Beroaldo quotes himself in dedications, and this practice is followed by others.[17] Beroaldo's dedication to Váradi is copied out by Johann Kresling of Buda, an orator at the 1515 Vienna meeting of Emperor Maximilian I and the Jagellonian kings of Poland and Hungary (Sigismund I and Wladislas II), where he changes the name of Váradi, archbishop of Kalocsa, to the name of George Szathmári, bishop of Pécs. It is amusing to see that parts of Kresling's oration were also copied out later in the dedication of the *Exhortatio ad proceres* of Martinus Thyrnavinus (Márton Nagyszombati) in 1523.[18]

the *Life of Beroaldo* by Pinus Tolosanus, quoted by Konrad Krautter, *Philologische Methode und humanistische Existenz. Filippo Beroaldo und sein Kommentar zum Goldenen Esel des Apuleius* (München: Fink, 1971), p. 24 and Julia Haig Gaisser, 'Teaching Classics in the Renaissance: Two Case Histories', *Transactions of the American Philological Association*, 131 (2001), 1-21 (p. 10 n. 28). Beroaldo replies to this joke in a hendecasyllabic poem at the end of his edition. See Mária Révész, 'Néhány adat Philippus Beroaldus maior magyar összeköttetéseihez' ['A few data concerning the Hungarian contacts of Filippo Beroaldo the Elder'], *Archivum Philologicum*, 65 (1941), 164-166.

[15] Gerézdi, 'A levélíró Váradi Péter', p. 83. According to Veress, Beroaldo wrote a short dedicatory poem to Peter Váradi already in 1490, but his reference is mistaken, and there is nothing to prove that Beroaldo had any contact with Váradi before the letter addressed to him in 1499 (See Garin, 'Note sull'insegnamento', pp. 379-387). Cf. *Olasz egyetemeken járt magyarországi tanulók anyakönyve és iratai* [*Matriculations and acts of Hungarian students at Italian universities*], ed. Endre Veress, (Budapest: Magyar Tudományos Akadémia, 1941), p. 58.

[16] The dedication edited by Károly Gulyás, 'Müvelödéstörténeti emlék a XV. századból' ['A 15th century relic of cultural history'], *Magyar Könyvszemle* 22 (1914), 161-163 and *Olasz egyetemeken*, pp. 62-69.

[17] His dedication of the *Symbola Pythagorea* to Tamás Bakócz in 1503 contains entire sections from the 1499 dedication to Peter Váradi.

[18] Gerézdi, 'Aldus Manutius', p. 125 and 'Nagyszombati Márton', p. 286.

The other, and perhaps more important issue here is the spreading of Apuleian style. As it is well-known, thanks to the research of John D'Amico,[19] Beroaldo was responsible for a new concept of Latin language, which drew upon the entire scope of Latin literature from Plautus to Boethius, allowing the speaker to use obsolete or foreign words, and even to create new words, when they fitted a known pattern. Beroaldo cherished the use of diminutives (*adolescentulus, nubecula, in virenti pubentique aetatulae flosculo*), the use of *-bundus* instead of participle imperfect (*laxabundus, meditabundus, peregrinabundus, cogitabundus*); he liked the absolute use of comparative, figura etymologica, alliteration, parataxis instead of hypotaxis, awkward nominal suffixes (*inmaculabilis, nauseosus, pensitator, lucubratorius*), to name just a few peculiarities of his style. He stated clearly the reason why he did so: Cicero and Virgil were readings appropriate for children, and therefore vulgar, too common for the taste of a humanist.[20] His stylistic influence was spread over the Alps by his former students and by dedicatory letters, orations and commentaries.[21] The use of diminutives was even more appropriate in dedications as a form of expressing modesty and humbleness vis-à-vis the dedicatee, and its popularity is attested already in antiquity in this context.[22] But if we look at the contemporary Central European publications, it is evident

[19] See the comprehensive study of John F. D'Amico, 'The Progress of Renaissance Latin Prose: The Case of Apuleianism', *Renaissance Quarterly*, 37 (1984), 351-392 and Krautter, *Philologische Methode*, pp. 84-92. Furthermore Remigio Sabbadini, *Storia del ciceronianismo* (Torino: Loescher, 1885), pp. 42-45 and Martin M. McLaughlin, *Literary Imitation in the Italian Renaissance. The Theory and Practice of Literary Imitation from Dante to Bembo* (Oxford: Clarendon, 1995), pp. 249-256. On the philological debates between Beroaldo and Poliziano see Paola da Capua, 'Poliziano e Beroaldo', in *Agnolo Poliziano poeta scrittore filologo*, eds. Vincenzo Fera, Mario Martelli (Firenze: Le Lettere, 1998), pp. 505-525.

[20] 'Vulgares scriptores sunt Vergilius et Cicero. Quid enim magis in ore vulgi est, quid usu populari magis detritum. Docti indoctique, urbani et rustici opifices omnes pueri mulierculae Virgilium Ciceronem nouere. Nihil uulgare magis. Uterque quotidie excutitur quotidie comprobatur, et cum ex illo proverbiali verbo, 'quot capita tot sententiae' fiat, ut scriptor qui uni placet, alteri displiceat, quod unus et alter probant, plusculi improbent: Virgilio Ciceroneque probando conspirant omnes tam amusoteri quam litterati.' *Oratio proverbiorum* (Bologna: Benedictus Hectoris, 1499), f. c8r-v.

[21] Ezio Raimondi, *Codro e l'umanesimo a Bologna* (Bologna: Mulino, 1987²), pp. 77-92; Eugenio Garin, 'Note sull'insegnamento di Filippo Beroaldo il Vecchio', in id., *La cultura filosofica del rinascimento italiano* (Firenze: Sansoni, 1961), pp. 364-387 (pp. 374-378), and id., 'Note in margine all'opera di Filippo Beroaldo il vecchio', in *Tra latino e volgare. Per Carlo Dionisotti* (Padova: Antenore, 1977), II, 437-456.

[22] Tore Janson, *Latin prose prefaces. Studies in Literary Conventions* (Stockholm: Almquist and Wiksell, 1964), p. 145.

that Beroaldian-Apuleian-Plautine style was an overwhelming success in these years in Central Europe, down to around 1520, to a much greater extent than could be explained by literary traditions, the influence of Plautus or Apuleius.[23] Since the aim of my study is not to explore the Beroaldian influence in Central Europe, I quote only one example: in 1504, Augustinus Moravus of Olomouc (a Moravian humanist at the court of Wladislas II in Buda) wrote letters to Celtis, using the expressions *aucupare* (a typical Plautine word), *opicus* (occurring only after Pliny and Juvenal), *locorum discapedine inveniamur secreti* (*discapedo* in not known in classical literature, but *discapedinare* occurs in Apul. *Flor.* 3).[24]

The dedication of Beroaldo to Péter Váradi claims that the students sent to him have studied well 'stilus latialis', and they can return to the North armed with Ciceronian ornaments,[25] but his choice of words and

[23] Among the 31 surviving books of Paul of Krosno, Beroaldo's works or editions amount to five, and there is one work of Beroaldo's over-zealous student, Giovan Battista Pio, too. See Gorzkowski, *Paweł z Krosna*, pp. 100-105. About the Czech contacts of Beroaldo see Bohuslaus Ryba, 'Filip Beroaldus', pp. 1-39; though Ryba does not treat stylistic issues. The most important Czech humanist of the period, Bohuslaus Hassenstein von Lobkowitz, owned six of Beroaldo's publicatons and wrote an epitaph to his memory (Ryba, 'Filip Beroaldus', p. 33). The modern editors of the *Theriobulia* (1520) of Joannes Dubravius, one of the most important literary works in the Czech-Hungarian Jagellonian Kingdom in this period, describe the archaic, Plautine and Apuleian style of this allegorical 'parliament of animals' in detail. See Josef Hejnic, 'Dubraviova Theriobulia a humanistická literární tradice', in Jan Dubravius, *Theriobulia – Rada zvířat*, eds. Miroslav Horna – Eduard Petrů (Prague: Academia, 1983), pp. 47-52. This could be connected to the influence of Beroaldo, too. About the translations of Mikuláš Konáč z Hodiškova from the works of Beroaldo (one of the earliest in Europe!) see Milan Kopecký, *Český humanismus*, (Prague: Melantrich, 1988), pp. 62-63 and id., *Literární dílo Mikuláše Konáče z Hodiškova* [*The literary work of M. K. of H.*] (Prague: SPN, 1962), 66-69. For the Polish contacts of Beroaldo see: Tadeusz Ulewicz, *Iter Romano-Italicum Polonorum, czyli o związkach umysłowo-kulturalnych Polski z Włochami w wiekach średnich i renesansie* [*About the cultural relations of the Polish with Italians in the Middle Ages and the Renaissance*] (Cracow: Universitas, 1999), pp. 138-139. An edition of the letters of Beroaldo and an appraisal of his European influence (including the later Czech, German, French, Hungarian translations of his works), as proposed by Silvia Fabrizio-Costa and Frank La Brasca would be welcome. See Silvia Fabrizio-Costa — Frank La Brasca, 'Un maître provincial précursor de la Grande Europe. Pour une édition de l'*Epistolario* de Filippo Beroaldo l'Ancien' in iid., *Filippo Beroaldo l'Ancien. Un passeur d'humanités* (Bern: Peter Lang, 2005), pp. 1-28.

[24] *Der Briefwechsel*, p. 566, pp. 571-572.

[25] 'tam diligenter indulget stilo latiali, [...] ut ad genitales terras in patrium larem sit elegantias italicas haud dubie secum relaturus, ut Tullianis ornamentis excultus possit inter suos non solum disertus, verum etiam eloquens haberi et doctrinae nitidioris honestamento nobilitari.' *Olasz egyetemeken*, p. 444. To my knowledge, the adjective 'latialis' connected to language, style, speech ('sermo latialis' etc.) occurs only in Ennodius, Macrobius and

expressions clearly reveals his real stylistic ideals. In his dedication of the *Golden Ass* to Péter Váradi he calls his new commentary "novicium animi nostri simulacrum vario effigiatu colore cultuque laborioso perpolitum",[26] religion is called "vitiorum expultrix", *doctrina* is "virtutis indagatrix", Pythagoras is "philosophiae primus nuncupator",[27] the genius of Péter Váradi is characterized thus "tua mens adipibus doctrinarum saginata pinguescit";[28] he uses words, such as *splendicare* (occurring only in Apul. *Met.* 5, 9; 7, 8 in Classical Latin), *dehonestamentum* (late Latin), *secretarium* (Apul. *Flor.* 17, *Mund.* 17), etc.

After the arrival of these Apuleian dedications and Beroaldian texts, there must have been some resentment against their style, since Ciceronian Latin was already well established in the Czech and Hungarian Kingdom (see e.g. the letters of Bohuslaus Hassenstein von Lobkowitz). As we can see from an undated letter of the Czech Rodericus Dubravus (Racek Doubravský), certain readers objected to the style of Beroaldo, and Dubravus was astonished to learn that some people even dared to criticise the excellent writings of Beroaldo, and to state that the master from Bologna was not at all as famous in Italy, as he was beyond the Alps.[29] Therefore, Dubravus assured Nicolaus Dieczki (Mikuláš Dětský), the recipient of his letter, that during the years when he studied in Italy, he hadn't met a better teacher and orator than Beroaldo. Dubravus' letter is written in Ciceronian Latin, as he was a student of Giovanni Garzoni,

Sidonius Apollinaris (carm. 2, 182: *latialibus libris*; ep. 4, 3, 1: *sermocinari latialiter*) in antiquity. Sidonius was a favourite author of Beroaldo and Giovan Battista Pio. 'Latialia verba', 'latialis suada' and similar expressions occur often in the works of H. Bebel, C. Celtis and Jac. Locher. Although the style of the paragraph is not Ciceronian, Beroaldo's opposition of 'eloquens' and 'disertus' is really taken from Cicero (*de orat.* 1, 21, 94).

[26] *Olasz egyetemeken*, p. 437. Cf. Apul. *met.* 11, 11; *apol.* 14, 3.

[27] *Olasz egyetemeken*, p. 437. Cf. Apul. *mund.*, Praef., and Cic. *Tusc.* 5, 2, 5; for Pythagoras cf. the chapter about the praise of the Samian sage in the *Florida*: 'primus philosophiae nuncupator et conditor' Apul. *flor.* 15.

[28] *Olasz egyetemeken*, 439. Cf. Apul. *met.* 10, 15: 'liberalibus cenis inescatus et humanis adfatim cibis saginatus corpus obesa pinguitie compleveram'.

[29] 'Dicunt enim ipsum [Beroaldum] illepidas et invenustas facere epistolas ac verbis abditis et inconditis uti, nec ipsum esse apud Italos tam celebri fama, quae de ipso apud Theutones percrebruit, et tam multo nomine, neque omnes Italiae oratores nostra memoria eum praestare.' *Dva listáře humanistické (I. Dra. Racka Doubravského, II. M. Václava Píseckého)* [*Two humanist epistolaries*, I: *Dr. Racek Doubravsky*; II: *Mgr. Václac Písecky*], ed. Josef Truhlář, (Prague: Česká akademie Františka Josefa, 1897), pp. 16-17. (Sbírka pramenův ku poznání literárního života v Čechách, na Moravě a v Slezsku II. 3.) Also quoted by Ryba, 'Filip Beroaldus', pp. 30-31, who refuses the date suggested by Truhlář (1501).

another master from Bologna, who followed Ciceronian principles in his teaching; still, he doesn't disapprove Beroaldo's style.[30]

Almost a decade after the death of Beroaldo, we can detect a stronger opponent of Beroaldian style in the person of Aldus Manutius, who used the dedication of his edition of the *Epistularum ad Atticum, ad Brutum, ad Quintum libri XX* (1513) to correct the intolerable licence of Apuleian style. He dedicated this work to Philip Csulai Móré, provost of Bács and later (1524-26) bishop of Pécs, who had been a student of Beroaldo for six years (1491-1496), as mentioned above. Manutius chose a subtle strategy of persuading Csulai Móré of the incorrectness of late Latinity: he praised the bishop for supporting Ciceronian style instead of "those writers who lived 1200 or 1300 years ago", although one can hardly imagine, that the bishop's enduring studies under Beroaldo did not have any influence on his style.[31] Thus, Manutius enlists the provost among Ciceronians, the winners of the current debate between Pietro Bembo and Gianfrancesco Pico before the wider public, and at the same time he informs Csulai Móré, that the style he learned at school with Beroaldo was becoming unfashionable, and that those who follow it, "despise white bread and eat mast".[32]

A very important component of Beroaldian stylistic complexity was the use of proverbs. His *Oratio proverbiorum* appeared in Bologna in

[30] About Garzone: Florio Banfi, 'Giovanni Garzoni ed il cardinale Tommaso Bakócz primate d'Ungheria', *L'Archiginnasio*, 31 (1936), 120-139 and R. Ridolfi, 'Giovanni Garzoni', in *Dizionario biografico degli Italiani*, 52 (Roma: Istituto della Enciclopedia Italiana, 1999), pp. 438-440.

[31] 'quod eo feci etiam libentius, quia valde delectari te dictione et eloquentia Tulliana prae te fers, nec laudandos ducis, qui eorum authorum, qui citra mille et ducentos trecentosve annos fuerunt stylo delectati, contemnunt Ciceronem, et quicunque Ciceronis est simillimus, ac si spreto et fastidito triticeo pane, glande vescantur. Doctos ais esse illos quidem, et legendos, sed stylum eorum non modo non imitandum, sed fugiendum pro viribus censes, et recte meo iudicio. Idem memini olim dicere Paulum quendam Pannonium, optimo iudicio adolescentem, ac condiscipulum meum, dabamus enim operam Baptistae, Guarini filio, in urbe Ferraria. Idem item Sigismundum Tursum, hospitem olim meum Venetiis.' See *Olasz egyetemeken*..., pp. 462-465 and *Aldo Manuzio editore: dediche, prefazioni, note ai testi,* introduction by Carlo Dionisotti, ed. Giovanni Orlandi (Milano: Il Polifilo, 1975), I, 117-120; II, 367. Unfortunately, we do not have anything written in Latin by Csulai Móré; nor could I identify the schoolmate of Manutius, Paulus Pannonius, who is supposed to have held the same opinion.

[32] This story has already been described by Gerézdi, 'Aldus Manutius magyar barátai' ['Hungarian friends of Aldus Manutius'], in id., *Janus Pannoniustól Balassi Bálintig* [From Janus Pannonius to Bálint Balassi] (Budapest: Akadémiai, 1968), pp. 204-266 (pp. 239-242), although he accepts Manutius' statement at face value, and considers Beroaldo a Ciceronian (actually, the dedication seems to suggest this!).

1499, dedicated to one of his students from Bohemia, Christopher Weitmüller. In this 60-page long declamation Beroaldo improvises on several proverbs (*Homo bulla, Lex et regio, Turture loquacior*), explaining and connecting them, and finally creating something, which is very difficult to follow. Partly this might have been the intention of Beroaldo, since already in the subtitle he calls this repository of proverbial wisdom "doctrina remotior", a book, which is "juicy, filled, embellished and decorated with the tasty marmalade of various doctrines, so that it would please both the palate, and the stomach".[33] Of course, his students tried to imitate him in his proverbial style: I quote a dedication of his former pupil and colleague, Giovanni Battista Pio, as the most frightening example. He dedicated his edition of Lucretius (1511) to the patron of his Hungarian students, George Szathmári, bishop of Pécs. While the first part of the dedication contains simple classical quotations, around half way through it, Pio starts to heap up a congeries of adages, one after the other, finally including almost any bookish expression that he can connect to his patron. A number of his quotations and adages can be found in the 1508 edition of the *Adagia* of Erasmus.[34] It seems that Pio also followed Erasmus' technique of creating new proverbs out of verses of classical poets. Erasmus calls this procedure *detorquere verba*, and this expression appears in the dedication of Pio as well.[35]

[33] 'libellus est succosus, fartilis, condimentisque doctrinae multifariae esculentioribus ita conditus concinnatusque ut et ad palatum faciat, et ad stomachum.' About the controversial relation of Beroaldo's *Oratio* to the *Adagia* of Erasmus see Myron Gilmore, 'Filippo Beroaldo senior', in *Dizionario biografico degli Italiani*, 9 (Rome: Istituto della Enciclopedia Italiana, 1967), p. 383, although E. Garin would deny any influence ('Note sull'insegnamento', 370. n.1).

[34] Pio mentions τῆς Ἑλλαδος Ἑλλάδᾳ (*Ad.* 2, 4, 92), Smyndirides (*Ad.* 2, 2, 65), anemonam rosae conferre (*Ad.* 2, 6, 41), εἷς ἀνήρ οὐ πάνϑ' δρᾷ (*Ad.* 1, 5, 40), καιρὸς πανδαμάτωρ (*Ad.* 1, 7, 70), Gygis anulus (*Ad.* 1, 1, 96), Plutonis galea (*Ad.* 2, 10, 74), sub leonis exuviis (*Ad.* 1, 3, 66), δμολοττῶν βοῦς and sixteen more adages in his dedication. Sometimes he even follows the order of the Erasmian *Adagia* when using them (just after 'canes Nilotici' – *Ad.* 1, 9, 80 – he mentions 'rhispaspides' occurring in *Ad.* 1, 9, 81). The ultimate proof of his exploiting of the *Adagia* is the quoting of 'obviis ulnis excipere', which is supposed to mean 'to receive something happily' and which occurs in the works of Quintilian according to Erasmus (*Ad.* 2, 9, 54). But actually this expression does not appear anywhere in classical literature and probably it was invented by Erasmus himself, to be copied eagerly by later humanists. See Desiderius Erasmus, 'Adagiorum chiliades', in *Opera omnia*, ordo II., t. IV., ed. Felix Heinimann – Emanuel Kienzle (Amsterdam: North Holland, 1987), pp. 248-249. Generally, about Pio see Valerio Del Nero, 'Note sulla vita di Giovan Battista Pio (con alcune lettere inedite)', *Rinascimento*, 2a s. 21 (1981), 247-263. This dedication of his edition of Lucretius (Bologna: Benedictis, 1511) is reprinted in *Olasz egyetemeken…*, pp. 452-459.

[35] This expression hardly occurs in classical Latin in this sense (Sen. *epist.*, 13, 12; Tac. *ann.*, 6, 5), and it always expresses a negative, pejorative misconstrual of the original

If we pick out any dedication from this period, almost inevitably we will find such Beroaldian sentences, as in the musicological work of Stephanus Monetarius (Münzer) of Kremnica, who dedicated his treatise about music to George Thurzó:

> Scholasticorum *saepicule adhortatus hortaciunculis*, ut huius disciplinae praecepta, et quidem emunctiora, quae sparsim classicorum autorum *latitarent* in voluminibus, summatim in unum colligerem in publicumque darem, quod mihi factu difficillimum esse dubitat nemo, ex quo smirnei vatis poemata *clanculorum* obtrectatorum non caruere morsibus, latinaeque genitoris linguae dicendi copia, non ab omnibus *uno fasce complexa* est: cum livor in summis (*tanquam gangrena*) late serpit: itaque mecum *cogitabundus* deambulans...[36]

An illustrative example of the new fashion in proverbs might be found in the dedication of the *Stauromachia,* the epic poem of Stephanus Taurinus (Stefan Stieröxel), a German by nationality from Moravia.[37] He chose a difficult subject for his epic poem: the history of the Hungarian peasant revolt in 1514. While the story was full of gory details, it completely lacked any heroism in the traditional sense, since the mass murder of peasants, armed with scythes, cannot be regarded as such. Even the

meaning of a word, while Erasmus uses it very often neutrally or positively in the *Adagia* (e.g. in the introduction 'De figuris proverbialibus' 13, and *Ad.* 1, 2, 54; 1, 3, 31; 1, 5, 49; 1, 10, 27; 2, 1, 33; 2, 4, 45 etc.). The typical wording is 'venustius erit [proverbium], si paulo longius detorqueatur', which seems to imply that the proverb is simply applied to a certain situation, and its meaning is not 'distorted' or 'misconceived'. This technique is a major source of his Homeric, Euripidian, Sophoclean 'proverbs', which Erasmus himself had created out of the texts. See Jacques Chomarat, *Grammaire et rhétorique chez Erasme* (Paris: Les Belles Lettres, 1981), II, 762. Pio says: 'Verba regis Pyrrhi de Fabricio pronuntiata ad Episcopum nostrum apposite detorquebimus.' Giovanni Battista Pio, *Elegidia* (Bologna: Giov. Ant. de Benedetti, 1509), f. A4v. The thought that almost any sentence of a classical poet (Homer) can be used as a proverb appears already with Macrobius *sat.* 5, 16. Unfortunately, I could not access the article of Claude Balavoine, 'Les principes de la parémiographie Érasmienne', in *Richesse du proverbe*, ed. François Suard (Lille: Univ. de Lille III, 1984), II, 9-23.

[36] Stephanus Monetarius (Münzer), *Epithoma utriusque musices practice* (Cracow: Ungler, 1518), f. 1v. (With a dedicatory poem of Valentin Eck). Reprinted in *Monumenta Musicae in Polonia,* I (Cracow: Polskie Wydawnictwo Muzyczne, 1975).

[37] The text is available in Stephanus Taurinus, *Stauromachia id est Cruciatorum servile bellum,* ed. Ladislaus Juhász (Budapest: Egyetemi Nyomda, 1944). The most comprehensive study is Sándor V. Kovács, 'A Dózsa-háború humanista eposza' ['The humanist epic of the Dózsa peasant war'], *Irodalomtörténeti Közlemények*, 63 (1959), 451-473. See also Franz Babinger, 'Der mährische Humanist Stephan Taurinus und sein Kreis', *Südost-Forschungen*, 9 (1954), 62-93 and Peter Wörster, *Humanismus in Olmütz. Landesbeschreibung, Stadtlob und Geschichtsschreibung in der ersten Hälfte des 16. Jahrhunderts* (Marburg: N. G. Elwert, 1994), pp. 101-103, 143-144.

nobles, whose party the poem naturally supports, often behave unheroically throughout the poem, except for the last book, where Francis of Várda, the bishop of Transylvania suppresses the rebels in a final battle and execution scene. Very aptly, Taurinus chose Lucan and his *Pharsalia* as his principal epic model,[38] since the paradoxical situation of the author, who had to become the immortaliser of a gruesome and unheroic event, fitted well the original epic problem of the Roman poet. However, Taurinus did more than simply imitate the *Pharsalia*; rather he made a cento of it, a process which he describes in detail in the dedication to Margrave Georg of Brandenburg: "Let them (the critics) grumble: 'Taurinus has compilated his *Stauromachy* from the hemistichs and even entire verses of Virgil, Catullus, Lucan, Martial, Horace, Ovid, Juvenal, Ausonius, Persius, Silius Italicus, Statius, Claudian, Giovanni Pontano and others', we will rebut their insolent petulance with the story about Virgil, which he used to direct against his own critics: 'it is very difficult to snatch away the lightning from Jove, the club from Hercules, or a line from Homer.'"[39] However, Taurinus forgot to mention that his long dedicatory epistle is also a cento: all of the numerous adages derive from the collection of Erasmus. We find *per transversum digitum* (*Ad.* 1, 5, 6), *ad umbilicum*

[38] For a reappraisal of this poem see László Szörényi, 'L'influenza della Farsaglia di Lucano sull'epopea tardoumanista latina in Ungheria (Stephanus Taurinus: Stauromachia)', *Neohelicon*, 27 (2000), 97-111, and László Jankovits, 'Aranykor a Mohács elötti Magyarországon: Taurinus Stauromachiájának felépítéséhez' ['Golden age in Hungary before Mohács: about the structure of the Stauromachia of Taurinus'], in *Religió, retorika, nemzettudat régi irodalmunkban* [*Religion, rhetoric and national consciousness in early Hungarian literature*], eds. István Bitskey and Szabolcs Oláh (Debrecen: Kossuth, 2004), pp. 74-82. The popularity of the *Pharsalia* in these years in the Viennese humanism is also attested by the *Poetica* of Joachim Vadianus, published in 1518. See Joachim Vadianus, *De poetica et carminis ratione*, ed. Peter Schäffer (München: Fink, 1973), I, 246-248.

[39] 'Mussitent illi: Taurinus ex Virgilii, Catulli, Lucani, Martialis, Horatii, Ovidii, Iuvenalis, Ausonii, Persii, Silii Italici, Statii, Claudii, Io. Pontani caeterorumque classicorum vatum hemistichiis ac etiam versibus Stauromachiam suam congessit; hanc eorum procacem petulantiam nos Maroniano apophthegmate retundemus, quod ipse suos in Virgilimastigas retorquere solebat, perquam funestum (?) esse vel Iovi fulmen eripere, vel clavam Herculis e manu Herculea extorquere.' Taurinus, *Pharsalia*, p. 3. Modern philological research has attested his claims: see Zoltán Császár, *A Stauromachia antik és humanista forrásai* [*Ancient and humanist sources of the Stauromachia*] (Budapest: Egyetemi Nyomda, 1937) and Ferenc Csonka, 'A Stauromachia utóélete a magyar szépirodalomban' ['Nachleben of the Stauromachia in Hungarian Literature'], in *Klaniczay Emlékkönyv*, ed. József Jankovics (Budapest: Balassi, 1990), pp. 143-167. From Neolatin poetry, beside Pontano, Taurinus also uses the translation of *Batrachomyomachia* by Reuchlin and the panegyricus of Guarino by Janus Pannonius. See V. Kovács, 'A Dózsa-háború', pp. 468-469.

*ducere* (*Ad.* 1, 2, 32), *sursum deorsumque* (*Ad.* 1, 3, 85), the story of Protogenes (*Ad.* 1, 3, 19), *Indus elephantus haud curat culicem* (*Ad.* 1, 10, 66), *vorsuram solvere* (*Ad.* 1, 10, 23). A quick look at the location of these proverbs in the Erasmian *Adagia* reveals that he must have used an edition of the *Collectanea adagiorum,* the first, shorter version of Erasmus' compendium (published first in 1500, and revised in 1505),[40] which later became the first chilias of the greater collection. However, Taurinus went even further, and copied the dedication of the *Collectanea adagiorum* as well, which, as is well known, is addressed to William Blount, Lord Mountjoy. Here, as a kind of humble excuse for the quality of the book, Erasmus complains of his fever (*febricula*), which prevented him from any serious work — at the doctor's orders, so all that he could accomplish was *nugae*, this collection.[41] Taurinus keeps the entire sequence of events (sickness — interruption of serious studies; law in the case of Taurinus — following the lighter Muses):[42]

> *Collectanea adagiorum veterum* (1500)
> [*Dedicatio*] Guilelmo Montiojo comiti cumprimis illustri. S. D. [...]
> Neque enim ignoro, delicatissimo tuo palato, quam vix etiam quae vulgo lautissima videntur, satisfaciant, tantum abest, ut haec placitura si[n]t, fiducia, *quae non modo ad severum unguem exacta non sunt, verum ne primam quidem manum totam dum acceperunt*... [...]
> At ego, juxta Plinium, perire ratus omne id temporis quod studio non impertiatur, committendum non putavi, ut rem tam pretiosam *morbus sibi totam abriperet,* maxime quod sine literarum commercio non video, quid haec habeat vita suave. Intermissis itaque gravioris operae lucubrationibus, hoc delicatiore studii genere, per varios authorum hortulos vagatus, adagiorum vetustissima quaeque maximeque insignia veluti omnigenos flosculos decerpsi, et tanquam in sertum concinnavi.

[40] Margaret Mann Phillips, *The 'Adages' of Erasmus, A Study with Translations* (Cambridge: Cambridge University Press, 1964), pp. 41-61. About the later influence of Erasmus in Hungary see Ágnes Ritoókné-Szalay, 'Erasmus und die ungarischen Intellektuellen des 16. Jahrhunderts', in *Erasmus und Europa: Vorträge*, ed. August Buck (Wiesbaden: Harrasowitz, 1988), pp. 111-128.

[41] Desiderius Erasmus, *Opus epistolarum*, ed. Percy Stafford Allen (Oxford: Clarendon, 1906), I, 290 (n. 126). In original editions e.g. Desiderius Erasmus, *Collectanea Adagiorum veterum*, ex secunda recognitione, (Strassburg: Schürer, 1509), f. A1v. (ELTE University Library Ant. 0380). The 1517 edition, quoted by Le Clerc (LB, II., vii) contains the same text: *Collectanea Adagiorum veterum* (Strasbourg: Schürer, 1517), f. A1v. (ELTE UL Ant. 0192). Taurinus included proverbs in the epic, as well, e.g. 'Sero sapiunt Phryges': *Stauromachia*, IV, 189 (cf. *Ad.* 1, 1, 28, though this adage is well known from classical literature, as well).

[42] Taurinus, *Stauromachia*, 2.

> *Stauromachia* (1519)
> [*Dedicatio*]... domino Georgio marchioni Brandenburgensi, serenissimi principis Lodovici Ungariae et Boemiae etc. regis potentissimi tutori dignissimo etc. domino suo gratioso humiliter commendat. [...]
> Hac, inquam, nugae nostrae *non modo ad severum unguem exactae non sunt, verum ne primam quidem manum totam acceperunt.*[...]
> Ego autem in Plinii sententiam pedibus iturus omne id temporis, quod studio non impertiatur, perire ratus committere nolui, ut sumptum pretiosissimum vilissimus corporis *morbus sibi totum abriperet*, praesertim cum hanc vitam velut alioqui caducam et incertam praeter literatoria otia nihil suavitatis habere, ita ad bonas literas perdiscendas plerisque breviusculam contigisse ipsa rerum experientia certiores facti sumus. Intermissis igitur iurisprudentiae aliisque gravioribus studiis redeunte pristino vigore humaniores delicatioresque Pegasidum et Charitum fontes delibare destinavi.

The only change that we can discover is stylistic: Taurinus seems to use the well-known school method of substituting synonyms for the original words of the text (*literatoria otia* for *commercium literarum*, etc.), but in a truly Apuleian-Beroaldian manner, he replaces the Erasmian adjectives (e.g. *pretiosam*) with superlatives (*pretiosissimam, vilissimus*) and adds a diminutive (*breviuscula*).[43] His stylistic preference is clearly anti-classical: the dedication itself contains *dedolare, suffarcinatus, loculosus, musteus, asciticius, sciolus, rumusculi, saepiusculi*, words which mostly come from Plautus or Apuleius.

The question, of course, here and in similar cases, is whether we can take seriously his 'data' about his own life, for which such dedicatory epistles were so highly valued by positivist research. Since Taurinus died around the time of the publication of his poem, we can surmise that he really did get sick, but the sequence of events in the dedication was already a literary and rhetorical reconstruction of an earlier scheme. We can recognise a similar method in another dedication from the previous year, 1518. The otherwise not very well-known poet, Francis Buzás of Újhely wrote a poem celebrating the wedding of Bona Sforza and King Sigismund I of Poland (*Carmen adventum... Bonae reginae*

[43] Taurinus: 'Hae, inquam, nugae nostrae non modo ad severum unguem exactae non sunt, verum ne primam quidem manum totam acceperunt.' Erasmus: 'quae non modo ad severum unguem exacta non sunt, verum ne primam quidem manum totam dum acceperant.' He also copies another sentence from the same dedication and a phrase from the dedication of the *Historia naturalis* of Pliny the Elder, which is one of the most popular sources of humanist dedications from Petrarch onwards. See Giuseppe Velli, 'Plinio nel proemio dell'*Africa*', *Giornale storico della letteratura italiana*, 166 (1989), 22-30.

*celebrans*).[44] After two years of study at the university of Cracow, Francis must have felt the need to produce something which he could show in his homeland, so he published this little poetic exercise together with the first known edition of the epigrams of Janus Pannonius, and dedicated it to his sponsor, a certain Benedict Ramocsay. Not surprisingly, the dedication contains some proverbs, which are there to prove the education Francis received at the university: most probably the reference to *Cleanthis lucerna* (*Ad.* 1, 7, 72) and to *Ne e quovis ligno Mercurius fiat* (*Ad.* 2, 5, 47) also derive from the *Adagia* of Erasmus. However, he wanted to sound somewhat more sophisticated, so he also picked out phrases from Beroaldo's dedication of the Apuleian *Golden Ass* to Péter Váradi, where he found the wordplay "psaltria pro psalterio" and from the dedication of the *Symbola Pythagorea* to Tamás Bakócz, from which he copied the definition of *Theosebia*.[45]

In a similar vein, Bartholomaeus Pannonius, the author of *Gryllus* (ca. 1519), a short comedy about a parasite following the *Captivi* of Plautus,

[44] *Opusculum Francisci Viihelini, aduentum serenissimae dominae Bonae Reginae, Coniugis inuictissimi principis domini, Domini Sigismundi Poloniae Regis declarans, Insunt praeterea Ioannis Pannonii Epigrammata*... (Cracow, Vietor, 1518). Its only known copy survives in the University Library of Uppsala (shelf n.: Kk 97.). See Gedeon Borsa, 'Janus Pannonius epigrammáinak legelsö kiadása' ['The very first edition of the epigrams of Janus Pannonius'], *Irodalomtörténeti Közlemények*, 95 (1991), 417-427. Besides, Buzás also published the *Ad Intemeratam Christi genitricem Mariam Elegiae XIII* of Marcus Antonius Sabellicus in Cracow, 1524 by Hieronymus Vietor (I have used the copy of Czartorysky Library in Cracow, shelf n.: Cim. I. 1880).

[45] Buzás, *Opusculum*, f. A2r: 'Quod ad eum esset mihi uirum scribendum, in quo praeter caeteras uirtutes affatim inesse conspiciuntur, ea quae doctor gentium Apostolus Paulus, Christiani gentis promptuarium, salutiferi nauigii gubernator constantissimus, in ecclesiastico tirone desiderat, utpote continentia, sobrietas, humilitas, modestia, constantia, patientia, frontis honos, studii grauitas, aetasque uirilis, quibus efficitur, ut nil agas dedecens nil iuuenile, nil uesanum, nec excors.' Beroaldo (*Olasz egyetemeken*..., p. 437): 'Apostolus Paulus in episcopo perfectissimo desiderat sobrietatem, prudentiam, sanctitudinem, continentiam, sanamque doctrinam, quae omnia in te uno affatim cumulata conspiciuntur'; Buzás, *Opusculum*, f. A2r: 'non ut plerique nostrae tempestatis sacerdotes, quibus pro psalterio psaltria et sacrosancto breuiario scortum accubat.' Beroaldo (*Olasz egyetemeken*..., p. 442): 'quod quotidianum sacerdos bonus Deo debet, suis horis absolutum inconstanter reddis [Váradi] in tantum dissimilis istis, quibus pro Psalterio psaltria est, pro sancto breviario scortum accubat.' Buzás, *Opusculum*, f. A2r: 'Quare magis Theosebiam (sic enim dei cultus appellatur), quam amasiam iudicas rem colorandam'; Beroaldo (*Olasz egyetemeken*..., p. 448): 'Tu [Bakócz] religione, qua constat vita mortalium, quae hominis propria est, quae nos deo cognatos efficit, ac vinculo pulcherrimo connectit, tanta praepolles, ut nihil quicquam apud te antiquis sit religione, ut Theosebiam, sic enim Dei cultus nominatur, rebus omnibus existimes esse anteponendam, ut saluberrimum illud documentum imprimis venerare deum memoriter memineris'.

uses some quotations and adages of Erasmus in his extremely elaborate and barely understandable dedication to Georg of Brandenburg.[46] Bartholomaeus mentions *Dares Entellum provocas* (*Ad.* 3, 1, 69), which in this form was created by Erasmus from a sentence of Jerome (*Ep.* 102, letter to St Augustine: 'memento Daretis et Entelli', referring to a scene of the *Aeneid*, 5, 369-460), so we can be quite sure Bartholomaeus borrowed it from the collection of Erasmus. However, we can only guess that he also borrowed his Greek quotation from an adage of Erasmus: the sentence "εἷς οἰωνὸς ἄριστος ἀμύνασθαι περὶ πάτρης" occurs in the famous adage *Meliores nancisci aves* (*Ad.* 2, 7, 20).

Generally, it can be said that the *Adages* of Erasmus was a great success in Central Europe, and gained great respect for the Dutch humanist, and the reception of his rhetorical teaching is documented in a much wider circle, than is that of his political and theological thought.[47] Even those authors who do not appear to include Erasmian adages in their dedications seem to have used him: an example might be the *De reipublicae administratione dialogus* (1520) of Valentine Eck, a teacher of the Cracow university and the Bardejov (Bártfa/Bartfeld) city school. Here Eck selects some adages of political content to describe ideal judicial practices or their opposite: he quotes *rex Tenedius* (*Ad.* 1, 9, 29), *Lesbia regula* (*Ad.* 1, 5, 93), *Heraclius lapis* (*Ad.* 1, 5, 84) and *Bocchiris* (*Ad.* 2, 9, 65) and we may be quite sure that he chose them from the collection of Erasmus, since in the copy of the Library of the Hungarian Academy of Sciences, the contemporary glosses (which seem to reflect the school teaching of Eck) quote the definitions of Erasmus word by word on the margin for each adage.[48]

[46] Bartholomaeus Frankfordinus Pannonius, *Opera quae supersunt*, ed. Anna Vargha (Budapest: Egyetemi, 1945), p. 3: 'Cum multum diuque mecum ipse cogito, princeps illustrissime, quo animo iam poene marcescentem in usum contraherem difficile ratus rubiginem vel semel mordicus contractam inviciata materia refellere, quare non absonum duxi hac saltem aetatula speculorum et paradigmatum totius humanae vitae [...] calcaneum aemulatione quadam (a longe saltem) sequi...'.

[47] Jacqueline Glomski, 'Erasmus and Cracow (1510-1530)', *Erasmus of Rotterdam Society Yearbook*, 17 (1997), 1-18. Glomski found evidence for the reception of the *Adages* in Cracow as early as in 1512. Erasmus became famous first for his rhetoric writings in Germany and even the *Encomium moriae* was read as a rhetorical *tour de force*: see James D. Tracy, 'Erasmus Becomes a German', *Renaissance Quarterly*, 21 (1968), 281-288 (pp. 281-282).

[48] Shelf number R. M. IV. 117/a, f. B3v. E.g. the gloss for *Lesbia regula* is 'Lesbia regula dicitur quociens praepostero modo non ad rationem factum sed ratio ad factum accommodatur', whereas Erasmus writes 'lesbia regula dicitur quoties praepostere, non ad

Of course, owning a good handbook of proverbs did not save an author from committing mistakes: we find an interesting example of this in the dedication of the *Rosarium* (1527) of John Sylvester,[49] the first published work of the Erasmian scholar who later translated the New Testament into Hungarian (1541). Here, in this youthful work, he wished to praise his patron, Simon, bishop of Eger, so he glorified him with the proverb: "Quocirca hos [uersiculos] tibi Reuerendissime in Christo pater, qui tua authoritate ex muscis (ut in prouerbio est) elephantos facere potes, nuncupamus." Probably, the bishop wouldn't have been very happy if he had known the real meaning of this expression (*Ad.* 1, 9, 69.). Erasmus explains simply that this adage means 'to glorify and amplify tiny things with words' ("res exiguas verbis attollis et amplificas"), and does not mention its ironic content, merely supplying a reference to Lucian. This short explanation must have misled John Sylvester.

In sum, I can only emphasize that dedications are important sources. They offer us essential information concerning the author, the dedicatee, their relationship, their stylistic preferences; however, one has to be very careful about drawing conclusions about the author's education, or his Greek knowledge on the basis of such data. The proper interpretation of a dedication requires the complete discussion of the direct sources of the text and its historical context. Dedications were written in order to achieve an immediate effect on the *respublica litteraria*, and especially on the dedicatee, therefore even the factual data provided by the dedication may try to be misleading. I hope I have successfully shown the presence of such strategies and distortions in the dedications of the first decades of the 16th century in Hungary.[50]

EÖTVÖS LORÁND TUDOMÁNYEGYETEM
Bölcsészettudományi Kar
Múzeum körút 4A
H – 1088 Budapest
farqas@index.hu

rationem factum, sed ratio ad factum accommodatur.' (*Ad.* 1, 5, 93.) In other sections, the gloss quotes several sources of the dialogue, which would have been very difficult to find out, unless we suppose that Eck himself dictated them.

49 The text was published by Katalin Németh S., 'Sylvester János Rosariuma' ['The Rosarium of John Sylvester'], *Acta Historiae Litterarum Hungaricarum*, 18 (1981), 11-20 (p. 14).

50 I want to thank Dr. William McCuaig for correcting my English.

# BEYOND THE MUSIC-THEORETICAL DISCOURSE IN FRANCHINO GAFFURIO'S TRILOGY: THE SIGNIFICANCE OF THE PARATEXTS IN CONTEMPLATING THE MAGIC TRIANGLE BETWEEN AUTHOR, OPUS, AND AUDIENCE

WALTER KURT KREYSZIG

*For Professor Dr. Ignace Bossuyt*

The central role accorded to the dedication of published Latin works and motets in the sixteenth century had its equivalent in the published books on music theory. This tradition dates back to the year 1480, which marks the first publication in music theory in the *Theoricum opus musice disci-pline* of Franchino Gaffurio (1451-1522).[1] For Gaffurio, the launching of his first major treatise also paved the way for three further volumes,[2] all printed in Milan,[3] namely, the revised version of the initial publication in

* The author wishes to thank Prof. Dr. Ignace Bossuyt (Professor of Musicology, Katholieke Universiteit Leuven) and the Organizing Committee of this Conference, in particular Prof. Dr. Philippe Vendrix (Director of Research, Center for Higher Studies, Université de Tours), Prof. Dr. Dirk Sacré (Professor of Classics, Katholieke Universiteit Leuven), cand. Dr. phil. Nele Gabriëls (Katholieke Universiteit Leuven) and Dr. Demmy Verbeke (Research Fellow, Centre for the Study of the Renaissance, University of Warwick), for their kind invitation to participate in this conference.

[1] Franchino Gaffurio, *Theoricum opus musice discipline* (Naples: Francesco di Dino, 8 October 1480); see Franchino Gaffurio: *Theoricum opus musice discipine*, Monuments of Music and Music Literature in Facsimile – Second Series: Music Literature, 100 (New York: Broude Brothers, 1967); *Franchino Gaffurio: Theoricum opus musice discipline*, ed. Cesarino Ruini, Musurgiana: Collana di Trattati di teoria musicale, storiografia e organologia in facsimile a cura dell'Istituto di Bibliografia Musicale di Roma, 15 (Lucca: Libreria Musicale Italiana, 1996).

[2] On the notion of the trilogy. see Luigi Salamina, 'La Triologia Gaffuriana', in Alessandro Caretta *et al.*, *Franchino Gaffurio* (Lodi: Edizioni Dell'Archivio Storico Lodigiano, 1951), pp. 137-153; Claudio Satori, 'Gaffurius (Gafori), Franchinus', trans. Anna Amalie Abert, in *Die Musik in Geschichte und Gegenwart*, 14 vols., ed. Friedrich Blume (Kassel: Bärenreiter, 1949-1968), IV (1955), 1241; Clement A. Miller, 'Gaffurius's *Practica Musicae*: Origin and Contents', *Musica Disciplina*, 22 (1968), 109.

[3] Mariangela Dona, *La stampa musicale a Milano fino all'anno 1770*, Biblioteca di Bibliografia Italiana (Supplemento a La Bibliofilia), 39 (Florence: Leo S. Olschki, 1961), pp. 41, 50-51, 73.

the *Theorica musice* (1492),[4] the *Practica musicae* (1496),[5] and the *De harmonia musicorum instrumentorum opus* (1518).[6] These volumes had already been conceived by 1480, as explicit references to these publications surface in the *Theoricum opus musice discipline*. Indeed, for Gaffurio the completion of these four volumes, which had a profound impact on the era of musical humanism and beyond,[7] meant an undertaking, encyclopedic in scope, unrivalled by his contemporaries.[8]

While the four volumes mentioned have survived in a number of *incunabula* and have also been made accessible to a larger group of scholars in facsimiles and English translations, and thus have entered into the discourse of twentieth- and twenty-first-century scholarship, hitherto no study has focussed on the important paratexts of these publications.

[4] Franchino Gaffurio, *Theorica musice* (Milan: Filippo Mantegazzi, 1492). The colophon of the *Theorica musice* reads: 'Printed at Milan by Magister Filippo Mantegazza, known as Castano, at the order and expense of Master Giovanni Petro de Lomazio in the year of our Saviour 1492, on the fifteenth day of December'; see Franchino Gaffurio, *The Theory of Music*, translated with introduction and notes by Walter Kurt Kreyszig, Music Theory Translation Series (New Haven, Connecticut-London: Yale University Press, 1993).

[5] Franchino Gaffurio, *Practica musicae* (Milan: Gulielmus Signer Rothomagensis, 1496). The colophon of the *Practica musicae* reads: 'Printed at Milan, in care of Ioannes Petrus de Lomatio, by Guilelmus Signer Rothomagensis, on the last day of September 1496, in the felicitous reign of Pope Alexander VI, August Caesar Maximilian, and the invincible Ludovicus Maria Sforza, Duke of Milan'; see *Franchinus Gaffurius: Practica musicae*, trans. Clement A. Miller, Musicological Studies and Documents, 20 (American Institute of Musicology, 1968); *The Practica musicae of Franchinus Gaffurius*, trans. Irwin Young (Madison, Wisconsin: University of Wisconsin Press, 1969). For a reference to the *Practica musicae* in the *Theoricum*, see Gaffurio, *Theoricum*, Book 5, chapter 6, line 386.

[6] Franchino Gaffurio, *De harmonia musicorum instrumentorum opus* (Milan: Gotardus Pontanus, 1518). The colophon of the *De harmonia musicorum instrumentorum opus* reads: 'Printed at Milan on November 27, 1518, by Gotardus Pontanus, in the thirty-fifth year of the author's prefecture, under the felicitous reign of Pope Leo X and the most Christian French King Francis, Duke of Milan'; see *Franchinus Gaffurius: De harmonia musicorum instrumentorum opus*, trans. Clement A. Miller, Musicological Studies and Documents, 33 (American Institute of Musicology, 1977).

[7] For a discussion of this impact, see, for example, Walter Kreyszig, 'Humanismus, musikalischer', in *Pauly's Realenzyklopädie der Klassischen Altertumswissenschaften: Rezeptionsgeschichte*, 3 vols. (Stuttgart: Metzler, 1998-), II (2000), 560-563; also in English translation as Walter Kreyszig, 'IV Music', in Manfred Landfester in collaboration with Hubert Cancik and Helmuth Schneider (eds.), *Classical Tradition*, 2: *Dem-Ius*, Brill's Encyclopaedia of the Ancient World: New Pauly (Leiden-Boston, MA: Brill, 2007), 1036-1039.

[8] Irwin Young, 'Franchinus Gaffurius: Renaissance Theorist and Composer (1451-1522)' (PhD diss. University of Southern California, 1954).

## II

At the outset of this examination, it is of interest to note that the number of paratexts and the authors associated with them varies greatly from the *Theorica musice* to the *Practica musicae* and in turn to the *De harmonia*. The discrepancy from volume to volume suggests an obvious correlation between the complexity of the particular discourse in the main treatise and the accompanying paratexts, though the precise relationship between the particular paratext and the corresponding treatise is subject to change, depending on the author of the paratext and the message(s) intended. With regard to Gaffurio's trilogy, the content of the individual volume indeed is indicative of the sheer number of paratexts, that is, from two paratexts in the *Practica musicae* — a treatise concerned with the rather contemporary topics of the Latin modes (Book 1), the notational symbols and properties of mensural notation (Book 2), the interaction of individual parts with one another in two-voice and three-voice counterpoint, the consonance-dissonance flow as well as issues of *musica ficta* and rules of decorum in singing (Book 3), and the definition and division of proportions as well as the discussion of the *species* and *genera* of *diapason*, *diapente*, and *diatessaron* (Book 4)[9] — to three paratexts in the *Theorica musice* — a treatise, which in comparison with the *Practica musicae* reveals a considerably wider array of topics, such as the disclosure of systems of classifying music (Book 1), the physical properties of sound[10] and the Pythagorean arithmetic proportions (Books 2 and 3), the musical intervals (Book 4) and the Greek *systema teleion*[11] and

[9] For a survey of the *Practica musicae*, see Clement A. Miller, 'Gaffurius's *Practica Musicae*: Origin and Contents', *Musica Disciplina*, 22 (1968), 105-128; see also James Haar, 'The Frontispiece of Gafori's *Practica Musicae* (1496)', *Renaissance Quarterly*, 27 (1974), 7-22; also in James Haar, *The Science and Art of Renaissance Music*, ed. Paul Corneilson (Princeton, New Jersey: Princeton University Press, 1998), pp. 79-92.

[10] Dorothea Baumann, 'Musical Acoustics in the Middle Ages', trans. Barbara Haggh, *Early Music*, 18/2 (1989), 199-209; see also Claude V. Palisca, 'The Science of Sound and Musical Practice', in *Science and the Arts in the Renaissance*, eds. John W. Shirley – F. David Hoeniger (Washington, D.C.-London-Toronto: The Folger Shakespeare Library-Associated University Presses, 1985), pp. 59-73; idem, 'Interactions Between Acoustics and Musical Practice in the Renaissance', in *Tiefenstruktur der Musik: Festschrift Fritz Winckel zum 75. Geburtstag am 20. Juni 1982*, eds. Carl Dahlhaus *et al.* (Berlin: Technische Universität, 1982), pp. 119-127.

[11] For an overview of the Greek *systema teleion*, see R.P. Winnington-Ingram, *Mode in Ancient Greek Music*, Cambridge Classical Studies (Amsterdam: Adolf M. Hakkert, 1968 = 1936); see also Stefan Hagel, *Modulation in altgriechischer Musik: Antike Melodien im Licht antiker Musiktheorie*, Quellen und Studien zur Musikgeschichte von der Antike bis in die Gegenwart, 38 (Frankfurt am Main-New York: Peter Lang, 2000).

the Guidonian solmization and hexachords[12] in juxtaposition (Book 5)[13] — and finally to nine paratexts in the *De harmonia* — a treatise in which the author fuses *musica theorica* and *musica practica*, thus requiring a heightened sense of attention and accordingly suggesting an urgency with regard to the subject matter at hand, specifically with regard to the dichotomy between the Greek and Latin systems of *musica* still unresolved, and unfortunately with no solution in sight by the conclusion of this treatise. In the *De harmonia*, there still remains the larger topic of the training of the consummate musician, that is, a training of the *musicus* (knowledgeable in both *musica theorica* and *musica practica*) as opposed to that of the *cantor* or *phonascus* (the one proficient only in the *ars musicae*).[14] Indeed, the diversity of issues and the complexity of the overriding larger concern fully justify the increase of paratexts in the *De harmonia* by some sixty-six percent over the *Theorica musice*.

Based on these preliminary observations, one may surmise that the paratexts in Gaffurio's trilogy are linked with the particular treatise in terms of its content. These texts shed light on one or more individuals intimately connected with the treatise, including the author, the dedicatee, the poet, the printer, and the engraver of the woodcuts, thus furnishing a window for a larger *scenario*, perhaps providing even an ultimate *raison d'être* and goal for compiling the principal treatise in the first place, in short,

[12] For an overview of the Guidonian system, see Gaston G. Allaire, *The Theory of Hexachords, Solmization, and the Modal System: A Practical Application*, Musicologial Studies and Documents, 24 (American Institute of Musicology, 1972).

[13] For a survey of the content of *Theorica musice*, Book 5, see Gaffurio, *The Theory of Music*, trans. Kreyszig, pp. xxvi-xxix.

[14] Further on this dichotomy, see Wilibald Gurlitt, *Zur Bedeutungsgeschichte von musicus und cantor bei Isidor von Sevilla*, Akademie der Wissenschaften und der Literatur: Abhandlungen der Geistes- und Sozialwissenschaftlichen Klasse, 7 (Mainz-Wiesbaden: Verlag der Akademie der Wissenschaften und der Literatur-Franz Steiner Verlag, 1950); also in Wilibald Gurlitt, *Musikgeschichte und Gegenwart: Eine Aufsatzfolge*, ed. Hans Heinrich Eggebrecht, 2 vols, Beihefte zum Archiv für Musikwissenschaft, 1 (Wiesbaden: Franz Steiner Verlag, 1960), Part I (*Von musikgeschichtlichen Epochen*), 18-30; Ernst Tittel, 'Musicus und Cantor: Ein paradigmatisches Kapitel aus der scholastischen Musikphilosophie', *Österreichische Musikzeitschrift*, 12 (1957), 13-18; Heinrich Hüschen, 'Berufsbewußtsein und Selbstverständnis von Musicus und Cantor im Mittelalter', in *Beiträge zum Berufsbewußtsein des mittelalterlichen Menschen*, eds. Paul Wilpert – Willehad Paul Eckert, Miscellanea Mediaevalia: Veröffentlichungen des Thomas-Instituts an der Universität Köln, 3 (Berlin-New York: Walter de Gruyter, 1964), pp. 225-238; Erich Reimer, 'Musicus-Cantor', in *Handwörterbuch der musikalischen Terminologie*, ed. Hans Heinrich Eggebrecht (Wiebaden: Franz Steiner, 1978), pp. 1-13; idem, 'Musicus und cantor: Zur Sozialgeschichte eines musikalischen Lehrstücks', *Archiv für Musikwissenschaft*, 35 (1978), 1-32; Ružena Mužiková, 'Musicus – cantor', *Miscellanea Musicologica (Praha)*, 31 (1984), 9-38; Christopher Page, 'Musicus and cantor', in *Companion to Medieval and Renaissance Music*, eds. Tess Knighton – David Fallows (London: J.M. Dent, 1992), pp. 74-78.

illuminating and clarifying the broader context in which the particular treatise fulfills one or more objectives.

## III

In fact, the many issues and questions posed above are noted in Gaffurio's letter of dedication to the *Theorica music*e, printed by the well-known Filippo Mantegazza of Milan.[15] At the very outset, Gaffurio addresses the dedicatee as 'to the magnanimous and most devout Lord Lodovico Maria Sforza, the Viscount, the Duke of the Most Distinguished Principality of Bari and Governor of the Milanese State: this theoretical work on the Art of Music of Franchino Gaffurio of Lodi, Music Director in the Choir of the greater church [cathedral].'[16] Gaffurio here fuses the *dedicatio* proper with a preamble. In fact, this carefully organized and clearly crafted document, both suggestive of and mirrored in Gaffurio's well thought-out overall plan of execution of the treatise proper, allows for the identification of salient ideas and issues with which he wishes to introduce the treatise itself. Gaffurio's letter of dedication to the *Theorica musice*, though verbose and colourful with regard to the choice of vocabulary and style of writing, is characterized by a meticulous organization — one which is divided into a number of readily recognizable subgroupings.

(a) Substantiating the reason for the writing of this treatise (Sentences 2-14): Following a decisively brief mention of the dedicatee — though those comments specifically referring to the dedicatee are poignantly restricted to some remarks of flattery, totally appropriate for this type of prose — Gaffurio provides the genuine reason for the compiling of this document, 'turning to free music by means of letters [i.e. prose writing] from its untidy neglect and abuse' (Sentence 11).[17] What undoubtedly

[15] Claudio Sartori, *Dizionario degli editori musicali italiana (Tipografi, incisori, librai-editori)*, Biblioteca di Bibliografia Italiana (Supplementi a La Bibliofilia), 32 (Florence: Leo S. Olschki, 1958), p. 94; Mario Emilio Cosenza, *Biographical and Bibliogaphical Dictionary of the Italian Printers and of Foreign Printers in Italy from the Introduction of the Art of Printing in Italy to 1800* (Boston, Massachusetts: G.K. Hall, 1968), p. 383.

[16] 'Ad magnanimum et pientissimum dominum Lodovicum Mariam Sphortiam vicecomitem, Bari ducem, principis excellentissimi, et rei Mediolanensis gubernatorem: Franchini Gafuri laudensis in delubri maioris choro phonasci Theoricum opus musice discipline'; as cited in: Franchino Gaffurio, *Theorica musice* (Milan: Filippo Mantegazza, Impensa Io. Petri de Lomatio, 15 December 1492), [folio unnumbered] [Dedication]; see Gaffurio, *The Theory of Music*, trans. Kreyszig, pp. 1-3.

[17] 'ad musicen litteris a squalore *et* iniu[r]ia asserenda*m* co*n*versus'; as cited in: Gaffurio, *Theorica musice*, [Prohemium].

lies behind this flowery statement is the current state of the *disciplina musicae*, specifically the obvious discrepancy between *musica theorica* and *musica practica* — the latter subdiscipline which has flourished foremost in composition and to a somewhat lesser extent in the writing on compositional practices, whereas *musica theorica*, at least in Gaffurio's opinion, which is unsubstantiated and accordingly appears to convey a personal bias, has been thoroughly neglected. Of course, this neglect assumed by Gaffurio provides yet another ample reason for the existence of the present volume, the *Theorica musice*. Unfortunately, the claim concerning the neglect or abuse of music-theoretical writing is not clarified or substantiated by specific examples. With regard to Gaffurio's forceful mention of 'the neglect of sources' at the time of his writing of the *Theorica musice*, quite on the contrary, a substantial contribution to *musica theorica* had already been made by numerous authors, such as Hieronymus de Moravia (died after 1271),[18] Walter Odington (flourished 1298-1316),[19] Jacobus of Liège (ca. 1260 – after 1330),[20] Johannes de Muris (ca. 1290/ 1295 – after 1344),[21] Marchetto da Padova (flourished 1305-1319),[22]

[18] Hieronymus de Moravia, *Tractatus de musica* (completed in Paris, shortly after 1272); for an edition, see Jerome of Moravia, *Tractatus de musica*, ed. Simon M. Cserba, Freiburger Studien zur Musikwissenschaft (Regensburg, 1999 = 1935). Further on Hieronymus de Moravia, see *Jérôme de Moravie: Un théoricien de la musique dans le milieu intellectuel parisien du XIIIe siècle – Actes du Colloque de Royaumont, 1989*, ed. Christian Meyer, Collection 'Rencontres à Royaumont', 4 (Paris: Créaphis, 1992); Michel Huglo, 'La *Musica* du Fr. Prêcheur Jérome de Moray', in *Max Lütolf zum 60. Geburtstag: Festschrift*, eds. Bernhard Hangartner – Urs Fischer (Basel: Wiese Verlag, 1994), pp. 113-116.

[19] Walter Odington, *Summa de speculatione musice*; see *Walter Odington: Summa de speculatione musicae*, ed. Frederick F. Hammond, Corpus scriptorum de musica, 14 (American Institute of Musicology, 1970).

[20] Jacobus of Liège, *Speculum musice*; see *Jacobi Leodiensis, Speculum musicae*, ed. Roger Bragard, Corpus scriptorum de musica, 3 (American Institute of Musicology, 1955-1973); see also Roger Bragard, 'Le 'Speculum musicae' du compilateur Jacques de Liège', *Musica Disciplina*, 7 (1953), 59-104, and 8 (1954), 1-17.

[21] Johannes de Muris, *Musica speculativa secundum Boetium* (completed 1323); see Christoph Falkenroth, *Die musica speculativa des Johannes de Muris: Kommentar zur Überlieferung und kritische Edition*, Beihefte zum Archiv für Musikwissenschaft, 34 (Stuttgart: Franz Steiner, 1992); *Johannes de Muris: Musica (speculativa)*, ed. Susan Fast, Wissenschaftliche Abhandlungen / Musicological Studies, 61 (Ottawa, Ontario: Institute of Mediaeval Music, 1994); see also Ulrich Michels, *Die Musiktraktate des Johannes de Muris*, Beihefte zum Archiv für Musikwissenschaft, 8 (Wiesbaden: Franz Steiner, 1970); Lawrence Gushee, 'Jehan des Murs and His Milieu', in *Musik und die Geschichte der Philosophie und Naturwissenschaften im Mittelalter: Fragen zur Wechselbeziehung von 'musica' und 'philosophia' im Mittelalter*, ed. Frank Hentschel, Studien und Texte zur Geistesgeschichte des Mittelalters, 62 (Leiden-Boston, Massachusetts: Brill, 1998), pp. 339-372.

[22] Marchetto da Padova, *Lucidarium* (written 1326-1327); see Jan W. Herlinger, *The Lucidarium of Marchetto of Padua: A Critical Edition, Translation, and Commentary* (Chicago, Illinois-London: University of Chicago Press, 1985).

Ugolino of Orvieto (ca. 1380-1452),[23] and Johannes Cotto, also known as Johannes Affligemensis (flourished ca. 1100).[24] On the other hand, when Gaffurio mentions the abuse of music-theoretical writings, he is undoubtedly making a blatant reference to the polemic writings on music which had flourished during the fifteenth century, though without providing any specific examples.[25] Gaffurio places emphasis on the manifold importance of the *Theorica musice*, relevant on the one hand for the reconstruction of the ancient tradition, and that as a basis for exploring contemporary music theory and practical application in the *practica musicae*, and on the other hand for the further exploration of the two strands of *musica practica* in the *De harmonia*, revealing indeed a *tour de force* in the fusion of ancient and contemporary music-theoretical thought.

(b) Providing a context for this treatise (Sentences 15-17): In his continuation of a partly biased view, Gaffurio turns directly to the ancient tradition, where he finds ample room and justification for the emulating of the Latin and early Greek authors, the latter whose treatises are accessible to Gaffurio solely through contemporary Latin translations,[26] many of which Gaffurio himself had commissioned from eminent translators,[27] including Hermolao Barbaro (1454-1493 or 1495),[28] Giovanni Francesco

[23] Ugolino of Orvieto, *Declaratio musice discipline* (ca. 1430); see *Ugolini Urbevetani: Declaratio musicae disciplinae*, ed. Albert Seay, 3 vols, Corpus scriptorum de musica, 7 (Rome: American Institute of Musicology, 1959-1962); see also Albert Seay, 'Ugolino of Orvieto, Theorist and Composer', *Musica Disciplina*, 9 (1955), 111-166; idem, 'The *Declaratio musice discipline* of Ugolino of Orvieto: Addenda', *Musica Disciplina*, 11 (1957), 126-133.

[24] Johannes Cotto, *De musica*; see *Johannes Afflighemensis: De musica cum tonario*, ed. Joseph Smits van Waesberghe, Corpus scriptorum de musica, 1 (American Institute of Musicology, 1950); see also *Hucbald, Guido and John On Music: Three Medieval Treatises*, trans. Warren Babb, Music Theory Translation Series (New Haven, Connecticut-London: Yale University Press, 1978), pp. 85-198; see also E. Fred Flindell, 'Joh[ann]is Cottonis', *Musica Disciplina*, 20 (1966), 11-30; idem, 'Corrigenda et Addenda', *Musica Disciplina*, 23 (1969), 7-11.

[25] Heinrich Hüschen, 'Kritik und Polemik in der Musiktheorie des 15. Jahrhunderts', in *Festschrift Arno Forchert zum 65. Geburtstag am 29. Dezember 1985*, eds. Gerhard Allroggen – Detlef Altenburg (Kassel: Bärenreiter, 1986), pp. 41-47.

[26] F. Alberto Gallo, 'Le traduzioni dal Greco per Franchino Gaffurio', *Acta Musicologica*, 35 (1963), 172-174.

[27] Walter Kreyszig, 'Franchino Gaffurio und seine Übersetzer der griechischen Musiktheorie in der *Theorica musice* (1492): Ermolao Barbaro, Giovanni Francesco Burana und Marsilio Ficino', in *Musik als Text: Bericht über den Internationalen Kongress der Gesellschaft für Musikforschung, Freiburg im Breisgau 1993*, eds. Hermann Danuser – Tobias Plebuch, 2 vols (Kassel: Bärenreiter, 1998), I, 164-171.

[28] *Paraphrasis in Aristotelem*, trans. Ermolao Barbaro (Treviso: Bartolomeo Confalomeri and Morello Gerardino, 1481). This volume comprises Themistius's *Paraphrases* on

Burana (1494-1539)[29] and Marsilio Ficino (1433-1499).[30] Though impressed by the tradition of scholarship carried out by the ancient authorities, especially with emphasis on the interdisciplinary nature of the investigation in the inclusion of the *artes liberales*[31] and the *artes mechanicae*,[32] Gaffurio does criticize their style of writing, at least indirectly, when he states that 'for the ancients — by means of the agreeable tie to the other arts and by that faculty of association inborn to a noble sharpness of mind and by a luxuriant wealth of words, as if by many stinging rays of light —

the *De anima* of Aristotle — a treatise known to Gaffurio (with the particular references to Themistius's *Paraphrases* identified in Franchino Gaffurio, *Theorica musice*, trans. Kreyszig, p. 217); see also Aubrey Diller, 'The Library of Francesco and Ermolao Barbaro', *Italia Mediaevalia e Umanistica*, 6 (1963), 253-262.

[29] *Musica e graeco in latinum conversa*, trans. Giovanni Francesco Burana (Verona: Biblioteca capitolare, MS CCXL (201), folios 1 recto – 25 verso; dated 15 April 1494 [manuscript]). This volume includes translations of Bacchius Geron, *Introductio artis musicae*, and of Aristides Quintilianus, *De musica* — treatises known to Gaffurio (with the particular references to Bacchius Geron and Aristides identified in Gaffurio, *Theorica musice*, trans. Kreyszig, pp. 216 and 218); see 'Bacchius Geron's *Introduction to the Art of Music*', trans. Otto Steinmayer, *Journal of Music Theory*, 29/2 (1985), 271-298; *Aristides Quintilianus: On Music in Three Books*, trans. Thomas J. Mathiesen, Music Theory Translation Series (New Haven, Connecticut-London: Yale University Press, 1983).

[30] *Plato: Opera omnia*, trans. Marsilio Ficino (Florence: Laurentius de Alopa, 1484-1485; second ed. Venice: Bernardinus de Choris de Cremona and Simon de Luere for Andrea Torresano d'Asola, 13 August 1491). That Gaffurio relied heavily on Ficino's translation may be gleaned from the references to Plato, especially in the *Theorica musice* (with the particular references to Plato, obviously with recourse to Ficino's translation, identified in Gaffurio, *Theorica musice*, trans. Kreyszig, p. 221); see also Otto Kinkeldey, 'Franchino Gafori and Marsilio Ficino', *Harvard Library Bulletin*, 1 (1947), 379-382. Presumably Gaffurio owned a complete set of Plato's *Opera*, for the "Opera Platonis duplicat. in duobis voluminibus" was among the sources which he donated to the Incoronato di Lodi; see Emilio Motta, 'I libri della chiesa dell'Incoronata di Lodi nel 1518', in *Il libro e la stampa*, 1 (1907), 105-112.

[31] Friedmar Kühnert, 'Zur Reihenfolge der artes liberales in der Antike', *Wissenschaftliche Zeitschrift der Universität Rostock*, 12 (1953), 249-257; see also David L. Wagner, *The Seven Liberal Arts in the Middle Ages* (Bloomington, Indiana-London: Indiana University Press, 1986 = 1983).

[32] Franco Alessio, 'La riflessione sulle "artes mechanicae" (XII-XIV sec.)', in *Lavorare nel medioevo – Atti del Convegno internazionale, Todi, 1980*, Centro di Studi sulla Spiritualità Medievale, 21 (Todi, 1983), pp. 259-294; George Orvitt, Jr., 'The Status of the Mechanical Arts in Medieval Classifications of Learning', *Viator: Medieval and Renaissance Studies*, 14 (1983), 89-105; see also Hans Martin Klinkenberg, 'artes liberales / artes mechanicae', in *Historisches Wörterbuch der Philosophie*, eds. Joachim Richter – Karlfried Gründer (Basel-Stuttgart: Verlag Schwabe, 1971-), I, 531-535; Charlotte Ziegler, 'Artes liberales / Artes mechanicae', in *Musik im mittelalterlichen Wien: Historisches Museum der Stadt Wien, 103. Sonderausstellung, 18. Dezember 1986 – 8 März 1987*, ed. Walter Pass (Vienna: Eigenverlag der Museen der Stadt Wien, 1986), pp. 176-177.

blinded the eyes of [their] students with [their] lectures' (Sentence 15),[33] though again there is little solid basis for such an argument, but rather this statement reflects Gaffurio's personal judgment. These remarks help underscore the urgency of Gaffurio's contribution to fifteenth- and early sixteenth-century music-theoretical discourse. Also rather weak with regard to Gaffurio's argumentation is his open criticism of 'the recent [authors who] talk idly about this art out of either laziness or ignorance, with incomparable damage, and they now and then publish what is part inanity, part error, confounded and confused by a dry and barren style in a barbarous manner' (Sentence 16)[34] — with the obvious intent, not dissimilar to his earlier based comments, to justify the present undertaking. Unfortunately, the errors of recent authors are not discussed in any detail so that we may only offer some conjecture. Perhaps, Gaffurio was thinking of the myth of the Pythagorean hammers in the smithy,[35] one of the most widely disseminated accounts, with its non-applicability to the other physical media, especially glass, bell and so forth, all of which properties unlike that of iron bells,[36] although Gaffurio himself transmitted this error in the woodcut included in Chapter 8 of Book 1 of the *Theorica musice*. And indeed one wonders how Gaffurio can testify to the rejuvenating of the doctrines of the ancients when, in fact, he is generally adopting information from these authors in a more or less unchanged fashion, resorting to one of the commonly acceptable forms of citation, namely, literal quotation, paraphrase, and so forth.[37]

[33] 'Q*uod* cum veteres illi caeterarum artium blanda copula *et* annexu innato egregio acumine *et* verborum luxuriante copia veluti multiplicibus radiis *et* aculeis discentium aciem oratione perstringant'; as cited in Gaffurio, *Theorica musice*, [Prohemium].

[34] 'Recentiores fere omnes incomparabili iactura seu ignavia seu ignorantia ad artem ipsam alucinantes insulsissima quandoq*ue* tum inania partim falsa *et* arenti barbarie ieiunoq*ue* stilo involuta *et* confusa prodiderint'; as cited in Gaffurio, *Theorica musice*, [Prohemium].

[35] Marius Schneider, 'Pythagoras in der Schmiede', in *Festgabe zum 60. Geburtstag von Willi Kahl am 18. Juli 1953* (Cologne, 1953), pp. 126-129; Hans Oppermann, 'Eine Pythagoraslegende', *Bonner Jahrbücher*, 130 (1925), 284-301; Ruth Michels-Gebler, *Schmied und Musik: Über die traditionelle Verknüpfung von Schmiedehandwerk und Musik in Afrika, Asien und Europa*, Orpheus-Schriftenreihe zu Grundfragen der Musik, 37 (Bonn-Bad Godesberg: Verlag für Systematische Musikwissenschaft, 1984).

[36] Klaus-Jürgen Sachs, 'Die Rolle der Mensura von Monochord, Orgelpfeiffen und Glocken in der mittelalterlichen ars musica', in *Mensura: Mass, Zahl, Zahlensymbolik im Mittelalter*, eds. Albert Zimmermann — Gudrun Vuillemin-Diem, Miscellanea Mediaevalia: Veröffentlichungen des Thomas-Instituts der Universität zu Köln, 16/2 (Berlin-New York: Walter de Gruyter, 1984), pp. 459-475.

[37] Paul Oskar Kristeller, 'Der Gelehrte und sein Publikum im späten Mittelalter und in der Renaissance', in *Medium Aevum Vivum: Festschrift für Walther Bulst*, eds. Hans Robert

(c) Aiming for the eradication of errors found in treatises of previous eras (Sentences 18-23): Gaffurio takes his unsubstantiated errors perceived in the writings of recent authors one step further, namely, as a pretext for his deeper *raison d'être* of his scholarly venture, that is, 'to cleanse the obscure and false' (Sentence 18)[38] found in previous treatises a rather bold statement which Gaffurio unfortunately did not fulfill. Indeed, there is ample proof to disqualify Gaffurio's aspiration. The most blatant example is Gaffurio's utter confusion of Greek tonoi[39] and Western modality[40] arising from the erroneous juxtaposition of the *systema teleion* and the Guidonian system. In this decision, Gaffurio was likely influenced by a remark in the *De architectura* of Vitruvius (flourished 1st century BC), who stated that Greek harmonics is 'an obscure and difficult subject to read and write about, particularly for those who do not know Greek letters,'[41] indeed pointing to a shortcoming in Gaffurio's

Jauss – Dieter Schaller (Heidelberg: Carl Winter Universitätsbuchhandlung, 1960), pp. 212-230; also in English translation as 'The Scholar and His Public in the Late Middle Ages and the Renaissance', in *Medieval Aspects of Renaissance Learning: Three Essays by Paul Oskar Kristeller*, ed./trans. Edward P. Mahoney, Duke Monographs in Medieval and Renaissance Studies, 1 (Durham, North Carolina: Duke University Press, 1974), pp. 3-25.

[38] 'Fucata *et* infecta repurgavimus ...'; as cited in Gaffurio, *Theorica musice*, [Prohemium].

[39] For an overview of the Greek *tonoi*, see Annemarie Jeanette Neubecker, *Altgriechische Musik: Eine Einführung*, Die Altertumswissenschaft: Einführungen in Gegenstand, Methoden und Ergebnisse ihrer Teildisziplinen und Hilfswissenschaften (Darmstadt: Wissenschaftliche Buchgesellschaft, 1977); Claude V. Palisca, 'Introductory Notes on the Historiography of the Greek Modes', *Journal of Musicology*, 3 (1984), 221-228; Jon Solomon, 'Towards a History of *Tonoi*', *Journal of Musicology*, 3 (1984), 242-251; Mindy B. Horowitz, 'Modulation and the Tonoi According to Aristides Quintilianus', *Theoria: Historical Aspects of Music Theory*, 1 (1985), 84-96.

[40] For an overview of the Latin system, see Günther Wille, *Musica romana: Die Bedeutung der Musik im Leben der Römer* (Amsterdam: Verlag P. Schippers, 1967); idem, *Einführung in das römische Musikleben*, Die Altertumswissenschaft: Einführungen in Gegenstand, Methoden und Ergebnisse ihrer Teildisziplinen und Hilfswissenschaften (Darmstadt: Wissenschaftliche Buchgesellschaft, 1977).

[41] Vitruvius, *De architectura*, 5, 3; as referred to in an indirect manner in Gaffurio, *Theorica musice*. Book 5, Chapter 6. Sentence 11; see Gaffurio, *Theorica musice*, trans. Kreyszig, p. 172. On the significance of Vitruvius in music, see Paul Thielscher, 'Vitruv und die Lehre von der Ausbreitung des Schalles', *Das Altertum*, 3 (1957), 159-173; Egert Pöhlmann, 'Vitruvs Schalltheorie und das antike Theater', in *Griechische Musik und Europa: Antike – Byzanz – Volksmusik der Neuzeit: Im Gedenken an Samuel Baud-Bovy – Symposium "Die Beziehung der griechischen Musik zur europäischen Musiktradition" vom 9.-11. Mai 1986 in Würzburg des Internationalen Zentrums für wissenschaftliche, ökumenische und kulturelle Zusammenarbeit e.V. – Griechisch-deutsche Initiative*, eds. Rudolf M. Brandl – Evangelos Konstantinou, Orbis musicarum, 3 (Aachen: Alano Verlag [Edition Herodot], 1988), pp. 37-50.

own training. Misled by the same terminology, namely Dorian, Hypodorian, Phrygian, Hypophrygian and so forth, that classifies the individual scales of the Greek *systema teleion* and the Latin modes, though the same terms denote scales not of similar but dissimilar interval content,[42] Gaffurio assumes the derivation of the Latin modes derived from the Greek modes. Such erroneous interpretation is compounded by Gaffurio's further confusion of basic terminology relating solely to the Greek system, specifically the terms octave species, modes, and *tonoi*[43] — all of which are clarified by Gaffurio in Chapter 32 of Book 2 of his *De harmonia*.[44] Beyond that, Giovanni Spataro (1458-1541), in his *Errori de Franchino Gaffurio*,[45] rightly accuses Gaffurio on a number of issues, including the inaccurate application of the mathematical term *incommmensuralibilitas*

[42] Claude V. Palisca, 'Theory, theorists', in *The New Grove Dictionary of Music and Musicians*, ed. Stanley Sadie, 29 vols (London: Macmillan, 2001), XXV, 361 ff.

[43] Walter Kreyszig, 'Franchino Gaffurio als Vermittler der Musiklehre des Altertums und des Mittelalters: Zur Identifizierung griechischer und lateinischer Quellen in der Theorica musice (1492)', *Acta Musicologica*, 65 (1993), 134-150. Further on the issue of terminology, see Margarete Appel, *Terminologie in den mittelalterlichen Musiktraktaten: Ein Beitrag zur musikalischen Elementarlehre des Mittelalters* (Bottrop in Westfalen: Wilhelm Postberg, 1935); Hans Peter Gysin, *Studien zum Vokabular der Musiktheorie im Mittelalter: Eine linguistische Analyse* (Amsterdam: Frits Knuf, 1958); Gottfried Scholz, 'Musikalische Terminologie im Bildungsgut des 16. Jahrhunderts: Musikalische Begriffe im Nomenclatur des Hadrian Junius — Übertragung und Kommentar', *Anzeiger der Philosophisch-Historischen Klasse der Österreichischen Akademie der Wissenschaften*, 129 (1992), 145-194; idem, 'Musikalische Terminologie in Bildungsgut des 16. Jahrhunderts — ein Bereich der Musikpädagogik', *Musik &: Jahrbuch der Hochschule für Musik und Darstellende Kunst in Wien*, 1 (1994), 289-303.

[44] On the significance of terminology in the theoretical discourse of Gaffurio, see Walter Kreyszig, 'Das *Lucidarium in arte musice plane* des Marchettus von Padua in musiktheoretischen Drucken des späten 15. Jahrhunderts: Terminologie und Etymologie aus rezeptionsgeschichtlicher Perspektive in Franchino Gaffurius *Theorica musice* (1492) und *Practica musicae* (1496)', in *Festschrift Floridus Helmut Röhrig zum 70. Geburtstag am 27. August 1997*, ed. Kurt Holubar, Jr., Jahrbuch des Stiftes Klosterneuburg, 16 (Vienna-Klosterneuburg: Verlag Mayer, 1997), pp. 93-111.

[45] *Errori de Franchino Gafurio da Lodi, da Maestro Ioanne Spatario, musico Bolognese, in sua deffensione, et del suo preceptore maestro Bartolomeo Ramis hispano subtilemente demonstrate* (Bologna, 1521); see also Claude V. Palisca, *Humanism in Italian Renaissance Musical Thought* (New Haven, Connecticut-London: Yale University Press, 1985), pp. 232-235; Bonnie J. Blackburn, 'The Dispute About Harmony, c. 1500 and the Creation of a New Style', in *Théorie et analyse musicales, 1450-1650: Music Theory and Analysis – Actes du colloque international, Louvain-la-Neuve, 23-25 septembre 1999 / Proceedings of the International Conference, Louvain-la-Neuve, 23-25 September 1999*, eds. Anne-Emmanuelle Ceulemans – Bonnie J. Blackburn, Publications d'histoire de l'art et d'archéologie de l'Université Catholique de Louvain – C: Musicologica neolovaniensia, Studia, 9 (Louvain-la-Neuve: Département d'histoire de l'art et d'archéologie, 2001), pp. 1-37.

(Error 1), and the overly dogmatic approach to the discussion of intervals on the monochord (Error 2). Interestingly enough, Spataro did not realize Gaffurio's inconsistent use of the terms *diesis* and *apotome*.[46] Regardless of these blatant errors that have crept into Gaffurio's prose, Gaffurio nevertheless vows for a presentation with the ideas unfolding in an unbroken sequence (Sentence 19) — a commitment which he fulfills on the whole.

(d) Commenting on the ranking of the inventor versus the cultivator of the art (Sentences 24-26): Here Gaffurio seems to reflect on his own position as a cultivator of the art, which in his own opinion ought to take precedence over the contributions of an inventor, presumably including the composer. Though somewhat curious, this statement is merely meant to underscore the preeminence of the *musica theorica* over the *musica practica*, with Gaffurio once again making every effort to justify his writing of the *Theorica musice*, characterized by the austerity of the materials presented.

(e) Acknowledging Jacopo Antiquario, the principal source of inspiration (Sentences 27-29): Indeed, little is known biographically about the humanist Jacopo Antiquario of Perugia (1474?-1512?), a man whom Gaffurio deems 'consummate' (Sentence 27) and 'most erudite in literature' (Sentence 48). A letter preserved in the Biblioteca Apostolica Vaticana,[47] in which one of the earliest musical humanists, Giorgio Valla (1447-1500),[48] author of five books on music,[49] discloses the completion of this *magnum opus* in December 1491, to Jacopo Antiquario, suggests considerable interest and involvement of the latter in humanist musical circles.

[46] Gaffurio, *Theoricum opus musice discipline*, Book 4, Chapter 3, Lines 136-139; see also Gaffurio, *Theorica musice*, Book 4, Chapter 3, Sentences 64a and 73a.

[47] Rome, Biblioteca Apostolica Vaticana, MS Vat. lat. 3537, folio 56, as mentioned in Palisca, *Humanism*, p. 69.

[48] On the significance of Giorgio Valla's contribution to musical humanism, see Johan Ludvig Heiberg, *Beiträge zur Geschichte Georg Valla's und seiner Bibliothek*, Beihefte zum Centralblatt für Bibliothekswesen, 16 (Nendeln, Liechtenstein: Kraus Reprint, 1968 = Leipzig: Otto Harrassowitz, 1896); Gianna Cardenal – Patrizia Landucci Ruffo – Cesare Vasoli, *Giorgio Valla tra scienza e sapienza*, ed. Vittorino Branca, Civiltà veneziana: Saggi, 28 (Florence: Leo S. Olschki, 1983 = 1981); Palisca, *Humanism*, pp. 67-87; Anne E. Moyer, *Musica scientia: Musical Scholarship in the Italian Renaissance* (Ithaca, New York-London: Cornell University Press, 1992), pp. 92-100.

[49] These books on music were published posthumously in 1501 by Gian Pietro Valla Cademusto, the adopted son of Giorgio Valla; see Claude V. Palisca, 'Valla, Giorgio', in *The New Grove Dictionary of Music and Musicians*, ed. Stanley Sadie, 29 vols (London: Macmillan, 2001), XXVI, 217.

Antiquario's position as Secretary to the Governor of Milan as well as his involvement in significant diplomatic missions is surmised from his *Oratio pro populo*, an oration addressed to Louis XII of France in the name of the Milanese populace. Following the victory of Louis XII over Milan in 1499, Antiquario joined the conqueror's side.[50] The cordial relationship between Gaffurio and Antiquario is also readily gathered from two documents. In a letter dated 1 September 1479, Jacopo Antiquario beseeches Lodovico Maria Sforza (1452-1508), also known as Lodovico il Moro ('The Moor')[51] for a benefice for Gaffurio.[52] In another letter of 10 December 1493, Antiquario discloses the qualifications of Gaffurio for yet another benefice.[53] In 1509, Gaffurio published Jacopo Antiquario's *laudatio* on Louis XII in celebration of his victory over Venice.[54]

(f) Returning to the dedication proper of this treatise to Lodovico Maria Sforza (Sentences 30-53): In the concluding passage of Gaffurio's letter of dedication, the reader learns more about the dedicatee of the volume, Lodovico Maria Sforza, praised as a staunch patron (Sentence 32) and promoter of the *artes liberales* (Sentence 34), as a contemplator of wise thoughts (Sentence 37) and an instigator of a superior style of governance (Sentence 40). Remarkable here is Gaffurio's gradual increase in the enumerating of Lodovico's superior overall qualities.

[50] Gaffurio, *The Theory of Music*, trans. Kreyszig, p. xvii.

[51] For a reference to 'Il Moro', see Gaffurio, *Theorica musice* [Prohemium], Sentence 40, trans. Kreyszig, p. 2. Lodovico Il Moro's involvement in the musical activity of the Court of Milan was captured in the *Storia di Milano* of Bernardino Corio (1459 – before 1512), who characterized the Court of Lodovico with the following comment: 'quivi de canti e soni da ogni generatione erano tante suave e dolcissime armonie che dal cielo pareano fussen ma[n]date a la excelsa corte' as cited in Bernardino Corio, *Storia di Milano*, ed. Anna Morisi Guerra, 2 vols, I Classici della storiografia ([Turin]: Unione tipografica-editrice torinese, 1978), II, 1480; in English translation 'There, singing and playing of every kind were of such beautiful and of such sweet harmony that they appeared to have been sent from heaven to that lofty court', as reproduced in Wilhelm Prizer, 'Music at the Court of the Sforzas: The Birth and Death of a Musical Center', *Musica Disciplina*, 43 (1989), 173.

[52] 'Pre[sbi]te[r] Franchino Gaffuro: quale insegna la musica qua'; as reproduced in Palisca, *Humanism*, p. 8, including English translation: 'Father Franchino Gaffurio, who teaches music here'.

[53] Milan, Archivio di Stato, Autografi, No. 94, busta 33: 'Pre[sbi]t[er] Franchino Gafforo Rectore qui del a chiesa de S[an] Marcellino: quale per benignita de la ex[cellen]tia V[ostra] come quella sa: lege publicamente musica in questa Inclyta Cita ...'; as reproduced in Palisca, *Humanism*, p. 8, including English translation: 'Father Franchino Gafforo, Rector here of S. Marcellino, who though the kindness of Your Excellency, as you know, lectures publicly on music in this illustrious city'.

[54] Ludwig Finscher – Walter Kreyszig, 'Gaffurio, Franchino', in *Die Musik in Geschichte und Gegenwart*, second rev. ed. Ludwig Finscher, 27 vols. (Kassel: Bärenreiter – Stuttgart: Metzler, 1994-2007), VII (2002), 395.

Although dedicated to one person, the long-time Governor of Milan, Gaffurio was under no illusion as to his intended broader well-known circle of readers of fifteenth- and sixteenth-century Europe, one which has been discussed widely in the secondary literature.[55] With that in mind, the *Ad lectorem* (To the Reader)[56] is meant to provide a desperately needed balance to the foregoing letter of dedication. After the brief return to the tone of the dedication in the opening lines of the *Ad lectorem*, Gaffurio suddenly includes a brief reference to Hrabanus Maurus (ca. 780-856),[57] whom Gaffurio mentions in passing in the opening chaper of the *Theorica musice* as a scholar who along with Calcidius (flourished 4th or early 5th century AD),[58] Macrobius (flourished first half of 5th century AD),[59] Censorinus (flourished 3rd century AD),[60] Cassiodorus (ca. 485 –

[55] Kristeller, 'Der Gelehrte und sein Publikum'; see also Paul Oskar Kristeller, 'Music and Learning in the Early Italian Renaissance', *Journal of Renaissance and Baroque Music*, 1 (1947), 255-274; idem, 'The Renaissance and Byzantine Learning', in *Renaissance Concepts of Man and Other Essays*, ed. Paul Oskar Kristeller (New York: Harper and Row, 1972), pp. 64-109.

[56] Gaffurio, *Theorica musice*, [folio unnumbered]: *Ad lectorem* [To the Reader]; see also Gaffurio, *The Theory of Music*, trans. Kreyszig, p. 5.

[57] For a comprehensive coverage of the thoughts of Hrabanus Maurus on music, see Albert Richenhagen, *Studien zur Musikanschauung des Hrabanus Maurus*, Kölner Beiträge zur Musikforschung, 162 (Regensburg: Gustav Bosse, 1989).

[58] On Calcidius as translator and commentator on Plato's *Timaeus*, see Jan Hendrik Waszink, *Studien zum Timaioskommentar des Calcidius*, Philosophia antiqua, 12 (Leiden: E.J. Brill, 1964); Michael Dunn and Carl A. Huffman, 'The Cheltenham Manuscript of Calcidius' Translation of the Timaeus', *Manuscripta*, 24 (1980), 76-88; see also Eduard Steinheimer, *Untersuchungen über die Quellen des Chalcidius* (Aschaffenburg: Druck von G. Werbrun, 1912); Thomas J. Mathiesen, *Apollo's Lyre: Greek Music and Music Theory in Antiquity and the Middle Ages*, Publications of the Center for the History of Music Theory and Literature, 2 (Lincoln, Nebraska-London: University of Nebraska Press, 1999), especially pp. 616-617.

[59] Ambrosius Aurelius Theodosius Macrobius, Commentary on *Somnium Scipionis* of Cicero; see *Commentary on the Dream of Scipio by Macrobius*, trans. William Harris Stahl, Records of Civilization: Sources and Studies, 48 (New York: Columbia University Press, 1990 = 1952); see also Matthaeus Schedler, *Die Philosophie des Macrobius und ihr Einfluß auf die Wissenschaft des christlichen Mittelalters*, Beiträge zur Geschichte der Philosophie des Mittelalters: Texte und Untersuchungen, 13/1 (Münster in Westfalen: Aschendorff'sche Verlagsbuchhandlung, 1916); Michael Bernhard, 'Überlieferung und Fortleben der antiken lateinischen Musiktheorie im Mittelalter', in *Rezeption des antiken Fachs im Mittelalter*, ed. Frieder Zaminer, Geschichte der Musiktheorie, 3 (Darmstadt: Wissenschaftliche Buchgesellschaft, 1990), pp. 7-35; see also Mathiesen, *Apollo's Lyre*, pp. 617-618.

[60] Censorinus, *De die natali*. For a Latin edition and German translation, see *Betrachtungen zum Tag der Geburt*, trans. Klaus Gunther Sallmann (Weinheim an der Bergstraße: VCH, 1988). On the significance of this treatise, see Lukas Richter, 'Die Geburtstagsschrift des Censorinus als musiktheoretische Quelle', in *Studien zur Geschichte und Philosophie*

ca. 580 AD),[61] Isidore of Seville (ca. 559-636),[62] Marcus Fabius Quintilian (30-35 AD – after ca. 94 AD),[63] and Vitruvius venerated the musical discipline with great assiduity.[64] Though Gaffurio does not include any specific mentioning of treatises, his general comment can be easily substantiated from three volumes of Hrabanus Maurus, namely, the *De clericorum institutione*,[65]

*des Altertums: Bericht des Kongresses für Klassische Philologie, Budapest 1962*, ed. János Harmatta (Budapest-Amsterdam: Akadémiai Kiadó-Verlag Adolf M. Hakkert, 1968), pp. 215-223; see also Mathiesen, *Apollo's Lyre*, pp. 614-616.

[61] Hermann Abert, 'Zu Cassiodor', *Sammmelbände der Internationalen Musikgesellschaft*, 3 (1901/02), 439-453; Leslie W. Jones, 'The Influence of Cassiodorus on Medieval Culture', *Speculum*, 20 (1945), 433-442; 22 (1947), 254-256; Georg Sowa, 'Die Musikanschauung Cassiodors' (PhD diss. Humboldt Universität Berlin, 1953); Hans Thurm, 'Handschriftenstudien zu Cassiodors Institutiones', *Codices manuscripti*, 12 (1986), 142-144; Åke J. Fridh, 'Cassiodorus' Digression On Music, Var. II 40', *Eranos*, 86 (1988), 43-51; Fabio Troncarelli, 'I codici di Cassiodoro: Le testimonianze più antiche', *Scrittura e civilità*, 12 (1988), 47-99.

[62] *Isidori Hispalensis episcopi Etymologiarum sive originum libri XX*, ed. Wallace Martin Lindsay, Scriptorum classicorum bibliotheca Oxoniensis (Oxford: Clarendon Press, 1962 = 1911). On the significance of this encyclopedic treatise, see Heinrich Hüschen, 'Der Einfluß Isidors von Sevilla auf die Musikanschauung des Mittelalters', in *Miscelanea en Homenaje a Monsenor Higino Anglés*, 2 vols (Barcelona: Consejo Superior de Investigaciones Cientificas, 1958-1961), I, 397-406; Michel Huglo, 'Les diagrammes d'harmonique interpolés dans les mansucrits hispaniques de la musica Isidori', *Scriptorium*, 48 (1994), 171-186; Walter Pass, 'Die Musikkapitel in der Isidor-Überlieferung der Österreichischen Nationalbibliothek in Wien', in *Mittelalterliche Musiktheorie in Zentraleuropa*, eds. Walter Pass – Alexander Rausch, Musica Mediaevalis Europae Occidentalis, 4 (Tutzing: Hans Schneider, 1998), pp. 107-131.

[63] *The Institutio oratoria of Quintilian*, ed./trans. Harold Edgeworth Butler, The Loeb Classical Library: Latin Authors (Cambridge, Massachusetts-London: Harvard University Press-Heinemann, 1920); see also Ulrich Müller, 'Zur musikalischen Terminologie der antiken Rhetorik: Ausdrücke für Stimmlage und Stimmgebrauch bei Quintilian, *Institutio oratoria*, 11, 3', *Archiv für Musikwissenschaft*, 26 (1969), 29-48 and 105 121; see Armin Krumbacher, *Die Stimmbildung der Redner im Altertum bis auf die Zeit Quintilians*, Rhetorische Studien, 10 (Paderborn: Verlag von Ferdinand Schöningh, 1920); also in English translation by George Raymond Roy Pflaum as 'The Voice-Training of the Orators in Antiquity up to the Time of Quintilian: A Translation' (Unpublished A.M. Thesis Cornell University, 1924); Blake McDowell Wilson, '*Ut oratoria musica* in the Writings of Renaissance Music Theorists', in *Festa Musicologica: Essays in Honor of George J. Buelow*, eds. Thomas J. Mathiesen – Benito Rivera, Festschrift Series, 14 (Stuyvesant, New York: Pendragon Press, 1995), pp. 341-368.

[64] Gaffurio, *Theorica musice*, Book 1, Chapter 1, Sentence 282. For an identification of the treatises of the respective authors, see Gaffurio, *The Theory of Music*, trans. Kreyszig, p. 28.

[65] Düsseldorf, Landesbibliothek, MS 113 [ninth century, School of Reims]; *B. Rabani Mauri, fuldensis abbatis et moguntini archiepiscopi, Opera omnia, juxta editionem Georgii Colvenerii anno 1617 coloniae Agrippinae datam, mendis quibus scatebat innumeris cura qua par erat expurgatam, novissime ad prelum revocata et novo ordine, chronologico scilicet, digesta; variis praeterea monumentis quae suppeditarunt Mabillonii, Martenii, et*

the *De sacris ordine*[66] and the *De universo*.[67] While the reference to Hrabanus Maurus is somewhat curious and difficult to account for in the particular otherwise rather general context, Gaffurio's inclusion of this noted scholar,[68] incidentally the only specific reference in the section *Ad lectorem*, bears again witness to the fact that the paratexts do not represent isolated documents but indeed are a conscious effort on the part of the author of the particular paratext to realize opportunities for linking these important documents to the music-theoretical treatise proper. After a brief allusion to the dedicatee of the *Theorica musice*, though without mentioning Lodovico Maria Sforza by name, Gaffurio closes the *Ad lectorem* with another dichotomy: *musica practica* existing in *natura* versus the desire (*libidum*) out of which the science (*scientia*) grew.

In the panegyric poem,[69] the poet of the court of the Sforzas in Milan, Lancinus Curtius (died 1511),[70] erudite in both Latin and Greek,[71] proceeds

*Dacherii collectiones memoratissimae, aucta et illustrata*, 6 vols (Turnhout: Brepols, 1960-1966 = Paris, 1851). For glosses on the writings of Hrabanus Maurus, see MS Wiener Hofbibliothek, hist. prof. 6297 m.ix.49.4. For a modern edition, see Rabanus Maurus, *De institutione clericorum libri tres*, ed. Detlev Zimpel, Freiburger Beiträge zur Mittelalterlichen Geschichte, 7 (Frankfurt am Main-New York: Peter Lang, 1996); see also Rabanus Maurus, *La formazione dei Chierici*, trans. Luigi Samarati, Fonti medievali, 25 (Rome: Città nuova, 2002); Rabanus Maurus, *Über die Unterweisung der Geistlichen*, ed./trans. Detlev Zimpel, Fontes Christiani, 61 (Turnhout: Brepols, 2006).

66 *B. Rabani Mauri, fuldensis abbatis et moguntini archiepiscopi, Opera omnia*.

67 Archivio dell'Abbazia di Montecassino, Codex Casinensis 132; *B. Rabani Mauri, fuldensis abbatis et moguntini archiepiscopi, Opera omnia; Rabanus Maurus: Opus de universo* (Mainz: Adolf Rusch, 1467). For a facsimile, see *Rabanus Maurus: De universo* (Turin: Priuli & Verlucca, 1994).

68 On the significance of Hrabanus Maurus, see Friedrich Kunstmann, *Hrabanus Magnentius Maurus: Eine historische Monographie* (Mainz: Kirchheim, Schott und Thielmann, 1841); Joseph Freundgen, *Des Hrabanus Maurus pädagogische Schriften*, Sammlung der bedeutendsten pädagogischen Schriften aus alter und neuer Zeit, 5 (Paderborn: F. Schöningh, 1909); Cletus Paul Kohake, 'The Life and Educational Writings of Rabanus Maurus' (PhD diss. Cornell University, 1948); *Hrabanus Maurus und seine Schule: Festschrift der Rabanus-Maurus-Schule*, ed. Winfried Böhne (Fulda: Rabanus-Maurus-Schule, 1980).

69 Gaffurio, *Theorica musice*, folio k v recto – k viii recto: *Carmen Lancini Curtii* [Poem of Lancinus Curtius]; see also Gaffurio, *The Theory of Music*, trans. Kreyszig, pp. 189-195.

70 For the poetry of Lancinus Curtius, see *Lancini Curtii Meditatio in hebdomada Olivarum* (Milan: Alexander Minutianus, 1508); *Lancini Curtii Epigrammaton libri decem decados secundae* (Milan: Apud Rochum & Ambrosium fratres de Valle impressores Philippus Foyot faciebat, 1521).

71 *Biographical and Bibliographical Dictionary of the Italian Humanists and of the World of Classcial Scholarship in Italy, 1300-1800*, ed. Mario Emilio Cosenza, 5 vols and 1 supplement (Boston, Massachusetts: G.K. Hall, 1962-1967), II (1962), 1163-1164; Gaffurio, *The Theory of Music*, trans. Kreyszig, p. xvi.

beyond the mere extolling of Gaffurio's heroic efforts, recounted only in the latter part of the poem (lines 200 ff.). Achieving a true *tour de force*, Curtius carefully crafts the poem so as to offer a succinct commentary and critical reflection on selected topics from the opening chapter of the *Theorica musice* in a carefully distilled fashion — with such careful linking of Gaffurio's prose and Curtius's poetry attesting to the latter's intimate familiarity with the theoretical discourse upon which he is commenting.[72]

## IV

Like the *Theorica musice*, Gaffurio also dedicated the second instalment of his music-theoretical discussion, the *Practica musicae*, to Duke Lodovico il Moro of Milan. Unlike the more austere subject matter of the *Theorica musice* — a fact which accounts for the sole printed edition of this treatise — the *Practica musicae* with its marked shift in emphasis from an abstract music-theoretical system to the practice of composition in the context of the French mensural notation,[73] characteristic of late fifteenth-century music-theoretical discourse on *musica practica*,[74] was met with great enthusiasm, and that judging merely from the history of publication. With altogether three editions in Brescia (namely, those of 1497, 1502, and 1508) and another three editions in Venice (namely, those of 1512, 1517, and 1526), the *Practica musicae* abounds in some one hundred and fifty examples of polyphony, a marked contrast to the *Theorica musice*, which includes a single musical example, the famous solmization hymn *Ut queant laxis*[75] in reference to the Guidonian hand (*manus*).[76] There is

[72] The editorial annotations to Lancinus Curtius's poem refer to the sentence numbers, which are part of the modern English translation; see Gaffurio, *The Theory of Music*, trans. Kreyszig, pp. 1-29.

[73] On French mensural notation in the exposition by Gaffurio, see Ernst Praetorius, *Die Mensuraltheorie des Franchinus Gafurius und der folgenden Zeit bis zur Mitte des 16. Jahrhunderts*, Publikationen der Internationalen Musikgesellschaft, 2 (Leipzig: Breitkopf & Härtel, 1905).

[74] This notion has been forcefully articulated in Klaus-Jürgen Sachs, *De modo componendi: Studien zu musikalischen Lehrtexten des späten 15. Jahrhunderts*, Veröffentlichungen des Staatlichen Instituts für Musikforschung, 12; Studien zur Geschichte der Musiktheorie, 2 (Hildesheim-Zurich: Georg Olms, 2002).

[75] Jacques Chailley, 'Ut queant laxis et les origines de la gamme', *Music Disciplina*, 56 (1984), 48-69; see also Carl-Allan Moberg, 'Die Musik in Guido von Arezzos Solmisationshymne', *Archiv für Musikwissenschaft*, 16 (1956), 187-206.

[76] Karol Berger, 'The Hand and the Art of Memory', *Musica Disciplina*, 35 (1981), 87-120; Susan Forscher Weiss, '"Disce manum tuam si vis bene discere cantum": Symbols of Learning Music in Early Modern Europe', *Music in Art*, 30/1-2 (2005), 35-74.

but one further similarity between the respective treatises. The *Theorica musice* arose from a significantly revised version of the *Theoricum opus musice discipline*; likewise, materials of the *Practica musicae*, specifically Book 2, existed in an earlier version in Italian, the *Tractato vulgare del canto figurato*. This point of contact between the *Theorica musice* and the *Practica musicae* explains the affinity between the letters of dedication of these respective treatises, both of which are destined for the same dedicatee.

While Gaffurio admittedly regarded the *Theorica musice* as a weighty tomb of scholarship, the drafting of the *Practica musicae* provided for a revival of the spirit, as becomes readily apparent from the overall tone of the dedication. In the *Practica musicae*, Gaffurio includes merely one brief reference to the *Theorica musice* — a volume crafted with an emphasis on the *musica speculativa*,[77] a tradition vastly disseminated in fifteenth-century Italian manuscripts,[78] with the Pythagorean arithmetic proportions providing the basis for such an inquiry, modelled after ancient authorities (though without identifying any specific authors). Gaffurio offers a justification for this obvious departure in content from his earlier efforts, so as to fill a self-perceived lacuna in scholarly writings addressing the core of the practical discipline — a consideration which is particularly dear to the heart of the dedicatee, who had left a milestone in the promoting of both sacred and secular repertories. Yet, in spite of the total shift of deliberation in the *Practica musicae*, Gaffurio's apparent ongoing deep seated preoccupation with the doctrine of the ancients leaves an unmistakable imprint on this letter of dedication, with references to the *De amicitia* of Marcus Tullius Cicero (106 BC – 43 BC)[79]

[77] For an overview of the *musica speculativa*, see Palisca, *Humanism*, pp. 226-279; see also Manfred F. Bukofzer, 'Speculative Thinking in Medieval Music', *Speculum*, 17 (1942), 165-180; Calvin M. Bower, 'The Role of Boethius's 'De institutione musica' in the Speculative Tradition of Western Musical Thought', in *Boethius and the Liberal Arts*, ed. Michael Masi, Utah Studies in Literature and Linguistics, 18 (Berne-Frankfurt am Main: Peter Lang, 1981), pp. 157-174; Richard J. Wingell, 'Medieval Music Treatises: *Speculatio* versus *Institutio*', in *Paradigms in Medieval Thought — Applications in Medieval Disciplines: A Symposium*, eds. Nancy van Deusen – Alvin E. Ford, Medieval Studies, 3 (Queenston, Ontario-Lewiston, New York: The Edwin Mellen Press, 1990), pp. 157-172.

[78] See, for example, in Brussels, Koninklijke Bibliotheek van België / Bibliothèque Royale de Belgique, MS II 785. For an inventory of this source, see Jan W. Herlinger, 'A Fifteenth-Century Italian Compilation of Music Theory', *Acta Musicologica*, 53 (1981), 90-105.

[79] See Wilhelmine Edinger, 'Ciceros Stellung zur Kunst (Dichtkunst, bildende Kunst, Musik) in seinen rhetorischen Schriften' (PhD diss. Universität Innsbruck, 1951).

and to the *De institutione oratoria* of Fabius Quintilian (30/35 AD – after ca. 94 AD), to Virgil (70 BC – 19 BC)[80] and Gaius Plinius Secundus, also known as Pliny the Elder (23 AD – 79 AD)[81] — all authors who played a prominent role in the main body of the *Theorica musice*[82] — and also to the *Timaeus* of Plato (ca. 429 BC – 347 BC),[83] the latter author known to Gaffurio through his commissioning of a translation of Plato's *Opera omnia* from Marsilio Ficino, the founder of the Academy in Florence.[84] In view of Gaffurio's extensive citations from Ficino's published Latin translation (with Gaffurio's own copy signed 6 May 1489[85]) in the *Theorica musice*, the reference to this important document provides further evidence of Gaffurio's intention in the letter of dedication of bridging the

[80] On Quintilian's and Virgil's significance in the context of musical humanism, see Wille, *Musica romana*, pp. 449-456 and 225 ff.; idem, *Einführung in das römische Musikleben*, p. 166 and pp. 131-134.

[81] On Pliny's significance in the context of musical humanism, see Wille, *Musica romana*, pp. 145 ff.

[82] Gaffurio, *The Theory of Music*, trans. Kreyszig, pp. 218, 230, 231.

[83] Plato, *Timaeus*; see also O. Tiby, 'Note musicologiche al Timeo di Platone', *Dioniso*, 12 (1949), 33-55; Jacques Handschin, 'The "Timaeus" Scale', *Musica Disciplina*, 4 (1950), 3-42; Lukas Richter, *Zur Wissenschaftslehre von der Musik bei Platon und Aristoteles*, Deutsche Akademie der Wissenschaften zu Berlin: Schriften der Sektion für Altertumswissenschaft, 23 (Berlin: Akademie-Verlag, 1961); Ernest G. McClain, 'A New Look at Plato's *Timaeus*', *Music and Man*, 1 (1975), 341-360; Gerhard Jahoda, 'Die Tonleiter des Timaios — Bild und Abbild', in *Festschrift Rudolf Haase*, ed. Werner Schulze (Eisenstadt: Elfriede Rötzer Verlag, 1980), pp. 43-80; see also Werner Schulze, 'Logos – Mesotes – Analogia: Zur Quaternität von Mathematik, Musik, Kosmologie und Staatslehre bei Platon', in *Festschrift Rudolf Haase*, ed. Werner Schulze (Eisenstadt: Elfriede Rötzer-Verlag, 1980), pp. 107-180; Andrew Barker, 'Ptolemy's Pythagoreans, Archytas, and Plato's Conception of Mathematics', *Phronesis*, 39 (1994), 113-135.

[84] For a modern edition of Marsilio Ficino's translation of Plato's *Opera*, see *Marsilio Ficino, Opera Omnia*, ed. Paul Oskar Kristeller, Monumenta Politica et Philosophica Rariora, Series I, 7-8 (Turin: Bottega d'Erasmo, 1962); *Supplementum Ficianum*, ed. Paul Oskar Kristeller, 2 vols. (Florence: Leo S. Olschki, 1973 = 1937); James Hankins – William Bowen, trans., and Michael J.B. Allen – John Warden., trans., *Marsilio Ficino: Platonic Theology*, I Tatti Renaissance Library (Cambridge. Mass. – London: Harvard, 2001-2003); see also *The Letters of Marsilio Ficino*, ed./trans. Paul Oskar Kristeller, 2 vols. (London: Shepheard-Walwyn, 1975). Further on Marsilio Ficino, see Paul Oskar Kristeller, 'Marsilio Ficino as a Beginning Student of Plato', *Scriptorium*, 20 (1966), 41-54; idem, 'The Scholastic Background of Marsilio Ficino (with an edition of unpublished texts)', *Traditio: Studies in Ancient and Medieval History, Thought and Religion*, 2 (1944), 257-318. Further on the dissemination of Plato's writings in this era, see James Hankins, 'Latin Translations of Plato in the Renaissance' (PhD diss. Columbia University, 1984); see also idem, *Humanism and Platonism in the Italian Renaissance*, 2 vols., Storia e letteratura, 215, 220 (Rome: Edizioni di storia e letteratura, 2003-2004); idem, *Plato in the Italian Renaissance* ([Leiden]: Brill, 2007).

[85] 'Franchini Gaffori musicis professoris est hic liber / die vi maii 1489 emptus', as reproduced in Palisca, *Humanism*, p. 168.

gap between *musica* as a *scientia philosophiae* and an *ars secularis*. Gaffurio's intention is fully justified in that the *disciplina musicae* literally begs for an interdisciplinary approach for assuring an education in the *artes liberales*, of which *musica* forms an indispensable part.[86] As in the *Theorica musice*, Gaffurio closes this letter of dedication in the *Practica musicae* in the characteristic vein of a subservient, with the self-acknowledging of his contribution in the *Practica musicae* regarded as a mere compilation of the work of his predecessors, so as to restrain the reader from his aimless wandering about and penetrating of writings that are obscure in subject matter.

The heaping of praises upon the dedicatee of the volume, Lodovico Maria Sforza, continues in the poem by the humanist and Milanese poet Lucinus Conagus.[87] In his glowing comments on both author and dedicatee, Conagus does not miss the opportunity to include a decisive reference to Pythagoras (flourished second half of sixth century BC) and Euclid (flourished ca. 300 BC),[88] obviously underscoring the importance of the Pythagorean arithmetic tradition,[89] significant to *musica theorica* and *musica practica*. This intersection of *musica theorica* and *musica practica* is witnessed by Gaffurio himself in his recourse to proportional notation of a number of pieces — incidentally subscribing to a direction also followed by members of the Netherlands School of Composition,[90]

[86] Edward A. Lippman, 'The Place of Music in the System of Liberal Arts', in *Aspects of Medieval and Renaissance Music: A Birthday Offering to Gustave Reese*, eds. Jan La Rue *et al.* (London: Oxford University Press, 1967), pp. 545-559; Karl Gustav Fellerer, 'Die Musica in den Artes Liberales', *Artes Liberales: Studien und Texte zur Geistesgeschichte des Mittelalters*, 5 (1976), 33-49.

[87] Gaffurio, *Practica musicae*, [folio unnumbered]: *Carmen Lucini Conagi* [Poem of Lucinus Conagus]; see *The Practica musicae of Franchinus Gafurius*, trans. Irwin Young (Madison and Milwaukee, Wisconsin: University of Wisconsin Press, 1969), pp. 7-8.

[88] André Barbera, *The Euclidean Division of the Canon: Greek and Latin Sources*, Greek and Latin Music Theory (Lincoln, Nebraska-London: University of Nebraska Press, 1991); see also Thomas J. Mathiesen, 'An Annotated Translation of Euclid's Division of a Monochord', *Journal of Music Theory*, 19 (1975), 236-258; André Barbera, 'Placing Sectio Canonis in Historical and Philosophical Contexts', *Journal of Hellenic Studies*, 104 (1984), 157-161.

[89] Charles André Barbera, 'The Persistence of Pythagorean Mathematics in Ancient Musical Thought' (PhD diss. University of North Carolina at Chapel Hill, 1980).

[90] For an overview of the important contributions of the Netherlands School of Composition, see Raphael Georg Kiesewetter, *Verhandelingen over de vraag: Welke verdiensten hebben zich de Nederlanders vooral in de 14e, 15e en 16e eeuw in het vak der toonkunst verworven; en in hoe verre kunnen de Nederlandsche kunstenaars van dien tijd, die zich naar Italien begeven hebben, invloed gehad hebben op de muzijkscholen, die zich kort daarna in Italien hebben gevormd?* (Amsterdam: J. Muller, 1829).

including Jacob Obrecht (1457/8-1505)[91] and Johannes Ockeghem (ca. 1410-1497).[92] In addition to words to the dedicatee and the author of the treatise, Conagus also offers some advice to the prospective reader of this volume, in particular to the singer, who in turn offers praises to the Creator, thus contemplating yet another magic triangle, namely that of the author, the performer, and God — indeed what is hardly perceived as a stretch of imagination but recognised as a cogent reflection on Milanese society. Obviously, the poet is interested in underscoring the analogy between the scientific approach of *musica theorica* and the artistic approach (that is, the approach to performance) to *musica practica*, intimating a similar rigor of application.

## V

In the *De harmonia*, Gaffurio returns to the central topic of the *Theorica musice*, the Pythagorean arithmetic proportions. While the *Theorica musice* included merely an elementary consideration of the Greek *systema teleion*, with its embedded *genera* of *diapason*, *diapente* and *diatessaron* (Book 5), the *De harmonia* focuses on a thorough exposition of the Greek *genera* and the Pythagorean tuning system in the larger context of the monochord division.[93] Undoubtedly, Gaffurio was the first theorist to

[91] See, for example, Jacob Obrecht, two-voice *Regina coeli*, preserved in Segovia, Archivo Capitular De la Cathedral, MS s.s., folio 200 verso, including the ascription 'Jacobus Hobrecht'. For an edition of this work, see *Jacob Obrecht: Motets I and II*, ed. Chris Maas, Jacob Obrecht: New Edition of the Collected Works, 15-16 (Utrecht: Koninklijke Vereniging voor Nederlandse Muziekgeschiedenis, 1995-1996), XVI, 63-64 (No. 22); see also Helen Hewitt, 'A Study in Proportions', in *Essays on Music in Honor of Archibald Thompson Davison* (Cambridge, Massachusetts: Harvard University, 1957), pp. 68-81.

[92] See, for example, Johannes Ockeghem, *Missa prolationum*, preserved in Rome, Biblioteca Apostolica Vaticana, Chigi Codex C. VIII. 234 and in Vienna, Österreichische Nationalbibliothek, Codex 11883. For an edition of this work, see *[Johannes Ockeghem]: Masses and Mass Sections IX-XVI*, ed. Dragan Plamenac, Johannes Ockeghem: Collected Works, 2 (American Musicological Society, 1966 = 1947), pp. 21-36. For a further discussion of this work, see Michael Eckert, 'Canon and Variation in Ockeghem's *Missa prolationum*', in *Johannes Ockeghem: Actes du XLe Colloque international d'études humanistes, Tours, 3-8 février 1997*, ed. Philippe Vendrix, Centre d'Études Supérieures de la Renaissance: Collection 'Épitome musical' (Paris: Éditions Klincksieck, 1998), pp. 465-479; Marianne Henze, *Studien zu den Messenkompositionen Johannes Ockeghems*, Berliner Studien zur Musikwissenschaft, 12 (Berlin: Verlag Merseburger, 1968); K. Schweizer, 'Interpolationen zur Missa prolationum [Ockeghem]', *Dissonance*, 27 (1991), 30-31.

[93] On the monochord division, see Sigfrid Wantzloeben, *Das Monochord als Instrument und als System entwicklungsgeschichtlich dargestellt* (Halle an der Saale: Verlag von Max

offer a comprehensive coverage of Ptolemy's syntonic diatonic,[94] an aspect of the Greek harmonic science (*harmoniai*)[95] which was to achieve importance in the scholarly discourse carried out during the later part of the sixteenth and seventeenth centuries. Towards the end of this treatise, Gaffurio returns once again to familiar territory, namely, to the exploration of the Boethian tripartite division of the *musica disciplina* into *musica mundana*, *musica humana* and *musica instrumentalis*.[96] Unlike the earlier

Niemeyer, 1911); J. Murray Barbour, *Tuning and Temperament: A Historical Survey*, Da Capo Press Music Reprint Series (East Lansing, Michigan: Michigan State College Press, 1953 = 1951; New York: Da Capo Press, [1972]); Cecil Adkins, 'The Theory and Practice of the Monochord' (PhD diss. State University of Iowa, 1963); Jacques Chailley, 'La monochorde et la théorie musicale', in *Organicae voces: Festschrift Joseph Smits van Waesberghe angeboten anläßlich seines 60. Geburtstages am 18. April 1961*, ed. Pieter Fischer (Amsterdam: I.M.M. Instituut voor Middeleeuwse Muziekwetenschap, 1963), pp. 11-20; Cecil Adkins, 'The Technique of the Monochord', *Acta Musicologica*, 39 (1967), 34-43; F. Joseph Smith, 'The Medieval Monochord', *Journal of Musicological Research*, 5 (1984), 1-33; *Mensura monochordi: La division du monochorde, IXe-XVe siècles*, ed. Christian Meyer, Publications de la Société française de musicologie, Series 2, Vol. 15 (Paris: Société Française de Musicologie and Éditions Klincksieck, 1996); see also Clyde W. Brockett, 'A Comparison of the Five Monochords of Guido of Arezzo', *Current Musicology*, 32 (1981), 29-42.

[94] Claudius Ptolemaeus, *Harmonicorum Libri tres (A Facsimile of the Oxford 1682 Edition)*, Monuments of Music and Music literature in Facsimile: Second Series – Music Literature, 60 (New York: Broude Brothers, 1977); Andrew Barker, 'Ptolemy', in Andrew Barker, *Greek Musical Writings, Vol. 2: Harmonic and Acoustic Theory*, Cambridge Readings in the Literature of Music (Cambridge: Cambridge University Press, 1989), pp. 270-391; see also Ingemar Düring, *Die Harmonielehre des Klaudios Ptolemaios*, Göteborgs Högskolas Ärskrift, 38/2 (Göteborg: Elanders Boktryckeri Aktiebolag, 1930); Bengt Alexandersson, *Textual Remarks on Ptolemy's Harmonics and Porphyry's Commentary* (Göteborg: Almquist & Wiksell, 1969).

[95] For an overview of the Greek *harmoniai*, see P. Bonnaventura Meyer, *APMONIA: Bedeutungsgeschichte des Wortes von Homer bis Aristoteles* (Zurich: Dissertationsdruckerei A.G. Gebr. Leemann, 1932) [PhD diss. Université de Fribourg, 1932]; Henrich Hüschen, 'Der Harmoniebegriff im Musikschrifttum des Altertums und des Mittelalters', in *Bericht über den Siebenten Internationalen Musikwissenschaftlichen Kongress Köln 1958*, eds. Gerald Abraham *et al.* (Kassel: Bärenreiter, 1959), pp. 143-150; Olof Gigon, 'Zum antiken Begriff der Harmonie', *Studium Generale*, 19 (1966), 539-547; Heinrich Hüschen, 'Der Harmoniebegriff in Mittelalter', *Studium Generale*, 19 (1966), 548-554; Thomas J. Mathiesen, 'Problems of Terminology in Ancient Greek Theory: APMONIA', in *Festival Essays for Pauline Alderman: A Musicological Tribute*, eds. Burton L. Karson *et al.* (Provo, Utah: Brigham Young University Press, 1976), pp. 3-17; Thomas J. Mathiesen, 'Harmonia and Ethos in Ancient Greek Music', *The Journal of Musicology*, 3 (1984), 264-279; William R. Bowen, 'Ficino's Analysis of Musical *Harmonia*', in *Ficino and Renaissance Neoplatonism*, eds. Konrad Eisenbichler – Olga Zorzi Pugliese, University of Toronto Italian Studies, 1 (Ottawa, Ontario: Dovehouse Editions, 1986), pp. 17-27.

[96] Obviously inspired by Boethius's threefold classification, Gaffurio returns to the *musica mundana* several times in his trilogy, with the importance of these deliberations underscored in the frontispiece of the *Practica musicae*; see Haar, 'The Frontispiece of Gafori's *Practica musicae*'.

exposition of this topic in the *Theorica music*, and the subsequent completion of an entire treatise on those aspects of the *musica disciplina* related to the subdiscipline of the *musica practica* (identified earlier), with special emphasis on the proportions as they relate to and in part define compositional practice (Book 5),[97] Gaffurio is now in a position to fulfill his ongoing quest, namely, to combine theory and practice, as emphatically underscored in the woodcut in Book 4 of the *De harmonia*, juxtaposing the muses, the fifteen steps of the *systema teleion*, the Latin modes, and the planetary order. This rather ambitious program of the *De harmonia* is also borne out in the number of paratexts included in both the manuscript version of the treatise (Vienna, Österreichische Nationalbibliothek, Codex Ser. nov. 12745)[98] and the final version of the treatise, the Milan print of 1518, meant to supercede the initial circulation of the treatise in manuscript. Notwithstanding differences in the content of the respective versions of the treatise and also in the arrangement and content of the paratexts (all of which have been alluded to in the prefatory materials by Clement A. Miller[99]), the present considerations will focus only on the final version of this treatise — in this way consciously paralleling the earlier consideration of the *Theorica music*. The content of the 1518 publication is reflected and elegantly captured in the numerous paratexts that grace the music-theoretical discourse. The opening epigram by Joannes Jacobus Lomatius, who as a loyal patron of music-theoretical discourse had borne the costs of publication of Gaffurio's earlier *Practica musicae*, appropriately sets the tone for the *De harmonia*. For the woodcut shows Gaffurio, flanked by the schematic representation of the arithmetic *proportionalitas*, graphically by the pipes and the circle for the monochord division,[100] as *professor musices*[101] at Ludovico's in Milan, lecturing

[97] Anna Maria Busse Berger, 'Musical Proportions and Arithmetic in the Late Middle Ages and the Renaissance', *Musica Disciplina*, 44 (1990), 89-118.

[98] Further on this illuminated manuscript, see Franz Unterkircher, 'Eine Handschrift aus dem Besitze Jean Groliers in der Österreichischen Nationalbibliothek', *Libri*, 1 (1950/51), 51-57.

[99] Gaffurio, *De harmonia*, trans. Miller, pp. 11 ff.

[100] Arthur Donald Steele, 'Über die Rolle von Zirkel und Lineal in der griechischen Mathematik', in *Zur Geschichte der griechischen Mathematik*, ed. Oskar Becker, Wege der Forschung, 33 (Darmstadt: Wissenschaftliche Buchgesellschaft, 1965), pp. 146-202.

[101] Caretta *et al.*, *Franchino Gaffurio*, p. 56. Further on this title, possibly in reference to the chair of music, see Paul A. Merkley – Lora L.M. Merkley, *Music and Patronage in the Sforza Court*, Studi sulla storia della musica in Lombardia: Collana di testi musicologici, 3 (Turnhout: Brepols, 1999), pp. 2-3.

to his disciples from a podium, uttering the statement, 'Harmonia est discors concordantia' — meant as a motto for the entire treatise. Placed below this woodcut, the epigram identifies the Secretary of Louis VII, Jean Grolier (1479-1565) of Lyons, as a promoter of the harmony of the spheres,[102] that bibliophile who earlier had been the recipient of a handwritten dedication by Gaffurio in the parchment codex, Manuscript Vienna, Österreichische Nationalbibliothek, Codex Ser. nov. 12745 — that version initially intended for Bonifacius Simonetta (ca. 1447-1502), the Cistercian Abbot of the Monastery of St. Stefano and author of *De christianae fidei romanorum Pontificum persecutationibus opus* (Milan, 1492), whom Gaffurio had extolled as a 'viro omnium scientiarum studiosissimo' ('a man most cultured in all the sciences').[103] The three paratexts preceding the letter of dedication — that is, the distich by Caesar Saccus of Lodi,[104] the hendecasyllabic poem by Stefano Negri

[102] On the harmony of the spheres, see Carl von Jan, 'Die Harmonie der Sphären', *Philologus*, 52 (1894), 13-37; Fritz Erckmann, 'Sphärenmusik', *Zeitschrift der Internationalen Musikgesellschaft*, 9 (1907/08), 417-425; Jacques Handschin, 'Die Lehre von der Sphärenharmonie', in *Gedenkschrift Jacques Handschin: Aufsätze und Bibliographie* (Berne and Stuttgart: Verlag Paul Haupt, 1957), pp. 359-364; idem, 'Die Sphärenharmonie in der Geistesgeschichte', in *Gedenkschrift Jacques Handschin: Aufsätze und Bibliographie*, pp. 365-369; James Haar, 'Musica mundana: Variations on a Pythagorean Theme' (PhD diss. Harvard University, 1960); Marius Schneider, 'Die musikalischen Grundlagen der Sphärenharmonie', *Acta Musicologica*, 32 (1960), 136-151; Kay Slocum, 'Musica coelestis: A Fourteenth-Century Image of Cosmic Music', *Studia Mystica*, 14/2-3 (1991), 3-12; see also Gustav Junge, 'Die Sphären-Harmonie und die pythagoreisch-platonische Zahlenlehre', *Classica et Mediaevalia*, 9 (1947), 183-194; James Haar, 'Pythagorean Harmony of the Universe', in *Dictionary of the History of Ideas: Studies of Selected Pivotal Ideas*, ed. Philip P. Wiener, 4 vols (New York: Charles Scribner's Sons, 1973), IV, 38-42; Hans Strohm, 'Aristoteles Lehre vom Kosmos und ihrem Verhältnis zu Platon', *Wiener Humanistische Blätter*, 17 (1975), 1-12; Hans Schavernoch, *Die Harmonie der Sphären: Die Geschichte der Idee des Welteinklangs und der Seelenstimmung*, Orbis Academicus: Problemgeschichten der Wissenschaft in Dokumenten und Darstellungen, 6 (Freiburg im Breisgau-Munich: Verlag Karl Alber, 1981); Friedrich Zipp, *Vom Urklang zur Weltharmonie: Werken und Wirken der Idee der Sphärenharmonie* (Berlin-Kassel: Verlag Merseburger. 1985); Hans-Georg Nicklaus, *Die Maschine des Himmels: Zur Kosmologie und Ästhetik des Klanges* (Munich: Wilhelm Finck Verlag, 1994); Lukas Richter, 'Griechische Planetentonleitern in römischer Rezeption', in *Elementos griegos antiguos en las tradiciones musicales posteriors: In memoriam Otto J. Gombosi (1902-1955)*, Vol. 3 of *Actas del XV Congreso de la Sociedad Internacional de Musicología "Culturas Musicales del Mediterraneo y sus Ramificaciones", Madrid, 3-10.4.1992*, eds. Ismael Fernández de la Cuesta – Alfonso de Vicente, Revista de Musicología, 16 (Madrid: Sociedad Española de Musicología 1993), pp. 1331-1340.

[103] Gaffurio, *De harmonia*, trans. Miller, p. 11.

[104] Gaffurio, *De harmonia*, folio a 1 verso: *Caesaris Sacci Laudensis Dysticon* [Distich of Caesar Saccus of Lodi]. For an English translation, see Gaffurio, *De harmonia*, trans. Miller, p. 26.

(died ca. 1450),[105] and the colloquy of Maurus Ugerius of Mantua[106] — speak to the central topic of the muses,[107] a recurring theme throughout the trilogy of Gaffurio.[108] Caesar Saccus focuses on the centrality of the muses responsible for bringing eternal glory to men. In addition to the muses, Stefano Negri invokes the sirens,[109] symbolically attesting, as it were in one's imagination, to Gaffurio's reviving of the humanist tradition in his treatises with a focus on Pythagoras[110] and in his compositions with recourse to the use of the tones (see line 13). In the trilogy, the paratext identified as *Ad lectorem*, plays a somewhat ambivalent role. In the *Theorica music*e, Gaffurio addressed the reader. In the *Practica musicae* this paratext is missing altogether. The poet Stefano Negri assumes this important role in the *De harmonia*, addressing the reader specifically in the concluding three lines of this hendecasyllabic poem. In the colloquy between Maurus Ugerius and the muses (line 39), preceding the coat of arms of Jean Grolier, there appears to be a reversal of roles, with Gaffurio now responsible for stimulating the muses. Beyond that, the Colloquy is unusual in that Maurus Ugerius is the first author of a paratext pertaining to Gaffurios' trilogy who makes explicit reference,

[105] Gaffurio, *De harmonia*, folio a 1 verso: *Nigri Cremonensis Endecasyllabon* [Poem of Negri of Cremona]; see also Gaffurio, *De harmonia*, trans. Miller, p. 26.

[106] Gaffurio, *De harmonia*, folio a 4 verso: *Mauri Ugerii Mantuani & Musarum Colloquium* [Colloquy of Maurus Ugerius of Mantua and the Muses]; see Gaffurio, *De harmonia*, trans. Miller, p. 31.

[107] On the significance of the muses, see Walter Friedrich Otto, *Die Musen und der göttliche Ursprung des Singens und Sagens* (Düsseldorf: E. Diederichs, 1956); Anastasios Giannarás, 'Das Wachthaus im Bezirk der Musen: Zum Verhältnis von Musik und Politik bei Platon', *Archiv für Musikwissenschaft*, 32 (1975), 165-183; see also John Richard Thornhill Pollard, 'Muses and Sirens', *The Classical Review*, 66 (Nouv. Series II) (1952), 60-63.

[108] See, for example, (a) Gaffurio, *Theorica musice*: Book 1, Chapter 1, Sentences 47, 58, 59, 118, 191, 205, 213, 275; Poem of Lancinus Curtius, lines 175, 191-192; trans. Kreyszig, pp. 11, 12, 17, 20, 22, 27, 194; (b) Gaffurio, *Practica musicae*: *Carmen Lucini Conagi*, Line 17, trans. Miller, p. 18; (c) Gaffurio, *De harmonia*: *Caesaris Sacci Laudensis Dysticon*, Line 1; *Nigri Cremonensis Endecasyllabon*, Line 25; *Mauri Ugerii Mantuani & Musarum Colloquium*, Lines 2, 9, 11, 12, 14, 25; Book 1, *Author alloquitur librum*, Lines 30, 35; *Pantaleonis Meleguli Laudensis Epigramma. Ad Lectorem*, Line 10; *Francisci Phylippinei Endecacyllabon*, Lines 2, 9, 12, 22, 26, 27, trans. Miller, pp. 26, 31, 34, 214-215.

[109] Warren Anderson, 'What Song the Sirens Sang: Problems and Conjectures in Ancient Greek Music', *Research Chronicle (Royal Musical Association)*, 15 (1979), 1-16; see also Pollard, 'Muses and Sirens'.

[110] Barbara Münxelhaus, *Pythagoras musicus: Zur Rezeption der pythagoreischen Musiktheorie als quadrivialer Wissenschaft im lateinischen Mittelalter*, Orpheus-Schriftenreihe zu Grundfragen der Musik, 19 (Bonn-Bad Godesberg: Verlag für Systematische Musikwissenschaft, 1976).

not to the theory but rather to the music of Gaffurio, however, without mentioning any particular piece or genre cultivated by the master.[111]

While Gaffurio in his letters of dedication to both the *Theorica musice* and the *Practica musicae* exhibits a tremendous degree of uniformity with regard to the writing style, content, and layout, he introduces a deliberate change in the parameters that tend to define or are indicative of the more traditional approach to dedications. In order to establish the tone of the more unusual dedicatory letter of the *De harmonia* from the outset, Gaffurio begins this paratext[112] with a brief preamble — with the author himself speaking to the book (*Author alloquitur librum*), so as to personify the volume at hand. What follows are Gaffurio's self-termed greetings to Jean Grolier, the chief treasurer of Milan. For the first time, Gaffurio here identifies a number of authors and their respective treatises from previous eras that have helped shape and justify his approach, especially with regard to the selecting of a dedicatee worthy of bestowing such an honor upon. Unusual and rare is the painstaking precision with which Gaffurio identifies these respective authors — an aspect not found in the other dedications, let alone in the body of the respective treatises. There we observe the general tendency of deliberately imprecise identifications, so as to conceal the authority or authorities and their specific borrowings, especially in the case of authors, contemporary to Gaffurio or of apparently altogether wrong attributions, as for example in the case of Marcus Porcius Cato's *De agricultura* and Marcus Terentius Varro's *De re rustica*.[113] When we further consider that Gaffurio had apparent difficulties in identifying the appropriate dedicatee — a fact which perhaps explains the eighteen-year hiatus between the completion of the manuscript and the release of the printed version — the extraordinary details accorded to this dedicatory letter are even less surprising. Towards the end of this dedication, Gaffurio changes his overall tone to become more personal, as he applauds the dedicatee Jean Grolier as a *tutor disciplinarum liberalium* (guardian of liberal studies, line 29) and an instigator of the muses to tumult and tempest (line 30), and that to such an extent that he equates this patron of the art almost with deity.

[111] For an inventory of Gaffurio's compositions, see Bonnie J. Blackburn, 'Gaffurio, Franchino', in Stanley Sadie (ed.), *The New Grove Dictionary of Music and Musicians*, 29 vols. (London: Macmillan, 2001), IX, 412-413; see also inventory prepared by Ludwig Finscher, included in Finscher-Kreyszig, 'Gaffurio, Franchino', pp. 396-397.

[112] Gaffurio, *De harmonia*, folio A1 recto – A1 verso: [Dedicatory Letter] of Franchino Gaffurio; see also Gaffurio, *De harmonia*, trans. Miller, pp. 33-34.

[113] Gaffurio, *Theorica musice*, Book 3, Chapter 3, Sentence 40; see Gaffurio, *The Theory of Music*, trans. Kreyszig, p. 85.

Most unusual as a paratext is the inclusion of Pantaleon Meleguli's biographical sketch of Gaffurio,[114] appended to the music-theoretical discourse of the *De harmonia*. In his prose, Pantaleon Meleguli of Lodi adopts a carefully selected approach, thereby reflecting on details of Gaffurio's biography that have a direct bearing on his music-theoretical discourse, including the identification of two treatises, now no longer extant, namely, the *Musice institutionis collocutiones* (ca. 1475-1476)[115] and the *Flos musicae* (ca. 1475-1476).[116] Although Meleguli mentions Gaffurio's receiving of an important stipend (line 35), he fails to provide the date of this stipend, 19 May 1483, and even more importantly the significance of this stipend in the overall career aspirations of Gaffurio. In fact, the stipend in question allowed Gaffurio to assume an appointment as *director musices* of the Church of *San Maria Maggiore* at Bergamo, where he also supervised the installation of an organ pedal by Battista da Martinengo.[117] As I have pointed out elsewhere, Meleguli, on the whole, provides at best a thumbnail sketch of Gaffurio's thirty-nine year sojourn in Milan, with his account gradually trailing off towards the end of this sketch.[118] While Meleguli recounts with precision such details as Gaffurio's paternal and maternal backgrounds, his training with special consideration of his education relating to the priesthood, and in a nearly comprehensive coverage Gaffurio's prolific literal contributions, referring to almost all of his treatises and even *summa summarum* identifying Gaffurio's extensive involvement in commissioning of Latin translations of original Greek texts,[119] he fails to touch on various biographical aspects which have a lasting effect on Gaffurio's preeminence as a consummate

[114] Gaffurio, *De harmonia*, folio N 5 recto – verso: *Ex scriptis Pantaleonis Meleguli Laudensis* [Biographical Sketch of Gaffurio by Pantaleon Meleguli of Lodi]; see also Gaffurio, *De harmonia*, trans. Miller, pp. 212-214.

[115] This no longer extant volume was dedicated to Carlo Pallavicino, Bishop of Lodi; see Finscher – Kreyszig, 'Gaffurio, Franchino', p. 397.

[116] This no longer extant volume was dedicated to Lodovico Gonzaga III (died 1478). Gaffurio includes a reference to the *Flos musicae* in his *Theorica musice*, Book 5, Chapter 8, Sentence 108a; see Gaffurio, *The Theory of Music*, trans. Kreyszig, p. 179.

[117] Finscher – Kreyszig, 'Gaffurio, Franchino', 394.

[118] Walter Kreyszig, 'Research and Teaching During the Era of Musical Humanism: Defending the Scholar-Teacher in Response to the Principles of Creation and Dissemination of Knowledge in the Italian University Curriculum and Cultural Milieu of the Court of the Sforzas, with Special Reference to Franchino Gaffurio (1451-1522)', in *What is a Teacher-Scholar? – Reflecting the Scholarship of Teaching and Learning at the University of Saskatchewan: Symposium Proceedings, November 9 & 10, 2001*, ed. Ron Marken (Saskatoon, Saskatchewan: University of Saskatchewan, 2002), pp. 97-132.

[119] Kreyszig, 'Franchino Gaffurio und seine Übersetzer', pp. 164-171.

musician, that is, as a contributor to *musica theorica* and *musica practica*, including his own polyphonic repertory, largely destined for the performance at the Duomo.[120] These important facets of his biography, omitted altogether or recounted in an incomplete manner by Meleguli, include the leading of the chapel choir of the *Duomo* from 1484 until his death.[121] After Josquin des Prez's earlier term as cantor of the Duomo,[122] Gaffurio was entrusted with manifold duties, among them his participating in the singing and the teaching of the choirboys, as well as the significant restructuring of the Chapel. The latter task amounted to a reduction of the ensemble from ten to five singers, as well as a reduction of performing forces in the *schola cantorum* from thirty to some ten to fifteen singers, and finally the hiring of a *magister* or *preceptor* to oversee the instruction of the choirboys in grammar.[123]

Completely absent from Meleguli's sketch are the many activities of Gaffurio outside the borders of Milan, such as his constant contact with musicians from the Netherlands, a trip to Mantua in 1490 to second the architect Luca Paperio for important work on the *Duomo de Milan*, a number of appointments, specifically beginning in 1494 as prior of the Church of *San Marcellino*, beginning in 1495 presumably as a cleric at *Pontirolo* in Bergamo, beginning in 1497 in taking on the role as leader of the Church of Melzo, and finally on a three-month stay in Venice in 1506 in an effort to restructure the Church of *San Maria al Monte*. Of a somewhat controversial nature, providing perhaps ample enough reason for the deliberate omission by Meleguli, is Gaffurio's contact since 1489, with Bartolomeo Ramos de Pareja (ca. 1440 – after 1490) on fundamental

[120] Knud Jeppesen, 'Die 3 Gafurius-Kodizes der Fabbrica des Duomo, Milano', *Acta Musicologica*, 3 (1931), 14-28; Claudio Satori, 'Il quarto codice di Gaffurio non è del tutto scomparso', *Collectanea Historiae musicae*, 1 (1953), 25-44; Masakata Kanazawa, 'Franchino Gafori and Polyphonic Hymns', in *Traditions and Its Future in Music: Report of the SIMS, Osaka 1990*, eds. Yosihiko Tokumaru *et al*. (Tokyo-Osaka: Mita Press, 1991), pp. 95-101. For modern editions of Gaffurio's music, see, for example, *Franchinus Gaffurius: Collected Works*, ed. Lutz Finscher, Corpus Mensurabilis Musicae, 11 (Rome: American Institute of Musicology, 1960).

[121] Claudio Satori, 'Franchino Gaffurio a Milano: Nuove notizie biografiche e documenti inediti sulla sua attività die maestro di Cappella e sulla sua riforma della Cappella del Duomo', *Universitas Europae*, 1 (1952-1953), Nos. 4-5, 8-9, 11-12; idem, 'La musica nel duomo e alla corte sino alla seconda metà del '500', *Storia di Milano*, 9 (1961), 721-748.

[122] Claudio Sartori, 'Josquin des Prés, cantore del Duomo di Milano (1459-1472)', *Annales musicologiques*, 4 (1956), 55-83; see also David Fallows, 'Josquin and Milan', *Plainsong and Medieval Music*, 5 (1996), 69-80.

[123] Lora Matthews, 'Reconstruction of the Personnel of the Ducal Choir in Milan, 1480-1499', *Musica e storia*, 6 (1998), 297-312.

questions of consonances, with special emphasis on the major third and minor third[124] – an issue rather vexing to many theorists ever since the appearance of the *Liber de arte contrapuncti* (1477) by Johannes Tinctoris (ca. 1435-1511).[125] In fact, a proposal in favor of a tempered tuning articulated by Ramos de Pareja in his *De musica practica* (Bologna, 1482),[126] and that in opposition to the Pythagorean tuning handed down in the writings of Boethius,[127] led to a vehement debate,[128] at times even with polemic undertones, initially between one of Ramos de Pareja's students, Giovanni Spataro (?1458-1541) and Gaffurio, the latter who ardently defended the doctrines of Boethius, as shown in the *Theorica musice*. In subsequent years, this debate widened considerably, as became evident in a series of publications, including Giovanni Spataro's *Honesta defensio* (Bologna, 1491),[129]

[124] For an overview of the monochord division proposed by Ramos de Pareia, see Palisca, *Humanism*, pp. 232-234.

[125] Johannes Tinctoris, *De arte contrapuncti*, ed. Albert Seay, Johannes Tinctoris: Opera theoretica, 2; Corpus Scriptorum de Musica, 22 (American Institute of Musicology, 1975); *Johannes Tinctoris: The Art of Counterpoint*, ed./trans. Albert Seay, Musicological Studies and Documents, 5 (American Institute of Musicology, 1961); see also Klaus-Jürgen Sachs, *Der Contrapunctus im 14. und 15. Jahrhundert: Untersuchungen zum Teminus, zur Lehre und zu den Quellen*, Beihefte zum Archiv für Musikwissenschaft, 13 (Wiesbaden: Franz Steiner, 1974); Bonnie J. Blackburn, 'On Compositional Process in the Fifteenth Century', *Journal of the American Musicological Society*, 40 (1987), 210-284.

[126] *Bartolomeo Ramis de Pareia: Musica practica*, ed. Clement A. Miller, Musicological Studies and Documents, 44 (American Institute of Musicology and Neuhausen-Stuttgart: Hänssler-Verlag, 1993); see also *Musica practica Bartolomei Ramis de Pareia Bononiae Impressa opere et industria ac expensis magistri Baltasaris de Hisberia MCCCCLXXXII* (nach den Originaldrucken des Liceo musicale mit Genehmigung der Comune von Bologna), ed./trans. Johannes Wolf, Publikationen der Internationalen Musikgesellschaft, 2 (Leipzig: Martin Brelauer, 1901); Luanne Eris Fose, 'The "Musica practica" of Bartolomeo Ramos de Pareia: A Critical Translation and Commentary' (PhD diss. University of North Texas, 1992); Elisabetta Torselli, 'Musica practica di Bartolomeo de Pareja: Nuove edizione, traduzione in italiano, studio e commento' (PhD diss. University of Pavia, 1992).

[127] Georg Schepps, 'Zu den mathematisch-musikalischen Werken des Boethius', in *Abhandlungen aus dem Gebiet der Klassischen Altertumswissenschaft. Wilhelm Christ zum 60. Geburtstag dargebracht von seinen Schülern* (Munich, 1891); Bruno Heller, 'Boethius in Lichte der frühmittelalterlichen Musiktheorie' (PhD diss. Universität Wien, 1939); Felix von Lepel, *Die antike Musiktheorie im Lichte des Boethius: Eine Studie* (Berlin-Charlottenburg, 1958).

[128] For an overview of this lengthy debate, see Ernst Apfel, *Geschichte der Kompositionslehre: Von den Anfängen bis gegen 1700*, Taschenbücher zur Musikwissenschaft, 75-77, 3 vols (Wilhelmshaven: Heinrichshofen's Verlag, 1981), I, 127-187; see also Hüschen, 'Kritik und Polemik in der Musiktheorie des 15. Jahrhunderts', pp. 41-47.

[129] Giovanni Spataro's *Honesta defensio Bartolomaei Ramis in Nicolai Burtii Parmensis opusculum* (Bologna, 1491); also as Facsimile edition, ed. Giuseppe Vecchi, Antiquae musicae Italicae Monumenta Bononiensis, 2/1 (Bologna: Forni Editore, 1967).

the *Apologia Franchini Gafurii Musici* (Turin, 1520),[130] and finally Spataro's *Dilucide et probatissime demonstratione* (Bologna, 1521).[131]

As far as the paratexts to Gaffurio's *De harmonia* are concerned, the inclusion of some comments framed under the heading *Ad lectorem* by the French engraver of the woodcuts of the treatise, are of particular interest. Master Guilelmus le Signerre of Rouen, in reference to his woodcuts in the *De harmonia*, raises the question, in a somewhat sarcastic vein, as to the inclusion of errors in the woodcuts, presumably soliciting a negative response from his readers.[132] Indeed, the woodcut showing Gaffurio seated at the organ console, perhaps not even Master Guilelmus's work — a hypothesis based on the fact that the very same woodcut is also included in both the *Practica musicae* and the *Theorica musice*, treatises in which the engraver does not identify his work — features an inaccurate graphic representation of the organ pipes. Here, details pertaining to the different lengths of pipes as well as different diameters in the design of the pipes are absent from the illustration. In fact, such details are deliberately omitted in numerous organ illustrations, provided these graphic representations were not included to serve organ builders as organological blueprints.

The subsequent epigram by Pantaleon Meleguli[133] may be seen as a continuation of Meleguli's sketch of Gaffurio (examined earlier). In this epigram, Meleguli calls upon the readers urging them to subscribe to one or another philosophical direction, in fact providing the option of emulating Socrates (ca. 470 BC – 399 BC) or Epicurus (341 BC – 270 BC). Meleguli presumably was cognizant of the fact that the philosophies of both Socrates and Epicurus have been identified in that trilogy, for example,

[130] *Apologia Franchini Gafurii Musici adversus Joannem Spatarium et complices musicos Bononienses* (Turin, 1520).

[131] Giovanni Spataro, *Dilucide et probatissime demonstratione de Maestro Zoanne Spatario Musico Bolognese contra certe frivole et vane excusatione, da Franchino Gafurio (Maestro de li errori) in luce aducte* (Bologna, 1521); see *Dilucide et probatissime demonstratione de Maestro Zoanne Spatario, musico Bolognese, contra certe frivole et vane excusatione da Franchino Gafurio (maestro de li errori) in luce aducte*, ed./trans. Johannes Wolf, Veröffentlichungen der Musik-Bibliothek Paul Hirsch, Frankfurt am Main, 7 (Berlin: Verlag von Martin Breslauer, 1925); Palisca, *Humanism*, pp. 234-235.

[132] Gaffurio, *De harmonia*, folio 5 N verso: *Magister Gulielmus Le Signerre Rothomagensis Figurarum Celator. Ad Lectorem* [To the Reader by Master Gulielmus Le Signerre of Rouen]; see also Gaffurio, *De harmonia*, trans. Miller, p. 214.

[133] Gaffurio, *De harmonia*, folio 6 N recto: *Pantaleonis Meleguli Laudensis Epigramma. Ad Lectorem* [To the Reader: Epigram of Pantaleon Meleguli of Lodi]; see also Gaffurio, *De harmonia*, trans. Miller, p. 214.

in Book 1 of the *Theorica music*e. Towards the close of the epigram, Meleguli makes a somewhat curious allusion to the 'new mysteries of the harmonic law which must be kept secret from unexpurgated men' (lines 10-11),[134] unquestionably alerting the reader to the complex arithmetic calculations underlying the indepth examination of the Pythagorean tuning system. Unprecedented in the *De harmonia* are the unusually high number of references directly drawing in the reader. Indeed, large portions of the closing paratext of the *De harmonia*, the hendecasyllabic poem of Franciscus Phylippineus,[135] once again call upon the reader, beseeching him to read the *De harmonia* (lines 15-19) as a basis of becoming a theorist, that is, an expert in both music theory and practice — what Isidore of Seville in his *Etymologiae sive origines* had captured, perhaps idealized, in the dichotomy of the *musicus* versus the *cantor* or *phonascus*[136] and likewise Guido of Arezzo (ca. 991-2 – after 1033) in his *Regulae rhythmicae* more sharply articulated as the dichotomy of the *musicus* versus the *animal*.[137] In this Epigram, the somewhat heavy-handed discourse is framed by the more familiar and readily acceptable rehearsing, once again, of the throngs of the muses, cultivated throughout Gaffurio's music-theoretical writings.

## VI

Indeed, the paratexts of Gaffurio's trilogy become an indispensable facet of the publication squarely placed within the magic triangle of author,

[134] 'Quippe nova harmonicae capiunt mysteria legis / Quae male purgatis sunt reticenda viris'; as cited in Gaffurio, *De harmonia*. For references to Socrates, see Gaffurio, *Theorica music*e, Book 1, chapter 1, sentences 162, 200, 259, 275; chapter 3, sentence 33. For references to Epicurus, see Book 1, chapter 1, sentence 279; Book 2, chapter 4, sentence 24.

[135] Gaffurio, *De harmonia*, folio 6 N recto: *Francisci Phylippinei Endecasyllabon* [Poem of Franciscus Phyllippineus]; see also Gaffurio, *De harmonia*, trans. Miller, pp. 214-215.

[136] See Footnote 14.

[137] Guido of Arezzo, *Regulae rhythmicae*; see 'Musicae Guidonis regulae rhythmicae', ed. Martin Gerbert, in *Scriptores ecclesiastici de musica sacra potissimum ex variis Italiae, Galliae et Germaniae codicibus manuscriptis collecti et nunc primum publica luce donati*, 3 vols (Hildesheim-New York: Georg Olms, 1990 = St. Blasien, 1784), II, 25-34; *Guidonis Aretini tres tractatuli editi cum apparatu critico: Regulae dictae Rhythmicae*, ed. Joseph Smits van Waesberghe,Vol. 4 of *Divitiae Artis (Series A)* (Buren: Frits Knuf, 1985); Dolores Pesce, *Guido d'Arezzo's Regule rithmice, Prologus in antiphonarium, and Epistola ad Michaelem: A Critical Text and Translation with an Introduction, Annotations, Indices, and New Manuscript Inventories*, Wissenschaftliche Abhandlungen / Musicological Studies, 73 (Ottawa, Ontario: Institute of Mediaeval Music, 1999), pp. 330-331.

opus and audience. As far as Gaffurio's trilogy is concerned, these paratexts extend beyond the traditional bridging of the gap between the world of the book and the society of late fifteenth and early sixteenth-century Europe. The resulting exemplary collaboration between the various stakeholders identified earlier attests to the ultimate success of this publishing venture, as is readily seen in the unprecedented dissemination of the music-theoretical discourse concentrated firmly on the key issues of the contemporary debate, namely, the Greek *systema teleion*, the Guidonian modes, and the hexachord system, and at last, the compositional ideologies rooted in fifteenth- and sixteenth-century practices of the mensural system of notation. Indeed, notwithstanding an overall positive mood, these paratexts help position the three seminal treatises of Gaffurio in the larger realm of contemporary scholarship, and that in their poignant references to various important aspects of his writing, such as the grounding of the *musica disciplina* in the educational system of the *septem artes liberales*.[138] Beyond that, these paratexts also carry an important message for scholars of subsequent eras, indeed paving the way for and assuring the continuation of an ongoing healthy debate of this lively discourse surrounding the Greek and Latin systems of music theory, characterized by an all too often unfortunate dependency of the Latin system on the Greek system — a fallacy to which Gaffurio himself succumbed in his *Theorica musice*. On the whole, this debate helps to articulate, justify and perpetuate the antiquarian thinking which continued to exist and flourish side by side with the contemporary discourse focussed on more recent practices and techniques fortuitous to contrapuntal instruction.[139]

[138] This notion is forcefully expressed in iconographical depictions of the *artes liberales*; see Michael Masi, 'Boethius and the Iconography of the Liberal Arts', *Latomus*, 33 (1974), 57-75; see also Philippe Verdier, 'L'iconographie des arts libéraux dans l'art du moyen âge jusqu'à la fin du quinzième siècle', in *Arts libéraux et philosophie au moyen âge: Actes du quatrième congrès international de philosophie médiévale, Université de Montréal, Montréal, Canada, 27 août – 2 septembre 1967* (Montréal-Québec: Institut d'Études Médiévales and Paris: Librairie Philosophique J. Vrin, 1969), pp. 305-354. Further on the significance of iconography in the graphic depiction of the *theorica musicae*, see Tilman Seebass, 'The Illustration of Music Theory in the Late Middle Ages: Some Thoughts on Its Principles and a Few Examples', in *Music Theory and Its Sources: Antiquity and the Middle Ages*, ed. André Barbera, Notre Dame Conferences in Medieval Studies, 1 (Notre Dame, Indiana: University of Notre Dame Press, 1990), pp. 197-234.

[139] On the continuation of this tradition, see Claude V. Palisca, *Music and Ideas in the Sixteenth and Seventeenth Centuries*, Studies in the History of Music Theory and Literature, 1 (Urbana-Chicago, Illinois: University of Illinois Press, 2006).

With the trilogy of Gaffurio thoroughly secured as a result of scholarship mentioned earlier, the examination of the paratexts fills an important lacuna, indeed the final link that now permits us to appreciate and assess with the utmost transparency the significant connections, with all the stakeholders identified and their individual contributions considered, as each individual, depending on the level and depth of his association with the particular treatise and/or with two or rarely all three treatises, sees the theoretical opus from an ever so different perspective, often in a precarious, at times in an even ambivalent position, yet in a position which when put together in this mosaic of views and perceptions, contributes to the larger content of this trilogy, specifically to the magic triangle between author, opus, and audience.

DEPARTMENT OF MUSIC
University of Saskatchewan
CND – Saskatoon, SK S7N OX1

ZENTRUM FÜR KANADASTUDIEN
UNIVERSITÄT WIEN
A – 1090 Wien
walter.kreyszig@usask.ca

# *"ACCIPE NON NOTI PRAECLARIA VOLUMINA MUNDI"* LES DÉDICACES DU *DE ORBE NOVO* DE PIERRE MARTYR D'ANGHIERA

Brigitte Gauvin

Pierre Martyr d'Anghiera, savant italien, quitta à trente ans l'Italie pour s'installer à la cour d'Espagne où il passa le reste de son existence. Grand épistolier, il a laissé un nombre considérable de missives sur les événements d'Europe qui sont une aide précieuse pour les historiens, et, à côté de celles-ci, un ensemble de lettres, consacrées uniquement à la découverte et la conquête du Nouveau Monde, intitulé *De Orbe Nouo Decades* ou plus simplement *De Orbe Nouo*, rédigé entre 1493 et 1526, date de sa mort. Dans ces lettres, adressées à divers interlocuteurs essentiellement Italiens ou résidant en Italie, tous de haut rang, Pierre Martyr transmet les plus importantes des informations qu'il collecte en interrogeant les acteurs de la conquête du Nouveau Monde ou en lisant leurs rapports. La diversité des interlocuteurs et la succession des éditions font que l'ouvrage offre une quinzaine de dédicaces.

Il nous faut, avant de les étudier, présenter rapidement ce système complexe. En 1511 paraît la première décade, dite *Décade Océane,* précédée de la *Legatio Babilonica* et suivie des *Poemata*. La *Décade* est accompagnée d'une carte du Nouveau Monde. Dans cette édition, la *Décade Océane* comporte dix lettres, baptisés livres, et un appendice. Les lettres s'organisent comme suit: on trouve d'abord deux lettres adressées à Ascanio Sforza, rédigées en 1493 et 1494; ces lettres n'ont pas de dédicace. Viennent ensuite huit lettres, rédigées en 1500, dédiées au cardinal Louis d'Aragon, commanditaire de l'œuvre au nom de son parent le roi Frédéric III d'Aragon; au moment de l'édition, Pierre Martyr ajouta pour ce groupe de lettres une seconde dédicace au souverain Pontife Jules II. Enfin la décade se clôt sur un "appendice" adressé et dédié au comte de Tendilla. Les lettres sont précédées d'une dédicace générale de la *Décade* au comte de Tendilla, déjà dédicataire et destinataire de l'appendice. Notons pour finir que la carte fait l'objet d'une dédicace particulière au cardinal Francisco Jiménez de Cisneros, dédicataire de la *Legatio Babilonica*.

En 1516 paraît la seule édition officielle, et reconnue comme telle, publiée du vivant de Pierre Martyr. Chaque décade comporte dix lettres.

La première décade présente bon nombre de différences avec l'édition de 1511: la dédicace générale adressée au comte de Tendilla a disparu; les livres IX et X ont été réunis en un seul, qui forme le livre IX, et l'appendice est devenu le livre X, toujours adressé au comte de Tendilla; le texte diffère sur un certain nombre de passages. Les deuxième et troisième décades sont l'une et l'autre adressées et dédiées au pape Léon X; chacune possède une brève dédicace. L'ensemble formé par les trois *Décades* est précédé de plusieurs dédicaces. On trouve d'abord deux poèmes liminaires adressés au lecteur: l'un de Giovanni Ruffo, nonce apostolique, archevêque de Cosenza, l'autre de Pierre Martyr d'Anghiera lui-même. Figure ensuite une dédicace générale à Charles Quint, qui vient d'être proclamé roi de Castille. La carte est reprise, mais sans dédicace.

Enfin en 1530 paraît le *De Orbe Nouo* dans son intégralité, soit huit *Décades*. C'est une édition complète, mais posthume car Pierre Martyr d'Anghiera est mort en 1526. Les trois premières *Décades* sont identiques, à quelques points de détail près, à l'édition de 1516, et cinq autres *Décades* viennent s'y ajouter. La dédicace à Charles Quint est maintenue; le poème de Giovanni Ruffo a disparu et celui de Martyr a été modifié. La quatrième Décade est adressée et dédiée à Léon X; la cinquième est dédiée à Adrien VI mais adressée à son successeur, Clément VII. La sixième Décade est adressée et dédiée au nonce Giovanni Ruffo, intime de Clément VII. La septième Décade est adressée et dédiée à Francesco II Maria Sforza, dernier duc de Milan, la huitième au souverain pontife Clément VII lui-même.[1]

Après avoir d'abord présenté les différents niveaux de dédicaces et les liens existant entre dédicace et dédicataire, nous nous attacherons dans un second temps à comprendre quelles sont les grandes fonctions des dédicaces de Pierre Martyr, souvent inspirées des modèles antiques; enfin nous étudierons comment Pierre Martyr établit, dans ses dédicaces, une véritable fiche d'identité de l'œuvre au travers de laquelle transparaît, parfois, son propre portrait.

## Nature des dédicaces et statut des dédicataires

Les nombreuses dédicaces du *De Orbe Nouo* ne sont pas toutes sur le même plan: elles diffèrent en effet par leur nature et par l'ampleur de

[1] Voir le tableau joint en annexe.

l’œuvre à laquelle elles sont attachées. Or le choix des dédicataires et le contenu de la dédicace semblent étroitement liés à l’importance de l’œuvre dédiée.

Il existe d’une part un premier type de dédicace situé au commencement de chaque Décade. A deux exceptions près, chacune s’ouvre donc le plus souvent sur une dédicace assez brève au destinataire de la décade. Les exceptions sont constituées par la première et la cinquième décades: la première possède trois destinataires différents, voire quatre si l’on prend en compte le fait que les livres 3 à 10 de la *Décade Océane* étaient dédiés à la fois à Jules II et à Louis d’Aragon: Ascanio Sforza, Louis d’Aragon et le pape Jules II et le comte de Tendilla. Parmi ces quatre destinataires, le premier n’a pas de dédicace, et c’est un cas unique dans le *De Orbe Nouo*. Sans doute est-ce parce que Pierre Martyr, au départ, n’a pas conçu les lettres sur les terres nouvellement découvertes comme vraiment séparées du reste de sa correspondance avec Ascanio Sforza, et qu’il n’était absolument pas sûr que les événements confirmeraient son désir d’élaborer une œuvre nouvelle consacrée au Nouveau Monde. La cinquième Décade présente une autre particularité: l’en-tête offre la Décade au souverain pontife Adrien VI, mais dès la première ligne du texte de la dédicace Pierre Martyr s’adresse à Clément VII, successeur d’Adrien VI tout juste décédé, tout en signalant qu’il laisse intentionnellement l’en-tête.[2] On peut y voir la volonté de rendre hommage à un prélat qu’il avait fréquenté, avant son élection, à la cour d’Espagne, quand il était encore Adrien d’Utrecht.

D’autre part, Martyr surimpose à chaque groupe de lettres ou de décades prêt à être édité une dédicace générale, qui adresse à un prestigieux destinataire l’ensemble de l’ouvrage et qui s’ajoute aux dédicaces particulières de chaque *Décade*. Ici, au fur et à mesure que l’œuvre se développe,

[2] ‘Ad Adrianum Sextum Pontificem Maximum eiusdem Petri Martyris Anglerii Mediolanensis quinta decas caput primum [...]. Quam [quintam decadem] Adriano Pontifici Maximo praedecessori tuo inscripseram; cum et ille fato functus sit ante receptionem, tu, vt dignitatis illius, ita meorum laborum heres esto erisque posthac omnium rerum si quid dignum historica lectione a me scribetur’ (VI). Sauf mention contraire, les passages figurant en note ne sont extraits que des dédicaces. Le chiffre entre parenthèses indique à quelle Décade appartient la dédicace citée. Nous ajoutons des précisions d’édition et de livre, si besoin est, pour les trois premières Décades. Pour tous les textes extraits de la *Décade Océane*, nous renvoyons à notre édition, Pierre Martyr d’Anghiera, *De Orbe Nouo Decades*, I: *Oceanea Decas / Décades du Nouveau Monde*, I: *La Décade Océane suivie du Quatrième Voyage de Christophe Colomb*. Edition, traduction et commentaire de Brigitte Gauvin, Les Classiques de l’Humanisme (Paris: Les Belles Lettres, 2003); nous la désignons simplement par ‘Martyr’.

le destinataire change: en 1511 l'édition ne comporte qu'une seule Décade, baptisée *Décade Océane*, dédiée au comte de Tendilla; en 1516, trois Décades, dédiées à Charles Quint; en 1530, huit Décades, soit le *De Orbe Nouo* dans son intégralité, de nouveau dédiées à Charles Quint: il est difficile de commenter significativement ce dernier cas dans la mesure où 1530 est une édition posthume, pour laquelle les éditeurs se sont contentés de reprendre la dédicace. Rappelons simplement que les dédicataires d'un ensemble de lettres ou de décades sont parmi les personnages les plus prestigieux de l'entourage de Pierre Martyr au moment de la publication, et que les dédicaces qui leur sont adressées sont plus longues que les autres.

Ensuite, on trouve dans les éditions de 1516 et 1530 des poèmes qui précèdent la dédicace au destinataire prestigieux et qui font entrer en scène un autre destinataire: le lecteur.[3] Ces poèmes, seules manifestations poétiques dans les *Décades*, apparaissent comme les pièces les plus fragiles des dédicaces: ils sont absents de l'édition de 1511, apparaissent dans celle de 1516, mais l'édition posthume de 1530 ne reprend qu'un des deux poèmes; encore ne le laisse-t-elle pas intact puisqu'elle en modifie les trois premiers vers. Leur seul objet semble être d'annoncer au lecteur les merveilles qui l'attendent, et, pour le texte de Giovanni Ruffo, d'en remercier l'auteur.

Enfin, la carte qui accompagne l'édition de 1511 présente un phénomène particulier: contrairement à ce qu'y annonce Pierre Martyr, elle n'est pas à la fin (*in calce*) de la *Décade Océane* mais avant elle, soit juste après la *Legatio Babilonica*, qui précède la *Décade* dans l'édition de 1511; plus étonnant encore, elle est dédiée au cardinal Jiménez de Cisneros, grand inquisiteur de Castille, qui est également le dédicataire de la *Legatio*, mais n'a jamais eu de lien avec les *Décades*. La place de la dédicace

[3] 'Ioannes Rufus Foroliuiensis Archiepiscopus Consentinus Legatus Apostolicus ad Lectorem De Orbe Nouo: Accipe non noti praeclara volumina mundi / Oceani et magnas noscito, lector, opes. / Plurima debetur Typhis tibi gratia, gentes / Ignotas et aues qui uehis Orbe Nouo. / Magna quoque autori referenda est gratia nostro / Qui facit haec cunctis regna videnda locis; Autor: Siste pedem, lector: breuibus compacta libellis / Haec lege, principibus uariis Decimoque Leoni / Pontifici Summo inscripta. Hic noua multa uidebis / Oceani magnas terras, vasta aequora, linguas / Hactenus ignotas, atque aurea saecula nosces / Et gentes nudas, expertes seminis atri / Mortiferi nummi populisque auroque feracem / Torrentem zonam. Parcat veneranda vetustas' (1516). 'AUTOR: Accipito haec, lector, breuibus compacta libellis. / Principibus variis scripta. Hic noua multa uidebis: / Oceani ingentes terras, vasta aequora, linguas / Hactenus ignotas, atque aurea saecula nosces / Et gentes nudas, expertes seminis atri / Mortiferi nummi gemmisque auroque feracem / Torrentem zonam. Parcat veneranda vetustas' (1530): cf. Martyr, p. 13.

comme le choix du dédicataire sont étranges. Le contenu de la dédicace se limite à un commentaire descriptif de la carte qui suit.

Ces différences entre les dédicaces font que tous les destinataires n'ont pas le même statut. Il existe en effet un lien très net entre le statut du destinataire, le contenu de l'envoi et celui de la dédicace qui l'accompagne. Rappelons rapidement quels liens unissent Martyr et ses dédicataires: dans la première Décade on trouve le cardinal Ascanio Sforza qui avait été son protecteur à la cour de Milan; il ne l'a pas revu après avoir quitté l'Italie, mais lui a écrit par la suite, avec une très grande régularité, pour l'informer des événements d'Espagne. Le cardinal Louis d'Aragon, en visite à la cour d'Espagne où il accompagne sa tante, la reine de Naples Juana, veuve de Ferdinand Ier, à l'occasion du mariage de sa fille, est un parent du roi d'Espagne et du roi de Naples Frédéric III d'Aragon: c'est au nom de celui-ci qu'il commande la suite de la Décade abandonnée, qu'il emportera avec lui. Enfin le comte de Tendilla, dédicataire de la dernière lettre et de la Décade dans son ensemble, fut à Rome le représentant des Rois Catholiques et c'est à cette occasion qu'il proposa à Pierre Martyr de venir avec lui en Espagne. Il fut un des grands combattants de la *Reconquista*, devint vice-roi de la province de Grenade après qu'elle eut été reprise aux Maures et commandant de la ville. C'est lui qui a envisagé de faire une publication officielle des *Décades* de Martyr. Les trois premiers dédicataires sont donc des proches de Martyr. Mais à partir de la deuxième Décade, c'est-à-dire après le succès de la première édition de 1511, Martyr n'adressa plus ses *Décades*, à une exception près, qu'à des personnages extrêmement prestigieux et toujours plus éloignés de lui: les papes, de préférence, Léon X, Adrien VI puis Clément VII, le roi Charles Quint, et, à défaut, le dernier duc de Milan, Francesco II Maria Sforza.

Il y a donc dans l'ensemble une très grande homogénéité de statut entre les dédicataires qui se répartissent en deux groupes, avant et après la première publication. On peut cependant noter deux exceptions. Un des destinataires l'emporte sur les autres: c'est le roi Charles Quint, choisi dès son avènement comme le destinataire de l'édition de 1516, donc d'un groupe de Décades, ce qui constitue un honneur particulier. De plus, on peut constater que la dédicace qui lui est consacrée est deux fois plus longue que les autres; Pierre Martyr, et c'est la seule fois, y raconte sa propre histoire; il expose ses sentiments sur sa nation d'origine et sa patrie d'accueil et termine sur une accumulation d'apostrophes hyperboliques qu'on ne retrouve, à un degré moindre, que dans la dédicace générale de la première Décade pour l'édition de 1511, au comte de Tendilla. A l'inverse, la sixième Décade est la seule qui soit dédiée à un personnage de rang secondaire, le nonce apostolique Giovanni Ruffo, évêque de Cosenza, ami de Martyr, cité dans d'autres dédicaces comme intermédiaire, auteur d'un des poèmes qui ouvrent l'édition de 1516. La dédicace ne cache pas les raisons de ce choix: Clément VII n'a pas répondu à l'offre faite par Martyr lorsqu'il lui a adressé la cinquième décade; Giovanni Ruffo n'est qu'un destinataire de substitution, chargé d'offrir la décade à Clément VII. Or non seulement la sixième Décade est cinq fois plus courte que toutes les autres, mais c'est le seul cas où le nom du dédicataire ne figure pas dans l'en-tête de la dédicace: seul apparaît le titre du destinataire véritable.[4] Il est donc patent que Pierre Martyr associe soigneusement chaque dédicataire à l'œuvre qu'il offre.

Le *De Orbe Nouo* présente donc, si on prend en compte les trois premières éditions, une quinzaine de dédicaces dont la plupart constitue un ensemble homogène par la forme comme par le fond. Attachons-nous désormais à étudier en quoi elles possèdent des fonctions et des éléments très traditionnels, voire conventionnels.

## Des dédicaces aux fonctions traditionnelles

Si Martyr reprend les caractéristiques habituelles des dédicaces et préfaces de l'Antiquité classique et, plus encore, de l'Antiquité tardive[5], tout cependant, dans ces figures imposées, est centré sur un même objectif: mettre en valeur l'œuvre et son contenu, pour inciter le dédicataire à la lecture.

Nous pouvons constater tout d'abord que l'auteur et le destinataire ne constituent dans les dédicaces que des figures mineures. De fait, sans être tout à fait absent, Pierre Martyr apparaît peu dans ses dédicaces. Son nom, son origine et ses qualités figurent dans l'en-tête de chaque dédicace, mais il ne parle que peu de lui par la suite, si l'on omet l'exception que constitue la dédicace à Charles Quint. L'allusion à des problèmes de santé semble purement conventionnelle.[6] L'évocation de sa tâche au sein

[4] 'Archiepiscopo Consentino praebenda Pontifici Petri Martyris Anglerii Mediolanensis sexta decas' *(VI)*.

[5] Nous reprenons ici, sur un certain nombre de points, les analyses menées par Tore Janson dans son ouvrage *Latin prose prefaces. Studies in literary conventions*, Studia Latina Stockholmiensia, 13 (Stockholm: Almqvist och Wiksell, 1964).

[6] 'Inter rerum angustias et valetudinarium hos me conscribere coegeris' (I, 3, cf. Martyr, p. 63); 'Laborabam tunc ego vti nosti aduersa valetudine' (I, 10, cf. Martyr, p. 221).

du conseil des Indes reste également unique[7], ainsi que l'expression d'un manque de goût pour la copie qui l'amène à chercher des secrétaires compétents.[8] On ne connaît guère mieux ses destinataires. Par deux fois, Martyr indique que son œuvre procurera une détente à ses destinataires accablés de soucis et de responsabilités.[9] Pour les destinataires en charge de fonctions politiques, Martyr rappelle leurs titres (la dédicace générale au comte de Tendilla commence ainsi par une énumération pompeuse des qualités et titres de celui-ci[10] et la dédicace à Charles Quint se termine par une envolée lyrique consacrée à la puissance du souverain[11]), tandis que pour les membres de l'Eglise il fait plutôt mention des qualités de pouvoir et de l'étendue de la puissance pontificale. Léon X est célébré en une phrase pour son autorité, Clément VII pour sa clémence et son ascendance morale, mais cela ne va jamais plus loin que des généralités. Dans tous les cas, il précise les liens de parenté des destinataires entre eux, s'il en existe, ou entre le destinataire et d'illustres personnages. Enfin, dans toutes les dédicaces aux papes, comme dans celle à Charles Quint, Martyr souligne que la découverte du Nouveau Monde est synonyme, pour ses dédicataires comme pour ce qu'ils représentent, d'un prodigieux accroissement de puissance.[12] Tous ces procédés font que l'attention du lecteur n'est pas centrée sur les deux acteurs de la correspondance.

[7] 'In nostro rerum Indicarum regio senatu' (IV).

[8] 'Rari quippe docti scriptores in hac vestra curia. Ego namque ineptum figo caracterem et negligenter quae semel chartae commendaui mea dextra repingo. Est ingenio meo non mediocriter durum bis rem eandem exarare' (dédicace au comte de Tendilla, 1511, cf. Martyr, p. 267).

[9] 'Suasitque vt Oceaneae Decadis meae libellos quos ipse manu habuit dispersos colligerem ad tuamque Sanctitatem exemplar eorum mitterem vt, si quando per otium liceat, Tua Sanctitas queat animum tanta mole negotiorum pressum noua lectione reficere' (I, 3, dédicace à Jules II, 1511, cf. Martyr, p. 289); 'inter tot rerum procellas, quibus Excellentia Tua concutitur, fore gratissimum leuamen curarum semel atque iterum iureiurando professus est' (VII).

[10] 'Bello paceque insignis comes, et prime a Mauris eiectis Granatensis arcis praefecte ac regni ipsius, vt hispane loquar, capitanee generalis, salue!' (dédicace au comte de Tendilla, 1511, cf. Martyr, p. 267).

[11] 'Veni ergo veni, Rex electe a superis ad nondum ab hominibus intellectum rerum aliquod culmen, veni et propera [...] hinc, hinc tenelle Rex clarissime instrumenta quibus totus tibi pareat orbis, comparabuntur' (dédicace à Charles Quint, cf. Martyr, p. 7).

[12] 'Quibus per Christophorum Colonum conciuem suum regiis auspiciis tam vasta littora incognita hactenus fuisse reperta conspiciet, vbi christiana religio quae Tuae Beatitudinis humeris inhaeret iam creuit in immensum in diesque magis atque magis coalescet' (I, 3, dédicace à Jules II, 1511, cf. Martyr, p. 289); 'petieruntque a me cum suo, tum Sanctitatis Tuae nomine, vt quae post ea tempora reperta sunt scriptis superadderem sibique exemplar ad Beatitudinem Tuam mittendum traderem, quo intelligat quantum, nostra

Si l'auteur et le destinataire n'ont guère d'importance, Martyr affecte de ne pas en attribuer davantage à la forme et au style de son ouvrage. On peut remarquer d'ailleurs que Martyr ne donne pas à ses dédicaces, textes programmatiques s'il en est, l'éclat qui caractérise les dédicaces antiques. Elles apparaissent même comme un peu bâclées.

Cela est immédiatement visible dans le manque total d'originalité qui caractérise la composition des dédicaces. Comme c'est le cas chez les auteurs chrétiens des IVème-Vème siècles, la préface et la dédicace se confondent. La préface épistolaire marque alors une nette séparation avec le corps de l'œuvre elle-même. Cette fusion entre la dédicace et la préface amène Pierre Martyr à faire de ses dédicaces un lieu de présentation de l'œuvre dont la composition est plutôt conventionnelle. Le plan le plus fréquent est le suivant: une en-tête présentant le dédicataire et l'auteur; les raisons pour lesquelles Pierre Martyr écrit une nouvelle Décade (ou donne une suite aux lettres précédentes) et ses motivations; les circonstances excusant un éventuel retard; l'histoire de l'œuvre et la succession des dédicataires; une brève présentation du contenu de la décade; l'affirmation que les découvertes, par leur grandeur et leurs richesses, entraîneront un accroissement du pouvoir du dédicataire et de ce qu'il représente. Dans ces éléments, présents dans toutes les dédicaces, le dernier est le plus original, et c'est sur le sujet de l'œuvre qu'il attire l'attention, c'est-à-dire sur le Nouveau Monde.

Un autre élément témoigne d'une certaine négligence. Si nous n'avons guère le temps d'étudier ici le style de l'auteur, nous pouvons au moins remarquer que Martyr reprend les mêmes images, les mêmes thèmes, voire les mêmes phrases d'une dédicace à l'autre: l'image des Néréides apparaît plusieurs fois[13], ainsi que celle de la fortune qui de mère bienveillante se change en marâtre[14], le réveil de l'écrivain assoupi par un

tempestate, foelicibus Hispanorum regum auspiciis, et humano generi decoris et militanti ecclesiae augmenti accesserit' (II); 'attentas nobis aures Tua Sanctitas praebeat et quae illis passim in re tanta euenerint serena fronte et gaudenti pectore suscipiat, quandoquidem non centurias solum et legiones sed innumeras hominum natio haec Hispana per uarios labores et multa uitae discrimina tuo sacro throno subdendas domat myriades' (III); cf. aussi note 32.

[13] 'Sed cum eruditos amice, detractores inuide, mordaces rabide in nostras formosas Nereides Oceaneas spumantia tela detorquere praesenties' (I, 3, dédicace à Louis d'Aragon, cf. Martyr, p. 63); 'vulgaribus ego tegminibus, quod sericea uel auro intexta non assequar, venustissimas amiciui Nereides, Oceani dico gemmatas insulas ab orbis initio latentes' (VIII).

[14] 'Per epistolas diarias quae gerebantur Ascanio Mariae Sfortiae Vicecomiti Cardinali Vicecancellario roganti per literas significabam. Fortuna eius ex benigna matre mutata in

ordre sans discussion[15], l'association de la chute d'Ascanio Sforza et de la perte de l'envie d'écrire[16], l'allusion à la lecture des dédicaces comme source de détente[17], la dédicace comme moyen de rendre célèbre celui qui l'a poussé à écrire[18] et d'autres encore.

Autre manifestation de cette désinvolture par rapport à la forme, Pierre Martyr ne manque pas de dénigrer son travail. Ce thème, déjà très présent dans les dédicaces en littérature classique, s'est amplifié dans la littérature chrétienne. Martyr quant à lui adopte une approche originale en insistant d'emblée sur la nécessité de distinguer le contenu de l'œuvre et sa forme.[19]

Pour commencer, Martyr a recours à toute sorte d'arguments pour expliquer les faiblesses de son œuvre, mais tous sont traditionnels, comme dans sa dédicace au cardinal d'Aragon, lorsqu'il allègue à la fois sa santé précaire et le peu de temps que lui a laissé son commanditaire pour rédiger les huit lettres qui complètent la première Décade.[20] Par ailleurs, de même que Macrobe[21] ou les panégyristes[22] insistaient sur le fait que le latin n'était pas leur langue maternelle et mettaient en avant leur origine provinciale pour s'excuser à l'avance de la *rusticitas* de leur langue, Martyr recourt à un argument proche lorsqu'il insiste sur le fait qu'il est

nouercam, cessi a scribendo' (dédicace à Charles Quint, cf. Martyr, p. 5); 'Rex Federicus, priusquam ex blanda matre in saeuam nouercam fortuna eius mutaretur' (VII).

15 'Fratre Ludouico a Gallis Mediolano eiecto, cuius autoritas torpescere me non sinebat' (I, 10, cf. Martyr, p. 219); 'Quem tu nunc tuique inclyti patrui Regis Federici literae ad me directae excussistis' (I, 3, dédicace à Louis d'Aragon, cf. Martyr, p. 63); 'apostolici nuncii summi Pontificis Leonis Decimi nomine, varii post eum principes, vt infra dicemus, dormitantem excitarunt' (dédicace à Charles Quint, cf. Martyr, p. 5, note 2); 'Donec me, Federici regis nomine, Ludouicus Aragonius [...] excitauit' (I, 3, dédicace à Jules II, cf. Martyr, p. 289).

16 'Quo cadente decidit et mihi animus a scribendo' (I, 3, dédicace à Louis d'Aragon et dédicace à Jules II, 1511, p. 63, 289); 'haud secus mihi fortuna detorsit ingenium a scribendo, atque Ascanium deturbauit a potentia. Cessit a suadendo ille procellis agitatus, cessit et mihi feruor ista perquirendi' (I, 10, cf. Martyr, p. 219); 'per epistolas diarias quae gerebantur Ascanio Mariae Sfortiae Vicecomiti Cardinali Vicecancellario roganti per literas significabam. Fortuna eius ex benigna matre mutata in nouercam, cessi a scribendo' (dédicace à Charles Quint, cf. Martyr, p. 5); 'Ascanio vita functo, ac me in desidiam, nemine stimulante, prolapso' (VII).

17 Cf. note 25.

18 'Ad quem epistulam, quae adest, conscripsi, vt qui me ad scribendum agitarent noscerentur' (I, 3, dédicace à Jules II, 1511, cf. Martyr, p. 289).

19 'Rem, non picturam, degustate' (I, 3, dédicace à Louis d'Aragon, cf. Martyr, p. 63).

20 Cf. note 14.

21 Macr. *Sat.* 1. pref. 11-13.

22 Janson, *Latin prose prefaces*, pp. 131-132.

né à Milan, qu'il a passé toute sa vie loin de Rome et qu'il ne peut donc se targuer de la maîtrise dont font preuve les *Latinissimi uiri* romains.[23]

Par ailleurs, certaines images visent à montrer que son talent n'est pas adapté au sujet qu'il traite.[24] S'il compare le Nouveau Monde à des Néréides, Martyr déplore de n'avoir su leur tailler que des vêtements ordinaires là où il eût fallu les soieries et les brocarts d'un Cicéron[25], et quand il le compare à une pierre précieuse, c'est pour dire qu'il l'a mal sertie.[26] Martyr lui-même se compare à un *stultus Phaeton*, dénigrant ainsi la forme et le style de l'œuvre sans toutefois jeter le discrédit sur son sujet.

Enfin, plusieurs autres procédés empruntés aux dédicaces antiques visent à faire acte d'humilité. Dans sa dédicace générale de 1511, adressée au comte de Tendilla, Martyr assure ne pas vouloir d'une édition qui l'exposerait aux attaques et demande la permission de n'écrire que pour le comte, qui lui suffit comme lecteur.[27] C'est dans la même perspective qu'il feint d'accepter à contre-cœur la charge qu'on lui impose, tout en affirmant savoir qu'il va faire la démonstration de son incompétence, et qu'il indique au destinataire que celui-ci partagera la responsabilité de l'échec annoncé de l'œuvre. Ces deux motifs conjugués apparaissent très clairement dans la dédicace au Cardinal Louis d'Aragon: contraint de céder à la demande pressante du roi Frédéric, transmise par Louis d'Aragon, Martyr, dans un premier temps, présente les critiques qu'il ne manquera pas de recevoir; puis, immédiatement après, il charge Louis d'Aragon de le défendre en expliquant aux détracteurs les circonstances dans lesquelles il a obligé Martyr à écrire.[28] L'affirmation selon laquelle

[23] 'Ascripturine sint ignorantiae, an incuriae plaeraque similia Latinissimi viri qui Adrianum incolunt aut Lygusticum, si ad eorum manus nostra deuenerint aliquando, vti primam Decadem vidimus nobis inconsultis impressorum prelis suppositam, neutro cruciari statuo ad summum, voloque sciant me Insubrem esse, non Latium et longe a Latio natum, quia Mediolani, et longissime vitam egisse, quia in Hispania' (II,7).

[24] Cf. Cic. *Arch.* 1, 1.

[25] 'Ciceronianos optassent haec talia tantaque spiritus, vti saepe in priorum discursu protestatus sum, vulgaribus ego tegminibus, quod sericea uel auro intexta non assequar, venustissimas amiciui Nereides, Oceani dico gemmatas insulas ab orbis initio latentes' (VIII).

[26] 'Pretiosum hunc lapillum plumbo inepte circundatum ambo accipietis' (I, 3, dédicace à Louis d'Aragon, cf. Martyr, p. 63).

[27] 'Nobis ista seruaremus cuperem, tum quia minoris fient si communia, tum etiam quia inepta incultaque' (Dédicace au comte de Tendilla, 1511, cf. Martyr, p. 221). On retrouve cette attitude chez Sulpice Sévère ou Jérôme (Janson, *Latin prose prefaces*, pp. 138-139).

[28] 'Sed cum eruditos amice, detractores inuide, mordaces rabide in nostras formosas Nereides Oceaneas spumantia tela detorquere praesenties, quam breui spatio, inter rerum angustias et valetudinarium hos me conscribere coegeris ingenue profiteberis' (I, 3, dédicace à Louis d'Aragon, cf. Martyr, p. 63).

il n'écrit pas pour faire œuvre d'historien mais pour éviter que ne se perde une précieuse matière première qui pourra être utile à d'autres[29], l'emploi du terme *libellos* qui revient assez souvent, ainsi que l'allusion aux veilles nocturnes au cours desquelles Martyr rédige son ouvrage[30] sont autant de procédés traditionnels de dépréciation.

Cependant, contrairement à nombre d'écrivains de la littérature tardive, et plus particulièrement de la littérature chrétienne, Pierre Martyr limite son autocritique à son œuvre, et encore ne concerne-t-elle que les aspects stylistiques de celle-ci. On ne trouve jamais par exemple les termes *mediocritas mea*, si fréquents dans la littérature chrétienne[31], et jamais le contenu de l'œuvre n'est dévalorisé, bien au contraire. Quand à la critique du style, elle est atténuée par les violentes attaques de Pierre Martyr contre les érudits romains, accusés d'avoir figé le latin. Selon le chroniqueur, limiter le latin au modèle cicéronien ne permet en aucun cas de rendre compte des réalités du temps, à moins de pratiquer une langue aussi imprécise qu'amphigourique. Il plaide au contraire pour un latin vivant et adapté à son époque, pour un latin qui n'ait pas peur des néologismes. Et, faisant de son œuvre un petit laboratoire linguistique, il introduit toutes sortes de termes vernaculaires, espagnols ou indigènes, dans le latin, justifiant crânement les néologismes dont se gaussent, dit-il, les érudits romains.[32]

Cependant, ainsi que l'a bien montré Tore Janson, toutes ces critiques ne sont finalement qu'un procédé supplémentaire pour attirer l'attention sur le contenu de l'œuvre.[33] Martyr procède de la même manière: après avoir détourné l'attention du lecteur de lui-même, du destinataire, et de la forme, il l'amène à s'intéresser à ce qui est pour lui l'essentiel: le sujet

[29] 'Satis rebus ipsis factum uideatur ut tua causa inuigilauerimus ne perirent' (III, 9).

[30] 'A vigiliis' (Dédicace au comte de Tendilla, 1511, cf. Martyr, p. 267); 'nunc vero meas vigilias ad Beatitudinem tuam destinaturus' (VIII).

[31] Janson, *Latin prose prefaces*, p. 125.

[32] 'Dico gossipium id lanuginis genus quod alias bombycinum appellatione vulgari Itala dixi. [...] Idem velim dictum genuinis Adriaticis siue Lygusticis Latio propioribus de Bergantinis, de Carauellis et Almiranto Adelantoque vulgari appellatione Hispana. Me quippe non latet Graecissantes Architalassum, Latinissantes simul et Graecissantes Nauarchum hos, Pontarchum illos garrire dici debere magistratus eius principem. De ceteris huiusmodi idem, dummodo tuae Sanctitati satisfactum iri credam hac simplici mea de tantis inuentis narratione' (II, 7); voir à ce sujet l'article de Martine Furno, 'Marques et limites de la modernité: l'insertion de mots latins dans quelques textes de Pedro Martir d'Angleria', à paraître dans les actes du colloque 'Humanismo y pervivienca del mundo clasico, IV', Alcañiz, 9-14 mai 2005.

[33] Janson, *Latin prose prefaces*, pp. 127-130, 133-134.

de ses écrits. Nous nous attacherons simplement à étudier trois procédés qui contribuent à cet effet.

D'une part, Martyr modifie la tradition selon laquelle l'écrivain assure n'écrire qu'à la demande d'un commanditaire. Ce motif, présent au début, laisse peu à peu la place à un second qui l'emporte sur le premier: c'est l'arrivée d'informations nouvelles et de bonne qualité en provenance du Nouveau Monde qu'il faut exploiter avant qu'elles se perdent. On trouve cet argument dans les décades III, IV, V, VI[34]. En montrant ainsi qu'il écrit non seulement à la demande mais aussi quand survient l'occasion d'améliorer son ouvrage, Pierre Martyr fait comprendre que l'œuvre est plus importante que le destinataire. C'est aussi de cette manière qu'il souligne ce qui fait le prix de son œuvre: celle-ci apporte des informations récentes, nombreuses, obtenues auprès des acteurs même de la découverte, et par ailleurs élaguées, ramenées à l'essentiel de ce qu'il faut savoir pour comprendre le déroulement de la conquête et ses enjeux.

D'autre part, une image particulière, presque un lapsus, révèle elle aussi cette fierté: dans la dernière Décade, dédiée et adressée au souverain pontife Clément VII, Pierre Martyr, pour justifier le fait que Clément VII ne vienne qu'après une longue série de destinataires, compare la huitième Décade au souverain Pontife qui s'avance après que de nombreux prélats lui ont ouvert la marche. Mais par cette métaphore Martyr ramène toute l'attention sur l'œuvre, et le souverain Pontife n'est plus qu'un comparant.[35]

Enfin la manière dont il parle du Nouveau Monde dans son poème, dans ses dédicaces, notamment celle à Charles Quint, le lyrisme débridé auquel il s'abandonne de manière tout à fait exceptionnelle confirme tout l'enthousiasme qu'il ressent devant la découverte et la fierté presque paternelle qu'il éprouve à la faire connaître.[36]

[34] 'Clauseram Orbi nouo portas, Beatissime Pater, satisque me per illius oras vagatum arbitrabar, quando nouae litterae allatae patefacere illas iterum et repositum sumere calamum coegerunt' (III); 'in nostro rerum Indicarum regio senatu, grauidae ambagibus epistolae ab ineptis quibusque missae quotidie legebantur, e quibus succi parum colligebamus' (IV); 'postea vero aliae a Fernando Cortesio, Caesaris classis praefecto, venerunt litterae ab illis terris, quas Hispanae tunc ditioni subigebat, in quibus res nouae et inauditae maximeque mirabiles continentur' (V); 'nunc ab Aegidio Gonsalo litteras habemus post biennium sub data ex Hispaniola illorum tractuum regia, pridie nonas Martii MDXXIIII' (VI).

[35] 'Nunc vero meas vigilias ad Beatitudinem Tuam destinaturus, operae pretium fore ratus sum, si haec praesentia praeteritorum exemplaribus, licet alteri dicatis, muniero, vti solet antistitum et purpuratorum ecclesiae principum caterua gradientem anteire pontificem, ita ducalis haec viam aperiet' (VIII).

[36] 'Sed pace maiorum dictum velim, quicquid ab initio mundi gestum scriptumque reperio, meo iudicio, parum est, si pensitauerimus, quas tibi, Rex potentissime, nouas

## Une carte d’identité de l’œuvre

Cependant ces différentes fonctions restent traditionnelles, et ce n’est pas là qu’il faut chercher l’originalité des dédicaces de Pierre Martyr. Si singularité il y a, c’est bien plutôt dans la manière dont Martyr fait partager à son destinataire l’histoire de l’œuvre et sa fabrication, tout en lui fournissant des éléments pour comprendre le contexte très spécifique dans lequel elle s’élabore.

L’histoire de l’œuvre commence par sa naissance. Dans la plus pure tradition classique, Martyr justifie systématiquement son activité d’épistolier et présente souvent son œuvre comme la réponse à une demande. C’est le cas dans les dédicaces à Louis d’Aragon[37], au comte de Tendilla[38], à Léon X[39], à Giovanni Ruffo[40], à Clément VII[41]. Il utilise toute la gamme des termes de sollicitation, des plus neutres (*hortor*) aux plus impérieux

terras, quae noua maria, quas uarias nationes et linguas, quales aurifodinas, quae margaritarum uiuaria, prouentibus aliis omissis, tibi pararunt. Quae qualia quantaque sunt tres hae meae decades patefacient. [...] Aequinoctialem tibi circulum latentem hactenus, et furentem atque ardore solis adustam antiquorum opinione zonam, paucis exceptis, tibi paratam habemus, populis refertissimam, amoenam, vberem, fortunatissimam, auro et candentibus margaritis coronatas mille insulas, et vno putatu continenti tres Europas offeremus. Veni nouum orbem amplexurus, nec tui nos desiderio vlterius macerato. Hinc, hinc, tenelle rex clarissime, instrumenta quibus totus tibi pareat orbis comparabuntur’ (dédicace à Charles Quint, cf. Martyr, p. 7).

[37] ‘Petis iterum vt Phoebaeos currus ineptus Phaeton gubernet [...] Nouum, vt ita dixerim, terrarum orbem [...] qui hactenus latitabat repertum, vt ego describam Federici Regis inclyti patrui tibi mihi litteras de hac re ostendens imperas’ (I, 3, dédicace à Louis d’Aragon; cf. Martyr, p. 63).

[38] ‘Distuli ad te mittere operum in mea officina tam libero quam irretito pede decussorum exemplaria quae per litteras te diu cupisse mihi significasti’ (dédicace au comte de Tendilla, 1511, cf. Martyr, p. 267); ‘nunc vero quandoquidem tu exemplar integrum meorum operum extorquere a me fueris conatus’ (I, 10, cf. Martyr, p. 221).

[39] ‘Nouae narrationis licet male comptae amore pellecti rem commendarunt petieruntque a me cum suo, tum Sanctitatis Tuae nomine, vt quae post ea tempora reperta sunt scriptis superadderem sibique exemplar ad beatitudinem Tuam mittendum traderem’ (II); ‘Beatissime Pater, Aegidius Viterbiensis Augustinianae professionis Eremitarum et sacri ordinis Cardinei lucidum exemplar, legatione sua functus a latere, discedens ex Hispania, Sanctitatis Tuae suoque nomine imperatum mihi reliquit, vt quae praegnans Oceanus pareret, post tres meas Decades, iam pridem ad Sanctitatem tuam missas, conscriberem’ (IV).

[40] ‘Quibus inter caetera inquis Summum Pontificem Claementem his significationibus non minus delectari, quam Leonem patruelem aut Adrianum praedecessores, per suas breues membranas imperantes mihi vt ea conscriberem’ (VI).

[41] ‘Beatissime Pater, ab anulo piscatoris de more, Pontificum habui membraneum a Beatitudine Tua diploma: duobus id concluditur capitibus, de rebus ex orbe nouo ad suos praedecessores a me directo vno laudatiuo, imperatiuo altero, ne patiar ab obliuionis vasto hiatu caetera quae successerunt absorberi’ (VIII).

(*impero*), mais, conformément à la tradition tardive[42], ce sont les termes les plus forts qui l'emportent progressivement. Grâce à ce procédé, Martyr présente la rédaction de son œuvre comme une manifestation de respect et d'obéissance dans laquelle n'entre aucun désir de gloire personnelle, tout en rehaussant l'autorité et le pouvoir de son dédicataire. La demande est plusieurs fois présentée comme incontournable.[43] Cette manière de faire amène Martyr à se montrer comme partagé entre son désir personnel, qui serait de ne pas écrire[44], et la demande parfois impérative de son destinataire.

Cependant l'insistance sur ces demandes est telle que l'on ne peut se contenter d'y voir un simple artifice rhétorique. Martyr insiste plus que les auteurs tardifs sur ce point, et il rappelle constamment qu'il a besoin d'être aiguillonné, sollicité pour écrire, affirmant même à plusieurs reprises que la poursuite de l'œuvre est strictement liée à cette condition. Il emploie un certain nombre d'images à ce propos dont celle, récurrente, du sommeil ou de l'inertie dont le tirent ses commanditaires. Ce sont toujours la disparition ou la chute du dédicataire qui justifient ses interruptions, comme le prouvent, dans la première Décade, l'interruption de sept ans après la mort d'Ascanio Sforza, et celle de dix ans qui suivit la chute du roi Frédéric III d'Aragon. Ces phénomènes sont rappelés de manière obsessionnelle, par la suite, dans les dédicaces.[45] Quand il n'obtient pas la certitude qu'on désire ses écrits, ce besoin d'être sollicité tourne même à une véritable détresse comme le montrent ses rapports avec le Souverain Pontife Clément VII dans les dédicaces des Décades V à VIII: Martyr commence par adresser la cinquième Décade à Clément VII, qu'il encense, tout en laissant la dédicace à Adrien VI; Clément VII fut-il vexé par le procédé? Toujours est-il qu'il semble n'avoir pas donné suite à la proposition explicite de Martyr puisque la sixième Décade est adressée à

[42] Janson, *Latin prose prefaces*, pp. 117-120.

[43] 'Quam breui spatio, inter rerum angustias et valetudinarium hos me conscribere coegeris, ingenue profiteberis [...] Infestabas namque me quotidie, tuum discessum obiiciens' (I, 3, cf. Martyr, p. 63); 'detrusit in praeceps Ascanium fortuna, fratre Ludouico a Gallis Mediolano eiecto, cuius auctoritas torpescere me non sinebat, quin assidue calamum in dextra haberem' (I, 10, cf. Martyr, p. 219); 'Placuit virorum sapientum et de Tua Sanctitate benemeritorum obtemperare mandatis, quippe qui, audito Beatitudinis Tuae nomine, nefas inexpiabile fore putassem nisi illico paruissem' (II).

[44] 'Laborabam tunc ego vti nosti aduersa valetudine' (I, 10, cf. Martyr, p. 221); 'clauseram Orbi nouo portas, Beatissime Pater, satisque me per illius oras vagatum arbitrabar, quando nouae litterae allatae patefacere illas iterum et repositum sumere calamum coegerunt' (III).

[45] Cf. notes 40 et 41.

Giovanni Ruffo, nonce apostolique, avec mission de la transmettre au Saint Père, et accompagnée de la précision que Martyr cessera d'écrire si le pape ne lui fait pas savoir qu'il souhaite recevoir d'autres Décades[46]. Demande qui resta elle aussi sans réponse immédiate car la Décade suivante (1525) est adressée au duc de Milan, en réponse, précise Martyr, à sa demande. Enfin Martyr indique qu'il a reçu du souverain Pontife Clément VII des encouragements et des sollicitations[47] et lui dédie la huitième et dernière Décade.

Notons d'ailleurs à ce sujet une autre spécificité de Pierre Martyr: même si la préface épistolaire marque une nette séparation avec le corps de l'œuvre elle-même, le dialogue entre auteur et dédicataire se poursuit ponctuellement dans le corps de l'œuvre: en effet, l'œuvre étant constituée de lettres, elle relève du même genre que la préface et l'on trouve de temps à autre des réflexions faites au lecteur, des précisions *ad hominem* ou une petite conclusion faisant écho à la dédicace, tous ces procédés établissant un lien entre la préface et le corps de l'œuvre. Cette habitude ôte *a posteriori* un peu du caractère factice et très artificiel de la préface dédicatoire. Elle permet aussi de prolonger le propos de la dédicace dans la mesure où la plupart de ces incises concerne la faiblesse stylistique de l'auteur ou le caractère à peine croyable de certaines informations.

Autre trait caractéristique des dédicaces, Pierre Martyr convie son dédicataire à suivre l'élaboration de l'œuvre. D'une part, chaque dédicace est pour lui l'occasion de rappeler, et ce de manière systématique, qui ont été les dédicataires et destinataires précédents, procédé qui fait connaître à chaque nouveau dédicataire l'histoire de l'œuvre, que nous avons suffisamment évoquée auparavant pour n'y plus revenir. D'autre part, la dédicace donne l'occasion de découvrir la manière dont Pierre Martyr élabore son œuvre et la rend publique. Ainsi, pour la composition, le lecteur apprend, dans la dédicace de la lettre X de la première décade, dans l'édition de 1516, comment les chapitres initialement numérotés 9 et 10 dans l'édition de 1511 ont été réunis en unique chapitre 9 tandis que l'épilogue initial devient le nouveau chapitre X.[48] Martyr profite aussi de

[46] ‘Collegi ad te pauca e multis, non ad Suam Beatitudinem dirigendam, quae si vti Leo patruelis, si vti successor eius Adrianus fecere, suis me imperiis impulerit ad scribendum, parebo libens, aliter ab eo labore abstinebo ne intemeritatis notam a labiis iniquis iudicer incidisse’ (VI).

[47] Cf. note 41.

[48] ‘De superstitionibus insularium solutum per se libellum scripseram ut Decadem impleret; nunc placuit perpendiculum ad te directum decimi capitis titulo munire, tanquam

la dédicace générale de l'édition de 1511 pour exprimer ses réticences concernant la publication, projetée par le comte de Tendilla, des lettres que Martyr, à sa demande, vient de réunir en une Décade complète.[49] En revanche, ce n'est jamais dans les dédicaces mais dans le corps du texte, en incise, que Martyr exprime son mécontentement devant la réalisation de ce projet et assure que la publication a été faite sans son approbation.

Enfin Martyr lève un voile sur ses méthodes de travail: il explique qu'il lit toutes les lettres qui arrivent du Nouveau Monde, dans un cadre privé tout d'abord, puis en tant que membre du conseil des Indes Occidentales.[50] Ensuite, il le dit presque dans chaque Décade, il se livre à une sévère sélection des informations qu'il va retenir.[51] Puis il rédige ses *archetypa*, ses "documents originaux": certains sont utilisés pour composer les *Décades*, d'autres sont conservés à d'autres fins.[52] Enfin s'il

huius turmae substitem et tergi ductorem prioremque decimum nono connectere, non sublata de ducatu decimi praepositione ne toties cogerer totum opus transcribere aut mittere lituratum. Propterea non miraberis si nonum legens promissum reperies irritum; non semper oportet stare pollicitis' (I, 10, 1516, cf. Martyr, p. 221).

[49] 'Quod vero Antonio Nebrissensi Hispaniae speculo, utriusque amico, illa te commendaturum vt pressorum praelis subiiciat inquias nescio utrum malim. Nobis ista seruaremus cuperem, tum quia minoris fient si communia, tum etiam quia inepta incultaque. Magis namque, ni fallor, carpemur a nuda textura quam laudabimur a vigiliis et ea describendi ne perirent sollicitudine: vnde in laborem non modo irritum sed insanum euademus. Tu ergo qui habes in hac fabrica non infirmum cubiculum ex Inacho de te, quando pro tuis regibus apud Innocentium Pontificem Maximum orator Itala bella sedasti cum iuuenescerem, a me conscripto, rei accurate matureque consulito, nec te cura haec praecipitet, quod ambo iam senescamus immineatque nobis et operibus Letheum discrimen. Satius namque est latere quam in compitis populari dente corrodi aut rhinoceroteo cornu terebrari' (dédicace au comte de Tendilla, 1511, cf. Martyr, p. 267).

[50] 'Distuli quia uana referebantur multa, digna memoratu pauca. In nostro rerum Indicarum regio senatu, grauidae ambagibus epistolae ab ineptis quibusque missae quotidie legebantur, e quibus succi parum colligebamus' (IV); 'postea vero aliae a Fernando Cortesio, Caesaris classis praefecto, venerunt litterae ab illis terris, quas Hispanae tunc ditioni subigebat, in quibus res nouae et inauditae maximeque mirabiles continentur' (V); 'ingens est cartarum volumen, quod minuta quaecumque longo temporis ac terrarum interuallo sibi acciderunt enarret' (VI).

[51] 'Pauca haec ex magno cumulo rerum quae relatu auctorum illas conquirentium accepi memoratu dignarum delegi' (I, 10, cf. Martyr, p. 221); 'est eius epistola Capreensi de Seiano grandior. Sed ea tantum ab illa caeterisque excerpsimus quae memoratu esse digna duximus' (III); 'referantur digna mihi uisa memoratu, praetermissis ambagibus. Breuibus dehinc aperiam quae in credito continenti sub sequenti tenore successerunt' (IV); 'more igitur nostro seruato, posthabitis scribentium minutis affectibus, quae necessaria cognitu fore arbitramur perstringemus' (VI).

[52] 'Haec igitur, uti apud me iacebant, Tua Sanctitas sibi habeat. Quae de praeclare gestis suis et animi constantia per commentaria adhuc apud me latentia, reliquis rebus memoratu dignis quae nostra tempestate in uniuerso acciderunt commixta, si uiuere dabitur, aliquando uidebit' (I, 3, dédicace à Jules II, 1511, cf. Martyr, p. 289); 'ab Oceani prima largaque

veut envoyer à son destinataire les décades précédentes, il se met en quête d'un secrétaire compétent dont il loue les services car il déteste recopier ses propres écrits.[53]

Une fois la Décade commandée et rédigée, il reste à la faire parvenir à son destinataire. Les dédicaces de Pierre Martyr permettent de comprendre comment une œuvre passait de main en main au XVIème siècle, quel chaîne d'intermédiaires assurait sa transmission. Résidant à la cour d'Espagne, Martyr écrit à des Italiens. Dans l'ensemble, les lettres sont adressées directement au dédicataire, mais les parcours sont parfois plus complexes. Dans la première décade, le deuxième groupe de lettres (les livres 3 à 9 de 1516) a été sollicité, nous dit Martyr dans la dédicace, par Frédéric III d'Aragon; mais c'est son parent, le cardinal d'Aragon, qui transmet la demande et veille à l'élaboration de sa réponse, car il s'est rendu à la cour d'Espagne à l'occasion du mariage de la fille de sa parente, la reine de Naples. Ce fait a des conséquences sur l'écriture puisque le cardinal veut ramener les lettres de Martyr avec lui et contraint donc l'épistolier à respecter un délai rigoureux.[54] Dans la quatrième Décade, on apprend que c'est Gilles de Viterbe, venu en ambassade à la cour d'Espagne, qui transmet à Martyr le désir de Léon X de lire une nouvelle Décade.[55] Dans la sixième Décade, dédiée et adressée à Giovanni Ruffo, Martyr profite de la dédicace pour rappeler que son destinataire, son ambassade terminée, repart en Italie et assure ainsi le transport de la

beneficentia, per Christophorum Colonum excitata, pereuntia cuncta vsque ad has narrationes, vno fasce Iacobus Pierius, hero suo, protonotario electo Catinense, ad vos nomine Caesaris ab hac legatione discedente, asportauit, Adriano pontifici offerenda: quae partim opera calchographorum erant in vulgus emissa, partim sua manu a meis archetypis scripta' (VII).

[53] 'Distuli ad te mittere operum in mea officina tam libero quam irretito pede decussorum exemplaria [...] quod sero reperi qui ea excriberet. Rari quippe docti scriptores in hac uestra curia. Ego namque ineptum figo caracterem et negligenter quae semel chartae commendaui mea dextra repingo' (Dédicace au comte de Tendilla, cf. Martyr, p. 267); 'scis namque me tanto celeriter ex Praefecti ipsius Marini Coloni archetypis pauca haec delegisse, quanto tuus a manu famulus, qui me dictante scribebat, poterat exarare' (I, 3, dédicace à Louis d'Aragon, cf. Martyr, p. 63).

[54] 'Nouum, vt ita dixerim, terrarum orbem Catholicorum Fernandi et Helisabeth regum tibi patruorum ductu ab occidente, qui hactenus latitabat repertum vt ego describam Federici Regis inclyti patrui tibi mihi litteras de hac re ostendens imperas [...] Infestabas namque me quotidie, tuum discessum obiiciens, vt nostri Regis sororem Parthenopaeam Reginam, tibi amitam, quam huc fueras comitatus, in patriam reduceres. Singulis interdum diebus singulos me libellos cudere adegisti' (I, 3, dédicace à Louis d'Aragon, cf. Martyr, p. 63).

[55] Cf. note 39.

Décade, qu'il pourra remettre au pape.[56] L'imminence de ce départ contribue peut-être à expliquer le brièveté surprenante de celle-ci. Cette Décade expose dans sa dédicace comment s'organise toute une chaîne de transmission entre commanditaire et auteur, les uns effectuant la demande, les autres veillant à ce que la rédaction ait lieu dans les délais impartis, d'autres encore se chargeant d'acheminer l'œuvre jusqu'à son destinataire, en Italie.

La présentation de l'œuvre, cependant, ne serait pas complète si l'auteur n'expliquait pas quel est le point de vue auquel il se place. Le *De Orbe Nouo* tire en effet beaucoup de son originalité de la position spécifique de Pierre Martyr, qui apparaît comme un homme à la croisée de deux nations, l'Italie et l'Espagne, et à la croisée de deux mondes, l'ancien et le nouveau, à une place privilégiée pour sentir les mutations profondes qui affectent l'univers.

L'actualité de l'Europe n'est présente, dans les dédicaces du *De Orbe Nouo*, que sous forme d'allusions. De plus, lorsque Pierre Martyr mentionne, en quelques phrases maximum, certains éléments de politique internationale, il se limite à ceux qui concernent ses destinataires et dédicataires. C'est ainsi qu'il signale la chute conjointe de Ludovico Sforza le More et d'Ascanio Sforza puis celle de Frédéric d'Aragon[57], les guerres entre les princes chrétiens et les conflits qui se déroulent sur le sol italien[58],

[56] 'Quibus inter caetera inquis Summum Pontificem Claementem his significationibus non minus delectari, quam Leonem patruelem aut Adrianum praedecessores, per suas breues membranas imperantes mihi vt ea conscriberem. Collegi ad te pauca e multis, non ad Suam Beatitudinem dirigendam, quae si vti Leo patruelis, si vti successor eius Adrianus fecere, suis me imperiis impulerit ad scribendum, parebo libens, aliter ab eo labore abstinebo ne intemeritatis notam a labiis iniquis iudicer incidisse' (VI).

[57] 'Duos in prima fronte alieno comperies nomine signatos, quod dum ista quaerebantur, ad infelicem Ascanium Sfortiam, tibi affinem Cardinalem Vicecancellarium scriptitare incoeperam; quo cadente cecidit et mihi animus a scribendo' (I, 3, dédicace à Louis d'Aragon, cf. Martyr, p. 63); 'detrusit in praeceps Ascanium fortuna, fratre Ludouico a Gallis Mediolano eiecto' (I, 10, cf. Martyr, p. 219); 'rex Federicus, priusquam ex blanda matre in saeuam nouercam fortuna eius mutaretur' (VII).

[58] 'Fixisse tamen pedem haudquaquam poenitet, tum quia nullibi terrarum hoc tempore aeque praeclaras res fieri uidebam, tum etiam, quod ex Christianorum principum dissidiis ruere omnia in praeceps: depopulari agros in uniuersa fere Italia, et humano sanguine impinguari, atque urbes hostiliter diripi, uirgines nuptasque cum bonis patriis in praedam trahi, miseros innocentes natos ac genitores intra proprios lares, inermes etiam, et gratuito crudeliter trucidari; querulis clamoribus non audiebam modo sed paene sentiebam. Nec enim affinium et propinquorum meorum sanguis ab ea fera saeuitia immunis euasit' (dédicace à Charles Quint, cf. Martyr, p. 5); 'eia ergo age vt coepisti, et inter Christianos Principes, Caesarem praecipue, Christianissimosque reges dissidentes, perpetuam compone pacem vexillaque salutiferae crucis in impios hostes tolle et aeterna tui nominis ac famae apud posteros quae nulla vnquam oblitterabit aetas, relinque monumenta' (V).

l’accession de Charles Quint au pouvoir en Espagne[59] puis son couronnement comme empereur[60] et le rétablissement de Francesco II Maria Sforza à la tête du duché de Milan.[61]

L’attachement de Martyr à l’Italie, sa terre d’origine, et à ses dirigeants est patent. Si l’on regarde en effet ses dédicaces, on constate qu’un an avant sa mort, il adresse la septième Décade au duc de Milan, redisant son attachement à sa région natale, et Ascanio Sforza, son protecteur à la cour de Milan et premier destinataire, est celui dont il fait le plus souvent mention dans les dédicaces qu’il adresse à d’autres. Notons aussi que si l’on excepte le cas un peu particulier de Charles Quint, il n’y a qu’un Espagnol à se voir jamais offrir un livre, puis une Décade (honneur qui lui sera ultérieurement retiré au profit du jeune roi): le comte de Tendilla, sans doute parce qu’il a amené Martyr en Espagne. Mais les rares observations sur l’Italie auxquelles il se livre dans ses dédicaces constituent un constat désespéré: il souligne en effet dans sa dédicace à Charles Quint comment l’Italie, qui tourne ses forces contre elle-même, a cessé d’offrir des perspectives intéressantes aux savants[62], raison pour laquelle il a lui-même choisi de rester en Espagne; il décrit aussi avec émotion les tueries qui ensanglantent la terre italienne.[63] Dans l’adresse à Clément VII qui ouvre la cinquième décade, il encourage le pape nouvellement élu à user de tout son pouvoir pour ramener la paix entre les princes.[64] En revanche il célèbre à plusieurs reprises la grandeur de l’Espagne et le statut de premier plan qu’elle a su obtenir par la *Reconquista* et la découverte du Nouveau Monde[65], statut que personnifie la figure emblématique

[59] ‘Nunc ad te uenio, Serenissime Rex, a quo parumper uagatus sum’ (dédicace à Charles Quint, cf. Martyr, p. 7).

[60] ‘Carente regibus Hispania, ob regis Caesaris discessum ad oblatam imperialem coronam capessendam’ (VI).

[61] ‘Priusquam id Beatitudinis tuae mandatum ad manus meas peruenisset, ad Franciscum Sfortiam Vicecomitem mei natalis ducem, quando eius fortuna liberum a Christianissimi Regis animo indefesso sinebat’ (VIII).

[62] ‘In Hispaniam concessi [...] quod inueni mihi rerum nouarum cupido nil praeberet Italia, vnde pascere ingenium quirem’ (dédicace à Charles Quint, cf. Martyr, pp. 3-5).

[63] ‘Tum etiam, quia ex Christianorum principum dissidiis ruere omnia in praeceps, depopulari agros in uniuersa fere Italia, et humano sanguine impinguari, atque urbes hostiliter diripi, uirgines nuptasque cum bonis patriis in praedam trahi, miseros innocentes natos ac genitores intra proprios lares inermes etiam et gratuito crudeliter trucidari, querulis clamoribus non audiebam modo sed paene sentiebam. Nec enim affinium et propinquorum meorum sanguis ab ea fera saeuitia immunis euasit’ (dédicace à Charles Quint, cf. Martyr, p. 5).

[64] Cf. note 58.

[65] ‘Fixisse tamen pedem haudquaquam poenitet, tum quia nullibi terrarum hoc tempore aeque praeclaras res fieri uidebam’ (dédicace à Charles Quint, cf. Martyr, p. 5).

de Charles Quint. A cheval entre deux nations, l'une déclinante, l'autre ascendante, Pierre Martyr choisit celle qui incarne l'avenir, comme ses dédicaces l'exposent clairement.

Mais Pierre Martyr apparaît aussi comme un homme à la croisée de deux mondes, l'ancien et le nouveau. Sa position privilégiée à la cour d'Espagne, où il reçoit dans son cabinet tous ceux qui arrivent du Nouveau Monde, puis son statut de secrétaire du Conseil des Indes Occidentales, qui lui permet d'avoir accès à tous les rapports, toutes les informations, le placent au cœur de l'événement. Sa curiosité, son étonnante absence de préjugés, sa capacité d'adaptation, la vivacité de son style et sa capacité de distinguer l'essentiel de l'anecdotique lui ont permis de tirer parti de cette extraordinaire position et ont fait de lui un témoin privilégié. Il est le premier à avoir employé, dès 1494, le terme d'*Orbis Nouus* et à avoir compris quel est l'enjeu principal, à ce moment, de la découverte du Nouveau Monde: outre le caractère extraordinaire de l'événement, c'est cette découverte, par l'extension inouïe qu'elle représente, par l'afflux de richesses qu'elle va provoquer, qui va fournir à l'Espagne de quoi nourrir ses prétentions à la domination et lui donner pour le siècle à venir un avantage contre lequel aucune nation d'Europe ne pourra lutter.[66]

En conclusion, nous pouvons donc constater que Pierre Martyr d'Anghiera, comme les écrivains de l'Antiquité, recourt à un modèle de dédicace relativement conventionnel et se plie aux figures imposées du genre. Il est flagrant cependant qu'il n'y déploie pas un zèle particulier, qu'il s'agisse du fond ou de la forme. En effet, si le fait que l'œuvre soit composée en Décades et que sa rédaction se soit échelonnée sur une trentaine d'années a entraîné la multiplication des dédicaces, celles-ci apparaissent toujours comme un passage obligé et le dédicataire comme une figure bien pâle, voire interchangeable. Pierre Martyr profite cependant de ce texte à part pour rappeler sa position si particulière entre deux pays et entre deux mondes, pour présenter l'ensemble de son œuvre à son destinataire et pour attirer l'attention de celui-ci sur ce qui est à ses yeux l'essentiel: le contenu de l'œuvre. C'est donc tout naturellement que Martyr trouve dans les dédicaces l'occasion de manifester la grande fierté qu'il éprouve à être le premier chroniqueur de la découverte du Nouveau Monde. Mais à travers les dédicaces se dessine aussi le portrait d'un

[66] Cf. note 11.

homme qui perçoit les enjeux des siècles à venir, qui ne craint ni d'innover dans la langue, ni d'aborder le récit géographique sous un angle nouveau, débarrassé cette fois du poids des influences antiques, toutes choses que confirme la lecture de l'œuvre à laquelle l'épistolier nous a conviés, dans ses dédicaces, avec tant d'adresse.

Université de Caen – Basse Normandie
F – 14032 Caen
brigitte.gauvin@unicaen.fr

## Annexe
## Les dédicaces du *De Orbe Nouo* de Pierre Martyr d'Anghiera

| | **Date** | **Dédicace** | **Dedicataire** | **Destinataire premier** | **Destinataire second** |
|---|---|---|---|---|---|
| **Edition de 1511 (1ère décade)** | | | | | |
| Carte | 1511 | Oui | Cardinal Jiménez | Cardinal Jiménez | |
| Dédicace générale | 1511 | Oui | Comte de Tendilla | Comte de Tendilla | |
| Préface d'Antonio de Nebrija | 1511 | | | | |
| Livres 1-2 | 1493-1494 | Non | | Ascanio Sforza | |
| Livres 3-10 | 1500 | Oui | Pape Jules II / Louis d'Aragon | Louis d'Aragon | Frédéric d'Aragon |
| Epilogue | 1510 | Oui | Comte de Tendilla | Comte de Tendilla | |
| | | | | | |
| **Edition de 1516 (I-III)** | | | | | |
| Poèmes | 1516 | Oui | Le lecteur | Le lecteur | |
| Dédicace générale | 1516 | Oui | Charles Quint | Charles Quint | |
| Préface d'Antonio de Nebrija | Modifiée 1516 | | | | |
| 1ère décade 1-2 | 1493-1494 | Non | | Ascanio Sforza | |
| 1ère décade 3-9 | 1500 | Oui, modifiée | Louis d'Aragon | Louis d'Aragon | |

| | | | | | |
|---|---|---|---|---|---|
| 1ère décade 10 | 1510 | Oui, modifiée | Comte de Tendilla | Comte de Tendilla | |
| 2ème décade | 1514 | Oui | Pape Léon X | Pape Léon X | |
| 3ème décade | 1516 | Oui | Pape Léon X | Pape Léon X | |
| | | | | | |
| **Edition de 1530 (I-VIII)** | | | | | |
| Poème | Modifié 1530 | Oui | Le lecteur | Le lecteur | |
| Dédicace générale | 1516 | Oui | Charles Quint | Charles Quint | |
| Préface d'Antonio de Nebrija | 1516 | | | | |
| 1ère décade | Cf. *supra* | Cf. *supra* | Cf. *supra* | Cf. *supra* | |
| 2ème décade | 1514 | Oui | Pape Léon X | Pape Léon X | |
| 3ème décade | 1516 | Oui | Pape Léon X | Pape Léon X | |
| 4ème décade | 1520-21 | Oui | Pape Léon X | Pape Léon X | |
| 5ème décade | 1523 | Oui | Pape Adrien VI | Pape Clément VII | |
| 6ème décade | 1524 | Oui | Nonce apostolique Giovanni Ruffo | Nonce apostolique Giovanni Ruffo | Clément VII |
| 7ème décade | 1525 | Oui | Francesco II Maria Sforza | Francesco II Maria Sforza | |
| 8ème décade | 1526 | Oui | Pape Clément VII | Pape Clément VII | |

# DÉDICACES ET INSCRIPTIONS LATINES DANS LES LIVRES DE MUSIQUE POUR VIHUELA (1536-1576)

PALOMA OTAOLA GONZÁLEZ

Parmi les nouveautés que la Renaissance instaure dans le domaine musical, on peut signaler le développement de la musique instrumentale et le goût pour la monodie accompagnée. Les livres de musique pour vihuela, imprimés en Espagne entre 1536 et 1576 témoignent de ces changements. Sept d'entre eux sont des recueils de musique pour vihuela seule ou pour vihuela et chant, en incluant quelques pièces pour guitare.[1] Deux autres sont des recueils de musique instrumentale pour clavier, harpe et vihuela: le *Libro de cifra nueva* de Venegas de Henestrosa et les *Obras de música* de Cabezón.[2]

On a très peu d'informations sur les auteurs de ces livres de musique. Certains étaient des nobles ou appartenaient à des familles de la haute bourgeoisie, avec un talent naturel pour la musique, comme c'est le cas de Luis Milán, de Diego Pisador ou d'Esteban Daza. D'autres étaient des musiciens professionnels au service de la Cour ou des maisons aristocratiques, comme Luis Narváez, Enríquez de Valderrábano, Miguel de

[1] Luis Milán, *Libro de música de vihuela de mano intitulado El Maestro* (Valence: Francisco Díaz Romano, 1535-1536; Genève: Minkoff, 1975); Luis de Narváez, *Los seis libros del Delphin de música de cifras para tañer vihuela* (Valladolid: Diego Hernández de Córdoba, 1538; Genève: Minkoff, 1980); Alonso Mudarra, *Tres libros de música en cifras para vihuela* (Séville: Juan de León, 1546; Monaco: Chanterelle, 1980); Enríquez de Valderrábano, *Libro de música de vihuela intitulado Silva de Sirenas* (Valladolid: Francisco Fernández de Córdoba, 1547; Genève: Minkoff, 1981); Diego Pisador, *Libro de vihuela* (Salamanque: [l'auteur], 1552; Genève: Minkoff, 1973); Miguel de Fuenllana, *Libro de música para vihuela intitulado Orphenica lyra* (Séville: Martin de Montesdoca, 1554; Genève: Minkoff, 1981); Esteban Daza, *Libro de música en cifras para vihuela intitulado El Parnaso* (Valladolid: Diego Fernández de Córdoba, 1576; Genève: Minkoff, 1979). Edition fac-similé des sept livres de musique pour vihuela sur CD-rom par Gerardo Arriaga y Carlos González (Musica Prima y Opera Tres [s.l.a.]).

[2] Luis Venegas de Henestrosa, *Libro de cifra nueva para tecla, arpa y vihuela* (Alcalá de Henares: Juan de Brocar, 1577), éd./trans. Higinio Anglés in *La música en la corte de Carlos V* (Barcelone: Consejo Superior de Investigaciones Científicas, 1944); Antonio Cabezón, *Obras de música para tecla, arpa y vihuela,* éd. par son fils Hernando (Madrid: Francisco Sánchez, 1578), éd./trans. Felipe Pedrell (Barcelone: Consejo Superior de Investigaciones Científicas, 1966).

Fuenllana et Antonio de Cabezón. D'autres, enfin, tels que Alonso Mudarra et Venegas de Henestrosa, étaient des clercs, maîtres de chapelle à la Cour ou à la cathédrale. Les contrats d'édition de ces livres, entre 1000 et 1500 exemplaires, reflètent l'essor de la musique pour vihuela qui n'était pas le privilège des milieux aristocratiques mais touchait également des secteurs plus larges de la société du seizième siècle.[3] Cependant, la popularité de la vihuela ne peut pas occulter le fait que les livres de musique s'adressent en premier lieu à un public savant, aristocratique et raffiné. En effet, les livres de vihuela constituent un intéressant et curieux mélange de musique profane et de musique sacrée, des adaptations de musique polyphonique et de nouvelles pièces créées pour l'instrument, de goût populaire et d'esthétique savante, de tradition et de modernité.[4]

Tous ces livres présentent une structure similaire: dédicace, concession des privilèges pour l'édition, lettres au bienfaiteur et au lecteur, suivies des instructions et autres conseils sur la musique, la tablature, la façon d'accorder l'instrument, les indications de *tempo*, etc. Certaines introductions sont très techniques, mais dans la plupart des livres, elles sont l'occasion de digressions, très imprégnées des traditions anciennes. De façon générale, les préfaces évoquent la splendeur et l'importance de la musique chez les Anciens, sa valeur éthique et son rôle dans l'éducation. Son origine divine, représentée par les mythes et légendes tant classiques que bibliques, place la musique au-dessus des autres arts et fait d'elle la meilleure expression de la louange à Dieu. Tous ces aspects soulignent le lien entre la musique instrumentale, notamment la musique pour vihuela, et une certaine conception de la musique, que l'on retrouve également dans les traités théoriques de la Renaissance. En effet, la littérature musicale de cette époque souligne le rôle irremplaçable de la musique, hérité des Anciens, dans la vie humaine et dans la société. La musique est considérée comme le sommet des arts et un moyen privilégié pour cultiver l'esprit.[5] Par ailleurs, les livres de vihuela montrent bien une

[3] John Griffiths, 'At Court and at Home with the *Vihuela de mano*: Current Perspectives on the Instrument, its Music, and its World', *Journal of the Lute Society of America*, 22 (1989), 1-27 (p. 8).

[4] Paloma Otaola González, 'Los Romances para vihuela del siglo XVI', in *Actas del XIV Congreso de la Asociación Internacional de Hispanistas*, éds. Isaías Lerner – Robert Nival – Alejandro Alonso (New York: Juan de la Cuesta, 2004), pp. 435-446.

[5] Sur la conception de la musique à la Renaissance en lien avec l'humanisme du seizième siècle, on peut voir Paloma Otaola González, *El humanismo musical en Francisco Salinas* (Pampelune: Newbook, 1997) et *Tradición y modernidad en los escritos musicales de Juan Bermudo. Del Libro primero (1549) a la Declaración de instrumentos musicales*

affinité esthétique et intellectuelle avec les autres manifestations artistiques et culturelles du seizième siècle.

Nous trouvons également dans ces livres des gravures qui illustrent ces idées qui viennent d'être évoquées. Généralement, les gravures sont accompagnées d'inscriptions en latin ou en castillan qui explicitent la scène. Il est fréquent d'y trouver aussi des épigrammes, des sonnets et des poèmes à la louange de l'auteur et de la musique, aussi bien en latin qu'en langue vernaculaire. Des emblèmes, accompagnés ou non d'inscriptions, sont présents dans les livres pour orner les pages de titre et très souvent dans le colophon, utilisés comme marques typographiques.

La langue de ces livres est le castillan. Cependant, parmi les pièces pour chant et vihuela, se trouvent des textes en latin, en portugais et en italien.[6]

Quel est le rôle des inscriptions latines dans ces livres et quel est le lien entre les textes latins et la conception de la musique de l'auteur ou du milieu dans lequel l'auteur évoluait? Ce sont les questions auxquelles nous essaierons de répondre à travers une réflexion sur les dédicaces et les inscriptions latines qui accompagnent les gravures, les emblèmes ainsi que les marques typographiques. Nous allons commencer par les textes en latin présents dans les dédicaces. Ensuite, nous aborderons les emblèmes et les marques typographiques et enfin, nous commenterons les gravures accompagnées d'une citation latine.

## Les dédicaces

Tous les livres de vihuela sont dédiés à un personnage important. Le plus souvent, ce sont des rois, des princes et des nobles, sans qu'il y ait toujours une relation personnelle entre l'auteur du livre et le destinataire. Ainsi, *El maestro* de Luis Milán est dédié à Jean III du Portugal tandis que le destinataire du livre de Pisador, de celui de Fuenllana et des œuvres de Cabezón est Philippe II. Dans d'autres cas, le destinataire est moins connue, mais il s'agit, en général, des personnes de haut rang du milieu ecclésiastique ou de la Cour.[7] Parfois la dédicace est accompagnée d'une

*(1555)* (Kassel: Reichenberger, 2000); Isabel Pope, 'La vihuela y su música en el ambiente humanístico', *Nueva Revista de Filología Hispánica*, 15 (1961), 364-376.

[6] Des chansons françaises figurent parmi les pièces pour vihuela seule.

[7] Luis Narváez dédie son ouvrage à don Fancisco de los Cobos, Grand Commandeur de León. Alonso Mudarra adresse ses trois livres à don Luis Zapata. Le livre de Valderrábano est dédié à don Francisco de Zuñiga, Comte de Miranda, à qui Bermudo dédie également sa célèbre *Declaración de instrumentos musicales* (Ossuna: Juan de León, 1555).

FIGURE 1. Luis Milán, *El maestro* (Valence: Diaz Romano, 1535-1536, fac-similé Genève: Minkoff, 1975), fol. 2v.
Avec l'aimable autorisation des éditions Minkoff.

épître adressée au destinataire. Comme nous l'avons déjà mentionné, la langue utilisée est le castillan, mais dans *El maestro* de Milán et dans *El Parnaso* de Daza des textes en latin accompagnent la matière préliminaire de l'œuvre.

## *El Maestro*

Le premier livre de musique pour vihuela publié en Espagne, *El maestro*, est dédié à Jean III, roi du Portugal. Sur la page de titre figure l'année 1535, mais la date du colophon est 1536. Précédant la dédicace, une gravure représente le monarque avec l'inscription: 'Invictissimus Rex Lusitanorum'.

Ce titre de *Invictissimus*, adressé aux empereurs romains, rappelle les épigraphies de monuments commémoratifs et des épitaphes.[8] La gravure elle-même, d'ailleurs, rappelle les sculptures en hommage aux rois et aux princes. Ce même titre était attribué souvent à l'empereur Charles V.[9] Dans les dédicaces en espagnol, en revanche, on préfère la formule 'Muy alto y muy poderoso señor' ('très grand et très puissant seigneur').[10]

En s'appuyant sur la dédicace et sur la présence de *villancicos* en portugais, il est communément admis que Milán a séjourné, dans sa jeunesse, à la Cour du Portugal, sans que l'on sache exactement quand, et s'il a eu des contacts personnels avec Jean III.[11] Quoi qu'il en soit, c'est probablement le renom du souverain, grand mécène des arts et des lettres, qui aurait motivé la dédicace.[12]

Jean III accède au trône en 1521, à l'époque de la grande expansion portugaise outre-mer, mais aussi des liens étroits du Portugal avec l'Espagne. Par ailleurs, son rôle de protecteur de la culture était connu au-delà des frontières. Des hommes célèbres, tels que le poète et dramaturge Gil Vicente et l'humaniste Francisco de Sá de Miranda avaient bénéficié de la protection de la Cour portugaise. Jean III avait également réformé

[8] Dalle sur la tombe de Charlemagne à Aix-la-Chapelle; épitaphe de Guillaume le Conquérant, Caen, Abbaye aux Hommes.

[9] Le titre d'*invictissimus* est inscrit sur la frise de l'une des "chambres de l'empereur" du Palais de Charles V à Grenade.

[10] Dédicace de Fuenllana à Philippe II, *Orphenica lyra*, page de titre.

[11] John Griffiths, 'Milán, Luis', in *Diccionario de la Música Española e Hispanoamericana*, éd. Emilio Casares (Madrid: ICCMU), VII (2000), 564-566 (p. 564).

[12] Le *Libro primero* de Juan Bermudo (Ossuna: Juan de León, 1549) est également dédié à Jean III roi du Portugal, même si le théoricien espagnol ne connaissait pas personnellement le monarque.

l'Université et créé un Collège des Arts.[13] Dans ce contexte, le nom du roi était comme un "label de qualité" pour introduire le livre de musique et son auteur dans un certain milieu aristocratique et humaniste.

Dans la dédicace rédigée en castillan, Milán justifie son geste en déclarant que la valeur d'un objet est rehaussée par celui qui le possède. Ainsi son livre aura plus de valeur dans les mains du roi du Portugal, pays où la musique est comprise et appréciée. Il fait allusion à une légende selon laquelle un savant philosophe avait jeté une pierre précieuse à la mer. Engloutie par une baleine qui échoua sur le rivage, elle fut finalement retrouvée par un roi, récupérant ainsi toute sa valeur. De même, le compositeur confie son œuvre au royaume du Portugal qui est pour la musique comme la mer de la légende. De plus, il demande au roi de le protéger des envieux, en sachant que le livre ne pouvait pas se trouver dans de meilleures mains.[14] D'après Samuel Rubio, cette dédicace lui aurait valu une pension de 7000 ducats et le titre de gentilhomme.[15] Ces données, cependant, restent invérifiables. Les informations le concernant attestent que Milán a passé la plupart de sa vie à Valence, sa ville natale.[16] Dans cette ville, il entre au service de la cour de Ferdinand II d'Aragon, Duc de Calabre, premier vice-roi de Valence, marié à Germaine de Foix.[17]

Milán incarne à la perfection le type du noble d'éducation raffinée, dépeint dans le *Cortegiano* de Castiglione.[18] En plus du livre de musique, il est l'auteur d'un ouvrage intitulé *El Cortesano*, adaptation de celui de l'humaniste italien, et d'un livre de poèmes sur des sujets de cour intitulé *Libro de motes de damas y caballeros*.[19]

*El Maestro* est le seul livre de musique pour vihuela qui ne contient pas d'adaptations d'œuvres de polyphonie vocale. Toutes les pièces sont originales et il ne contient pas non plus d'œuvres religieuses. Parmi les compositions pour vihuela, se trouvent également des sonnets en italien,

[13] Sur l'histoire du Portugal au seizième siècle, on peut voir Mário Domingues, *D. João III: o homem e a sua época: evocaçao histórica* (Lisbonne: R. Torres, 1962).

[14] Milán, *El maestro*, fol. 3r.

[15] Samuel Rubio, *Historia de la música española*, vol. 2: *Desde el ars nova hasta 1600* (Madrid: Alianza Editorial, 1998), p. 221.

[16] Griffiths, 'Milán', p. 564.

[17] Après la mort d'Isabelle la Catholique en 1504, Ferdinand II d'Aragon, plus connu sous le nom de Ferdinand le Catholique, épousa Germaine de Foix en 1506.

[18] Baldassar Castiglione, *Libro del Cortegiano* (Venise: Aldo Manuzio, 1528).

[19] Luis Milán, *Libro intitulado: El cortesano* (Valence: Ioan de Arcos, 1561); *Libro de motes de damas y caballeros intitulado: El juego de mandar* (Valence: Francisco Díaz Romano, 1535).

ce qui laisse supposer que l'auteur ait séjourné en Italie. L'œuvre est composée de deux livres de difficulté croissante. Le premier est précédé d'une prière en latin où l'auteur invoque la protection de Dieu et de sa Mère, la Vierge Marie. Une invocation similaire se trouve à la fin de l'ouvrage, dans le colophon.

*El Parnaso*

La deuxième dédicace, accompagnée d'un texte en latin, est celle d'Esteban Daza, auteur du livre de musique pour vihuela intitulé *El Parnaso*. Le titre évoque le mont Parnasse où se déroulaient, dans l'Antiquité Grecque, des concours poétiques et musicaux sous la protection des Muses et d'Apollon. Ce recueil est le dernier des livres pour vihuela et le seul imprimé sous le règne de Philippe II. *El Parnaso* comprend des fantaisies originales et des adaptations d'œuvres vocales, religieuses et profanes, pour chant et vihuela.

Les informations que l'on possédait jusqu'à présent sur l'auteur étaient celles qu'il fournit dans l'introduction de son œuvre, mais les recherches de John Griffiths ont apporté de nombreuses données sur la famille et l'entourage du vihueliste.[20] Il résidait à Valladolid, ville où son livre paraît chez l'imprimeur Diego Fernández de Córdoba. D'après Griffiths, Daza appartenait à une famille prestigieuse. Il n'était pas musicien professionnel mais jouait de la vihuela dans ses loisirs, ce qui apparemment n'était pas bien vu dans sa famille, jusqu'au succès de la publication de son livre.[21] Celui-ci est dédié au 'Licenciado Hernando de Habalos de Sotomayor', du Conseil Suprême de sa Majesté, avocat de la Chancellerie royale et ami de la famille Daza.[22] Le titre de *licenciado*, probablement en droit étant donné sa fonction d'avocat, suggère qu'il s'agissait d'une personne cultivée ayant fait des Études Supérieures. La faculté de droit ainsi que celle de théologie étaient les deux établissements d'Enseignement Supérieur les plus réputés à Valladolid.

La dédicace est écrite en castillan, mais elle commence par une citation de Martial: 'Victurus liber debet habere genium', traduite ensuite par l'auteur: 'El libro que ha de durar [...] ha de tener genio'.

[20] John Griffiths, 'Esteban Daza: A Gentleman Musician in Renaissance Spain', *Early Music*, 23/3 (1995), 437-449.

[21] John Griffiths, 'Esteban Daza: el enigma desvelado de un vihuelista español', *Hispanica Lyra*, 5 (2007), 8-15.

[22] Griffiths, 'Esteban Daza: el enigma', p. 11.

Al muy Illuſtre Señor, el Señor Licenciado
Hernando de Habalos de Soto mayor del Conſejo ſupremo
Eſteuan Daça ſu ſeruidor. P. F. y S. deſca.

ICTVRVS liber debet habere genium, El libro que ha de durar (muy Illuſtre Señor) dize Marcial, que ha de tener genio, deſſeando pues yo con aquel amor que cada vn padre tiene a ſus hijos, por mas que ſean feos, y lagañoſos, que eſte mio dure, y viua largos años, no ſupe a qual genio mejor pudieſſe darle que a v. m. cuya eminencia de letras, valor de perſona, reſ-

FIGURE 2. Esteban Daza, *El Parnaso* (Valladolid: Diego Fernández de Cordoba, 1576, fac-similé Genève: Minkoff, 1979), fol. 2. Avec l'aimable autorisation des éditions Minkoff.

Ce vers de Martial, 'Victurus genium debet habere liber' (*Epigrammes*, VI, 60, 10),[23] figure également dans la préface d'Antonio Nebrija au *De Orbe Novo* de Pierre Martyr d'Anghiera: 'An quod liber victurus, ut ait poeta, debet habere genium'.[24] Nebrija ne mentionne pas le nom de Martial mais la sentence est la même, bien que l'ordre de la phrase soit altéré. La dédicace de Daza est plus proche de celle de Nebrija que de l'original.

On pourrait supposer que la famille Daza possédait l'œuvre d'Anghiera, préfacée par Nebrija, ce qui ne serait pas improbable. En effet, Martyr d'Anghiera était l'un de grands humanistes espagnols, célèbre par ses *Décades du Nouveau Monde*.[25] Nebrija également possédait une grande notoriété en tant qu'humaniste et professeur de rhétorique à l'Université

[23] Martial, *Épigrammes*, t. I, éd./trad. H-J. Izaak (Paris: Les Belles Lettres, 1961), p. 195.

[24] Je tiens à remercier Brigitte Gauvin qui m'a communiqué la présence de la citation de Martial dans la préface de Nebrija à l'œuvre de Pierre Martyr d'Anghiera, *Décades du Nouveau Monde, I: La décade océane*, édition, traduction et commentaire de Brigitte Gauvin (Paris: Les Belles Lettres, 2003), pp. 8-9.

[25] D'origine italienne, Pierre Martyr d'Anghiera entra au service des Rois Catholiques en 1492. Très apprécié par la reine Isabelle, il était chargé de l'éducation des nobles de la Cour. Nommé directeur de l'École Palatine, il jouissait d'une certaine notoriété. Après la mort d'Isabelle, il est nommé Secrétaire du Conseil des Indes en 1524. Il passe au service de Charles V les dernières années de sa vie jusqu'à sa mort à Grenade en 1526. Parmi ses œuvres le récit de la découverte du Nouveau Monde connut une grande popularité. La première décade est publiée en 1511 à Séville chez l'imprimeur Jacob Cromberger. L'édition préfacée par Nebrija est imprimée en 1516 à Alcalá chez Arnao Guillén de Brocar. Pierre Martyr d'Anghiera, *Décades du Nouveau Monde, I: La décade océane*, ed. Gauvin, pp. XV-XIX et LXXVI.

de Salamanque. C'est dans cette ville qu'il imprime sa *Gramática castellana*, le premier texte à fixer les normes d'une langue vernaculaire.[26] Probablement, ces deux œuvres faisaient partie des bibliothèques des personnes aisées et cultivées. Dans ce cas, Esteban Daza aurait pu s'inspirer de la préface de Nebrija. Cependant, Griffiths signale que la maison des Daza était très austère, sans œuvres d'art ni meubles précieux ou autres objets de luxe. De plus, il est surprenant, commente-t-il, de noter l'absence de livres parmi les biens de son père.[27] En réalité, c'est la popularité de Martial en Espagne au seizième siècle qui est à l'origine de cette coïncidence.

Le vihueliste utilise le vers de Martial pour confier son œuvre à Hernando de Habalos, car il n'a pas pu trouver meilleur génie protecteur que lui.[28] Il lui dédie son ouvrage en espérant que les nombreuses qualités du *Licenciado* suffiront à défendre sa musique des "langues envieuses". En même temps, la citation en latin peut être interprétée comme un hommage à l'érudition du destinataire et à sa familiarité avec le monde des "Lettres latines". En effet, ces citations savantes, en latin, des auteurs anciens dans un texte en langue vernaculaire évoquent un milieu érudit, sensible à la mouvance humaniste. L'épigramme *De Stephano Dazza Colloquium inter Mussas & Appollinem,* d'auteur anonyme, est une autre manifestation du milieu intellectuel dans lequel évoluait le vihueliste.

Les deux dédicaces — les seules enrichies d'expressions en latin — reflètent, si l'on tient compte également des dédicaces en langue vernaculaire, que, dans certains cas, il n'y a pas de relation personnelle entre le compositeur et la personnalité à laquelle sont dédiés les livres de musique. Dans d'autres cas, la dédicace peut répondre à une relation de service: maître de chapelle, musicien de la cour ou d'amitié, comme dans le cas du livre de Daza.[29] En général, la dédicace n'est que la formule

[26] Antonio de Nebrija, *Grammatica castellana* (Salamanque: s.n., 1492).

[27] John Griffiths, 'Daza, Esteban', in *Diccionario de la Música*, IV (1999), 413-416 (p. 414).

[28] Le mot *genium* dans le vers de Martial est un peu ambigu. On pourrait l'interpréter dans le sens de Génie protecteur ou bien dans le sens de *ingenium*, talent. Dans la dédicace de Daza, l'appel à la protection du *Licenciado* semble privilégier la première interprétation. D'autre part, Gauvin l'a aussi interprété dans ce sens dans la traduction de la préface de Nebrija, p. 8.

[29] Luis Narváez était au service de Francisco de los Cobos, destinataire de son livre de musique. Cf. John Griffiths, 'Narváez, Luis de', in *Diccionario de la Música*, VII (2000), 976-979 (p. 976). Par ailleurs, la dédicace du livre de Valderrábano a été interprétée comme un indice de l'appartenance du vihueliste au service du Comte de Miranda. Cf. John Griffiths, 'Valderrábano, Enríquez de', in *Diccionario de la Música*, X (2002), 630-633 (p. 630).

habituelle pour demander la protection à l'égard des envieux, des malveillants et des détracteurs, et contre toute sorte de contrefaçon. En effet, plusieurs cas de plagiat ou d'édition frauduleuse se sont produits parmi les livres de musique imprimés au seizième siècle. Miguel de Fuenllana dénonce en 1555 une édition frauduleuse de son livre et envoie son domestique pour récupérer les exemplaires de cette édition.[30] Un autre exemple est celui de la *Declaración de intrumentos* de Bermudo, entièrement copiée par Martin Tapia et publiée en 1570 sous le titre de *Vergel de musica,* sans aucune mention de l'auteur de la *Declaración*.[31] Cette idée de protection est également évoquée par la citation de Martial dans la dédicace de Daza.

Par ailleurs, la dédicace constitue, d'une part, un hommage aux œuvres de mécénat de la part des princes et des nobles et, d'autre part, une façon de reconnaître la valeur de l'œuvre en lui octroyant une certaine noblesse, comme le suggère la dédicace de Milan. Quant aux expressions latines des deux dédicaces, elles répondent probablement au prestige des lettres classiques dans les milieux humanistes.

## Les emblèmes

Le succès du *Livre d'Emblèmes* d'Alciat, paru pour la première fois en 1531, entraîna un grand engouement pour les emblèmes, les devises et les hiéroglyphes. En effet, le livre d'Alciat connut nombre d'éditions et de traductions.[32] Les images (*pictura*) introduites par une sentence (*inscriptio*) en latin ou en grec, accompagnées le plus souvent d'une épigramme, généralement de sources classiques, eurent un énorme succès comme le montrent les recueils d'emblèmes publiés aux seizième et dizseptième siècles.[33] Outre l'aspect symbolique et moralisant de l'emblème,

[30] John Griffiths, 'Fuenllana, Miguel de', in *Diccionario de la Música*, vol. 7 (2000), pp. 273-274 (p. 274).

[31] Martin Tapia Numantino, *Vergel de musica spiritual, speculativa y activa* (Burgo de Osma: Diego Fernández de Córdoba, 1570). Pour plus de détails voir Francisco José Leon Tello, *Estudios de historia de la teoría musical* (Madrid: CSIC, 1962), pp. 313-335.

[32] Andrea Alciato, *Emblematum liber* (Augsburg: Steyner, 1531). Édition latin-français (Paris: Wechel, 1536). Plusieurs traductions furent réalisées à Lyon: André Alciat, *Livre d'Emblèmes* (Lyon: Macé Bonhomme, 1548, 1549, 1550, 1551). L'édition consultée pour ce travail est celle de André Alciat, *Les Emblèmes*, éd. Pierre Laurens (Lyon: Macé-Bonhomme, 1551, fac-similé, Paris: Klincksieck, 1997).

[33] Barthélémy Aneau, *Picta poesis. Ut pictura poesis erit* (Lyon: Macé-Bonhomme, 1552); Juan de Horozco y Covarrubias, *Emblemas morales* (Segovie: Juan de la Cuesta,

un certain côté initiatique du monde de l'érudition se répand, touchant tous les milieux concernés par la culture: les nobles et les aristocrates, les artistes eux-mêmes et les imprimeurs.[34]

En ce premier siècle d'imprimerie, l'édition n'est pas seulement une affaire technique ou commerciale. Les maisons d'édition essaient de produire des œuvres qui aient en elles-mêmes une valeur artistique et manifestent ainsi l'érudition de l'imprimeur. Cela explique la présence d'emblèmes, généralement sans l'épigramme, sur la page de titre ou à côté du colophon, utilisés comme marque typographique. Par ailleurs, les marques d'imprimeurs sont parfois originales, mais le plus souvent sont copiées d'imprimeurs étrangers, ce qui contribue à créer une certaine communion d'esprit avec une intention didactique.

Nous allons présenter l'emblème de la paix du livre de Mudarra et celui d'Hercule d'*Orphenica lyra*, de Fuenllana. Les deux emblèmes présentent, à notre avis, un lien avec le monde culturel et intellectuel de la musique.

### *Emblème de la paix*

Cet emblème apparaît à la fin de chaque livre et à côté du colophon des *Tres libros de música* de Mudarra. D'après les informations connues sur Alonso Mudarra, il était chanoine de la cathédrale de Séville, poste qu'il occupa à partir de 1546. Il y restera jusqu'à son décès en 1580.[35] Séville était au seizième siècle une ville riche et cosmopolite grâce notamment au commerce avec le Nouveau Monde. Son essor économique contribua, sans doute, à faire de cette ville un centre important de diffusion de l'humanisme.[36]

1591); Hernando de Soto, *Emblemas moralizadas* (Madrid: Juan Iñiguez de Lequerica, 1599); Juan de Borja, *Empresas morales* (Bruxelles: François Foppens, 1680); Sebastian de Covarrubias Horozco, *Emblemas morales* (Madrid: Luis Sánchez, 1610); Juan Francisco Fernandez de Heredia, *Trabajos y afanes de Hércules* (Madrid: Francisco Sanz, 1682).

[34] Sur le genre emblématique on peut consulter: Robert Clements, *Picta Poesis. Literary and Humanistic Theory in Renaissance Emblem Books* (Rome: Edizione di Storia e Letteratura, 1960); *L'emblème à la Renaissance*, éd. Yves Giraud (Paris: Société d'édition d'enseignement supérieur, 1982); Antonio Bernat Vistarini, *Enciclopedia de emblemas españoles ilustrados* (Madrid: Akal, 1999); *Estudios sobre emblemática española*, éd. Sagrario López Poza (A Coruña: Sociedad de Cultura Valle Inclán, 2000); *Los días de Alción: emblemas, literatura y arte del Siglo de Oro*, éds. Antonio Bernat Vistarini – John T. Cull (Palma de Mallorca: Sociedad española de emblemas, 2002).

[35] Rubio, *Historia de la música española*, p. 224.

[36] Vicente Lleó, *Nueva Roma, mitología y humanismo en el renacimiento sevillano* (Séville: Diputación Provincial, 1979).

Les trois livres de musique pour vihuela, furent publiés dans un seul volume par Juan de León en 1546.[37] Les deux premiers livres contiennent uniquement de la musique instrumentale. Certaines pièces sont des adaptations des extraits de messes de Josquin. Le troisième livre est composé de pièces pour chant et vihuela: motets, romances, chansons, sonnets, *villancicos*, etc. L'œuvre comprend également des pièces pour guitare. Mudarra est l'un des vihuelistes loué par Bermudo.[38]

L'édition de l'œuvre de Mudarra est très soignée: elle comporte plusieurs emblèmes et gravures qui enrichissent la présentation du livre. Ses aspects décoratifs laissent penser que Juan de León était un homme cultivé qui fréquentait sans doute les milieux humanistes. Il commence son activité d'imprimeur à Séville, mais en 1549, il déménage à Ossuna, nommé imprimeur officiel du *Studium Generale* fondé par don Juan Téllez de Giron, comte d'Ureña. Juan de Leon est également l'imprimeur de trois écrits de Bermudo: *Libro primero* (1549), *Arte Tripharia* (1550) et *Declaración de instrumentos musicales* (1555). Son activité s'arrête à partir de cette année.

Dans l'œuvre de Mudarra se trouve une gravure qui représente un heaume avec plume entouré de l'inscription suivante: 'Ex bello pax, ex pace concordia, ex concordia musica constat.'

Cette illustration garde une grande parenté avec l'un des emblèmes d'Alciat regroupés sous le titre de la paix. Dans l'image d'Alciat, on voit des abeilles qui ont fait leur ruche dans un heaume abandonné; l'inscription est brève: 'ex bello pax'.

Le heaume symbolise la guerre tandis que les abeilles évoquent le miel et la cire, symboles de l'abondance en temps de paix. Sa signification morale énonce le lien entre la guerre et la paix. En quelque sorte la seule justification de la guerre est le rétablissement de la paix.

Dans le livre de Mudarra, l'inscription plus développée modifie un peu sa signification car elle s'applique à la musique en tant qu'harmonie. On pourrait voir ici une allusion non seulement à la musique sonore mais aussi à l'harmonie universelle ou musique des sphères d'origine pythagoricienne.[39]

[37] Klaus Wagner, 'Los libros del canónigo y vihuelista Alonso Mudarra', *Bulletin Hispanique*, 92 (1990), 655-675; Juan Delgado Casado, *Diccionario de impresores españoles: (siglos XV-XVI)* (Madrid: Arco Libros, 1996).

[38] Bermudo, *Declaración*, fol. 29v.

[39] On pourrait également interpréter, comme me l'a signalé Anna-Laura Puliafito lors du Colloque, que la paix est nécessaire au développement de la musique, des arts et de la culture.

FIGURE 3. Mudarra, *Tres libros de música* (Séville: Juan de León, 1546, fac-similé Monaco: Chanterelle, 1980), fol. 58v.
Avec l'aimable autorisation de Chanterelle-Verlag.

Ex bello pax.

FIGURE 4. Alciat, *Les Emblèmes* (Lyon: Macé Bonhomme, 1551, fac-similé Paris: Klincksieck, 1997), n° 177.
Avec l'aimable autorisation des éditions Klincksieck.

L'harmonie des sphères ou harmonie cosmique est l'une des traditions qui a influencé la pensée musicale à la Renaissance.[40] Pour les Pythagoriciens, le cosmos, l'univers est harmonie, *harmonia*, dont la signification est à la fois métaphysique et musicale. L'harmonie implique l'union des éléments contraires dans une tension en équilibre. Dans la pensée grecque, harmonie, équilibre et accord sont des notions étroitement liées.

Nous retrouvons les échos de la tradition de l'harmonie des sphères dans les livres de vihuela. Remarquons que, au Moyen Âge, cette doctrine de l'harmonie céleste s'est christianisée, de telle façon que c'est Dieu lui-même qui a accordé les mouvements des astres dans une proportion admirable. Ainsi, dans la préface à l'œuvre de Cabezón, son fils Hernando affirme que la musique n'est pas seulement l'art des voix et des instruments, mais qu'elle se trouve dans l'admirable machine de ce monde. L'univers est le premier instrument, accordé par la main de la sagesse divine dans une grande consonance et proportion.[41]

L'harmonie universelle se reflète également dans la musique. C'est pourquoi, les pythagoriciens appelaient harmonie et la musique des planètes et la gamme musicale comprise à l'intérieur d'une octave.

Des idées analogues sont exprimées par Fuenllana qui décrit la musique comme une admirable 'concordancia', mot dérivé de *concordia* et que nous traduisons par 'harmonie':

> Il est donc raisonnable que la musique, dont Dieu se sert tant, rende heureux les hommes; car elle est si excellente que même le tout puissant

[40] La littérature sur la tradition de l'harmonie des sphères est très abondante. Le lecteur pourra trouver de plus amples informations dans les titres suivants: Théodore Reinach, 'La musique des sphères', *Revue des études grecques,* 13 (1900), 432-449; Pierre Boyancé, 'Les Muses et l'harmonie des sphères', in *Mélanges à la mémoire de Félix Grat*, (Paris: Pecqueur-Grat, 1947), pp. 3-16; Claude V. Palisca, *Musical Humanism in Italian Renaissance Musical Thought* (New Haven: Yale University Press, 1985); Paloma Otaola, 'Pervivencia del mundo clásico en los libros de música para vihuela y tecla del siglo XVI', in *Humanismo y Pervivencia del mundo clásico* (Cádiz: Université de Cadiz, 1993), pp. 710-712; Joscelyn Godwin, *The Harmony of the Spheres: a Sourcebook of the Pythagorean Tradition in Music* (Rochester: Inner Traditions International, 1993); Gary Tomlinson, *Music in Renaissance Magic: Toward a Historiography of Others* (Chicago: University of Chicago Press, 1993); Jamie James, *The Music of the Spheres. Music, Science and the Natural Order of the Universe* (New York: Copernicus Press, 1995); Thomas J. Mathiesen, *Apollo's Lyre: Greek Music and Music Theory in Antiquity and the Middle Ages*, Publications of the Center for the History of Music Theory and Literature, 2 (Lincoln, Nebraska-London: University of Nebraska Press, 1999).

[41] Cabezón, *Obras*, p. 14.

> créateur du ciel et de la terre n'a pas voulu les laisser sans cette admirable harmonie.[42]

Dans le sens musical, l'*harmonia* est la *concordia* en latin, d'où est issu le vocable espagnol *concordancia* qui signifie la concordance ou l'équilibre entre les sons aigus et les graves. Les mots 'harmonie', 'accord', 'consonance' et 'concordance' sont utilisés par les théoriciens pour décrire les bonnes relations entre les sons dans la composition musicale. Ainsi, dans le contexte de l'alternance ou diversité de consonances dans le contrepoint, Bermudo utilise le mot *concordancia* comme synonyme de consonance:

> Après une quinte, vous mettez une sixte, puis une octave et ainsi vous composez à l'aide de diverses *concordances*. Plus la diversité des *consonances* est grande, plus la musique sera parfaite et d'une plus grande sonorité et mélodie.[43]

On pourrait interpréter dans ce sens les paroles de la devise: 'Ex bello pax; ex pace concordia; ex concordia musica constat'. La musique est harmonie en tant que résultat de l'accord entre les sons consonants. D'autre part, parmi les effets bienfaisants de la musique figure celui de répandre l'harmonie et la paix. D'après Valderrabano, grâce à la musique, grandissent l'harmonie et l'amitié parmi les hommes.[44]

Même si cet emblème, choisi probablement par l'éditeur dans le but d'embellir son livre, n'a pas au premier abord de lien direct avec l'auteur ni avec son entourage, il reflète néanmoins la conception de la musique que l'on retrouve dans les préfaces des livres de vihuela et dans les écrits des théoriciens.

La pensée musicale du seizième siècle récupère donc l'image de l'harmonie de l'homme et de l'univers, résultat de l'union des éléments contraires, du corps et de l'esprit pour l'homme, et des différents éléments qui composent le cosmos pour l'univers. Cette même idée, appliquée à la

[42] 'Porque cosa [la música] con que tanto se sirve Dios, razón es que con ella tengan contento los hombres, por ser tan qualificada que aun la machina de cielo y tierra no quiso su potentissimo artifice dexarla sin esta admirable concordancia.' Fuenllana, *Orphenica Lyra*, fol. 3r.

[43] 'Después de una quinta dais una sexta, luego una octava y así vais componiendo con diversas concordancias. Cuanto mayor fuere la diversidad de consonancias tanto será la música mas perfecta y de mayor sonoridad y melodía.' Bermudo, *Declaración*, fol. 131r.

[44] 'Con esta [la música] crece la concordia y la amistad entre los hombres.' Valderrábano, *Silva de sirenas*, fol. A3v.

musique, explique l'harmonie agréable et douce, capable de ravir l'esprit de celui qui écoute, qui naît de l'union des différents sons et instruments bien accordés.

*Emblème d'Hercule*

Ce deuxième emblème figure sur la page de titre du deuxième livre d'*Orphenica lyra* de Miguel de Fuenllana. Ce vihueliste, aveugle de naissance selon son propre témoignage dans la dédicace à Philippe II, est l'auteur de l'un des plus beaux recueils de musique pour vihuela. On ignore, comme pour la plupart des vihuelistes, les dates de sa naissance et de sa mort. D'après Bermudo, Fuenllana était musicien au service de la Marquise de Tarifa.[45] Ce qui est certain est qu'à partir de 1562, il faisait partie de la Cour d'Isabelle de Valois.[46] Il est très probable aussi que Fuenllana ait vécu à Séville à l'époque où son livre paraît dans cette même ville.[47] Il était très renommé de son vivant selon le témoignage de Bermudo qui le considère parmi les meilleurs instrumentistes de son époque.[48]

*Orphenica lyra*, dont le titre est un hommage à la mémoire d'Orphée, se compose de six livres de musique pour vihuela et quelques pièces pour guitare. La plupart des pièces sont des arrangements de compositeurs célèbres, notamment Josquin, Morales, Flecha, Guerrero, Gombert, Willaert, Verdelot, Archadelt... D'autres sont des fantaisies originales. Chaque livre est précédé d'une page de garde sur laquelle est indiqué sommairement le contenu du livre. Ces indications sur le type de pièces contenues dans chaque livre sont encadrées par une décoration de type architectural sur laquelle on trouve des inscriptions en latin, généralement en deux vers, l'un dans la partie supérieure de la frise et l'autre dans la partie inférieure de la page.

C'est une très belle édition de Martin de Montesdoca, imprimeur de rénom à Séville et connu également pour sa culture et son érudition. Ses épigrammes en latin sont un exemple de la production latine des écoles poétiques à Séville au seizième siècle.[49]

[45] Bermudo, *Declaración*, fol. 30r.

[46] Rubio, *Historia de la música española*, p. 229.

[47] Griffiths, 'Fuenllana', p. 274.

[48] Bermudo, *Declaración*, fol. 29v.

[49] José Solis de los Santos, 'Epigramas latinos del impresor Martin de Montesdoca', in *Los humanistas españoles y el humanismo europeo* (Murcie: Université de Murcie, 1990), pp. 237-241 (p. 237). Voir aussi Klaus Wagner, *Martin de Montesdoca y su prensa:*

Au moins douze des quinze exemplaires connus représentent deux variantes de l'édition de 1554. Les différences entre les deux versions se trouvent dans la matière préliminaire: pages de titre, poèmes de louange et colophon.[50]

La page de titre du livre II présente l'emblème d'Hercule avec l'inscription 'labor omnia vincit'. Cette inscription reprend les trois derniers mots du vers 145 du premier livre des *Géorgiques* de Virgile: 'labor omnia vicit'. Le texte de Virgile est modifié car le temps du verbe chez Fuenllana est au présent. Des paroles similaires apparaissent dans les *Bucoliques* (10, 69): 'Omnia vincit amor', mais ici, la structure de la phrase est différente.[51] Comme pour la citation de Martial, la forme du texte a été modifiée. La devise est probablement une déformation du texte des *Géorgiques* car l'emblème d'Hercule symbolise l'effort pour vaincre les difficultés.

On pourrait se poser la question de la relation entre l'emblème et la musique contenue dans le deuxième livre. Celui-ci est un recueil d'adaptations de motets et de fantaisies de l'auteur. On ne trouve aucun indice d'un lien éventuel. Néanmoins, l'emblème d'Hercule peut être mis en rapport avec l'idée que l'étude et le travail sont nécessaires pour l'apprentissage de la musique.[52] La musique est une science; elle n'est pas le fruit du seul talent naturel. Par ailleurs, les musiciens, instrumentistes ou compositeurs, sont encouragés à apprendre la théorie et les fondements rationnels de l'art des sons, comme nous le rappellent les théoriciens de l'époque, notamment Juan Bermudo: 'Il n'y a rien d'aussi dur et d'aussi

*contribución al estudio de la imprenta y de la bibliografía sevillanas del siglo XVI* (Séville: Université de Séville, 1982).

[50] Les deux versions d'*Orphenica lyra* ont été classées dans deux groupes. Les exemplaires du groupe A sont ceux de la Biblioteca Nacional de España (R. 5647), British Library, Bodleian Library, Bibliothèque Nationale de France, Bibliothèque du Conservatoire de Paris et Nassauische Landesbibliothek (Wiesbaden). Les exemplaires du groupe B, Biblioteca Nacional de España (R. 9283), Biblioteca de El Escorial, Koninklijke Bibliotheek van België / Bibliothèque Royale de Belgique, New York Public Library, Newberry Library (Chicago), présentent des lacunes notamment du colophon et des aspects décoratifs sur les pages de titre: Griffiths, 'Fuenllana', p. 274. Ainsi l'inscription *Soli Deo honor et gloria* figure dans le fac-similé de l'édition de Minkoff mais pas dans l'édition numérique d'*Opera prima*.

[51] Virgile, *Géorgiques*, 1, 145, texte et traduction par Eugène de Saint-Denis (Paris: Les Belles Lettres, 1963), p. 7. *Bucoliques*, 10, 69, texte et traduction par Eugène de Saint-Denis (Paris: Les Belles Lettres, 1963), p. 71.

[52] En fait, dans le premier livre, la première pièce est le duo de la *Messe d'Hercules* de Josquin, mais nous ne pensons pas qu'il y ait une relation avec la gravure du deuxième livre.

FIGURE 5. Fuenllana, *Orphenica lyra* (Séville: Martin de Montesdoca, 1554, fac-similé Genève: Minkoff, 1981), fol. 14.
Avec l'aimable autorisation des éditions Minkoff.

résistant que le travail et la constance ne puissent ramollir et maîtriser, ni rien aussi difficile que la persévérance ne rende facile.'[53]

D'après Vindel, l'emblème d'Hercule a été utilisé comme marque typographique par Juan de León pendant son activité à Séville en 1545.[54] Étant donné que les deux imprimeurs travaillaient dans cette ville à la même époque, on peut supposer que les mêmes illustrations circulaient chez les différents imprimeurs.

## Marques typographiques

Certains imprimeurs prennent des emblèmes comme marque typographique, ce qui montre leur popularité. Parfois, la marque de l'imprimeur figure sur la page de titre, mais le plus souvent elle est située à côté du colophon.

[53] 'No hay cosa tan recia y dura que la continuación y trabajo no ablande y cave, ni tan dificultosa, que la perseverancia no haga fácil.' Bermudo, *Declaración*, fol. 60r.

[54] Francisco Vindel, *Escudos y Marcas de impresores y libreros en España durante los siglos XV a XIX* (Barcelone: Orbis, 1942), n° 185.

*Marque typographique de Juan de León*

Sur la page de titre de chacun des livres de l'œuvre de Mudarra figure un emblème qui représente la croix sur le Golgotha avec les trois clous, symboles de la Passion, Jérusalem au fond.[55] L'image est entourée par une banderole circulaire portant l'inscription: 'Soli Deo honor et gloria'.

FIGURE 6. Mudarra, *Tres libros de música*, page de titre.
Avec l'aimable autorisation de Chanterelle-Verlag.

Le même emblème figure au colophon des deux premières œuvres de Bermudo, éditées aussi par Juan de León, avec une variante: au pied de l'image est inscrite la légende 'Sola fides sufficit' qui n'apparaît pas dans les livres de Mudarra. En fait, les deux inscriptions sont fréquemment utilisées par d'autres imprimeurs, unies parfois à d'autres images.[56] L'inscription 'Soli Deo honor et gloria' apparaît également sur la page de titre du cinquième livre d'*Orphenica lyra*.[57]

[55] Giuseppina Zapella, *Le Marche dei tipografi e degli editori italiani del Cinquecento* (Milan: Editrice Bibliografica, 1986), p. 136.

[56] 'Soli Deo honor et gloria' est utilisé par Pierre Regnard, imprimeur à Tours, 1566-1569 et 'Sola fides sufficit', par Martin Lempereur, imprimeur à Anvers, 1528-1537. Louis-Catherine Silvestre, *Marques typographiques* (Paris: Jannet, 1853, fac-similé Amsterdam: Grüner, 1971), marques 1121 et 16.

[57] Cette inscription, comme nous l'avons mentionné précédemment, n'apparaît pas dans tous les exemplaires d'*Orphenica lyra*. Elle est dans l'exemplaire utilisé par Minkoff, mais elle n'apparaît pas dans l'édition numérique qui reproduit l'exemplaire de la Biblioteca Nacional de España, R. 9283.

L'emblème ou l'inscription seule apparaissent à des dates et à des endroits différents chez plusieurs imprimeurs. Leur présence est en relation avec le sens religieux qui imprégnait la société de l'époque. Par ailleurs, les préfaces des livres de musique rappellent au lecteur que la finalité principale de la musique est de rendre gloire à Dieu. La marque de Juan de León exprime par l'image et son inscription les mêmes idées que nous retrouvons dans les préfaces des autres livres et des traités théoriques de l'époque.[58]

*Marque typographique de Fernández de Córdoba*

Francisco Fernández de Córdoba est l'imprimeur de *Silva de Sirenas* de Enríquez de Valderrábano. Nous avons très peu d'informations sur Valderrábano, hormis les données qui figurent sur la licence pour l'impression du livre.[59] D'après Bermudo, Valderrabano était vihueliste au service du Comte de Miranda à Peñaranda de Duero, près de Burgos.[60] Cette information, probablement tirée de la dédicace, n'a pu être vérifiée.[61] *Silva de Sirenas* est un grand recueil de musique pour vihuela composé de sept livres. Le titre évoque les sirènes, divinités marines qui attiraient par leurs chants les marins naviguant à proximité. La dénomination de *Silva* ('forêt') répond à la variété de compositions musicales recueillies dans le livre.[62] Comme dans d'autres livres, beaucoup de pièces sont des arrangements de compositions polyphoniques de Josquin, Gombert, Willaert, Morales, etc.

À côté du colophon apparaît une représentation de Mercure qui lève un bras ailé au ciel tandis que l'autre pend vers la terre, attaché à une grosse pierre. L'inscription qui sert à encadrer l'image est la suivante: 'Ne ingenium volitet/ Paupertas deprimit ipsum'.

Dans d'autres livres de cet imprimeur, la marque présente quelques variantes, notamment dans la structure grammaticale de l'inscription, mais le message reste le même.[63] Cette image, sans l'inscription, figure dans le colophon de *El Parnaso*.

[58] Dans le colophon du livre de Milán, *El maestro*, bien qu'il ne contienne pas de pièces religieuses, on peut lire une formule similaire: 'pour l'honneur et la gloire de Dieu', fol. R6.

[59] Rubio, *Historia de la música española*, p. 225-226.

[60] Bermudo, *Declaración*, fol. 29.

[61] Griffiths, 'At Court', p. 10.

[62] Valderrabano, *Silva de sirenas*, fol. A3r.

[63] Vindel, *Escudos y Marcas de impresores y libreros en España*, nº 174.

FIGURE 7. Valderrábano, *Silva de Sirenas*, fol. 104v.
Avec l'aimable autorisation des éditions Minkoff.

La marque de Fernández de Córdoba garde une grande similitude avec l'un des emblèmes d'Alciat regroupés sous le nom de *Fortuna*. Toutefois, les images et les inscriptions varient d'une édition à l'autre, tout en conservant le même enseignement: 'Paupertatem summis ingeniis obesse, ne provehantur'.

L'inscription de l'emblème énonce que la pauvreté est un obstacle à la réussite pour des personnes de talent. Cet emblème de la fortune n'est pas en rapport avec le monde de la musique. C'est plutôt une manière indirecte

Paupertatem ſummis ingenijs obeſſe, ne prouehantur.

FIGURE 8. Alciat, *Emblèmes*, n° 120.
Avec l'aimable autorisation des éditions Klincksieck.

de rappeler l'importance du mécénat et de la protection des grands pour le développement de la musique et des arts. En même temps, la parenté avec les emblèmes d'Alciat montre bien à quel point ce genre d'illustrations était apprécié en dehors des recueils du genre.

## Inscriptions latines

Les inscriptions latines, outre celles des emblèmes, accompagnent également les gravures pour renforcer ou expliciter la signification de l'image. Parfois, elles y figurent seules, en guise d'ornement.

Les pages de titre des livres quatre, cinq et six d'*Orphenica lyra* ne portent pas d'emblème, mais uniquement une inscription poétique:[64]

> Livre 4: 'Delphinas mulsit vocalis Arion in undis. / Haec Orphaea chelys pectora nostra rapit'
>
> Livre 6: 'Accipe divinam quae venit ab aethere musam / Hac poteris curas attenuare Lyra'

Les inscriptions des deux livres sont enracinées dans la tradition ancienne. Celles du quatrième livre évoquent la légende d'Arion sauvé des eaux par les dauphins et le mythe d'Orphée, qui charmait au son de sa cithare les hommes et les bêtes sauvages.[65]

En effet, les légendes d'Orphée et d'Arion connaissent une grande popularité dans la littérature musicale de l'époque, notamment dans les livres de vihuela. Orphée incarne le pouvoir pacificateur et civilisateur de la musique. Cabezón lui attribue l'origine des cités et de la civilisation. Selon lui, les hommes vivaient autrefois comme des bêtes, éparpillés dans les montagnes, sans loi, sans ordre ni éducation. Le premier qui commença à les unir fut Orphée dont la musique les attirait tous.[66]

La tradition met en relief la douceur et le charme de cette musique qui apaisait les fauves, faisait s'incliner les branches des arbres et toutes sortes d'animaux accouraient pour l'écouter. Certains le considèrent comme le père de la musique pour vihuela;[67] d'autres soulignent les effets de sa musique sur les fauves et sur la nature. Miguel de Fuenllana fait référence au récit d'Eurydice libérée des Enfers par le chant d'Orphée qui réussit à tempérer la rigueur des ministres de Pluton par la douceur de sa vihuela.[68] Le rôle civilisateur de la musique, qui rend douce et pacifique l'âme sauvage, lié au mythe d'Orphée, apparaît également chez Salinas.[69]

[64] Nous avons déjà parlé de l'inscription du cinquième livre 'Soli Deo honor et gloria'.

[65] Le récit d'Arion apparaît dans Hérodote, *Histoires*, tome I, I, 23-24, éd./trad. Philippe-Ernest Legrand (Paris: Les Belles Lettres, 1995). Il est cité par Aulu-Gelle, *Les nuits attiques*, tome IV, 16,19, éd./trad. Yvette Julien (Paris: Les Belles Lettres, 1998) et par Virgile, *L'Enéide*, 3, 332, éd. Henri Goelzer, trad. André Bellessort (Paris: Les Belles Lettres, 1961). Pour le mythe d'Orphée, voir entre autres: Virgile, *L'Enéide*, 5, 252.

[66] Cabezón, *Obras*, p. 20.

[67] Au fol. 6v du livre de Milán, *El maestro*, une gravure représente Orphée en train de jouer de la vihuela. Cette gravure est accompagnée d'une inscription en espagnol, raison pour laquelle nous n'en parlons pas dans ce travail.

[68] Fuenllana, *Orphenica lyra*, fol. 3r.

[69] Francisco Salinas, *De musica libri septem* (Salamanque: Mathias Gasthius, 1577). *Siete Libros sobre música*, traduction espagnole par Ismael Fernández de la Cuesta (Madrid: Alpuerto, 1983), p. 23.

Quant à Arion, il est le musicien et poète célèbre de la Grèce antique qui fut jeté à la mer par les pirates qui lui avaient volé ses biens. Les dauphins attirés par sa musique s'étaient rassemblés autour du bateau et l'un d'eux le conduisit sain et sauf jusqu'au rivage, ne recevant comme récompense d'un tel voyage que la musique qu'il entendait.[70] C'est en l'honneur de cette légende que Narváez donne à son livre le titre de *Six livres du dauphin*. Dans ce même livre, au folio 4, une gravure représente Arion sur un dauphin en train de jouer de la vihuela.[71]

Outre la popularité de ces deux légendes, l'allusion à Arion et à Orphée est une façon de rappeler l'ancienneté de la musique et de la vihuela.

L'inscription du sixième livre fait allusion au pouvoir de la musique pour apaiser l'âme troublée par les soucis de la vie quotidienne. Les effets de la musique sur l'âme humaine, soulignés par la tradition pythagoricienne, rejoignent les sources bibliques dans les livres de vihuela. Nous aborderons cet aspect de la musique dans les commentaires aux gravures et illustrations.

## Gravures et Illustrations

Les trois gravures qui comportent une inscription latine se trouvent dans l'œuvre d'Alonso Mudarra, *Tres Libros de música*.

### *Mercure, père de la lyre*

Cette gravure est accompagnée d'un distique d'Horace, Ode X, *Ad Mercurium*, du premier livre d'Odes:

> *Te canam magni Iovis, et deorum*
> *Nuntium, Curvaeque lirae parentem*

La représentation de Mercure, père de la lyre, renforce l'idée que la musique est d'origine divine. En effet, les Grecs avaient entouré de légendes l'origine de la musique, afin de lui accorder une place privilégiée parmi les arts. Apollon était le dieu de l'Olympe, protecteur de la musique et des instruments à cordes. Hermès (Mercure) est considéré comme l'inventeur de la lyre, faite avec la carapace d'une tortue et les nerfs d'un bœuf.

[70] Cabezón, *Obras*, p. 20.

[71] Cette illustration ne comporte pas de texte.

FIGURE 9. Alonso Mudarra, *Tres libros de música*, fol. 4v.
Avec l'aimable autorisation de Chanterelle-Verlag.

Cette légende est transmise par la tradition et recueillie dans les sources musicales du seizième siècle. Valderrábano cite Mercure parmi les premiers musiciens et poètes[72] et Cabezón lui attribue l'invention de la musique avec les neufs Muses.[73]

La présence du mythe de Mercure comme inventeur de la lyre permet l'association de la vihuela avec l'instrument grec, d'où découle son prestige. Ce lien entre la lyre et la vihuela semble être évoqué par ces paroles de Valderrábano dans le prologue à *Silva de Sirenas*:

> Cette [harmonie] Dieu ne l'a mise en aucune créature terrestre avec une telle mesure et perfection comme chez l'homme, ni en aucun instrument à cordes comme dans la vihuela. Ainsi donc, tout ce que les savants anciens,

[72] Valderrábano, *Silva de Sirenas*, fol. A4r.
[73] Cabezón, *Obras*, p. 16.

> et tous les autres, ont écrit à la louange de la musique, il semble évident qu'on doit l'attribuer à plus forte raison à la vihuela, car elle est la plus parfaite consonance de cordes.[74]

Comme le fait remarquer Bermudo, la source de la légende de Mercure, inventeur des instruments à cordes, est le *De institutione musica* de Boèce.[75] Le théoricien espagnol aborde dans le quatrième livre de la *Declaración*, consacré aux instruments, la question sur l'origine de la vihuela et de la guitare. Le premier à inventer la guitare fut Tubal, personnage biblique mentionné par la Sainte Ecriture, ce qui montre en outre l'antériorité des récits bibliques par rapport aux récits païens et donc leur supériorité sur eux. Après lui, ce fut Mercure. Puis Orphée, qui en ajoutant deux autres cordes, peut être considéré comme l'inventeur de la vihuela.

> Cherchant qui avait été le premier à utiliser la vihuela ou la guitare après son inventeur Tubal (ce dont témoigne la Sainte Ecriture), comme le dit Boèce dans le chapitre vingt du premier livre, j'ai trouvé ce que j'étais en train de chercher. Ce saint docteur affirme, en prenant à témoin l'ancien Nicomaque, que Mercure fut l'inventeur d'un instrument de musique à quatre cordes à l'instar des quatre éléments. Cet instrument perdura ainsi jusqu'au temps du grand Orphée [...]. Des propos de Boèce je déduis que Mercure utilisa la guitare et qu'Orphée la développa en la rendant vihuela.[76]

A partir de cette légende, Bermudo donne à la guitare ancienne à quatre cordes le nom de *guitare de Mercure*. Cela montre la popularité de cette légende sur l'invention du premier instrument à cordes qui est présente dans les différentes sources de la littérature musicale espagnole du siezième siècle.

[74] 'Esta [armonía] en ninguna criatura terrena la puso Dios con tanta razón y perfectión como en el hombre, ni en los instrumentos de cuerdas como en el de vihuela, Y assí es que lo que los sabios antiguos y todos los demás en loor de la música escrivieron, parece claro que con más razón se deve atribuir a la vihuela, en que es la más perfecta consonancia de cuerdas.' Valderrábano, *Silva de Sirenas,* A2v.

[75] Boèce, *Traité de la musique*, 20, 6, introduction, traduction et notes Christian Meyer (Turnhout: Brépols, 2004), p. 62.

[76] 'Andando a buscar el primero que usó la vihuela, o guitarra después del inventor Tubal (de lo qual da testimonio la Sacra Scriptura) de las palabras de Boecio en el capítulo veynte de libro primero saqué, lo que desseava. Dize este sancto doctor trayendo por testigo a Nichomaco antiguo, que Mercurio fue el inventor de poner la música en quatro cuerdas a imitación de los quatro elementos: y duró esta manera de instrumento hasta el tiempo del gran músico Orpheo [...]. De las palabras de Boecio saco que Mercurio usó guitarra y Orpheo la augmentó y la hizo vihuela.' Bermudo, *Declaración*, fol. 96v.

FIGURE 10. Mudarra, *Tres libros de música*, fol. 58r.
Avec l'aimable autorisation de Chanterelle-Verlag.

*Le prophète Elisée*

> *Cumque caneret psaltes, facta est super eum manus Domini*
> (IIII. Reg. Caput iii [2, Rois, 3, 15-16]) [77]

La gravure représente le moment où Elisée fait venir un musicien pour accompagner sa prière au son de la cithare. Alors, les cieux s'ouvrent, et Dieu fait à Elisée la prophétie de la victoire sur Moab. Cette gravure est accompagnée d'une citation du livre des Rois, où l'on raconte la scène.

Une image similaire se trouve dans la page de titre du troisième livre d'*Orphenica lyra* de Fuenllana, mais l'inscription qui l'accompagne est tirée du psaume 150: 'Laudate Deum in cithara: laudate Deum cordis, & organo.'

Les versets du psaume 150, 'Louez Dieu au son de la cithare; louez Dieu sur les cordes et le fifre', nous encouragent à louer Dieu au son des instruments.

Le sens religieux de la musique s'enracine également dans le Monde Antique. En effet, la musique avait un rôle important dans la société grecque lors de cérémonies religieuses.[78] On sait que Platon, dans plusieurs

[77] Les références bibliques des livres de vihuela renvoient à la *Vulgate* tandis que les éditions modernes reprennent l'ordre de la *Néo-Vulgate*.

[78] Adolfo Salazar, *Teoría y práctica de la Música a través de la historia*, I, *La Música en la cultura griega* (Mexico: Colegio de México, 1954), p. 105.

FIGURE 11. Fuenllana, *Orphenica lyra*, fol. 59.
Avec l'aimable autorisation des éditions Minkoff.

passages des *Lois* et de la *République*, considérait la musique au-dessus des autres arts, parce qu'elle contribuait à forger le caractère et disposait l'homme à acquérir la vertu.[79] L'assimilation chrétienne de la tradition platonicienne, notamment à partir de saint Augustin, octroie à la musique la capacité de détacher l'âme des choses terrestres pour l'amener vers la contemplation, favorisant ainsi la prière et la méditation.[80]

[79] Platon, *République*, éd./trad. E. Chambry (Paris: Les Belles Lettres, 1970), III, 400 c-e; Werner Jaeger, *Paideia* (Mexico: Fondo de Cultura Económica, 1971), p. 620.

[80] Saint Augustin, *De musica*, texte, éd./trad. G. Finaert – F. J. Thonnard (Paris: Desclée de Brouwer, 1947), 6, 1; Paloma Otaola González, *El De musica de san Agustín y la tradición pitagórico-platónica* (Valladolid: Estudio Agustiniano, 2005) pp. 111-112.

Cette tradition est reprise dans les livres de vihuela dans lesquels les auteurs nous rappellent que la musique nous rapproche de Dieu. Ainsi, Venegas de Henestrosa considère la musique comme un moyen privilégié pour l'oraison, pour élever l'esprit vers le Créateur qui a tout crée en harmonie et musique.[81] Par la musique, affirme Valderrábano, grandissent la charité, la piété et la dévotion. L'esprit s'enflamme et l'âme s'élève en louange et reconnaissance à Dieu. D'où l'importance de la musique liturgique, dont la finalité est de louer Dieu dans les chœurs et dans les Messes, comme l'affirme Bermudo: 'Il est grandement utile de savoir que par la musique, Dieu nous accepte dans cette vie comme ses serviteurs et dans l'autre comme des chanteurs éternels en compagnie des Anges.'[82]

Par ailleurs, le répertoire pour vihuela, qui comprend aussi bien des pièces profanes que de la musique sacrée, montre bien le sens religieux de la musique.

*David jouant de la harpe*

La troisième gravure représente David en train de jouer de la harpe pour calmer la mélancolie de Saül. L'image est accompagnée du texte du récit des effets apaisants de la musique sur Saül.

> *Quandocumque spiritus domini malus arripiebat Saul, David tollebat citharam et percutiebat manu sua & refocillabatur Saul; & levius habebat. Recedebat enim ab eo spiritus malus*
> (I. Regum, Caput XVI [Samuel I, 16, 23])

Le pouvoir de la musique d'agir sur les émotions et sur la psychologie humaine a été développé par les Pythagoriciens. La musique aide à récupérer l'équilibre perdu et à guérir certains troubles. Cette conviction de son bienfait sur la vie humaine se reflète dans l'habitude de Pythagore de jouer de la lyre et de chanter plusieurs fois par jour:

> Le soir, lorsque ses compagnons se préparaient au sommeil, il les débarrassait des soucis du jour et du tumulte et il purifiait leur esprit agité, leur donnant un sommeil paisible, plein de beaux rêves [...]. Lorsqu'ils se levaient, il les débarrassait de leur torpeur nocturne, de leur faiblesse et de l'engourdissement de la nuit au moyen de certains chants et mélodies particuliers.[83]

[81] Venegas de Henestrosa, *Libro de cifra nueva*, p. 152.

[82] 'Grande utilidad es esta, que por la música Dios nos reciba en esta vida por criados: y en la otra por cantores perpetuos en compañía de los Angeles.' Bermudo, *Declaración*, fol. 8v.

[83] Jamblique, *Vie de Pythagore*, éd./trad. Luc Brisson – A. Ph. Segonds (Paris: Les Belles-Lettres, 1996), p. 65.

I, Regum Caput, XVI.

¶ Q̃ñdocũq; spũs dñi malus arripiebat Saul, David tollebat citharã et percutiebat manu sua: & refocillabatur Saul; & leuius habebat. Recedebat enim ab eo spũs malus.

FIGURE 12. Mudarra, *Tres libros de música*, fol. 60v.
Avec l'aimable autorisation de Chanterelle-Verlag.

Les musiciens du seizième siècle héritent donc ces traditions en leur accordant une place dans leurs réflexions sur la musique, tout en ajoutant aux sources classiques la tradition biblique, dans laquelle David joue un rôle principal. En général, tous les auteurs reprennent le cas de Saül soulagé de sa mélancolie par le chant de David, comme nous pouvons le lire dans ce texte de Bermudo, qui reprend la scène de la gravure du livre de Mudarra, mais sans citer le vihueliste:

> On raconte de Saül dans le premier livre des Rois, chapitre seize, que lorsque l'esprit mauvais s'emparait de lui, David jouait doucement de la harpe et le roi Saül se consolait et son cœur s'épanouissait et s'élargissait par la musique. Il se sentait tellement soulagé que l'esprit mauvais le quittait.[84]

[84] 'De Saúl se dize en el libro primero de los Reyes capitulo diez y seys, que cuando le tomava el spiritu malo, tañía David suavemente la Harpa, y el Rey Saul era consolado

Après avoir présenté les faits, il ajoute ses propres commentaires sur les effets bienfaisants de la musique:

> La musique du musicien David avait trois effets sur Saül. Le premier était d'épanouir, d'élargir et de réjouir son cœur, ce qui est le contraire de la mélancolie; en effet, celle-ci attriste l'homme tandis que la musique le réjouit. Le deuxième était qu'il se sentait mieux, car en écoutant la musique, il recouvrait la santé. Troisièmement, la musique le délivrait de cette maladie.[85]

Par ailleurs, la tradition pythagoricienne des effets de la musique sur les émotions et les sentiments est largement commentée dans les préfaces des livres de vihuela, notamment dans *Silva de sirenas*, *Orphenica lyra* et dans les *Obras de música* de Cabezón.

## Conclusion

Pour tenter de répondre aux questions posées au début de ce travail sur le rôle des inscriptions latines, nous les avons classées en trois catégories:

Une première catégorie est représentée par l'*Invictissimus* inscrit sur la gravure de Jean III de Portugal. Cette formule était courante en latin comme forme de louange aux monarques et aux princes, en perpétuant la tradition des empereurs romains. Comme nous l'avons mentionné, elle rappelle les épigraphies latines des monuments commémoratifs.

La deuxième est constituée de citations bibliques. Étant donné que, dans les pays catholiques, la traduction de la Bible en langue vernaculaire était interdite, il est normal que les passages de l'Écriture soient cités en latin. Cependant, il est intéressant de constater que les citations explicitent les images qu'elles accompagnent. Or, les images sont parlantes en elles-mêmes pour celui qui est familier de l'histoire sacrée. Le fait donc d'expliciter par le texte la scène représentée peut correspondre à l'énorme succès des livres d'emblèmes. Les deux gravures des livres de vihuela

y su coraçon se dilatava y ensanchava con la Musica, era aliviado en tanta manera que el spiritu malo huía del.' Bermudo, *Declaración*, fol. 7r.

[85] 'Tres effectos hazía la música del tañedor David en Saúl. El primero, que se dilatava, estendia y alegrava el coraçon de Saúl: lo qual es contrario a la melancholía: que entristece al hombre, y la música lo alegra. Lo segundo se sentía mejor. Que como oía la Musica iba cobrando mejoría en la salud. Lo último dize, que era libre de la tal enfermedad.' Bermudo, *Declaración*, fol. 7r.

(Elisée et David) dont la source est l'Écriture utilisent la même technique que les emblèmes d'Alciat: une image, un texte et un enseignement moral. Dans le cas d'Élisée, le message est celui de l'efficacité de la musique pour la prière. Pour David, le texte comme l'image soulignent la capacité de la musique pour soulager la mélancolie et la tristesse.

Quant au troisième type d'inscriptions latines, il est constitué des citations classiques (Martial, Horace, Virgile). Ces dernières reflètent l'engouement pour les auteurs latins, caractéristique de la Renaissance. La présence du latin dans des livres de musique, non seulement accompagnant les gravures, mais dans des épigrammes et des poèmes à la louange de la musique et de l'auteur, confirme en quelque sorte que la musique de vihuela s'adressait en premier lieu à un public cultivé et raffiné. D'autre part, le latin reste la langue d'érudition, alors que le castillan se développe comme la langue littéraire et de la culture. Il est curieux de constater que tous les livres de musique instrumentale sont édités en castillan, or les livres de motets et autres compositions de musique sacrée sont souvent en latin. Quant aux traités théoriques, hormis celui de Salinas, ils sont tous écrits en langue vernaculaire.

Les trois catégories d'inscriptions, seules ou avec images, de source biblique ou classique, ont un rôle de rappel et d'évocation. Elles répondent aux idées diffusées dans les milieux humanistes autour de la musique et au désir d'imiter les anciens, en accordant à la musique l'importance et la splendeur qu'elle avait dans le Monde Antique. Parmi les thèmes que l'on retrouve aussi bien dans les textes, prologues et traités théoriques, que dans tous ces aspects décoratifs du livre imprimé, nous pouvons donc mentionner: l'origine divine de la musique; la doctrine pythagoricienne de l'harmonie cosmique; les effets de la musique sur l'âme; la valeur éthique de la musique et l'importance de la musique comme expression de louange à Dieu. Le retour aux sources anciennes, en lien avec les traditions et les mythes classiques autour de la musique (Orphée, Mercure, inventeur de la vihuela, Hercule symbolisant l'effort, Arion sauvé par les dauphins, etc.), mettent aussi en évidence le désir de rattacher la musique de cette époque à la tradition et à la culture antiques.

Bien évidemment, les gravures et illustrations ont surtout une fonction esthétique et c'est sans doute leur première finalité. Mais, on peut constater que les mêmes *topos*, textes et images, sont repris par différents imprimeurs indépendamment de l'auteur ou de la musique contenue dans le livre. De plus, les mêmes sujets sont abordés par les théoriciens, notamment par Bermudo et par Salinas, ce qui montre la diffusion d'une tradition commune. En somme, on pourrait penser que les imprimeurs et les auteurs, ainsi que les nobles auxquels les livres sont dédiés, respiraient une même atmosphère imprégnée d'érudition et de culture antique.

Pour finir, les emblèmes et les inscriptions latines constituent une forme condensée de l'expression d'une conception de la musique qui était partagée par les vihuelistes, par les théoriciens, par les imprimeurs et vraisemblablement par le public, destinataire de cette musique.

UNIVERSITÉ JEAN-MOULIN LYON 3
F – 69007 Lyon
otaola@univ-lyon3.fr

# *"PER PATRONOS, NON PER MERITA GRADUS EST EMERGENDI"* LIPSIUS'S CAREFUL CHOICE OF *PATRONI* AS A WAY OF CAREER PLANNING[*]

Jeanine De Landtsheer

From the first century A.D. on, starting a work with a dedicatory letter had become quite fashionable. Author and dedicatee could be equals (friends), but more often the relation was one of subordination (*cliens-patronus*). In both cases, though, the mechanism was essentially the same: the former had obtained a service or a gift from the other and thus felt obliged to repay this service or gift by showing gratitude through presenting a work. According to the rules of the *ars rhetorica*, which prescribed a humble approach in the preface, the author would express doubt about his own capacities either to treat the subject in a proper way, or to do so in an appropriate style. Hence the preface became important for self presentation, with thankfulness and (pseudo-)modesty as its most emphasized qualities. The subject, on the other hand, was often cried up a bit to match the dedicatee's reputation.

## Cui et qua causa

Lipsius applied his classical models faithfully in his dedicatory letters.[1] The selection of a dedicatee could be extremely important for more than

* My sincere thanks to Dr Paul Arblaster, who corrected my English.

1 I have strictly limited myself to the dedicatory letters, without taking into account the 'Prefaces to the reader' occurring in almost every work as well. In the latter Lipsius usually explains his way of approaching his subject, which, however interesting, does not meet the conference's subject and might be examined at another occasion. A complete list of Lipsius's works and their dedicatory letters, together with a reference to the description of the work in BBr is given in appendix [BBr = Ferdinand Vander Haeghen, *Bibliotheca Belgica: Bibliographie générale des Pays-Bas*, ed. Marie-Thérèse Lenger, 7 vols (Brussels, 1964-1975)]. For any references to Lipsius's letters the abbreviation ILE will be used, referring either to the volumes already available in the series *Iusti Lipsi Epistolae*, ed. by Alois Gerlo, Marcel A. Nauwelaerts, Hendrik D.L. Vervliet *et al*. (Brussels, 1978-) — up to nine volumes now —, or to A. Gerlo – H.D.L. Vervliet, *Inventaire de la correspondance de Juste Lipse, 1564-1606* (Antwerp: Éditions scientifiques Érasme, 1968). In case of the already published letters the Roman numeral of the corresponding part is added.

the obvious, 'honorable' and 'honorific' reasons. Going through the list of dedicatees, one notices immediately that most of his patrons were chosen from among people who were socially his superiors — prominent people in the service of Church or State, or illustrious members of the *res publica literarum*.[2] Occasionally the names of fellow-humanists or friends occur, but never those of people who were subordinated, such as his students or the young scholars he wanted to recommend. Taking into account the background of Lipsius's life, one can understand that he hardly ever offered his books to someone out of mere friendship. Guided by higher aspirations, he presented his books either as a discreet reminder that favours and support were welcome, or as an acknowledgement of benefices or favours and support already given. In a few cases the name put in front of the dedication was supposed to act as a guarantee of Lipsius's orthodoxy and a protection against criticism and even slander. Sometimes the reason for the selection of a patron is expressed quite clearly, whereas in other cases the author prefers more general and vague terms as *benignitas* or *beneficium*, or even conceals his motives entirely. The link between the dedicatee and the theme of the work is not always obvious. A few examples may suffice by way of illustration.

The first treatise after Lipsius's farewell to Calvinist Leiden, published when he was already lecturing at the Catholic University of Leuven, offers a clear example of career planning.[3] It was dedicated to the States of Brabant who had agreed to his appointment. However, instead of completing the treatise on the Roman army on which he had been working for more than a year,[4] he preferred to focus on another aspect of antiquity, the cross and crucifixion as a form of punishment, because this

[2] The alphabetical index at the end of Gerlo-Vervliet, *Inventaire*, pp. 517-536 is in a way misleading: Lipsius did not really keep up a correspondence with several of the dignitaries named on the list. Pope Paul V, Emperor Maximilian II, and a number of princes and cardinals only occur because one of Lipsius's works was dedicated to them.

[3] Lipsius left Leiden in the middle of March 1591. After a few weeks to cure his health in Spa, he settled in the neutral principality of Liège, where he devoted himself entirely to his studies and his correspondence, until he could safely return to the Southern Netherlands. On 9 August 1592 he finally arrived in Leuven, where he was offered the chair of Ancient History and Latin at the University. A detailed account of Lipsius's itinerary can be found in J. De Landtsheer, 'From North to South: Some New Documents on Lipsius' Journey from Leiden to Liège' in *Myricae. Essays on Neo-Latin Studies in Memory of Jozef IJsewijn*, eds. Dirk Sacré – Gilbert Tournoy, Supplementa Humanistica Lovaniensia, 16 (Leuven, 2000), pp. 303-331.

[4] Lipsius's *De Militia Romana Libri Quinque, Commentarius Ad Polybium. E parte prima Historicae Facis* only came from the press in the middle of June 1595.

theme would be recognized as an evidence of his devotion to the true Faith, which was still under suspicion after a thirteen-year stay at Protestant Leiden. Hence with his *De Cruce*, a somewhat ambiguous title, Lipsius killed two birds with one stone: he expressed his gratitude towards the country who had welcomed a Prodigal Son, and he stressed the fact that he ought to be considered a good Catholic.[5]

He also tried to ingratiate himself with persons who were politically important or might become so. In September 1579, the *Electorum liber* I was dedicated to the Emperor's youngest brother, Archduke Matthias of Austria, who had been hailed as governor general of the Southern Netherlands by the anti-Spanish party. Although Lipsius fully enjoyed the peaceful haven of the Northern Low Countries and had settled down firmly, he wanted to provide for the future and secure his relations with the South, now that his native country had embarked upon a new, more independent course. Once back in the Southern Netherlands, Lipsius time and again established good contacts with its governors general. *De militia Romana* was meant to be dedicated to Archduke Ernest of Austria, who had arrived in the Netherlands in 1594 to succeed Alexander Farnese († December 1592). After Ernest's untimely death in February 1595, however, the treatise was finally presented to the Crown Prince of Spain, the future Philip III, in the hope that the King might grant Lipsius the title of *Historiographus regius* which indeed happened on 14 December 1595 bringing with it an annuity of 1,000 florins, even more than Lipsius earned as a professor.

Other dedicatees were selected because they were a guarantee against possible calumnies. This was for instance the case with the *Adversus Dialogistam*, a refutation of the harsh criticism Dirck Volckertsz. Coornhert vented on Lipsius's *Politica*: 'You, whose present this is, protect me with your shield, and do not permit *innocence to be exposed more to danger than esteem*,' Lipsius wrote in his dedicatory letter to the States of Holland.[6] The *Politica*, addressed more generally 'to the Emperor, the Kings and the Princes'[7] because Lipsius saw it as a theoretical manual in

[5] See J. De Landtsheer, 'Justus Lipsius's *De Cruce* and the Reception of the Fathers', *Neulateinisches Jahrbuch*, 2 (2000), 97-122.

[6] Cf. ILE III, [90 10 00], 'Vos, quorum id munus, me meaque auctoritatis vestrae clypeo tegite neu patiamini *innocentiae plus periculi quam honoris esse*.'

[7] It is regrettable that this letter, even though it has no specific dedicatee, was not inserted in its appropriate place, in ILE III. Presumably the initiators of the series, Alois Gerlo and Hendrik D.L. Vervliet, excluded it because they considered it fictitious. This was also the reason why they left out most of the letters collected in the *Epistolicae Quaestiones*, even though all of them were addressed to a definite person.

politics, kept stirring up trouble. Soon after his appointment at Leuven University the work was in danger of being put on the Index of Forbidden Books.[8] Jesuit friends in Rome urged him to revise the treatise and gave him good advice to avoid further criticism from Rome. Lipsius followed their suggestions and adapted his *Politica* in collaboration with one of the Leuven censors, Henricus Cuyckius. Yet to be even more on the safe side, he reworked and enlarged the final section of *Notae*, which in the new 1596 edition he dedicated to Johannes Saracenus (Jean Sarazin), a generous patron of arts and particularly of literature, who had encouraged many humanists, Lipsius among them, even with financial support.[9] Saracenus, however, was also, as the Abbot of St Vedast in Arras, an influential politician, who had proved his allegiance to the king of Spain by reconciling the rebellious Walloon provinces. Consequently he had been appointed as a member of the Council of State.[10] By claiming Saracenus's patronage for his *Ad politicorum libros notae*, Lipsius showed not only his esteem and gratitude for the Abbot's benevolence, but ensured himself — as well as his controversial treatise — of a powerful protector. He challenged more or less possible opponents to attack or question a work appealing to such a paladin of Church and State. In the *Monita et Exempla*, dedicated to Archduke Albert, a simile was used: 'Thus, we address ourselves to you. To which avail? To procure lustre

[8] Lipsius's *Politica* was listed on Pope Sixtus V's *Index librorum prohibitorum* with the restriction *donec corrigatur*. This Index had come from the presses, but was not yet dispersed when the pope passed away on 27 August 1590. Probably as many of the few copies already circulating were destroyed as possible. In April 1592 Pope Clement VIII charged the congregation to review the list of his predecessor. Cf. Franz Heinrich Reusch, *Der Index der Verbotenen Bücher. Ein Beitrag zur Kirchen- und Literaturgeschichte* (Bonn, 1883-1885), pp. 501-531 (on the Index of Sixtus V); pp. 532-538 (on the Index of Clement VIII). Lipsius's Jesuit friends in Rome urged him to review his *Politica* immediately and suggested a close collaboration with Henricus Cuyckius, theologian and censor of books to Leuven University, cf., e. g., ILE VI, 93 02 10 B and 93 07 31 BEN. See also a recent edition with introduction, English translation and annotations by Jan Waszink, *Justus Lipsius, Politica. Six Books of Politics or Political Instruction. Politicorum sive Civilis Doctrinae libri sex*, Bibliotheca Latinitatis Novae (Assen: Van Gorcum, 2003).

[9] On 21 February 1594 Saracenus offered Lipsius twenty crowns to meet the expenses of his *De Cruce* (cf. ILE VII, 94 02 21, 14-17). In ILE VII, 94 07 20 SA the abbot opened his purse once more and offered Lipsius one hundred florins as a contribution to the house he was restoring and urged Lipsius to send him the bill once the window provided with his coat of arms was finished (l. 20-25).

[10] On Johannes Saracenus, cf. *Biographie Nationale* (Brussels, 1866-1986), 21, 402-410; Hubert De Schepper, *De kollaterale raden in de katholieke Nederlanden van 1579 tot 1609. Studie van leden, instellingen en algemene politiek*, 3 vols, unpubl. doct. diss. (Leuven, 1972), 170-173.

and defence for this, our writing. As we attach your coat of arms to our dwellings, official buildings, and country-seats against violence or impudence, so we use these venerable names against slander and spite.'[11]

A final example proving Lipsius's insecurity and longing for protection can be found in both Virgin treatises, giving accounts of a number of miracles which occurred through her mediation in two of her sanctuaries. The *Diva Virgo Hallensis* (Antwerp, 1604) was dedicated to Guillaume de Berghes, who — as Archbishop of Cambrai — held the jurisdiction over Halle. One year later the *Diva Sichemiensis sive Aspricollis* was offered to Archduchess Isabella who, together with her husband, Archduke Albert of Austria, was to become one of the main promoters of this sanctuary.[12] Writing about miracles brought Lipsius, of course, very near to the theologian's field and he rightly foresaw criticism, not only from the Protestant side, but from Catholic theologians as well, for they might accuse him of meddling with a subject which was definitely not his own. Hence Lipsius invoked the patronage of prominent people whose piety and orthodoxy was behind doubt, to shield his miracle treatises.

A final category is that of dedications to fellow humanists, inspired by admiration and/or affection. These are the only cases when the book's subject matches the dedicatee's interest. A first example can be found in the second part of *De amphitheatro* (1584). Lipsius was grateful for the willingness of his friend Abraham Ortelius to give him useful information and to share his impressive collection of books with him.

The next year, Lipsius presented his *Electorum liber alter* to two of his dearest Leiden friends, Janus Dousa Sr, the driving power in bringing Lipsius to Leiden, and Jan van Hout, secretary of the town and the University.[13] Lipsius expressed his sincere and loyal affection for both of

[11] Cf. ILE 05 01 18: 'Ergo ad Te imus: et quo fine? Ut splendorem huic scriptioni mutuemur, et tutelam. Sicut insignia vestra aedibus, praetoriis, villis appendimus contra vim aut proterviam, sic nomina haec sacra contra calumniam aut livorem.'

[12] Sharp Hill or Montaigu, part of Zichem, was a solitary hill before the Archdukes decided to found a new town, on which privileges, rights and tax exemptions were conferred by a number of letters patent. Church and town of Scherpenheuvel were conceived as a bulwark of the Counter Reformation in the Southern Netherlands. See the well-documented study by Luc Duerloo – Marc Wingens, *Scherpenheuvel. Het Jeruzalem van de Lage Landen* (Leuven: Davidsfonds, 2002), pp. 51-56, and Piet Lombaerde, "Dominating Space and Landscape: Ostend and Scherpenheuvel", in Luc Duerloo – Werner Thomas (eds), *Albert & Isabella 1598-1621. Essays* (Turnhout: Brepols, 1998), pp. 173-183 (esp. 177-81).

[13] On this *Trias amicorum*, cf. Chris L. Heesakkers, 'Lipsius, Dousa and Jan van Hout: Latin and the vernacular in Leiden in the 1570s and 1580s', in *Lipsius in Leiden. Studies*

them. From their first meeting on, in Leuven 1571, he was enchanted by Dousa's candour and the sweetness of his character. He was introduced to Van Hout in Leiden and even enjoyed his hospitality during the first months of his stay. 'And since that moment, though we had separate dwellings, we were not seperated in contacts or in mind. For as if we had concluded a triumvirate of Friendship, we had frequent meetings, discussions, parties'[14]. The main part of the letter focuses upon their favourite pastime — literature — and praises the poetry of both Lipsius's companions: Dousa, who continued along the old, Latin way and Van Hout, who preferred the new paths of their mother tongue. Although using different languages, both were equally gifted and skilled poets writing elegy, comedy, epigrams, satires and odes alike. Need it to be said that Lipsius enhanced the expression of his sympathy towards these two close friends by a well-polished and appropriate style, viz. in a persistence of bipartite sentences?

## Quomodo

In the next part I will briefly dwell upon the formal aspect: I will deal with the question if and, possibly, how Lipsius brings up the subject of the publication in his dedicatory letters. Secondly I will focus on two particular topoi: praise (of the dedicatee) and (pseudo-)modesty towards his own achievements.

### *Presentation of the Subject*

Quite often the author elaborates on his treatise by presenting its subject or stressing its importance. This is primarily the case for the antiquarian treatises and, of course, for the successive editions of Tacitus and the edition of Seneca. Moreover, Lipsius often tries to establish a link between his subject and the patron chosen, and even with the contemporary situation.

The dedication of the edition of the philosophical works of Lucius Annaeus Seneca to Pope Paul V, for instance, is explained by the fact that,

*in the Life and Works of a Great Humanist on the Occasion of his 450th Anniversary*, ed. Karl Enenkel – Chris L. Heesakkers (Voorthuizen: Florivallis, 1997), pp. 93-120. ILE II, 85 02 01, the dedicatory letter of the *Electorum liber* II, is translated and discussed pp. 99-101.

[14] ILE II, 85 02 01, 13-15.

according to Lipsius, the Roman philosopher had undoubtedly earned the highest esteem among all Latin authors; his emphasis on an ethically sound life turned him almost into a Christian. Since Seneca spent the larger part of his life in Rome, it is evident that the patron of his works should have his residence in Rome as well. Finally, the Fathers of the Church were unanimous in their belief that Seneca and St Paul were very close, hence the dedication to another Paul seemed appropriate.

The dedicatory letter of *De militia* stresses that a good leader has to be an expert general as well. Together with his crown, Philip will inherit an immense realm, with just one formidable adversary, the Ottomans. Military art will be of vital importance to consolidate his power. Rome is the best evidence that the better the nations organize their laws and state of affairs, the better they are at perfecting their army. Even the former inhabitants of Spain, however warlike and courageous — here Lipsius alludes to the Crown Prince's geographical roots, adding a flattering touch — finally had to give in to the Romans, who enhanced their own merits by giving praise to their enemies. Lipsius hopes that a better knowledge of Roman military practice might be useful to the future king.

A striking exception is *De cruce*, a treatise which must be counted among Lipsius's antiquarian works, as its subtitle indicates. The author might even have referred to similar ways of punishment in his own time — the gallows, for instance (*crux* in sixteenth-century Latin) and the stake, both of them mentioned in *De cruce* III —, yet he does not breathe a single word about the real intention of his book. Instead, he praises the States of Brabant for not giving in to the bad times, but being aware of the Muses in the midst of the trumpets of war. Only in the final sentences of the dedicatory letter Lipsius refers to the main part of the title: the States should take up and bear their cross. Such as a column keeps upright and stands even more firmly when a heavier weight is put in top on it, so the States should keep their heads high and straight, not yielding to the burden, but striving.[15] The reason for this exception has already been touched upon before: Lipsius wanted primarily to prove himself a good Catholic.

[15] ILE V, 92 11 04, 30-32: 'Interea CRUCEM accipite atque etiam ferte. Ut columna quae recta stat, imposito magis pondere firmatur, sic altas rectasque mentes oportet non cedere oneri, sed obniti.' In *De cruce* I, 5 Lipsius had pointed out that the word *crux* could as well refer to a single, erected beam, hence the simile with the column.

*Laudatio*

That *laudatio* should be a component of a dedicatory letter is only obvious. Lipsius praises or underlines his addressee's superior character, his origin, citizenship, position. Quite often he emphasizes that the dedicatee already had or might possibly have a positive influence either on the political state of affairs, or on the *res publica litterarum*. When a publication is dedicated to a city council, Lipsius nearly always stresses the importance of the place for the origin of the work. The '*catalogue of virtues*' attributed to the various dedicatees is, of course, enormous. The most frequently used are the general *virtus* and, more specifically: *prudentia*, synonyms as *benignitas, amor, comitas, benificentia* or also *doctrina*, *eruditio* and *benignitas erga litteras* or *erga studiosos*.

The dedicatee's origin is stressed in *De militia*: Lipsius recalls the military achievements of Ferdinand and Isabella (the seizure of Granada in 1492 ending the Reconquista), Charles V and Philip II, the latter inviting him to draw a parallel between the crown prince and Alexander the Great. In the *Diva Sichemiensis* 'los Reyes católicos' are called upon as well: Archduchess Isabella is praised for following the model of piety and modesty set by her namesake.

The *national* element is referred to in the dedication of the *Manuductio* and the *Physiologia*: both treatises are meant as an introduction to the Spanish-born Seneca, hence they should be offered to Spaniards. That the same Seneca afterwards became a citizen of Rome, was given as a reason why Lipsius dedicated Seneca's *Opera omnia* to the head of the Roman church, as already pointed out.

The *position* of the dedicatee is alluded to, for example, in the *Variae lectiones* (to Antoine, Cardinal of Granvelle, King Philip II's councillor), the editions of the major works of *Tacitus* (to Emperor Maximilian II) and *Seneca* (to Pope Paul V), the *Centuria ad Italos* and the *Diva Hallensis* (to respectively Federico Borromeo, Cardinal-Archbishop of Milan, and Papal Nuncio Ottavio Mirto Frangipani).

*Modestia*

A first, obvious manifestation of reducing his own merits is the frequent use of diminutives such as *opella*, *opusculum* or *munusculum*. Expressions such as *quantulumcumque* and *hoc quodcumque est* are also a commonplace indication of (pseudo-)modesty. Especially in his earlier works,

Lipsius used the topos of (feigned) *incompetence* or *careless work*, sometimes in combination with the excuse of *young age*. In the *Satyra menippaea*, dedicated to the French scholar Josephus Justus Scaliger, he characterizes his own satirical efforts as 'without bite, without bile, seasoned with only a few grains of wit, and that so poor, that I fear it will go sour before it comes into your hands.'[16]

A particular kind of *humilitas affecta* is used in the dedicatory letters of collections. In his letter collections, for example, Lipsius apologizes because the *Centuriae* are only a gathering of letters, each having already its proper 'owner'. The *Centuria miscellanea* I, for instance, is called

> Epistolas meas, novum et veterem ingenii partum; novum dispositu, compositu veterem. Sed partum profecto infirmum aut informem et quem per diuturni hoc morbi taedium nec fingere nec polire mihi mens, quemque abiecisse verius videor quam peperisse.
>
> My letters, a new, as well as an old fruit; new because of its order, old because of its contents. But weak or unshapely anyway. Because of the loathing of this lasting illness I could not bring myself to shape or polish them. It seems rather as if I had it thrown out instead of begotten it.[17]

The metaphor of his book being a child is continued, when he claims the members of the Utrecht city council as the *Centuria*'s protectors, or rather its fathers, who should touch and accept the offspring and in the first place defend it with the shield of their authority against the bite of envy and spite.[18]

In other works Lipsius contrasted the importance of his subject and his own limited merits. No modesty was, of course, needed in connection with Tacitus, the poor value of his own work was compensated by that worthy Roman author. In *De recta pronunciatione*, on the contrary, which he dedicated to Sir Philip Sydney, Lipsius apologized for touching upon a theme which was highly obscure and to which no decisive answer was possible. But this was immediately countered by attributing the responsibility for dwelling upon such matters to his correspondent: it was impossible to neglect the request of such a noble and successful man. In the *Dissertatiuncula*, the elaborated version of the public lecture held

[16] See ILE I, 81 00 00 S, 9-10.

[17] ILE II, 85 11 13, 16-20.

[18] ILE II, 85 11 13, 20-22: 'Vos ei tutores, imo patres advoco; tangite, tollite expositam hanc prolem et inprimis auctoritatis vestrae scuto defendite contra maligni livoris dentem.'

in Leuven in the presence of the Archdukes and dedicated to them, this modest touch becomes

> Et a me quidem res parva est; splendorem tamen a vobis habet et (fas sit dicere) vos ab ea aliquem, ut dimanet ad exteros aut posteros singularis hic vester in optimas artes vel amor vel honor; dimanet, inquam, in laudem vestram, in aliorum exemplum.
>
> And whereas it is only a small achievement from my part, it will have its splendour from you and — if I may say so — you will get some lustre from it, as your singular interest in or esteem of literature and the arts is spread abroad or about future generations; as it is spread, I say, to sing your praise and to set an example to others.[19]

After being seriously ill for many months at the turn of 1584-1585, poor health too was included on the list of possible excuses, though not always without reason, for Lipsius was indeed suffering from a liver disorder, and particularly in his later years also from respiratory infections, as is sufficiently proved by his correspondence. Often 'not feeling well' was combined with 'too much work'. Its first occurrence was in the *Opera omnia quae ad Criticam spectant* (Leiden, 1585), dedicated to Bailiff, Burgomasters, and city council of Leiden, after a period of serious illness from the end of August 1584 until March 1585.[20]

Occasionally Lipsius also pointed to his numerous adversaries to apologize for being less prolific in his writings or rather modest in the choice of his subjects, as is the case in the edition of the historiographer Velleius Paterculus: 'Quite recently we have felt Calumny's sharp teeth, so that we do not improperly recoil from all serious writing.' Particularly in his later writings, slander occurs time and again in the dedicatory letters, certainly in letters claiming the dedicatee's protection.[21] Fear of backbiting was also among the main reasons why Lipsius postponed a further edition of

[19] Cf. ILE XIII, 00 04 12, 9-13. See on this lecture Toon Van Houdt, 'Justus Lipsius and the Archdukes Albert and Isabella', in *The World of Justus Lipsius: A contribution towards his intellectual biography. Proceedings of a colloquium held under the auspices of the Belgian Historical Institute in Rome (Rome, 22-24 May 1997),* ed. Marc Laureys, together with Christoph Bräunl, Silvan Mertens, Reimar Seibert-Kemp (= Bulletin van het Belgisch Historisch Instituut te Rome, 68) (Brussels – Rome, 1998), pp. 405-432.

[20] Cf. ILE II, 85 02 03, 15-16: 'Valetudinem hanc videtis? Etsi melior ea nunc paullo mitiorque, tamen, ni fallam, remisit potius morbus quam dimisit et cathena me etiamnunc ligat, etsi magis laxa.' (Do you see my health? Although I am feeling slightly better now and more comfortable, yet, if I am not mistaken, my ailment has slackened, rather than left me, and its chains are still fettering me, albeit in somewhat more loosely).

[21] Cf. ILE 91 01 03: '[...] a calumniae telo, cuius aciem ita recenter sensimus, ut non iniuria abhorreamus a seria omni scriptione.'

his correspondence for almost ten years, despite the encouragements and the urgent requests of many of his friends.

## Conclusion

Lipsius was very well aware of the limitations tradition imposed both on the selection of his patrons and on the dedications. Two letters to Johannes Moretus, definitly not intended for publication and written when the five *Centuriae* of letters issued in 1602 were about to come from the press, reveal that he did not feel strongly about his dedicatory letters: one had to accord with what had been common practice for centuries and, moreover, the author was not allowed a free choice of his friends and dearest colleagues, for instance, but had to coax and flatter prominent politicians, who did not deserve to be a dedicatee.

> Ie vous aij escript dernierement des Dedicatoires. Ie ne fais chose au monde plus enuis, et si ie men pouvoy passer ou excuser honestement, nij auroit aultre qu'une *Préface au Lecteur.* Il fault flatter, louer etc. et sans aultre fruict ou fin que de complaire a tels qui en vérité ne le méritent. Sed mos gerendus publico mori.[22]

Nearly one month later Lipsius repeated once more:

> Monsieur, ienvoye a vostre fils la derniere preface, bien aise d'avoir achevé une si fascheuse besoigne. Le temps me commande de m'adresser a telles gens et la dependence que iaij de la court; aultrement ie suivroij mon interieur iugement. Patience.[23]

Unfortunately, no matter how careful Lipsius was in selecting his dedicatees, the very name in front of a publication might turn against him as well. Some of the dedications risked being a stumbling block after his return to the Catholic and Spanish Southern Low Countries, for the Catholic Church was not inclined to grant an *approbatio* for the mere reissue of a treatise which had been published in the Calvinist Leiden and had been dedicated, for example, to its University Board, as was the case with *De amphitheatro*.[24] And of course, the dedications of the *Centuria Ia et*

[22] Cf. ILE 02 02 09, in Alois Gerlo, Hendrik D.L. Vervliet, and Irène Vertessen, *La correspondance de Juste Lipse conservée au Musée Plantin-Moretus* (Antwerp, 1967), no 118, 10-15.

[23] Cf. ILE 02 03 02, in *ibid*., no 124, 1-4.

[24] Hence Moretus's advice that Lipsius should make slight alterations, so that they could put 'editio nova et auctior' or a similar formula on the title page.

*IIa* to respectively the city council of Utrecht and Thomas Cecil, the later Lord Burghley, one of the commanders of the English garrisons in the North, were frowned upon as well.[25]

Since addressing dedicatory letters seems to have been an onerous task for Lipsius, one can easily understand that it was often procrastinated until the *Officina Plantiniana* had almost completed the printing of the publication. Time and again either Johannes or Balthasar Moretus even had to urge the author to send his text within the next week.[26] Yet in spite of Lipsius's belittleling of these dedications in his correspondence with the Moretuses, they were always very carefully phrased and stilistically well-elaborated, as a more detailed analysis of both argumentation and style of some of the most revealing letters would prove.

SEMINARIUM PHILOLOGIAE HUMANISTICAE
Katholieke Universiteit Leuven
Blijde-Inkomststraat 21 (Box 3316)
B – 3000 Leuven
Jeanine.Delandtsheer@arts.kuleuven.be

[25] The troubles with *De amphitheatro* were easily overcome, because its subject itself was inoffensive and strictly limited to ancient history. As to the letter collections, containing also a number of 'notorious' addressees, who had proved their adherence to Calvinism or who played an active part in the government of the rebellious provinces, Moretus found a simple way to get around the difficulty. Once Lipsius's new *Centuria ad Italos et Gallos* had been approved by the book censor, he simply changed the title preferred by Lipsius into *Epistolarum selectarum centuria miscellanea tertia*, as if it were a mere sequel to the long-awaited reissue of the *Centuria prima et altera*. At the end of the third part he added its *approbatio*, but without a date, thus suggesting that the *approbatio* given in december 1600 for the *Centuria ad Italos et Hispanos* prevailed for the whole.

[26] See for instance concerning *Lovanium sive opidi et academiae eius descriptio. Libri III* (Antwerp, 1605), presented by Lipsius as a wedding gift to Charles, Duke of Croÿ and Aarschot, and his niece Dorothea de Croÿ, the post script of ILE 05 11 04: '*Praefationes ad Lovanium* mitti nobis tempestivius optemus, quo citius corrigendos remittamus' (We would like you to send us the Prefaces to your *Lovanium* well in time, so that they can be returned for correction more quickly). The request was repeated more urgently four days later in ILE 05 11 08 M: 'Praefationes exspectamus, si non crastino per Colibrant, proximo mulieris huius reditu' (We are waiting for the prefaces, if not tomorrow when Colibrant returns, then with the return of the woman [who is bringing the present quires]).

## Appendix
## Index Epistolarum Dedicatoriarum

**1.** *Variarum lectionum libri IIII* (Antwerp, 1569)
BBr. 3, 993-995
ILE I, 68 00 00 [spring 1568]; from ed. 2a on: 1 June 1566
to Antoine Perrenot de Granvelle

**2.** *C. Cornelii Taciti Historiarum et Annalium libri qui exstant* (Antwerp, 1574)
BBr. 5, 289-290
ILE I, [74 07 00] M
to Maximilian II of Habsburg

Part two, *Taciti opera minora*
ILE I, 74 07 00 S
to Joannes Sambucus (Zsámboky)

**3.** *Antiquarum lectionum commentarius tributus in partes quinque, in quibus varia scriptorum loca, Plauti praecipue, illustrantur aut emendantur* (Antwerp, 1575)
BBr. 3, 992-993
ILE I, 74 11 00
to Thomas Rehdiger

**4.** *Epistolicarum Quaestionum Libri V. In quibus ad varios scriptores pleraeque ad T. Livium notae* (Antwerp, 1577)
BBr. 3, 1064-1065
ILE I, 76 08 18
to Jan Scheyfve

**5.** *Leges Regiae et Leges X.virales I. Lipsii opera studiose collectae* (Antwerp, 1576)
BBr. 3, 995-996
No dedication

**6.** *Titus Livius, Historiarum ab Urbe condita liber I, recensuit I. Lipsius* (Antwerp, 1579)
BBr 3, 1126
No dedication

**7.** *Electorum Liber I. In quo praeter censuras, varii prisci ritus* (Antwerp, 1580)
BBr. 3, 927-928
ILE I, 79 09 17
to Archduke Matthias of Austria

**8.** *Ad Annales Corn. Taciti liber commentarius sive notae* (Antwerp, 1581)
BBr. 3, 1077
ILE I, 81 00 00 H
to the States of Holland

**9.** *Satyra Menippaea. Somnium. Lusus in nostri aevi criticos* (Antwerp, 1581)
BBr. 3, 1073-1074
ILE I, 81 00 00 S
to Josephus Justus Scaliger

**10.** *Saturnalium sermonum Libri Duo, qui de gladiatoribus (*Antwerp, 1582)
BBr. 3, 1068-1073
ILE I, 82 01 00
to Augerius Gislenus Busbecquius

**11.** *De constantia libri duo, qui alloquium praecipue continent in publicis malis* (Leiden, 1584)
BBr. 3, 902-918
ILE I, 83 09 00
to Burgomasters, city council and citizens of Antwerp

**12a.** *De amphitheatro liber. In quo forma ipsa loci expressa, et ratio spectandi* and *De amphitheatris quae extra Romam libellus. In quo formae eorum aliquot et typi* (Leiden, 1584)
BBr. 3, 895-899
ILE I, 84 01 05 C
to the members of Leiden University Board: Janus Dousa Sr, Paulus Buys and Abraham van Almonde

**12b.** *De amphitheatris quae extra Romam libellus. In quo formae eorum aliquot et typi* (Leiden, 1584)
BBr. 3, 895-899
ILE I, 84 [01 05] O
to Abraham Ortelius

**13.** *Ad libros Historiarum notae* (Leiden, 1585)
Not in BBr.
ILE II, 84 08 04 $D^2$
to Andreas Dudith

**14.** *Electorum Liber secundus, in quo mixtim ritus et censurae* (Leiden, 1585)
BBr. 3, 928-929
ILE II, 85 02 01
to Janus Dousa Sr and Jan van Hout

**15.** *Opera omnia quae ad criticam proprie spectant. Quibus accessit Electorum liber secundus, novus nec ante editus. Cetera item varie aucta et correcta* (Leiden, 1585)
BBr. 3, 1055-1056
ILE II, 85 02 03
to the city council of Leiden

**16.** *C. Iulii Caesaris commentarii de bello Gallico et civili. Eiusdem librorum qui desiderantur fragmenta* (Leiden, 1585)
BBr. 1, 418-419
no dedication

**17.** *Epistolarum selectarum centuria prima* (Leiden, 1586)
BBr. 3, 929-933
ILE II, 85 11 13
to the city council of Utrecht

**18.** *De recta pronunciatione Latinae linguae dialogus* (Leiden, 1586)
BBr. 3, 1061-1064
ILE II, 86 03 17
to Sir Philip Sydney

**19.** *Ad C. Cornelium Tacitum curae secundae* (Leiden, 1588)
BBr. 3, 1077-1078
ILE III, 88 00 00 R[1]
to Henricus Ranzovius

**20.** *Auctarium inscriptionum* (Leiden, 1588)[27]
Not in BBr.
ILE III, 88 01 01 D
to Pietro Delbene[28]

**21.** *Iusti Lipsi Animadversiones. In tragoedias quae L. Annaeo Senecae tribuuntur* (Leiden, 1588)
BBr. 3, 900; 1116-1117
no dedication[29]

**22.** *Politicorum sive civilis doctrinae libri sex. Qui ad principatum maxime spectant* (Leiden, 1589)
BBr. 3, 1040-1052
Not in ILE
to the Emperor, the Kings and the Princes

**23.** *Adversus dialogistam liber de una religione* (Leiden, 1590)
BBr. 3, 1065
ILE III, [90 10 00]
to the States of Holland

**24.** *Epistolica institutio, excepta e dictantis eius ore, anno M.D. I). LXXXVII mense Iunio. Adiunctum est Demetrii Phalerei eiusdem argumenti scriptum* (Leiden, 1591)
BBr. 3, 985-991
no dedication

**25.** *Epistolarum centuriae duae. Quarum prior innovata, altera nova* (Leiden, 1590)
BBr. 3, 933-938
ILE III, 90 04 11
to Thomas Cecil, the later Lord Burghley

[27] Addendum to Martinus Smetius' *Inscriptionum Antiquarum quae passim per Europam liber. [...] Accessit Auctarium a Iusto Lipsio* (Leiden: Raphelengius, 1588).

[28] In ILE III mistakenly also ILE III, 88 03 01, to the Leiden University Board.

[29] The whole is conceived as a letter to Franciscus Raphelengius Jr.

**26.** *C. Velleius Paterculus cum animadversionibus I. Lipsii*, (Leiden, 1591)
BBr. 3, 1121-1122
ILE, 91 01 03
to Theodorus Leeuwius

**27.** *De cruce libri III ad sacram profanamque historiam utiles. Una cum notis* (Antwerp, 1593)
BBr. 3, 918-925
ILE V, 92 11 04
to the States of Brabant

**28.** *De militia Romana libri quinque, commentarius ad Polybium. E parte prima Historicae facis* (Antwerp, 1595-1596)
BBr. 3, 1002-1005
ILE VIII, [95 04 21] P
to Philip, Crown Prince of Spain

**29.** *Ad libros politicorum notae*
BBr.: cf. *Politica*
ILE VIII, 95 12 26 S
to Johannes Saracenus (Sarazin)

**30.** *Poliorceticωn sive de machinis, tormentis, telis libri quinque. Ad historiaum lucem* (Antwerp, 1596)
BBr. 3, 1037-1040
ILE 96 02 15 B
to Ernest of Bavaria, Prince Bishop of Liège

**31.** *Admiranda, sive de magnitudine Romana libri quattuor* (Antwerp, 1598)
BBr. 3, 883-884; 892-895
ILE 98 03 01 A
to Archduke Albert of Austria

**32.** *Dissertatiuncula apud Principes item C[aii] Plini Panegyricus* (Antwerp, 1600)
BBr. 3, 925-927
ILE XIII, 00 04 12
to Archdukes Albert and Isabella

**33.** *Centuria ad Italos et Hispanos* (Antwerp, 1601)
BBr. 3, 940-943
ILE XIII, 00 12 31 B
to Federico Borromeo, Archbishop of Milan

**34.** *Centuria ad Germanos et Gallos* (Antwerp, 1602)
BBr. 3, 943-944
ILE 02 02 11 F
to Ottavio Mirto Frangipani

**35.** *Centuria prima ad Belgas* (Antwerp, 1602)
BBr. 3, 944-947

ILE 02 02 21
to Balthasar de Zuñiga

**36.** *Centuria altera ad Belgas* (Antwerp, 1602)
BBr. 3, 944-947
ILE 02 02 23 C
to the Privy Council [Brussels], nominatim to Jean Richardot and Christophe D'Assonleville

**37.** *Centuria tertia ad Belgas* (Antwerp, 1602)
BBr. 3, 944-947
ILE 02 02 25 A
to the city council of Antwerp

**38.** *Centuria miscellanea tertia* (Antwerp, 1602)
BBr. 3, 944
ILE 02 02 25 D
to Jan van Drenckwaert

**39.** *De bibliothecis* (Antwerp, 1602)
BBr. 3, 900-902
ILE 02 06 20
to Charles, Duke of Croÿ and Aarschot

**40.** *Dispunctio notarum* (Antwerp, 1602)
BBr. 3, 925
ILE 02 06 24 C
to Charles, Duke of Croÿ and Aarschot

**41.** *De Vesta et Vestalibus syntagma* (Antwerp, 1603)
BBr. 3, 1080-1081
ILE 03 06 13 H
to Matthias Hovius, Archbishop of Mechelen

**42.** *Diva Virgo Hallensis* (Antwerp, 1604)
BBr. 3, 974-985
ILE 04 07 15
to Guillaume de Berghes, Archbishop of Cambrai

**43.** *Manuductionis ad Stoicam philosophiam* (Antwerp, 1604)
BBr. 3, 1074-1076
ILE 04 02 27
to Juan Fernández de Velasco

**44.** *Physiologiae Stoicorum libri III* (Antwerp, 1604)
BBr. 3, 1074-1076
ILE 04 02 28
to Pedro Enriquez Fuentes, Governor of the Duchy of Milan

**45.** *Monita et exempla politica* (Antwerp, 1605)
BBr. 3, 1005-1010

ILE 05 01 18
to Archduke Albert of Austria

**44.** *Diva Sichemiensis sive Aspricollis* (Antwerp, 1605)
BBr. 3, 1010-1014
ILE 05 04 17 I
to Archduchess Isabella Clara Eugenia

**45.** *L. Annaei Senecae philosophi opera quae exstant omnia* (Antwerp, 1605)
BBr. 3, 1117-1118
ILE 05 06 27
to Pope Paul V

**46.** *Lovanium sive opidi et academiae eius descriptio. Libri III* (Antwerp, 1605)
BBr. 3, 996-998
ILE 05 [10 18]
to Charles, Duke of Croÿ and Aarschot

# LES DÉDICACES LATINES DES LIVRES DE MOTETS DE RENÉ DEL MEL (ca. 1554-ca. 1598)

EMILIE CORSWAREM

## René del Mel, un dernier exemple de la transhumance franco-flamande

La dédicace comme procédé de double présentation — celle du recueil de musique et celle du compositeur — est illustrée de manière éloquente chez René del Mel.[1] Précieux à l'historien de la musique, les textes dédicatoires de ses quatre recueils de musique religieuse et treize recueils de musique profane conservés livrent des indications plus ou moins précises relatives à sa biographie, à la chronologie de ses œuvres mais aussi à ses ambitions, ses employeurs et dans une certaine mesure, à la réception de sa musique. Outre quelques rares mentions dans les archives, le contenu de ces textes constitue la source quasi unique concernant le compositeur.

L'origine de René del Mel est désormais établie. Dès avant 1547, sa famille réside à Malines.[2] Le jeune del Mel y fait ses premières études musicales comme choral à la cathédrale de Saint-Rombaut à partir de 1562.[3] Les années qui suivent sont mal documentées mais il est probable

[1] Cette conception du geste de la dédicace est formulée par Peter Schaeffer à propos des textes dédicatoires de Georg von Logau: 'Humanism on Display: The Epistles Dedicatory of Georg von Logau', *Sixteenth Century Journal*, 17/2 (1986), 215-223 (p. 215).

[2] En 1547, le père du musicien, François del Mel, apparaît dans les archives communales de la ville, relativement à un remboursement de rentes hypothéquant sa maison; Malines, Archives communales, série G, actes scabinaux, reg. I 170, f° 90v, le 18 avril 1547. Voir aussi Georges van Doorslaer, 'René del Mel, compositeur du XVIe siècle', *Annales de l'Académie royale d'archéologie de Belgique*, 69 (1921), 221-288 (p. 226).

[3] La maîtrise de Saint-Rombaut est alors dirigée par Rombaut van den Scriecke. C'est toutefois Séverin Cornet qui est en charge l'éducation des enfants dès 1564 en tant que *zangmeester van de koorkinderen*. Jacobus Peetrinus (1561) et Guillielmus Nick (1564) figurent entre autres parmi les enfants de chœur à la même période. A ce sujet voir Georges van Doorslaer, 'Notes sur les jubés et les maîtrises des églises des Saints-Pierre-et-Paul, de Saint-Jean, de Notre-Dame au-delà de la Dyle et de Saint-Rombaut', *Bulletin du Cercle archéologique littéraire et artistique de Malines*, 16 (1906), 119-216 (pp. 145-181); Emile Steenackers, 'L'école des choraux de l'église métropolitaine de Saint-Rombaut à Malines', *Bulletin du Cercle archéologique, littéraire et artistique de Malines*, 31 (1926), 53-94; Georges van Doorslaer, *Notes sur la musique et les musiciens à Malines*

qu'à la suite du sac de Malines en 1572, le musicien ait quitté la ville. Un premier voyage le mènerait à Lisbonne. Selon Giuseppe Baini, il occupe le poste de *maestro* à la cour du roi Sébastien Ier (1554-1578), puis d'Henri dit lc Cardinal (1512-1580).[4] Qu'il ait ou non assumé cette fonction n'est à ce jour pas attesté. Cette hypothèse n'est toutefois pas inconcevable vu le lien de parenté entre Sébastien Ier et Renée de Lorraine (1544-1602), membre d'une famille avec qui René del Mel entretient d'étroites relations tout au long de sa carrière.[5] A la mort du roi Henri, le Portugal est agité par une série de troubles, qui se soldent par son annexion à l'Espagne en 1580. Si del Mel se trouve alors à Lisbonne, il n'y reste guère et se met en recherche d'un milieu plus favorable. Il se rend à Rome où il aurait rencontré Palestrina (1525/26-1594).[6] En janvier 1580, son nom apparaît dans les archives de Santa Maria in Campo Santo Teutonico, lié à l'achat de nouvelles cloches pour l'église.[7] Difficile de préciser la fonction de René de Mel à Rome à cette époque. Peut-être s'illustre-t-il comme chantre à Campo Santo ou occupe-t-il déjà quelque fonction pour le cardinal Gabriele Paleotti (1522-1597), au service duquel le compositeur figurera ultérieurement.[8] Une chose est sûre: René del Mel compose et publie son premier recueil en 1581.[9]

Jusqu'en 1587, sa carrière se déroule principalement dans la région de Rome et à Venise. La date et le lieu où sont signées les dédicaces mettent au jour les pérégrinations du compositeur (voir tableau en

(Malines: Dierickx-Beke, 1934) ou encore Joseph Kreps, 'Cinq siècles de maîtrise: Saint-Rombaut à Malines', *Musica Sacra*, 41 (1960), 141-164.

[4] Giuseppe Baini, *Memorie storico-critiche della vita e delle opere di Giovanni Pierluigi da Palestrina*, 2 vols (Hildesheim: Olms, 1966/Reprod. 1828), II, 126-127.

[5] Sébastien Ier, petit-fils de Charles Quint, est le cousin sous-germain de Renée de Lorraine, petite-fille de la sœur de l'empereur, Isabelle.

[6] Baini, *Memorie storico-critiche della vita e delle opere di Giovanni Pierluigi da Palestrina*, II, 126.

[7] Van Doorslaer, 'René del Mel', p. 225. Cette information a pu être vérifiée dans les archives du Campo Santo; Rome, Archivio di Campo Santo Teutonico, Libro secondo dei conti, ricevute e ordinazioni di Campo Santo dall'anno 1580 sin'all'anno 1600, janvier 1580 (volume non folioté).

[8] Van Doorslaer, interprétant erronément Baini, avance que del Mel est déjà à cette époque au service de Gabriel Paleotti à Rome. Rien ne permet cependant de l'affirmer avec certitude; Van Doorslaer, 'René del Mel', 231 et Baini, *Memorie storico-critiche della vita e delle opere di Giovanni Pierluigi da Palestrina*, I, 23.

[9] *Liber primus ... mottettorum quae partim quaternis, partim quinis, partim senis, ac unum septenis, alterum vero octonis vocibus concinuntur* (Venise: Gardano, 1581; *Einzeldrucke vor 1800*, Répertoire international des sources musicales – Internationales Quellenlexikon der Musik – International Inventory of Musical Sources (Kassel-Basel-Tours-London, 1971-) [ensuite: RISM], no. M 2193).

appendice).[10] Au premier recueil de motets dont la dédicace est signée à Rome (1581), succèdent un premier livre de madrigaux à quatre, cinq et six voix (1583) et l'année suivante un livre de madrigaux à cinq voix, tout deux signés à Chieti. Il se peut qu'alors, René del Mel s'illustre dans quelques fonctions au service des Valignani, dont l'un des membres est le dédicataire du second livre de musique signé à Chieti.[11] Dans le texte de la dédicace, le compositeur se décrit comme étant au service de cette famille depuis longtemps. Si tel fut le cas, il s'agit probablement d'une expérience brève, malgré ce qu'exprime le compositeur ou comme le suggère Van Doorslaer, d'une activité exercée sous la forme de compositions musicales offertes aux Valignani puisque, dans les années qui précèdent, René del Mel se trouverait successivement au Portugal puis à Rome.[12]

Il semble que Venise ait constitué l'étape ultérieure (1584). La même année, le compositeur est nommé maître de chapelle à la cathédrale de Rieti. Ses nombreuses absences lui valent toutefois de perdre prématurément sa nouvelle fonction.[13] C'est au service de Girolamo d'Acquaviva (1554-1592), duc d'Adri, que del Mel se trouve ensuite pour une courte période. En 1585, il signe la dédicace de son premier livre de madrigaux et cinq et six voix à Aquila.[14] Le texte dédicatoire révèle que c'est grâce aux recommandations de Mario Valignani, que le compositeur est admis au service du duc, sans doute suite à la perte de son poste à la cathédrale de Rieti. Chieti (1585), Sabine (1586) et encore Venise (1587) sont les destinations des années suivantes. La carrière ultérieure de del Mel constitue une parenthèse lors de laquelle il regagne des régions proches de son lieu d'origine. Il signe un livre de madrigaux à six voix et un livre de motets à Liège, respectivement en 1587 et 1588.[15] Jusqu'en 1589, il est au service du prince évêque Ernest de Bavière (1554-1612) à Liège. C'est bien d'une parenthèse qu'il s'agit puisque les six derniers livres de René del Mel sont à nouveau signés (et imprimés) en Italie, en région romaine

[10] Ces indications ont permis à Van Doorslaer de réaliser la première reconstitution de la vie du compositeur en 1921.

[11] *Il primo libro de madrigali a cinque voci* (Venise: Scotto, 1584; RISM M 2200) est dédicacé à Mario Valignani.

[12] Van Doorslaer, 'René del Mel', p. 230.

[13] Angelo Sacchetti-Sassetti, 'La cappella musicale del duomo di Rieti', *Note d'archivio per la storia musicale*, 18 (1941), 49-88 (p. 71).

[14] *Il primo libro de madrigali a cinque et sei voci* (Venise: Scotto, 1585; RISM M 2201).

[15] *Sacrae cantiones ... V, VI, VII, VIII ac XII vocum, cum litania de B[eata] Maria Virgine V vocum* (Anvers: Phalèse et Bellère, 1588; RISM M 2195) et *Madrigali ... a sei voci* (Anvers: Phalèse et Bellère, 1588; RISM M 2206).

essentiellement: Calvi (1593), Sabine (1594 et 1595) et Rome (1594, 1595 et 1596). Son retour en Italie est sans doute lié à son entrée en fonction auprès de Paleotti dans ces années.[16] La dédicace du cinquième livre de motets atteste qu'il est au service du cardinal en 1595.[17] Peut-être y demeure-t-il jusqu'à la mort de Paleotti en juillet 1597? Sur les dernières années de la vie de René del Mel, les sources ne parlent guère plus que sur le début de sa carrière. Le fait qu'en 1593 et en 1594 le compositeur dédie deux recueils aux membres de la famille Valignani indique que del Mel est resté en contact avec certains de ses premiers protecteurs.[18] A la même époque, le compositeur intensifie également les dédicaces à destination des membres de la famille Lorraine-Bavière.[19] En 1598, del Mel publie huit chansons françaises dans le *Rossignol musical*, imprimé à Anvers chez Phalèse.[20] Si ce recueil ne permet nullement d'affirmer que le compositeur est revenu dans les Pays-Bas, il peut toutefois constituer l'indice d'un tel retour à la mort de Paleotti.

Il convient ici d'envisager les textes dédicatoires de René del Mel dans ce qui leur donne naissance et ce qui les légitime grâce à l'étude des relations que le compositeur entretient avec ses dédicataires et les convictions qu'il tient à mettre en évidence. Au-delà de l'aspect apologétique contingent au genre, les dédicaces dévoilent des stratégies mises en œuvre par le compositeur pour exploiter au mieux un cadre formel.[21]

[16] Baini, *Memorie storico-critiche della vita e delle opere di Giovanni Pierluigi da Palestrina*, I, 23.

[17] *Liber quintus motectorum ... quae partim senis, partimque octonis, ac duodenis vocibus concinuntur* (Venise: Gardano, 1595; RISM M 2197), voir n. 36 de cet article.

[18] *Il quinto libro de madrigali a cinque voci* (Venise: Gardano, 1594; RISM M 2209) est dédié à Lucio Savello, lié aux Valignani par l'épouse de Mario Valignani, Paola Savello. *Il terzo libro delli madrigali a sei voci* (Venise: Gardano, 1595; RISM M 2211) est dédié à Mario Valigano.

[19] *Il secondo libro de madrigali a sei voci* (Venise: Vincenti, 1593; RISM M 2207) est dédicacé à Minutio Minucci, notamment actif comme conseiller à la cour de Guillaume de Bavière; *Il terzo libro delli madrigaletti a tre voci* (Venise: Gardano, 1594; RISM M 2210) à Maximilien de Bavière; et le livre des *Madrigaletti spirituali libro quarto a tre voci* (Venise: Gardano, 1596; Emil Vogel, *François Lesure et Claudio Sartori*, Bibliografia della musica italiana vocale profana pubblicata dal 1500 al 1700 (Pomezia: Staderini, 1977 [éd. rév. 1982]), n° 717) à Dorothée de Lorraine.

[20] *Rossignol musical des chansons de diverses et excellens autheurs de nostre temps a 4, 5 et 6 parties* (Anvers: Phalèse, 1598; RISM 1598$^5$).

[21] Les dédicaces latines de René del Mel ont fait l'objet d'une édition critique par Demmy Verbeke, *"Ad musicae patronos" — Latijnse dedicaties en inleidende teksten in motettenbundels van componisten uit de Nederlanden (ca. 1550 – ca. 1600)*, 4 vols (PhD diss. Katholieke Universiteit Leuven, 2005). Cette thèse de doctorat est consultable en ligne: http://hdl.handle.net/1979/160. Outre les extraits cités dans le cadre de cet essai,

## La dédicace comme geste de reconnaissance

Le lieu commun selon lequel la dédicace relève de la recherche d'un protecteur ou d'une tentative pour attirer l'attention trouve bien sûr une application dans les dédicaces des recueils de del Mel.

Offrir un recueil de musique imprimée peut aussi faire simplement office de remerciement pour des faveurs obtenues. Se justifie de la sorte la dédicace du premier livre de motets de René del Mel à Christine de Danemark (1521-1590) en 1581. De manière classique, le texte dédicatoire s'ouvre sur l'énumération des nombreux titres de la princesse sous les auspices de laquelle se place le compositeur. Le texte proprement dit n'est guère qu'une vaste justification du présent que del Mel fait à Christine, gage de son souvenir pour l'assistance qu'elle a portée à la famille du compositeur: à ses ancêtres, ses frères de même qu'à lui-même.[22] Del Mel, à peine arrivé en Italie, espère peut-être briguer une fonction officielle auprès de Christine de Danemark qui depuis 1578, s'est retirée entre Milan et Gênes, dans son domaine de Tortona.[23]

> Serenissimae Principi et Dominae D[ominae] Christiernae Daciae, Sueciae, Norvegiae, etc. Reginae natae, Mediolanique, Lotharingiae, Barri Duci ac Derthonae Marchioni etc. Rinaldus del Mel s[alutem] d[icit].
>
> Cum sepe animo volverim, Princeps serenissima, quantis qualibusque maiores olim et nunc fratres meos, qui familiari ministerio tibi assistunt, meque ipsum prosequuta fueris et in dies prosequaris beneficiis et favoribus, cogitavi aliquoties quid propterea liberalitati et benegnitati tuae a me retribuendum foret.[24] (Rome, le 5 août 1581 – RISM M 2193)[25]

le lecteur trouvera les textes entiers des dédicaces, leur traduction en néerlandais ainsi qu'un appareil critique et une bibliographie sommaire.

22 Le père du compositeur fut chambellan à la cour de Lorraine; Malines, A.C., actes scabinaux, reg. 174, f° 10v, le 29 octobre 1550. Voir aussi Van Doorslaer, 'René del Mel', 227.

23 Julia Cartwright, *Christina of Denmark Duchess of Milan and Lorraine: 1552-1590* (Londres: Murray, 1913), pp. 496-509.

24 Verbeke, *'Ad musicae patronos'*, III, 122. 'René del Mel salue la Princesse Sérénissime et Maîtresse Christine, née reine de Dacie, de Suède, de Norvège etc. duchesse de Milan, de Lotharingie, de Bar et marquise de Tortona etc. Alors que je méditais souvent, Princesse Sérénissime, sur les grand et bons bienfaits et faveurs par lesquels autrefois tu as soutenu et tu soutiens encore de jour en jour mes ancêtres, aujourd'hui mes frères, qui t'assistent comme serviteurs, ainsi que moi-même, j'ai pensé un certain nombre de fois qu'il me faudrait rendre à ta générosité et à ta bonté.' Nous remercions vivement Bruno Rochette, Professeur à l'Université de Liège ainsi que Grégory Dolcimascolo, Catherine Stans et Annick Delfosse pour leur aide précieuse à la traduction des dédicaces.

25 La date et le lieu de la dédicace sont donnés lors de la première citation d'un recueil. Pour les extraits suivants issus du même recueil, seules les références RISM sont mentionnées.

La formule conclusive de la dédicace qui ouvre le recueil de *Sacrae Cantiones*[26] offert à la fille de Christine de Danemark et de François Ier de Lorraine (1517-1545), Renée, procède de cette même légitimation de la dédicace par un devoir de gratitude dont le compositeur veut s'acquitter.[27]

> Quapropter, ne accepti tanti beneficii immemor viderer, aeternae memoriae perpetuaeque gratitudinis et observantiae ergo, sacrum hocce munusculum, pro tenuioris fortunae atque ingenioli mei qualitate, V[estrae] sereniss[imae] Cels[itudini] offero, dedico atque consacro; obnixe postulans, ut tametsi conspectu suo indignum, serena fronte id e manibus humillimi sui clientuli suscipere dignetur. (Liège, le 15 octobre 1588 – RISM M 2195)[28]

Alors que la dédicace à Christine de Danemark révèle que des membres de la famille du compositeur ont été actifs à son service, celle des *Sacrae Cantiones* donne plus de détails quant à la nature des relations de la famille de Lorraine à celle de del Mel. Outre le fait que Renée de Lorraine est la marraine du compositeur, cet extrait de dédicace renseigne également que la sœur de del Mel, Marie, est élevée à la cour avant que Renée de Lorraine n'épouse Guillaume de Bavière (1548-1626).[29]

> Nam ut de sorore mea Maria, olim tam in sereniss[imae] matris, Reginae Daniae, quam ipsiusmet V[estrae] Cels[itudinis] antequam cum serenissimo Bavariae Duce Guilhelmo contraxisset, servitiis feliciter enutrita, audire memini, non solum me Cels[itudo] V[estra] e sacro fonte suscepit, sed benevolentiae testatione suo ipsius nomine donavit, ac Renatum vocari voluit.[30] (RISM M 2195/2196)

Le tableau en appendice reprend la liste des éditions musicales avec leurs références complètes.

[26] Ce recueil a fait l'objet d'une édition critique, voir Johan Akkermans, 'De bundel "Sacrae Cantiones V, VI, VII ac XII vocum", van Renatus del Melle, Antwerpen, 1588', 2 vols (mémoire de licence, Katholieke Universiteit Leuven, 1984).

[27] Sur l'échange hommage-protection que permet la dédicace, voir Gérard Genette, *Seuils* (Paris: Seuil, 1987), pp. 122-123.

[28] Verbeke, *'Ad musicae patronos'*, III, 124. 'C'est pourquoi, pour éviter de sembler être oublieux d'un si grand bienfait dont j'ai été gratifié, j'offre, je dédie et je consacre ce petit cadeau sacré, à la mesure de ma modeste condition et de la petitesse de mon talent à Votre Excellence, en mémoire éternelle de ma perpétuelle gratitude et déférence, en lui demandant avec insistance de daigner le recevoir des mains de son modeste et humble serviteur, même s'il est indigne de son regard.'

[29] Sur les festivités du mariage de Renée de Lorraine et de Guillaume de Bavière, voir Klaus Lazarowicz, 'Konzelebration oder Kollusion? Über die Feste der Wittelsbacher', in *Europäische Hofkultur im 16. und 17. Jahrhundert: Vorträge und Referate gehalten anläßlich des Kongresses des Wolfenbütteler Arbeitskreises für Renaissanceforschung und des Internationalen Arbeitskreises für Barockliteratur in der Herzog August Bibliothek Wolfenbüttel*, ed. August Buck, Wolfenbütteler Arbeiten zur Barockforschung, 9 (Hambourg: Hauswedell, 1981), pp. 301-317.

[30] Verbeke, *'Ad musicae patronos'*, III, 124. 'En effet, tout comme ma sœur Marie élevée autrefois avec bonheur tant dans les services de la Sérénissime Mère danoise que dans

Le cinquième livre de motets (1595) est dédicacé au cardinal Gabriele Paleotti à l'époque où celui-ci est le patron de del Mel. Dès sa jeunesse, Paleotti manifeste un intérêt pour la musique. Formé auprès de Domenico Maria Ferrabosco (1513-1585) avec qui il demeure en contact, il continue à l'âge adulte à chanter et à improviser au luth et ce, 'dans la meilleure tradition de la Renaissance'.[31] Son implication est considérable lors du Concile de Trente, en particulier dans la formulation des décrets relatifs à la musique.[32] Lors de la session XXII en septembre 1562, la première des trois sessions lors desquelles la musique est envisagée, il semble que ce soit Paleotti qui énonce les canons touchant aux abus de la messe. Selon son biographe, Paolo Prodi, les décrets de réforme musicale des deux dernières sessions (XXIV et XXV) lui seraient dus pour l'essentiel.[33] Il est vrai que c'est à lui et à Egidio Foscarari, évêque de Modène, que la session XXV fut commandée.[34] Après avoir été nommé archevêque de Bologne (1582) et suburbicaire d'Albano (1589), Paleotti devient suburbicaire de Sabine (1591). Le 26 janvier 1593, il fonde le séminaire de Sabine, le troisième fondé en Italie après le Concile.[35]

Dans la dédicace adressée à Gabriele Paleotti en 1595, René del Mel mentionne ses nouvelles fonctions. C'est le parcours du compositeur qui confère ici sa légitimité au geste dédicatoire. Le titre du recueil retient

ceux de Votre Excellence avant qu'elle n'ait été liée au Sérénissime Duc de Bavière Guillaume, je me souviens avoir entendu dire que non seulement Votre Excellence m'a porté sur les eaux saintes du baptême mais qu'elle m'a aussi donné son nom, en témoignage de sa bienveillance, et qu'elle a voulu que je sois appelé Renatus.'

[31] Craig A. Monson,'The Council of Trent Revisited', *Journal of the American Musicological Society*, 55 (2002), 1-37 (p. 13). Sur la formation musicale de Paleotti, voir du même auteur, 'The Composer as "Spy": The Ferraboscos, Gabriele Paleotti, and the Inquisition', *Music & Letters*, 84/1 (2003), 1-18 (p. 4).

[32] En témoigne son *Diarium*, journal sur le déroulement du concile. Le texte complet est publié dans *Concilium Tridentinum. Diariorum, Actorum, Epistularum, tractatuum nova collectio, editio secunda stereotypa*, ed. Societas Goerresiana, 13 vols (Fribourg-en-Brisgau: Herder, 1901-1976), III (1931), 231-761.

[33] Paolo Prodi, *Il Cardinale Gabriele Paleotti (1522-1597)*, Uomini e dottrine, 7 (Rome: Edizioni di Storia e Letteratura, 1959).

[34] Craig Monson fait remarquer que cette session, souvent négligée par les historiens de la musique est en réalité la seule qui présente à la congrégation générale un décret restrictif concernant la musique, celle des moniales. A l'automne 1563, l'attention de nombreux prélats se tourne progressivement vers leurs préoccupations propres. Monson émet l'hypothèse que le décret restrictif présenté à la congrégation générale du 20 Novembre soit l'œuvre d'un seul homme, Gabriele Paleotti. Voir 'The Council of Trent Revisited', pp. 19-21.

[35] Outre Prodi, voir la notice synthétique consacrée à Paleotto dans *The Cardinals of the Holy Roman Church*, base de données accessible en ligne, réalisée par Salvador Miranda (Florida International University Library): http://www.fiu.edu/~mirandas/cardinals.htm.

déjà l'attention de l'historien de la musique. Il précise que le compositeur est maître de chapelle de la cathédrale de Sabine et qu'il est nommé professeur au séminaire.

> Liber quintus motectorum Raynaldi del Mel chori ecclesiae cathedralis ac seminarii Sabinen[sis] praefecti, ab illustrissimo et Reverendissimo D[omino] Gabriele S[anctae] R[omanae] E[cclesiae] Cardinale Paleoto Episcopo Sabinen[si] deputati. (Sabine, le 1er mars 1595 – RISM M 2197)[36]

Plus loin dans le texte, le compositeur ne manque pas de réitérer la mention de sa nouvelle fonction au séminaire.

> Seminarium clericorum (in fundamento cuius maximae difficultates dudum exoriebantur) mira sane prudentia addidisti, ad bonas artes capessendas plurium facultatum professores in eo constituens; meque etiam licet indignum, quo alumni scientia musices imbuantur, habere voluisti. (RISM M 2197)[37]

L'usage d'un tel procédé dans le cadre d'une dédicace place Paleotti, instigateur de la promotion du compositeur, face à la concrétisation de sa reconnaissance des qualités de del Mel. La mention des postes récemment obtenus vient faire la preuve de l'estime en laquelle le cardinal tient le compositeur. Elle confère sa justification au choix d'un tel dédicataire et légitime pleinement le don du recueil. René del Mel opte pour un dédicataire qu'il n'a plus à conquérir. Le compositeur choisit l'un des seuls moyens à sa disposition afin de témoigner à Paleotti sa gratitude pour les bienfaits reçus de lui. Il n'y a pas d'enjeu véritable sinon celui de demeurer dans sa bonne considération. Nommé au poste prestigieux de maître de chapelle, le compositeur inscrit donc la dédicace de ce recueil non plus au sein d'un processus de persuasion mais de confirmation.

## De l'importance du dédicataire

Une fois le geste dédicatoire légitimé, reste à obtenir du dédicataire l'acceptation du recueil. Le dédicataire est le trait d'union entre la composition

36 Verbeke, *'Ad musicae patronos'*, III, 125. 'Livre V de motets. René del Mel, maître de chœur de la cathédrale et préfet du séminaire de Sabine salue le très illustre et révérend Gabriel Paleotti, cardinal de la Sainte Eglise Romaine, évêque de Sabine.'

37 Verbeke, *'Ad musicae patronos'*, III, 125. 'Tu as ajouté le séminaire des Clercs (pour la fondation duquel de très grandes difficultés s'étaient levées) avec une sagesse tout à fait admirable, afin d'y acquérir les beaux arts en y établissant des professeurs de nombreuses disciplines et tu as voulu m'avoir aussi, moi qui en suis indigne pourtant, pour abreuver les élèves de la science de la Musique.'

et sa révélation publique. En acceptant le don du compositeur, il permet en effet l'accomplissement du processus de création. Par son prestige, par le caractère unique et exceptionnel de la relation qu'il entretient avec le compositeur ou encore par sa bonne connaissance de la musique, il est ainsi investi du pouvoir de décider ou non de l'aboutissement de l'œuvre. L'acceptation du recueil est pourvoyeuse de grands bienfaits pour le compositeur, ainsi que l'expose del Mel dans le texte dédicatoire du recueil des *Sacrae Cantiones*.

> Quod si impetrabo et ingens me beneficium accepisse sentiam, et ingratus sim, nisi Deum opt[imum] Max[imum] pro diuturna nominis vestri incolumitate interpellem. (RISM M 2195)[38]

Le dédicataire est aussi le protecteur de l'œuvre musicale. Dans l'exemple de la formule finale du livre III de motets dédié en 1585 à Carlo Valignani, archevêque de Teate (Chieti)[39] et membre d'une famille déjà mentionnée à qui del Mel dédie d'autres recueils, le compositeur enjoint Valignani à protéger et à défendre son œuvre 'avec la défense avec laquelle il a l'habitude de défendre les autres choses'.

> Quo igitur soles alia munire munimine munias, qua tueri tutela tuearis, postremoque qua defendere defensione defendas meque famulum tuum perpetuis beneficiis devinctum esse certo scias, et vale. (Chieti, le 13 novembre 1585 – RISM M 2194)[40]

Christine de Danemark est elle aussi investie des espoirs du compositeur dans la dédicace du premier livre de motets. La grandeur de sa personne rejaillit sur la musique et rehausse la valeur du recueil. Grâce au nom de la princesse, la musique est honorée et protégée. La dédicataire personnifie un maillon indispensable. Son rôle, effectif à la diffusion et à la reconnaissance de la musique apparaît ici clairement:

> Audeo hos sacrae lectionis modulos, rudis ingenii mei primitias licet agrestes, Cels[itudini] tuae consecrare non tam in pietatis erga te meae argumentum,

[38] Verbeke, *'Ad musicae patronos'*, III, 124. 'Si j'y parviens, que je sente que j'ai reçu cet énorme bienfait. Et que je sois ingrat si je n'invoque pas Dieu Très Grand pour la longue vie de ton nom.'

[39] Ville d'Italie centrale, dans la région des Abruzzes. Proche de la côte Adriatique, Chieti se trouve au sud-ouest de Pescara.

[40] Verbeke, *'Ad musicae patronos'*, III, 123. 'Puisses-tu les protéger [ces œuvres] de la protection avec laquelle tu as l'habitude de protéger les autres choses, y veiller avec la vigilance avec laquelle tu as l'habitude de veiller aux autres choses et enfin les défendre avec la défense avec laquelle tu as l'habitude de défendre les autres choses. Sois sûr que je suis ton serviteur, lié par tes bienfaits perpétuels. Porte-toi bien.'

> quam quod sub nomine tuo in lucem prodeuntes decorentur et tutentur. (RISM M 2193)[41]

Dans la dédicace à Renée de Lorraine en 1588, bien qu'indirecte, l'association est plus forte encore. René del Mel met en évidence plusieurs éléments: la recherche d'immortalité, la diversité des solutions pour y parvenir et la voie idéale selon lui: la vertu.

> Ea est humanae naturae conditio, serenissima Princeps, ut quotquot fluxa hac luce fruimur, immortalitati assequendae certatim, tametsi modis diversis, incumbamus. Ad quam tamen, cum unica sanctarum virtutum scala ascensum certissimum praestet, ii profecto magis ea digni videntur, qui illuvie quadam vitiorum depulsa, per eiusmodi aeternae gloriae semitam, ardentioribus ad eam studiis evehuntur.[42] (RISM M 2195)

Le compositeur insiste ensuite sur les nombreuses qualités de Renée de Lorraine, son passe-droit pour l'immortalité. Le fait de se placer sous la protection d'un tel personnage fait immanquablement retomber une part de caractère exceptionnel sur le recueil. L'allusion à l'immortalité ne doit rien au hasard. Le compositeur prétend lui aussi y accéder. La publication de l'écrit — qu'il s'agisse d'une épître dédicatoire ou de pièces musicales — est un geste révélant la volonté de laisser une trace, de s'inscrire dans le temps. C'est le moyen d'un compositeur pour tendre sinon vers l'immortalité, du moins vers la reconnaissance. Au service de ce même objectif, la dédicace et les pièces musicales sont consubstantielles. La dédicace, au même titre que les notes de musique qu'elle précède, fait partie du recueil qui est le don. Sans les notes, le texte ne se légitimerait guère et sans le texte, les notes ne trouveraient pas leur destination. La dédicace donne sa justification au recueil. En cela, elle lui est nécessaire. Dans le texte de la dédicace à Renée de Lorraine, le premier thème qu'expose le compositeur fait rimer l'aspiration à l'immortalité avec un

[41] Verbeke, *'Ad musicae patronos'*, III, 122. 'Aussi osè-je dédicacer à ton Eminence ces melodies sacrées, prémices — certes agrestes — de mon talent maladroit, non tant pour témoigner de ma piété envers toi que parce que publiés sous ton nom, ils seraient honorés et protégés.'

[42] Verbeke, *'Ad musicae patronos'*, III, 125. 'La nature humaine est ainsi faite, Sérénissime Princesse, que, aussi longtemps que nous jouissons de cette lumière éphémère [la vie], nous nous attachons à l'envi à atteindre l'immortalité et ce, de façons diverses. Cependant, puisque l'échelle des saintes vertus est la seule qui permette une ascension tout à fait assurée vers cette immortalité, il me semble que ceux qui en sont le plus dignes sont ceux qui, après s'être débarrassés d'une boue de vices, se sont élevés, par le sentier d'une gloire éternelle de cette espèce, par des efforts plus ardents vers elle.'

personnage qui pourrait y prétendre, telle une inspiratrice idéale[43], caution morale du recueil.[44]

> Qua in re quum sereniss[ima] Cels[itudo] V[estra] maxime etiam supra foeminei sexus vires eniteat, utpote quae (ut stirpem regiam, iudicii maturitatem, animi mansuetudinem, morum suavitatem atque id genus alia laudabilia permulta sileam) pietatem illam avitam, admirandam (inquam) tot hisce turbulentissimis contra Romanam Ecclesiam exortis tempestatibus, catholica in religione pectoris sui plane regii, constantiam, non sine magna divinae Maiestatis providentia, cum evidentissima subditorum suorum utilitate, inconcussam gloriosissime semper conservaverit; non abs re mihi visum fuit, si ad summi Dei gloriam ac Cels[itudinis] V[estrae] immortalitatem, hasce sacras cantiones, licet rudioris Minervae, in lucem emitterem. (RISM M 2195)[45]

Comme pour renforcer cette stratégie à peine voilée d'association du dédicataire à l'acte créateur, le compositeur manifeste sa volonté d'afficher des convictions tant religieuses que politiques, qu'il partage avec Renée de Lorraine. Del Mel insiste sur la fidélité de Renée à l'Eglise catholique. Mentionnant sa piété ancestrale, le compositeur a peut-être plusieurs faits à l'esprit. Renée de Lorraine incarne en effet une véritable force catholique que bien des circonstances auraient pu faire vaciller. A la mort de son premier époux, François Sforza (1495-1535), la mère de Renée décline la demande en mariage adressée à son oncle Charles Quint pour elle par le roi d'Angleterre Henri VIII (1491-1547), gardant intacte son appartenance confessionnelle catholique.[46] Petite-fille de Christian II (1481-1559), ex-roi de Danemark, de Norvège et de Suède, Renée de Lorraine voit son

[43] Roger Chartier va plus loin encore en considérant que le dédicataire, 'loué comme l'inspirateur primordial, l'auteur premier du livre qui lui est présenté', fait sienne l'œuvre qui lui est présentée et par là, devient lui-même poète ou savant; *Culture écrite et société: L'ordre des livres (XIV<sup>e</sup>-XVIII<sup>e</sup> siècle)* (Paris: Albin Michel, 1996), p. 102.

[44] Le rôle de caution morale du dédicataire est également mis en évidence par Genette, *Seuils*, pp. 138-139.

[45] Verbeke, *'Ad musicae patronos'*, III, 124. 'Puisque Votre Sérénissime Excellence brille absolument en ce domaine, même au-delà des qualités du sexe féminin, elle qui a toujours, avec beaucoup de gloire, conservé inébranlable sa constance (pour ne pas parler de sa souche royale, de la maturité de son jugement, de la bonté de son âme, de la douceur de ses mœurs et de ses nombreuses autres qualités louables de ce genre) — admirable dis-je, alors que l'Église romaine était secouée par tant de tempêtes si turbulentes — non sans la grande providence de la Majesté divine, dans la religion catholique qui emplit sa poitrine royale, avec un profit tout à fait évident pour ses sujets, il ne m'a pas semblé incongru de mettre au jour ces *Sacrae Cantiones*, malgré leur finition grossière, pour la gloire de Dieu Très Grand et l'immortalité de Votre Excellence.'

[46] *Histoire de la Lorraine: les Temps Modernes*, ed. Guy Cabourdin, 2 vols (Metz-Nancy: Editions Serpenoises-Presses universitaires de Nancy, 1990-1991), I (1990), 52.

héritage échouer entre les mains des luthériens. En 1568, Renée épouse Guillaume de Bavière. Elle se retrouve désormais à la tête d'un territoire aux traditions catholiques fortement enracinées, allié essentiel de Rome dans un Empire miné de part en part par les protestants.[47] La suite de la dédicace des *Sacrae Cantiones* relate un épisode marquant de l'histoire de la Lorraine: la prise des évêchés de Metz, Toul et Verdun en 1552 par Henri II (1519-1559). La Lorraine, déclarée au traité de Nuremberg de 1542 'liber et non incorporatus' par l'empereur et 'principauté et souveraineté libre, franche et non attirée, ni comprise aux enclaves du Saint-Empire' par le roi de France se retrouve dix ans plus tard dans l'orbite d'Henri II.[48] Christine de Lorraine perd la tutelle du duc héritier Charles III, le frère de Renée; la régence qu'elle exerce jusqu'alors avec Nicolas de Vaudémont (1524-1577) incombe désormais seulement à ce dernier. Dans un premier temps, elle s'installe avec ses filles Renée et Dorothée (1545-1621) dans ses terres à Blâmont et à Denœuvre. Elle se réfugie ensuite avec Anne de Lorraine (1522-1568), la sœur de son époux défunt à Schlestadt.[49] Del Mel insiste sur le contexte défavorable du duché de Lorraine jadis libre et souverain et désormais dans le giron français. Trente ans après les faits, le compositeur estime utile de faire allusion à l'épisode de 1552. Procédant de la sorte, del Mel caractérise politiquement sa dédicace. Les termes utilisés ne laissent aucun doute. C'est en partisan de la Lorraine qu'il se présente, se remémorant 'les hostiles hordes de Gaulois' qui envahissaient 'avec grande barbarie' la 'très florissante Lotharingie'.

> Aderat tecum tum temporis et illustriss[ima] Ducissa Arschotana Sleistadii, quo se ab hostilibus Gallorum copiis, magna feritate florentissimam vestram Lotharingiam invadentium, una cum serenissima Maiestate Reginae matris receperat. (RISM M 2195)[50]

La volonté du compositeur à mettre en évidence des convictions de nature religieuse et politique est éloquente. Ce sont autant d'éléments venant

[47] Dès la seconde moitié du XVIe siècle, la Bavière est une alliée considérable de Rome grâce notamment aux rapports entretenus entre la nonciature d'Allemagne et la Curie. Pour une étude approfondie de ces relations, voir notamment Bettina Scherbaum, *Bayern und der Papst: Politik und Kirche im Spiegel der Nuntiaturberichte 1550 bis 1600*, Forschungen zur Landes und Regionalgeschichte, 9 (St. Ottilien: E.O.S. Verlag Erzabtei, 2002).

[48] *Histoire de la Lorraine*, I, 53-54.

[49] Cartwright, *Christina of Denmark*, pp. 370-375.

[50] Verbeke, *'Ad musicae patronos'*, III, 124. 'A cette époque, l'illustrissime Duchesse d'Aarschot était avec toi à Schelstadt où elle s'était réfugiée en même temps que sa sérénissime Majesté la Reine-mère, loin des troupes hostiles des Gaulois [Français] qui envahissaient avec grande barbarie votre très florissante Lotharingie.'

s'ajouter au lien ancien entre le compositeur et la maison de Lorraine-Bavière, dont del Mel fait état dès la dédicace à Christine de Danemark. Le rappel du lien qui unit le compositeur à sa dédicataire-marraine d'une part et d'autre part l'affirmation d'un nouveau type de lien, politique, corroborent à personnaliser la relation que del Mel entretient avec Renée de Lorraine et par là même, à la renforcer.

La relation du compositeur à son dédicataire, qu'elle qu'en soit la nature, est par ailleurs rendue publique, accessible au lecteur. La dédicace est un geste ostentatoire, un geste qui "affiche" et qui ne possède que l'apparence du geste privé; cela a déjà été mis en évidence. Le lecteur du recueil est "pris à témoin" de cette relation et de son caractère privilégié.[51]

Les textes dédicatoires de del Mel laissent en outre apparaître des éléments participant de la conception de la musique à cette époque. Dans la dédicace adressée à Christine de Danemark en 1581, le compositeur fait apparaître la musique comme une activité que la princesse cultive en dilettante, lorsque ses occupations sérieuses cessent de l'interpeller.[52] Définie de la sorte, la place réservée à la musique est dotée d'un intérêt secondaire, sinon d'une importance moindre que celle des affaires définies comme "sérieuses". Cependant, la musique — selon René del Mel — enrichit la princesse. Cette capacité confère immanquablement une certaine distinction à l'art musical. L'expérience musicale de Christine de Danemark est considérée comme une qualité, au même titre que 'ses innombrables vertus héroïques de corps et d'esprit'. La musique contribue donc à part entière à la haute considération en laquelle Christine de Danemark est tenue.

> Doctus attamen quod inter innumeras corporis animique tui heroicas etiam supra sexum virtutes, musices peritia polleas non modica eiusque armonicis modulationibus, dum gravium tuarum curarum cessat interpellatio, aliquando oblecteris [...] (RISM M 2193)[53]

[51] Genette, *Seuils*, pp. 134-138.

[52] Cette fonction de *diletto*, fréquemment formulée dans les dédicaces est examinée par Florence Alazard, *Art vocal, art de gouverner: La musique, le prince et la cité en Italie à la fin du XVI^e^ siècle* (Paris-Tours: Minerve-C.E.S.R. 'Ricercar', 2002), p. 98. Voir aussi Stefano Lorenzetti, *Musica e identità nobiliare nell'Italia del Rinascimento: Educazione, mentalità, immaginario* (Florence: Olschki, 2003).

[53] Verbeke, *'Ad musicae patronos'*, III, 122. 'Averti cependant que, parmi tes innombrables vertus héroïques de corps et d'esprit, même au-delà du sexe [féminin], tu es estimée d'une connaissance non négligeable de la musique et que, lorsque cesse l'obligation des tâches sérieuses, tu te laisses charmer de temps à autres par les modulations harmonieuses de cet art [la musique].'

## La dédicace, clé de lecture de la relative autonomie du musicien face à son employeur

Sans transgresser la coutume de se placer sous la bienveillance de son patron — certains exemples détaillés ci-dessus en attestent — le compositeur fait montre d'une détermination à conserver une allégeance vis-à-vis de la famille Lorraine-Bavière. Il multiplie les témoignages de sujétion malgré son attachement à un autre employeur. Cette fidélité interpelle.

Outre un premier livre de motets dédicacé en 1581 à Christine de Danemark et un livre de madrigaux en 1583 à Guillaume de Bavière, son beau-fils,[54] la succession rapprochée de recueils offerts à la maison de Lorraine-Bavière s'amorce en 1587. René del Mel dédie alors son livre de madrigaux à six voix au prince-évêque de Liège et archevêque de Cologne Ernest de Bavière, le frère de Guillaume.[55] En 1588, il dédie un recueil de *Sacrae Cantiones* à Renée de Lorraine, la fille aînée de Christine de Danemark. Minutio Minucci (1551-1609) reçoit en 1593 le second livre de madrigaux à six voix. Dans son texte dédicatoire, del Mel relate l'estime que voue Guillaume de Bavière à Minucci, qui s'est distingué en de nombreuses occasions au service du duc.[56] L'année suivante, c'est encore un Wittelsbach qui est le dédicataire d'un nouveau recueil: à Maximilien (1573-1651), le fils de Guillaume V de Bavière, est dédié le troisième livre de madrigaux de del Mel, dont la dédicace est signée à Rome le 27 mars 1594. Deux ans plus tard enfin, Dorothée de Lorraine, la seconde fille de Christine de Danemark reçoit le recueil de madrigaux spirituels à trois et quatre voix.

D'une manière ou d'une autre, chacun des textes dédicatoires adressés à l'un de ces personnages énonce l'antique sujétion du compositeur à la famille. Dans le livre de madrigaux dédicacé à Guillaume de Bavière, del Mel évoque le livre de motets offert à Christine de Danemark, se

[54] *Madrigali a quattro, cinque et sei voci* (Venise: Gardano; RISM M 2198).

[55] Ce recueil est le premier livre de madrigaux à six voix consacré à un même compositeur publié aux Pays-Bas. Le second, imprimé chez Phalèse également, est un recueil de madrigaux de Jean de Turnhout dédicacé à Alexandre Farnèse; dans Sandrine Thieffry, 'Jean de Turnhout, compositeur et maître de chapelle à la Cour de Bruxelles (ca. 1550-1614)', *Revue belge de Musicologie*, 58 (2004), 23-44.

[56] Nommé Secrétaire d'Etat des affaires allemandes par Innocent IX en 1591, Minucci exerce antérieurement déjà la fonction d'agent de la Bavière en tant que conseiller du duc Guillaume V. Voir Meinhard Pohl, 'Minucci', *Neue Deutsche Biographie*, ed. Historische Kommission bei der Bayerischen Akademie der Wissenschaften, 22 vols (Berlin: Duncker-Humblot, 1953-1994), XVII (1994), 547-549. Voir aussi Scherbaum, *Bayern und der Papst*, pp. 110-121.

revendiquant par ailleurs tant le serviteur affectionné du duc que celui de sa belle-mère. Le propos de la dédicace au prince-évêque Ernest va dans le même sens. Mention est faite des recueils offerts à Christine et Guillaume. Le compositeur ne craint pas, une fois de plus, d'insister sur l'allégeance qu'il conserve vis-à-vis de la famille de Lorraine-Bavière. Citons surtout le recueil dédié à Maximilien de Bavière, dans la préface duquel le compositeur affirme avoir dédié 'la majeure partie de son œuvre à cette famille'.

> Havendo io messo insieme il Terzo Libro di Madigaletti à Tre Voci, non meno delettevoli che artificiosi, e volendoli dar in luce, mi è parso non solo conveniente ma debito della antica servitù mia dedicarlo all'Altezza vostra, si come la maggior parte dell'opere mie sono dedicate alla Serenissima Casa di Baviera, e di Lorena, sicuro de sotto l'ale, e protettione di V[ostra] A[ltezza] Sereniss[ima] saranno grate al mondo, e principalmente alla Regal Casa sua dove tanto aggradisce si nobil scienza [...] (Rome, le 27 mars 1594 – RISM M 2210).[57]

Durant ces années, le compositeur ne cesse de manifester sa déférence à la même maison. C'est seulement dans une moindre mesure que la fidélité du compositeur décrite ici peut être comparée à celle que témoigne del Mel à l'égard des Valignani. De 1584 à 1594, il maintient certes d'évidents contacts avec des membres de cette famille et leur entourage. Toutefois, il semble que del Mel n'y ait occupé de fonctions que sporadiquement, peut-être principalement sous la forme de compositions musicales, à l'exception des années qui suivent son licenciement de la cathédrale de Rieti,

[57] La transcription de la dédicace a été réalisée au départ de l'édition musicale originale dont les dédicaces des deux parties conservées ne présentent pas de différence (Bologne, Civico Museo Bibliografico Musicale, T 91, parties de ténor et de basse). L'orthographe et la ponctuation de la source ont été respectées, le "&" est transformé en "e" et le "u" en "v" lorsqu'il s'inscrit entre deux voyelles. Les abréviations sont résolues entre crochets. Cette dédicace, comme la majeure partie de celles des autres recueils du compositeur a toutefois fait l'objet d'une transcription, où subsistent quelques menues erreurs dans Sylvie Janssens, *"Il secondo libro delli madrigalietti a tre voci (1586) di Rinaldo del Mel": Analyse et transcriptions*, 3 vols (mémoire de licence Université Libre de Bruxelles, 1995), I, 121 et dans Van Doorslaer, 'René del Mel', p. 283. 'Ayant compilé le Troisième livre de Madrigaletti à trois voix, non moins agréables que remplis d'artifices, et voulant les mettre au jour, il m'a semblé non seulement une chose convenable mais surtout un devoir, de le dédicacer à Votre Altesse en raison de mon antique sujétion, comme la plus grande partie de mes œuvres dédiées à la sérénissime maison de Bavière et de Lorraine, sûr que sous l'aile et la protection de Votre Altesse Sérénissime, elles [mes œuvres] plairont au monde et principalement à votre maison royale où l'on apprécie tant une si noble science [la musique].' Nous remercions vivement Laurence Wuidar et Peter de Laurentiis pour leurs conseils dans les traductions des extraits italiens de cette étude.

comme exposé en introduction de cet essai. Si dans les années 1584-1585, l'attitude de del Mel se justifie certainement par la recherche d'un emploi officiel, il n'en va pas de même à la fin de sa carrière, tandis qu'il se trouve au service de Gabriel Paleotti. Le compositeur démontre alors sa gratitude pour les faveurs reçues. Le travail de mémoire développé dans les dédicaces destinées aux membres de la maison de Lorraine-Bavière ne trouve pas d'équivalent dans les autres épîtres dédicatoires du compositeur, même si à plusieurs reprises, il ne manque pas de faire mention des services rendus aux Valignani et de l'assistance dont il a pu bénéficier. Pour donner au lien qui l'unit aux Lorraine-Bavière son caractère unique et privilégié, le compositeur rappelle la protection assurée à sa famille, il met en lumière des éléments biographiques, des étapes de son parcours de compositeur, particularisant encore et toujours la relation qu'il prétend maintenir avec ses dédicataires. Or, René del Mel n'est lié d'un point de vue professionnel qu'à de très courtes reprises à la famille de Lorraine-Bavière.

## René del Mel à la cour de Lorraine-Bavière

Dans la dédicace adressée en 1581 à Christine de Danemark, le compositeur dit se souvenir de l'attention avec laquelle la princesse a écouté l'année précédente à Tortona certaines de ses compositions. Les problèmes récurrents de santé de Christine la déterminent à s'établir dans cette région au climat plus doux. En août 1578, elle quitte Nancy. Après un pèlerinage à Lorette, elle se rend à Tortona, entre Milan et Gênes.[58] Cette dédicace établit la présence de René del Mel dans la ville durant l'année 1580.

> Memor item quod Derthonae anno proxime acto quibusdam a me editis cantionibus dum te coram concinerentur, quam gratis auribus arriseris, audeo hos sacrae lectionis modulos, rudis ingenii mei primitias licet agrestes, Cels[itudini] tuae consecrare non tam in pietatis erga te meae argumentum, quam quod sub nomine tuo in lucem prodeuntes decorentur et tutentur. (RISM M 2193)[59]

[58] Cartwright, *Christina of Denmark*, pp. 450-497.

[59] Verbeke, *'Ad musicae patronos'*, III, 122. 'Je me souviens aussi de l'attention avec laquelle tu as écouté l'année passée à Tortona, certaines chansons éditées par mes soins lors d'une exécution en ta présence. Aussi osè-je dédicacer à ton Éminence ces mélodies sacrées, prémices — certes agrestes — de mon talent maladroit, non tant pour témoigner de ma piété envers toi que parce que publiés sous ton nom, ils seraient honorés et protégés.'

Or, cette année-là, les registres de la confrérie de Notre-Dame à Santa Maria in Campo Santo de Rome mentionnent l'obole du compositeur pour l'achat de cloches. L'année suivante, il semble que del Mel soit encore dans l'Urbs où est signée la dédicace à Christine de Danemark.[60] Peut-être la duchesse a-t-elle accueilli dans le Milanais le jeune compositeur et encouragé ses premières tentatives? Dans le même texte dédicatoire, le compositeur insiste sur les dispositions exceptionnelles de la princesse à la compréhension de la musique. Il mentionne encore la bienveillance de Christine envers ses ancêtres et ses frères mais aussi à son propre égard. Derrière la grandiloquence habituelle à la dédicace, se cache donc peut-être un pan non exploré de la carrière de René del Mel et des dernières années de Christine à Tortona. Del Mel aurait-t-il voulu rendre hommage à Christine de Danemark suite à son entrée en la ville de Tortona le 17 juin 1579? Il semble que le compositeur ait eu quelques engagements dans cette ville puisque dans le texte de la dédicace du livre des madrigaux spirituels à trois et quatre voix qu'il offre à Dorothée de Lorraine en 1596, René del Mel fait mention d'un privilège dont sa protectrice l'aurait gratifié à Tortona, sans pour autant en préciser la période.

> E poi per haverla servita per suo Gentil'huomo facendomi degno dell'honoratissimo privilegio di che nel mio partir da Tortona mi fece dono, che prima di me stesso che di tanto beneficio dimenticar mi posso [...] (Rome, le 20 août 1596 – Vogel 717)[61]

Si dans la dédicace du recueil de madrigaux à six voix que René del Mel adresse à Ernest de Bavière le compositeur ne se présente pas comme étant au service du prince, c'est sans doute parce qu'il ne l'est pas encore. Un an plus tard, dans le titre du recueil de *Sacrae Cantiones* qu'il dédie à Renée de Lorraine, la belle-sœur du prince-évêque, René del Mel fait apparaître sa fonction de 'sereniss[imi] utriusque Bavariae Ducis Ernesti ... musices praefectus'. Les archives liégeoises confirment que le compositeur est alors maître de chapelle d'Ernest. Dès le mois d'août 1588,

[60] Voir note 7 et tableau en appendice.

[61] La transcription de la dédicace a été réalisée au départ de l'édition originale du recueil (Cracovie, Biblioteka Jagiellońska, Mus. Ant. Pract. D 147, partie de canto). Pour les principes éditoriaux, voir note 57. Elle est néanmoins également éditée dans Janssens, *Il secondo libro delli madrigalietti a tre voci (1586) di Rinaldo del Mel*, I, 124-125 et dans Van Doorslaer, 'René del Mel', pp. 283-284. Le sens exact de cette proposition n'est pas clair et le reste de la dédicace ne l'explicite guère. Il semble que le compositeur s'estime privilégié du fait que Dorothée de Lorraine l'ait considéré comme un serviteur à sa cour. L'activité de del Mel à Tortona n'est pas connue à ce jour.

René del Mel reçoit régulièrement des paiements en cette qualité.[62] L'attention est néanmoins attirée par le fait qu'un paiement est octroyé en avril de la même année à Antoine Goswin (ca. 1545 – ca. 1600), décrit comme 'magister capellae'.[63] Il semble que dès le mois d'août, ce soit del Mel qui le remplace; Antoine Goswin apparaît comme pridem magister capellae'.[64] Del Mel reçoit des paiements en septembre de la même année, sans toutefois être associé à la même fonction mais bien à celle de 'cantor' ou 'musicus'.[65] Dès janvier de l'année suivante, René del Mel est à nouveau décrit comme maître de chapelle du prince, de même qu'à la date du 17 février 1589 à laquelle il touche des arriérés de six mois.[66] Il semble que del Mel occupe le poste de maître de chapelle au moins jusqu'en mars 1589 puisque le 8 de ce mois un paiement est fait à un certain Jean Stas qui a logé 'René del Mel, maître de chapelle' durant les trois derniers mois.[67] Il s'agit de la dernière mention du compositeur dans les archives liégeoises, remplacé ensuite par Antoine Goswin qui réintègre son ancienne fonction.

[62] 'Ite[m] p[ro] eod[em] me[n]se [augusto 1588] solui Rinaldo del melle m[a]g[ist]ro capellae VI scuta XVIII fl[orenos] b[ra]b[antiae]'; Liège, Archives de l'Etat, Comptes généraux de la Chambre des comptes de Liège, reg. 197 (recettes et dépenses, 1587-1588), f° 164. Ultérieures références au même fonds: A.E.L., Ch.C. Nos remerciements vont à Jean Mornard, pour son aide à la lecture des extraits d'archives cités ici.

[63] 'Ite[m] le xxvi ap[ri]lis 1588 soluit M. Jacobus Gerardinius receptor g[e]n[er]alis quos illi restitui iux[ta] cedula[m] Thomae principe Anthonio Gosswin magistro capellae quinque scuta p[er] manus Piere Masteels xv fl[orenos] b[ra]b[antiae]'; A.E.L., Ch.C., reg. 197, f° 160.

[64] 'Ite[m] xvii augusti an[n]o 1588 seu potius xix eiusd[em] solui iux[ta] cedula[m] sue Cels[itudinis] M[a]g[ist]ro Anthonio Gosswin p[ri]de[m] Magistro Capelle vig[in]ti flor[enos] aureos q[uam]vis cedula de 50 faciat me[n]tione[m] l fl[orenos] b[ra]b[antiae]'; A.E.L., Ch.C., reg. 197, f° 165.

[65] 'Item tertia septe[m]bris 1588 solui Riinaldo del Mell ca[n]tori p[ro] me[n]se septe[m]bris sed ille pretendit p[ro] me[n]se augusto sex scuta facien[te]s xvii fl[orenos] xiiii sol[idos] b[ra]b[an]t[iae]'; A.E.L., Comptes Ch.C., reg. 197, f° 173 et 'Item eod[em] die [15 septembris 1588] solui M[agistro] Jo[hann]i Stas qui Rinaldu[m] musicu[m] hospitu[m] [*sic*!] p[rae]buit a 21 februarii ad p[rim]am septembris an[n]o 1588 xix fl[orenos] iiii sol[idos] b[ra]b[an]t[iae]'; A.E.L., Ch.C., reg. 197, f° 174v.

[66] 'Ite[m] eod[em] die [17 février 1589] solui de ma[nda]to aeconomi Lynde[n] Rinaldo del Mel m[a]g[ist]ro capellae p[ro] no[n]nullis retardatis eid[em] debitis videlicet iv coronatoru[m] p[ro] singulis sex mensibus iux[ta] cedula[m] facit lxii fl[orenos] brab[antiae]'; A.E.L., Ch.C. reg. 198 (recettes et dépenses, 1588-1589), p. 224. Van Doorslaer a mis en évidence ce paiement comme première et unique mention de del Mel dans les archives du prince-évêque de Liège; 'René del Mel', 235-236.

[67] 'Ite[m] 8 Martii a[n]no 1589 solui Johan[n]i Stas qui trib[us] lectis quibus excepit Rinald[um] del Mel m[a]g[istr]um capellae Maturino et Sr Pedro a p[rima] januarii ad p[ri]mam martii 1589 xvii fl[orenos] xiii sol[idos] brab[antiae]'; A.E.L., Ch.C., reg. 198, p. 226.

René del Mel ne demeure donc pas au service du prince de Liège. Comment comprendre cet état de fait? Ernest de Bavière cumule de nombreuses dignités ecclésiastiques. Prince électeur d'Empire, archevêque de Cologne, il est à la tête des évêchés de Freising en Bavière, de Hildesheim et de Liège et administrateur de la principauté de Stavelot-Malmédy.[68] A la cour d'Ernest, réapparaissent certains musiciens employés jadis à Munich. Parmi ceux-ci figurent son organiste, Bernardino Mosto (fl. 1575-1594)[69] et Antoine Goswin. Tous deux quittent probablement la cour d'Albert V (1528-1579), victimes des restrictions budgétaires faisant suite à la mort du duc.[70] En 1588, Bernardino Mosto dédie un livre de madrigaux à Ernest, faisant état de sa fonction d'organiste auprès du prince.[71] Si les documents font défauts pour la dizaine d'années qui suit, certains éléments indiqueraient que Bernardino n'abandonne pas son poste auprès du prince-évêque[72] et qu'Ernest de Bavière tisse pour lui des liens vers Cologne.[73] Peut-être del Mel n'a-t-il pas bénéficié de telles perspectives? L'insistance dont il fait preuve dans la dédicace adressée au prince-évêque

[68] Max Braubach, 'Ernst v. Bayern', *Lexikon für Theologie und Kirche*, eds. Joseph Höfer – Karl Rahner, 14 vols (Fribourg-en-Brisgau: Herder, 1957-1968), III (1959), 1036; Franz Bosbach, 'Ernst, Herzog von Bayern (1554-1612)', in *Die Bischöfe des Heiligen Römischen Reichen, 1448 bis 1648: Ein biographisches Lexikon*, ed. Erwin Gatz (Berlin: Duncker & Humblot, 1996), pp. 163-171.

[69] En 1578, les trois frères Mosto sont à Munich. Francesco Mosto perçoit 20 gulden 'abermalen auf die Reiss nach Italien' et un salaire annuel de 180 gulden. Son frère, Nicolas bénéficie du même salaire ('mit gleichem Sold angeschaft'). Bernard Mosto reçoit quant à lui seulement 80 gulden. Dans Wolfgang Boetticher, *Orlando di Lasso und seine Zeit (1532-1594): Repertoire-Untersuchungen zur Musik der Spätrenaissance*, 3 vols (Kassel-Basel: Bärenreiter, 1958), I, 500.

[70] Voir notamment Annie Cœurdevey, *Roland de Lassus* (Paris: Fayard, 2003), pp. 269 270, 283-284.

[71] *Madrigali ... a cinque voci* (Anvers: Phalèse et Bellère, 1588; RISM M 3811).

[72] Un motet de Bernardino Mosto figure dans l'anthologie de musique pour luth d'Adrien Denss, qui réside alors à Cologne (*Florilegium omnis fere generis cantionum suavissimarum ad testudinis tabulaturam accomodatarum*, Cologne: Grevenbruch, 1594; RISM 1594[19]). Son ancrage à la cour d'Ernest aurait peut-être permis à son frère, le compositeur Giovanni-Battista Mosto d'espérer trouver un emploi à la cour de Cologne, où il rejoint le prince-évêque avec le musicien Matteo Foresto en 1594. Une lettre de Matteo Foresto au duc de Mantoue la même année révèle que le prince les emmène avec lui successivement à Bonn et à Bruxelles. Voir Pietro Canal, *Della musica in Mantova. Notizie tratte principalmente dall'Archivio Gonzaga* (Genève: Minkoff, 1978/Reprogr. 1881), p. 89.

[73] Sur la vie musicale sous Ernest de Bavière, voir Emilie Corswarem, Katelijne Schiltz et Philippe Vendrix, 'Der Lütticher Fürstbischof Ernst von Bayern als Musik-Mäzen (1580-1612)', communication au colloque international *Das Erzbistum Köln in der Musikgeschichte des 15. und 16. Jahrhunderts*, Cologne, Maternhaus, 23-25 septembre 2005 (actes sous presse, éd. Klaus Pietschmann).

de Liège sur l'âge vieillissant de Lassus pourrait laisser penser que le compositeur rêve d'autres cours.

> Di che' l'huom tanto meno maravigliarsi deve, havendo tutto tre le Altezze V. comme heredità, oltre tante altre lodatissime parti, ancor questa (dico l'amore ed affetto alla musica, e la tanta intelligenza d'essa) da quella, che risplendeva, vi é piu ch'in altro qual si voglia Principe, nella gloriosa et immortale memoria del Sereniss[imo] Duca Alberto loro padre, come à tutto il mondo è notissimo; ed altrimenti ne possono far chiarissima fede le liberalità di quel realissimo Principe tanto honoratamente impiegate in eccellenti Musici: e, tra loro, l'eccellentissimo M[agistro] Orlando Lasso: il quale, antico servitore d'essa gloriosa memoria, in questi suoi anni piu maturi feliceme[n]te vive, si riposa, e co[n] ogni suo agio, e benignissimo trattenimento s'essercita nell'arte Musica, sotto l'o[m]bra et protettione della Sereniss[ima] casa di Baviera. (Liège, le 14 juillet 1587 – RISM M 2206)[74]

Cet élément, joint à la succession ininterrompue à partir du recueil de madrigaux dédié à Ernest de Bavière d'un nombre signifiant de dédicaces aux membres de la famille Lorraine-Bavière suggère que del Mel considère le poste qu'il occupe à Liège comme un tremplin vers de meilleurs auspices. Les dates des dédicaces (1593, 1594 et 1596) correspondent étrangement à l'extrême fin de la carrière de Roland de Lassus (ca. 1532-1594) à la cour de Munich et à la vacance, à sa mort, du poste de maître de chapelle. Johannes de Fossa (ca. 1540-1603) n'est pas encore nommé premier *Kapellmeister* et Lassus a déjà délégué une partie de ses attributions à son fils Ferdinand depuis 1584. René del Mel aurait-il entrevu la concrétisation d'une fin de carrière brillante? Rien ne le contredit.

[74] La transcription de la dédicace a été réalisée au départ de l'édition originale du recueil. Le texte dédicatoire en reproduit à l'identique au début de chacune des parties (Munich, Bayerische Staatsbibliothek, 4 Mus.pr.2718, parties de canto, alto, tenor, basso et quinto). Pour les principes éditoriaux, voir note 57. La dédicace est néanmoins également éditée dans Janssens, *Il secondo libro delli madrigalietti a tre voci (1586) di Rinaldo del Mel*, I, 115-116 et par Van Doorslaer, 'René del Mel', pp. 277-278. 'Il ne faut pas moins s'émerveiller de cet homme qui, ayant les trois altesses [Albert, Ferdinand et Guillaume] pour hérédité et tant d'autres illustres parents, a encore celle-ci (à savoir l'amour, l'affection et l'intelligence pour la musique), laquelle resplendissait, pour vous plus que pour tout autre qui se veut prince, dans la gloire et l'immortelle mémoire du Sérénissime Duc Albert votre père, dont tout le monde connaît et peut faire clairement foi de la libéralité avec laquelle il a employé si honorablement d'excellents musiciens, et parmi eux, le très excellent Maître Orlando di Lasso, lequel, serviteur de longue date à la glorieuse mémoire de celui-ci [du prince], se trouve heureux en ces années plus mûres et s'exerce confortablement, si bien traité, dans l'art de la musique sous l'ombre et la protection de la Sérénissime Maison de Bavière.'

## Conclusion

Certes, la lumière doit être faite sur certaines périodes de la carrière de del Mel. La chronologie des postes qu'il obtient demeure imprécise. Il n'empêche: l'importance des informations que recèlent les dédicaces apparaît clairement. Leur intérêt se révèle surtout lorsqu'est prise en compte la relation du compositeur avec le dédicataire et le sujet pour lequel il opte dans la dédicace. Il ne s'agit donc pas de tergiverser sur la finalité du texte dédicatoire, que ce dernier soit avoué ou non puisque force est de reconnaître qu'il n'est pas désintéressé. Il obéit dans la plupart des cas à une stratégie pour attirer et conserver l'attention d'un protecteur ou le remercier. La succession ininterrompue, à partir du recueil de madrigaux dédié à Ernest de Bavière, d'un nombre signifiant de dédicaces aux membres de la famille Lorraine-Bavière est sans doute la manifestation la plus éloquente de la reconnaissance de del Mel pour l'assistance dont lui et sa famille ont bénéficié.

Les caractéristiques des livres de motets de René del Mel, en particulier celles des livres I et des *Sacrae Cantiones* révèlent une intimité avec la Maison de Lorraine-Bavière que le compositeur entretient grâce à d'incessants dons de recueils. En dépit de nominations à d'éventuels postes ou d'octroi de gratifications, le compositeur développe un travail de mémoire et non de projection, tel la formulation d'une espérance professionnelle future. Il semble que les moyens mis en œuvre par del Mel tendent à un perpétuel affermissement du lien ancien.

Bien plus qu'une éloge du dédicataire, les textes dédicatoires recèlent d'autres types d'informations relatives à la vie du compositeur, à son œuvre, à la fonction dont il investit le mécène qu'il choisit et surtout à la mise à profit par le compositeur de l'espace de liberté qui subsiste à l'intérieur du cadre apologétique de la dédicace.

Université de Liège – Fonds National de la Recherche Scientifique
B – 4000 Liège
E.Corswarem@ulg.ac.be

TABLEAU. EDITIONS DE RENÉ DEL MEL[75]

| TITRE DU RECUEIL | ANNÉE DE LA PUBLICATION / DATE DÉDICACE | LIEU ÉDITION / DÉDICACE | IMPRIMEUR | DÉDICATAIRE | CATALOGUE |
|---|---|---|---|---|---|
| Liber primus … mottettorum quae partim quaternis, partim quinis, partim senis, ac unum septenis, altero vero octonis vocibus concinuntur | 1581 / 5 août 1581 | Venise / Rome | Angelo Gardano | Christine de Danemark | M 2193 |
| Madrigali a quattro, cinque et sei voci | 1583 / 1er avril 1583 | Venise / Chieti | Angelo Gardano | Guillaume de Bavière | M 2198 |
| Il primo libro de madrigali a cinque voci | 1584 / 1er janvier 1584 | Venise / Chieti | Girolamo Scotto | Mario Valignani | M 2200 |
| Il primo libro de madrigali a sei voci | 1584 / 8 janvier 1584 | Venise / Venise | Angelo Gardano | Horatio Henrici | M 2199 |
| Il primo libro de madrigali a cinque et sei voci | 1585 / 30 janvier 1585 | Venise / Aquila | Girolamo Scotto | Girolamo Acquaviva | M 2201 |
| Liber tertius … motectorum partim quinis partim senis vocibus concinuntur | 1585 / 13 novembre 1585 | Venise / Chieti | Angelo Gardano | Carlo Valignani | M 2194 |
| Il secondo libro delli madrigaletti a tre voci[76] | 1586 / 9 février 1586 | Venise / Sabine | Angelo Gardano | Camillo Henrici | M 2202 |

[75] Ce tableau fait la liste des éditions *principes* uniquement. Lorsqu'elles font défaut, c'est la seconde édition qui est reprise.

[76] Ce recueil, réédité en 1596 (Venise: Gardano; RISM M 2203) possède le même texte dédicatoire que l'édition princeps de 1586, daté du 20 août 1596. Le recueil est à nouveau réédité en 1604 (Venise: Gardano; RISM M 2204). La même dédicace est reproduite, avec la date de la première édition, le 9 février 1586.

| | | | | | |
|---|---|---|---|---|---|
| Il terzo libro de madrigal a cinque voci | 1587 / 2 janvier 1587 | Venise / Venise | Angelo Gardano | Donat'Antonio Tauldino | M 2205 |
| Madrigali … a sei voci | 1588 / 14 juillet 1587 | Anvers / Liège | Pierre Phalèse et Jean Bellère | Ernest de Bavière | M 2206 |
| Sacrae cantiones … V, VI, VII, VIII ac XII vocum, cum litania de B[eata] Maria Virgine V vocum | 1588 / 15 octobre 1588 | Anvers / Liège | Pierre Phalèse et Jean Bellère | Renée de Lorraine | M 2195 |
| Il primo libro de madrigaletti a tre voci … novamente ristampato[77] | 1593 / 21 janvier 1585 | Venise / Rome | Angelo Gardano | Filippo Valignani | M 2208 |
| Il secondo libro de madrigali a sei voci | 1593 / 20 mars 1593 | Venise / Calvi | Giacomo Vincenti | Minutio Minucci | M 2207 |
| Il terzo libro delli madrigaletti a tre voci | 1594 / 27 mars 1594 | Venise / Rome | Angelo Gardano | Maximilien de Bavière | M 2210 |
| Il quinto libro de madrigali a cinque voci | 1594 / 1er mai 1594 | Venise / Sabine | Angelo Gardano | Lucio Savello | M 2209 |
| Liber quintus motectorum … quae partim senis, partimque octonis, ac duodenis vocibus concinuntur | 1595 / 1er mars 1595 | Venise / Sabine | Angelo Gardano | Gabriele Paleotti | M 2197 |
| Il terzo libro delli madrigali a sei voci | 1595 / 15 octobre 1595 | Venise / Rome | Angelo Gardano | Mario Valignani | M 2211 |
| Madrigaletti spirituali libro quarto a tre voci | 1596 / 20 août 1596 | Venise / Rome | Angelo Gardano | Dorothée de Lorraine | Vogel 717 |

[77] La date de dédicace indique une probable édition *princeps* de 1585. Le catalogue Vogel mentionne une édition en 1590, non consultée (Milan: Tini; Vogel 711 bis3).

# DEDICATION AND DEVOTION IN SIMONE MOLINARO'S *MOTECTORUM QUINIS, ET MISSAE DENIS VOCIBUS, LIBER PRIMUS* (1597)

PETER S. POULOS

Simone Molinaro (ca. 1570-1636) was a leading musician in Genoa who rose to the position of chapel master at the cathedral of San Lorenzo in 1601, and later held the same title at the ducal palace. Molinaro's name first appears on record in 1589 as the nephew and disciple of Giovanni Battista Dalla Gostena on the title page of the latter's *Il secondo libro di canzonette a quattro voci*.[1] Dalla Gostena was chapel master at San Lorenzo from 1584 to 1589 and exerted a deep influence on the musical life of his nephew. While Dalla Gostena had published no sacred works by the time of his death in 1593, Molinaro produced at least ten books of sacred music between 1597 and 1616, the most by any Genoese composer of that time. Only the first and last of these books were provided with Latin dedications. The *Passio domini nostri Iesu Christi* from 1616 was published in Molinaro's own print shop in Loano and is a rare complete setting of the four Gospel passion stories.[2] The unaccompanied monophonic musical treatment of the *Passio* was also unusual for its time. Molinaro's ascetic approach to this composition, along with his dedication to the Doctors of Divinity, the Prefect, and the Canons of San Lorenzo, appears as a pious gift to the ecclesiastical scholars of the church. No less a work of reverence, the *Motectorum* from 1597 contains some of Molinaro's most elaborate and complex music.[3] The collection is a significant achievement in the history of sacred music in Genoa, and

[1] *Il secondo libro di canzonette a quattro voci* (Venice: Giacomo Vincenti, 1589; RISM D 813 [i.e. the number attributed to musical sources by the *Répertoire international des sources musicales*; henceforth: RISM]). Dalla Gostena notes on the title pages to the parts 'con una sestina di Simone Molinaro suo nepote, e discepolo'.

[2] *Passio domini nostri Iesu Christi secundum Matthaeum, Marcum, Lucam, et Joannem* (Loano: Francesco Castello, 1616; RISM M 2942). The only surviving copy of this work is held in the archives of the Vatican Library, call number Casimiri.III.471(6).

[3] *Motectorum quinis, et missae denis vocibus, liber primus* (Venice: Giacomo Vicenti, 1597; M 2930).

the product of a composer who had previously published only one book of light secular songs.[4]

Molinaro dedicated the *Motectorum* to Matteo Senarega, Doge of the Republic of Genoa. But there was also an internalized dedication that honored the memory of his uncle found within the writing of the music. The dedication letter, offered to one of the most visible political and cultural figures in Genoa, was a perfectly directed instrument by a young composer who sought to succeed his mentor Dalla Gostena as the chapel master at the cathedral.

Senarega was a learned aristocrat who wrote a tract on Genoa's city-state form of government entitled *Discorso sopra la Città e la Repubblica di Genova*,[5] and who also published his own Italian translation of Cicero's letters to Atticus (fig. 1).[6] Senarega's reputation, virtues, eloquence, and musical tastes are celebrated in the elaborately overwrought rhetorical language of he dedicatory letter.[7] A conceit is constructed whereby the 'worthlessness' of Molinaro's humble offering is contrasted to the 'unbelievable harmony' of the Doge's goodness, and a thread of self-promotion is woven through the juxtaposition of the two ideas. The propriety and utility of the works for church performance are asserted through the declaration that they are intended for the celebration of sacred events and the liturgy. Molinaro assures the Doge of his industry and diligence in the production of his musical lucubration, and offers that if so encouraged, he would eagerly complete greater tasks in the future that have already been conceived. Molinaro closes the dedication by announcing that his work represents an everlasting pledge and sign of respect, and a commitment to the future artistic glory and honor of the Doge.

The Senarega family were among the most notable patrons of the cathedral of San Lorenzo towards the end of the century.[8] In 1579 Matteo's brother Giovanni Senarega became patron of the chapel of Saint Sebastian and agreed with the requirements of the Fathers of the Commune to

[4] Molinaro's first known publication of music is *Il primo libro di canzonette a tre e à quattro voci* (Venice: Angelo Gardano, 1595; RISM M 2929).

[5] Cited in Massimiliano Spinola, *La restaurazione della Repubblica Ligure nel MCCCXIV. Saggio storico* (Genova: Tipografia dei Sordi Muti, 1863), pp. 410-411.

[6] Cicero, *Le pistole di Cicerone ad Attico, fatte volgari da M. Matteo Senarega* (Venice: Aldo Manuzio,1555).

[7] The text of the dedication letter is included in Appendix I.

[8] For a discussion of the history of the patronage of the Senarega family at the cathedral of Genoa see Michael Bury, 'The Senarega Chapel in San Lorenzo, Genoa', *Mitteilungen des kunsthistorischen Instituts in Florenz*, 31 (1987), 327-356.

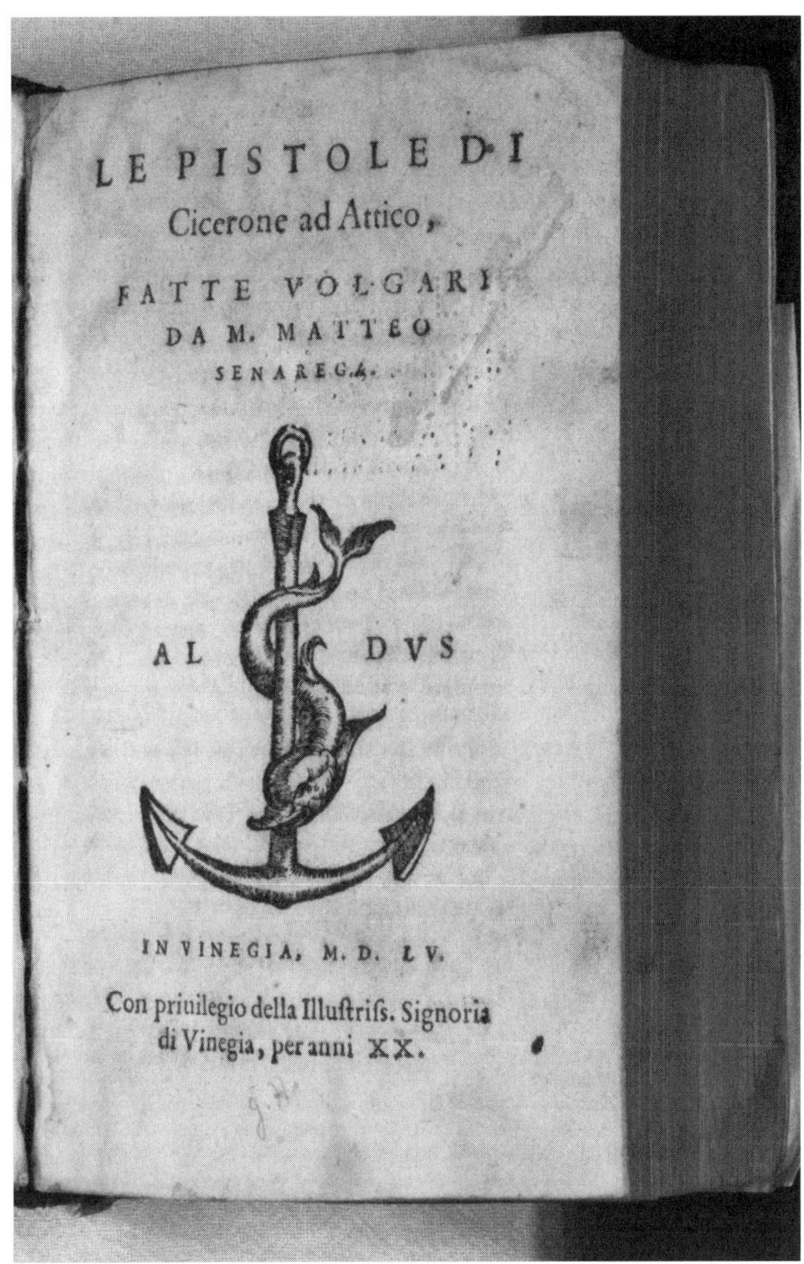


FIGURE 1. *Title Page of Le pistole di Cicerone ad Attico*, 1555
(by permission of the Oberlin College Library)

fund the chapel's renovation. Giovanni stipulated in his will that the chapel hold dedications to saint John the Evangelist, Giovanni's Patron saint; to the Virgin Mary; to the Holy Cross, as well as to Saint Sebastian.[9] This latter requirement was made to satisfy the dictates of the Commune who established that the dedication to Saint Sebastian be maintained in perpetuity.[10] Giovanni indicated that a Mass for the Dead and a solemn Mass be performed in his memory, and that the text of the Medieval sequence *Stabat Mater* be sung weekly. Payments were to be provided to the singers who would participate in the liturgical celebrations of his intercessory prayers. Funds were set aside for the construction of a second organ next to the chapel of Saint Sebastian towards the purpose of increasing the divine devotion through music.

However, Giovanni died in 1582 before any renovations were begun. The Commune agreed to transfer the patronage to Matteo, through whose efforts the main renovations of chapel were completed in 1593. The final design consisted of an ornate funerary chapel containing six over-life-sized allegorical statues of the saintly namesakes of the brothers of the Senarega family (Giovanni, Matteo, Stefano, Ambrogio, Geronimo, and Bartolomeo) along with effigies of the original patrons, Giovanni and Matteo, situated above sarcophagi.[11] In 1587 Matteo began negotiations for a commission from the leading Italian altar painter, Federico Barocci (1526-1612), for a work that would bring together the themes in the dedication of the chapel and complete its beautification.[12]

Barocci's *The Crucifixion with Three Saints* (fig. 2), completed in 1596, combined both the descriptive and the devotional elements of the various dedications envisioned by the patrons in such a superb manner that the altarpiece is counted among the painter's finest efforts. Senarega's

[9] Extracts from the will are reprinted in Bury, 'The Senarega Chapel', pp. 354-355. The original is held in the Archivio di Stato di Genova (ASG), Notarile, scansia 341, filza 9.

[10] Other requirements were that a sarcophagus for Giovanni's remains be built in the chapel. Bury, 'The Senarega Chapel', p. 354.

[11] The statues of Sts John, Matthew, Bartholomew, and Stephen have been attributed to the Flemish sculptor Pietro Francavilla (1548-1615) while the statues of Sts Jerome and Ambrose were fashioned by the Italian sculptor Taddeo Carlone (1543-1615). Carlone also produced the effigies of Giovanni and Matteo for the chapel as well as the sarcophagi. Bury, 'The Senarega Chapel', pp. 336, 347-350.

[12] That Senarega obtained the commission was as bit of a coup for the Genoese nobleman as Barocci was known to be a slow and deliberate worker who did not produce a large number of works. Barocci was also a highly sought-after artist who turned down many requests and counted the Pope and the Emperor among his patrons. See Bury, 'The Senarega Chapel', p. 341, and Harald Olsen, *Federico Barocci* (Copenhagen: Munksgaard, 1962), p. 29.

understanding and appreciation of the artistic and technical achievement of the altarpiece is revealed in a letter of appreciation addressed to Barocci dated 5 October 1596.[13] The Genoese noble praised the painter's ability to elicit and balance the complex of emotions and religious symbolism represented by the saintly images.

The 1000 scudi Barocci received for his work was one of the largest payments to any artist of the time for an altarpiece.[14] The huge sums that were spent on the newly decorated chapel represented an ostentatious display of familial and civic pride, social prestige, and religious devotion. One does not find it hard to imagine that the glories spoken of by Molinaro in his dedication to the Doge reflect upon the circumstances of these events. The earliest documented evidence of Molinaro's official association with the ecclesiastical institutions of Genoa date from December of 1595 when the musician received the first tonsure. This rite was the first step in the preparation to receive holy orders and to the priesthood, a prerequisite for all singers and the chapel master in San Lorenzo, and is the first suggestion of Molinaro's intention to seek employment there.[15] Nearly three years later in 1598 the now Reverend Molinaro was elected to his first official position in the cathedral as a chaplain of the Mass where he served until he was discharged the following year by directive of the cathedral chapter.[16] Molinaro's name next appears in the registers of the cathedral on 31 October 1601 in the record of his election as master of the chapel choir.[17] It is during this period and within this context that Molinaro began to publish his first volumes of sacred music.

[13] The letter is held in the Archivio Storico del Comune, Genova (ASCG), Arch. de' Ferrari, registro no. 141, fol. 131; transcribed in Bury, 'The Senarega Chapel', pp. 355-366.

[14] See Ian Verstegen, 'Federico Barocci, Federico Borromeo and the Oratorian Orbit', *Renaissance Quarterly*, 56 (2003), 1-30 (pp. 12-14).

[15] On the requirements for priesthood in the chapel of San Lorenzo see Peter S. Poulos, *The Life and Sacred Music of Simone Molinaro (ca. 1570-1636), Musician of Genoa* (PhD diss. University of Cincinnati, 2004), pp. 24-32.

[16] The report reads that 'Dario who had gone to Rome was in fact released from the Mansionaria by P…. [the ellipsis points are in the original text] Fiesco on 31 July, and in place of him I have posted Reverend Simone Molinari whom the Chapter passed on August 7.' The following year Marana writes 'Mansionario Simon Molinari was removed by the Chapter of the Mansionaria 16 March in proceedings [recorded by] Marcantonio Molfino [in] the yearbook, by sentence given by Signor Vicario at the request of the Chapter.' Reproduced in Maria Rosa Moretti, 'Simone Molinaro, Maestro di Cappella di Palazzo: Contributo per una nuova biografia', in *Musica a Genova tra Medio Evo e eta Moderna: Atti del convegno di studi* (Genoa: Associazione Ligure per la Ricerca delle Fonti Musicali, 1989), pp. 45-83 (p. 49).

[17] ASG, Notai, Roccatagliata, Gio. Antonio, ng. 3477 (1600-1601).

FIGURE 2. Federico Barocci, *Crucifixion with Three Saints*, 1596[18].

[18] Photo by Antonio Campostano, in *The Cathedral of Genoa* (Genoa: Sigla Effe Publications, 1959), p. 129.

Molinaro's first published book of sacred music, the *Motectorum* from 1597, comprises texts of great solemnity and devotion.[19] A number of these texts are well known in the motet literature while others appear to have no analogues in the repertoire of the time and may have been newly compiled or composed for the purpose of this publication. The text of the antiphon for the feast of Corpus Christi *O sacrum convivium*, for example, was one of the most popular text choices of composers in northern Italy around 1600, and was also the most frequently treated sacred text by Molinaro with eleven settings by him.[20] Of the two Marian-themed texts, Molinaro's version of *Quae est ista* is derived in part from a verse in the Song of Songs[21] that includes a second part of unknown derivation that serves as gloss to the Biblical text. The text of the motet *Virgo mater sponsa*, on the other hand, appears to have been newly fashioned in its entirety, or possibly pieced together from multiple sources, as it is not found in any work list or in any religious or liturgical books that I have searched.

The Psalms are a major source of texts used in the *Motectorum*, accounting for six of the eleven motets in the book. Among the works in this group are several that stand apart from settings in all of Molinaro's later publications in their extraordinary somber tone. The triple motet *Domine ne in furore-Convertere Domine-Laboravi gemitu meo*, for example, is based on eight verses from Psalm 6, a penitential psalm that stands liturgically in the Office for the Dead at Matins in the Roman rite. This motet is matched in severity in this collection only by the funereal motet *Versa est in luctum* with its combination of dark images from the book of Job.[22] The propitiatory tone is continued in the motets *Erravi sicut ovis*,

19 A transcription of the motet texts is given in Appendix II.

20 On the popularity of the setting of the text of *O sacrum* by Molinaro and other northern Italian composers see Poulos, *The Life and Sacred Music of Simone Molinaro*, pp. 125, 199-212; Michele Fromson, 'A Conjunction of Rhetoric and Music: Structural Modeling in the Italian Counter-Reformation Motet', *Journal of the Royal Musical Association*, 117-2 (1992), 208-246; and Michele Yvonne Fromson, *Imitation and Innovation in the North-Italian Motet, 1560-1605* (PhD diss. University of Pennsylvania, 1988).

21 A musical setting of this text was also made by Palestrina.

22 Alonso Lobo's version of *Versa est in luctum* was purportedly written for Philip's memorial at Toledo Cathedral. It was published in the composer's *Liber primus missarum* (Madrid: Joannes Flandre, 1602) and is headed 'Ad exequias Philip.II Cathol. Regis Hisp.'. The text also appears as part of Tomas Luis de Victoria's *Missa pro defunctis* (1605) (written in memory of Maria, Archduchess of Austria and Infanta of Spain (1528-1603)). This text was not, however, part of the Tridentine standardization of the Latin Requiem Mass.

*Recogitandis donis tuis*, and Molinaro's other setting from the Penitential psalms, *Miser factus sum.*

Molinaro solemnizes some texts through the employment of compositional archaisms not found in his later publications. Parallel movement sonorities, used here to color particular phrases of text, recall the fauxbourdon technique of fifteenth-century sacred music and reveal an austere and retrospective approach.[23] These motets are also among his most spacious works. Spare use is made, for example, of note values faster than a minim,[24] and an aural sobriety is created by textures often reduced from five to three voices. The alternating fifths and octaves in the opening of *Versa est*, contribute to a starkness of harmony that convey the dark and disquieting expressions of the text. These and other artifices reveal Molinaro's sensitivity to text expression and ally these settings to late sixteenth-century musico-rhetorical principles, which are amply displayed in his setting of Psalm 6.[25] The text inspired one of his most eloquent compositions marked by a variety of musical figures, harmonic color, and strong contrasts of rhythm and textures.

The first eight of the ten verses of the psalm are utilized and divided into the three parts of the motet. The first two parts are supplications for mercy and the third part a testimony of suffering. By omitting the fourth and more hopeful part, in which the psalmist acknowledges the promise of redemption, Molinaro maintains a unified and central theme of sorrow in the motet. Each phrase of music and text is organized as a distinct subsection within the piece distinguished by unique figurations. This idea is particularly apparent in the setting of the entreaty *miserere mei Domine*, where the litany for mercy is treated with a three-fold repetition of the phrase. The section is unified by a forlorn motive (ex. 1) on the word

[23] Molinaro seems to have employed this technique to underscore words or phrases of particular importance in this collection, such as *quaere servum tuum*, *non est in morte*, *recogitandis*, *ira*, and *mens impletur*.

[24] The motets *Erravi sicut ovis, Recogitandis donis tuis,* and *Miser factus sum* exhibit this characteristic.

[25] For an overview of the associations between rhetoric and music in the literature of music theorists of the fifteenth and sixteenth centuries see Blake McDowell Wilson, '*Ut Oratoria Musica* in the Writings of Renaissance Music Theorists', in *Festa Musicologica: Essays in Honor of George J. Buelow*, Festschrift Series No. 14 (Stuyvesant, N.Y.: Pendragon Press, 1995), pp. 341-369; Claude Palisca, '*Ut Oratoria Musica*: The Rhetorical Basis of Musical Mannerism', in *The Meaning of Mannerism*, eds. F. W. Robinson – S. G. Nichols, Jr. (Hanover, N.H.: University Press of New England, 1972), pp. 37-65; and also Blake Wilson, 'Rhetoric and Music', in *The New Grove Dictionary of Music Online*, ed. L. Macy (Accessed 1 September 2002), http://www.grovemusic.com.

Ex. 1. Simone Molinaro, *Domine ne in furore* mm. 22-27.

*miserere* signified by a stepwise descent of an interval of a third. The motive features flat pitches and repeated notes, both standard cues for the affects of sadness and lament in music of the period that reinforce the downcast and doleful mood of the text.[26]

Molinaro also employed figures that were not necessarily intended to be audible, but designed instead for their visual impact on the printed page.[27] The first device is an arrangement of elements used to convey the religious symbolism of the cross on the phrase *salvum me fac* sung to the chromatically altered notes of a rising tetrachord of A-B-C#-D in the tenor and cantus voices (ex. 2), a musical figure often used as a sign of anguish in the music of this period.[28] The cross symbol of the diesis

[26] On this convention in music of the period see Bernhard Meier, *The Modes of Classical Vocal Polyphony*, trans. Ellen S. Beebe (New York: Broude Brothers Limited, 1988), p. 245.

[27] Such so-called eye music recalls Quintilian's comments on the ability of rhetorical figures to place the subject before the eyes (*sub oculos subiiciendis*), a theme that was taken up by music theorists and humanists of the time. See Palisca, 'Ut oratoria musica', p. 40.

[28] This symbol is used in the music of Claudio Monteverdi to express similar emotions. See Jeffrey Kurtzman, 'A Taxonomic and Affective Analysis of Monteverdi's "Hor Che'l Ciel e la terra"', *Music Analysis*, 2 (1993), 169-195, at p. 182.

Ex. 2. Simone Molinaro. *Convertere Domine*, mm. 67-70.

or sharp sign, used here to raise the pitch of the Bb and C by a step, also contributes to the allusions implied in the setting. In addition, the figure is accompanied by a cruciform arrangement of the pitches in the music notation. The litany for salvation is intoned three times in an antiphonal arrangement between groups of the lowest and highest vocal parts, with each statement set off by rests for emphasis.

Another graphic image occurs at the words *lacrimis meis stratum* where the bass voice sings long held notes of breves and semibreves in the style of an older cantus firmus motet shown in the third stave of figure 2. The diamond-shape design of the semibreve is also used in this setting to serve as a metaphor for the falling tear, here descending over an octave. Molinaro extends the symbolic association at the words *turbatus est a furore oculus meus* where the notational coloration or blackening of the semibreves has the musical effect of shifting the meter, but the now blackened tears visually underscore the textual phrase at the words "my eye is troubled" signifying a metaphorical blindness and spiritual darkness. Such ornamental music was intended for literati who were attuned to the complexity of the allusions in the relationships between the musical figures and the text.[29]

[29] See Palisca's discussion of the term *musica reservata*, 'Ut oratoria musica', pp. 57-59.

FIGURE 3. Simone Molinaro. *Laboravi*, Bassus Part
(by permission of the Museo internazionale e biblioteca della musica di Bologna)

Much like a religious icon or painting, the figures also fulfilled the need to exalt and inspire to devotion.[30]

[30] This thought was expressed in the late-thirteenth-century *Catholicon* (also known as the *Summa Grammaticalis*) of John of Genoa as one of the functions of religious paintings: 'to excite feelings of devotion, these being aroused more effectively by things seen than by things heard.' Reproduced in Michael Baxandall, *Painting and Experience in Fifteenth-Century Italy*, 2nd ed. (London: Oxford University Press, 1988), p. 41.

No documentation exists that gauges Matteo Senarega's reception of Molinaro's work. As we have seen, the contents of Molinaro's *Motectorum* were in general accord with the substance of the requirements and the qualities esteemed by the patrons for the ceremonies and art that would adorn the chapel: a large Mass; works suitable to be performed in a requiem Mass; motets in honor of the Virgin; sensitivity to the allusions in the texts and the depth of technical mastery to express them.

In the months after becoming chapel master, Molinaro continued efforts to execute the goals of the cathedral patrons regarding the musical resources of the church. In December, 1602 he addressed a petition to the senate of the republic. Echoing the intentions of Giovanni and Matteo Senarega, Molinaro requested that more financial resources be allocated not only for the support of the current choir but also for the addition of new singers.[31]

Molinaro's endeavors to enhance and diversify the performing resources of the cathedral are again seen in August of 1603. At this time Simone and his brother Benedetto Molinaro acted as witnesses to a contract between representatives of San Lorenzo and the organ builder Giuseppe Vitani for the construction of a new organ to be located next to the chapel of Saint Sebastian. As was noted earlier, funding for a second organ was established in 1579 through Giovanni Senarega's donation, but it was likely Benedetto Molinaro, who guaranteed 300 of the total cost of 700 ducats for the construction, that finally made the plan a reality.[32] With the completion of the second organ, the behest of Senarega was fulfilled.

At the same time Molinaro was attempting to establish himself as a church musician in Genoa he was also working to secure the legacy of

[31] 'Il Reverendo P. Simone Molinari maestro di Capella delli musici nella chiesa catedrale desidera grandemente compire a quanto si dovrebbe per lode d'Iddio e per consolatione spirituale dei cittadini, ma non può sodisfare al pio desiderio mentre che il redito della Capella è tanto poco che non si può mantenere il numero e la qualità de cantori i quali sariano necessari per rendere sufficientemente armonioso il coro, che se egli havesse il modo di dare provisione mag[g]iore a i cantori potrebbe dare ancora maggiore sodisfattione con le sue fatiche le quali va preparando a questo effetto egli perciò ha havuto ricorso a Prestantissimi Padri di Commune acciochè per l'interesse che hanno in detta chiesa volessero sovenire a opera cosi pia con assignarle qualche soma di danari per dispensarla ogn'anno a chi canta nella capella, i quali certamente sariano stati pronti a farlo quando la loro bailia glielo condedesse'. Original text located in ASCG, Pratiche pubbliche 1601-1615, filza 221, n. 265, and printed in Maria Rosa Moretti, *Musica e costume a Genova tra cinquecento e seicento* (Genoa: Francesco Pirella, 1992), p. 253.

[32] The contract is published in Moretti, 'Simone Molinaro', pp. 68-72; and is held in ASG, notaio Giov. Stefano Sivori e Matteo Biscotto, sc. 656, filza 1, n.g. 5274, n. 45.

his uncle and mentor Giovanni Battista Dalla Gostena. The two activities were inextricably linked in the life of Molinaro by the influence that the uncle had upon the nephew. Dalla Gostena was the first important Genoese madrigalist and a superb composer for the lute who also produced a body of sacred music. Much of this music was published for the first time by his nephew in two complete volumes under Dalla Gostena's name and through pieces inserted into the collections of Molinaro's own music.[33] In addition to the legacy preserved by this editorial work, Molinaro honored his uncle's memory in the dedication letters to four books published between 1596 and 1601.[34] The near-poetic tone of these tributes is captured in a letter from 1601 addressed to the Bishop of Sarzana where Molinaro wrote:

> I have always tried to imitate Giovanni Battista Dalla Gostena, ... in all that he knew, ... and I claim to be his remaining heir of these two things; in that I learned from him the little that I know, and to Your Reverence, I am, as he was, your much obliged servant. And because I know the desire and intention that he had to present to you (had he lived) his work, and I profess to have the memory of his wishes, I come with these motets of mine to satisfy in part the soul of he who was the servant, and to me a father and teacher, and to demonstrate to you that within me lives by succession the same spirit that was in him.[35]

[33] Giovanni Battista Dalla Gostena, *Il secondo libro de madrigali a cinque voci* (Venice: Angelo Gardano, 1595; RISM D 814) and *Il primo libro di madrigali a quattro voci* (Venice: Giacomo Vincenti, 1596; RISM D 815). Molinaro notes on the title page of the former 'Novamente dato in luce da Simone Molinaro', and on the title page of the latter 'Nuovamente Ristampati, & Corretti'. Publications under Molinaro's name that include works of his uncle are *Il primo libro de madrigali à cinque voci* (Milan: Heirs of Simon Tini, & Francesco Besozzi, 1599; RISM M 2931), *Intavolatura di liuto, libro primo* (Venice: Ricciardo Amadino, 1599; RISM M 2932), *Il primo libro de Magnificat à quattro voci* (Milan: Heirs of Simon Tini, & Filippo Lomazzo, 1605; RISM M 2936), *Il terzo libro de moteti à cinque voci* (Venice: Alessandro Raverii, 1609; RISM M 2938), and *Fatiche spirituali, libro secondo* (Venice: Ricciardo Amadino, 1610; RISM M 2940).

[34] Molinaro mentions his uncle in the dedication letters to *Il primo libro de madrigali à cinque voci*, *Intavolatura di liuto*, *Il secondo libro de motetti à voci* (Milan: Heirs of Simon Tini, & Giovanni Francesco Besozzi, 1601; RISM M 2934), and in his edition of Dalla Gostena's *Il primo libro di madrigali a quattro voci.*

[35] 'Io procurai sempre d'imitare Gio Battista dall Gostena mio zio di buona memoria, in tutto quello ch'egli seppe, e nella servitù che tenne vivendo con V. S. Reverendiss. e pretendo esser rimaso suo herede di queste due cose; in quanto da lui hò imparato, quel poco ch'io vaglio, & à V. S. Reverendiss. sono, com'era lui obligatissimo servitore. Et perche sò il desiderio & intentione ch'egli haveva di presentargli (se havesse havuto vita) un'opera sua, & io professo d'haver memoria de' i suoi desiderij, come son ricordevole de i favori che V. S. Reverendiss. ne hà sempre fatto. Vengo con questi miei Motetti à

There is no mention of Dalla Gostena in our dedication of the *Motectorum* nor were any works by him included in this book. The absence of any overt reference is unusual within the context of other information that we now know regarding Molinaro's devotion to Dalla Gostena. Perhaps Molinaro did not wish in any way to divert attention away from his own superb collection by bringing into comparison the music or the memory of another excellent composer. Yet, this would seem to contradict all previous and later efforts by Molinaro to specifically draw an association between himself and his uncle when such juxtaposition was beneficial. Nor does it take into account Molinaro's endeavors to promote the music of other Genoese composers, many of whose works are known only through his own publications. Molinaro alluded to this idea in the dedication of his Passion settings from 1616 where he declared that 'I have always sweated with toil to benefit others, and I do not direct my mind or hand other than to support the well being of those who compete in the arena of music'.[36]

An examination of information regarding Dalla Gostena's career at San Lorenzo may shed some light on this point. We find that the musician's tenure was tainted by a scandal stemming from a dispute between him and the chaplains of the Mass of San Lorenzo during a procession for the feast of Corpus Domini on 4 June 1589, resulting in the ceremony being performed without music.[37] After this incident Dalla Gostena abandoned his duties and was subsequently dismissed from his position. In 1593 the musician was assassinated, possibly due to entanglement in a love affair.[38] Molinaro may have wanted to avoid any recollection of

sodisfar in parte all'animo di chi le fù servitore, & à me in loco di padre e maestro, & à dimostrarle che in me vive come per successione l'istesso animo ch'era in lui. ...'. Molinaro, *Il secondo libro de motetti à otto voci*.

[36] 'Alienis commodis mea semper desudat industria, nec alio mentem manumue dirigo, quam ut bonis in musica arena decertantium studeam'. Molinaro, *Passio domini nostri Iesu Christi*.

[37] See Moretti, *Musica e costume*, p. 86.

[38] The circumstance of Dalla Gostena's murder was immortalized in a poem by Gabriello Chiabrera, see Moretti, *Musica e costume*, p. 87. Molinaro referred to his uncle's death in a dedication letter to Gregorio Spinola in the edition of Dalla Gostena's *Il secondo libro de madrigali a cinque voci*: 'All'Illustrissimo, et Signore, e Patrone mio osservandiss, Il Signor Gregorio Spinola. Sodisfarò con la publicatione di questi Madrigali à due debiti principali che mi trovo; l'uno è con la memoria di M. Gio: Battista dalla Gostena mio Zio, che poco prima dell'infelice caso della morte sua, gli haveva cosi ordinati per istamparli; l'altro con V. Sign. alla quale dovendo un'obligata & perpetua riverenza, non so per hora come meglio manifestarla al mondo che per questa via ...'.

the embarrassing details of his uncle's firing and violent death under undignified circumstances that might have offended the pious sensibilities of the Duke. In this instance it was probably more advantageous to publicize his work without any obvious association with his teacher, and instead avoid any outward reference to Dalla Gostena in the work. In addition, such overt references to Dalla Gostena, whom the Duke may or may not have had any dealings with, would have been out of place in the formal setting of this highly laudatory letter.

There are, however, some subtle links to the uncle internalized within the writing of the music of the *Motectorum*. There is an oblique connection between Dalla Gostena and Molinaro's *Missa Nasce la pena mia*. The Mass is structured on the well-known madrigal of the same title by the Italian composer Alessandro Striggio. [39] Many composers utilized the music of the madrigal at this time for the basis of instrumental compositions.[40] The only other composer besides Molinaro to use this music as the structural basis for the setting of the Mass, however, was the Flemish composer Philippe de Monte. The significance of this can once again be found through the uncle. Dalla Gostena referred to himself as a disciple of Monte and served with him at the court of Maximilian II in Vienna.[41] The Genoese musician also received the singular distinction of having one of his madrigals represented in the numerous madrigal publications of the older master.[42] Molinaro's use of the model then raises the question of whether he intended to demonstrate his compositional abilities by inviting a comparison between his skill and that of the Flemish

[39] The esteem with which Striggio's madrigal was held during the period was recounted by Giulio Cesare Monteverdi in the foreword to Claudio Monteverdi's Fifth Book of Madrigals when he refers to the harmony as a "divine" example of the First Practice. Translated in *Source Readings in Music History*, ed. Oliver Strunk (New York: W.W. Norton, 1950), p. 412. The author of the text of the madrigal is unknown. See *Alessandro Striggio. Il Primo libro de madrigali a sei voci*, ed. David S Butchart (Madison, WI: A-R Editions, 1986), p. xix.

[40] See Richard Erig – Veronika Gutmann, *Italienische Diminutionen* (Zürich: Päuler, 1979), pp. 291-305; *The Bottegari Lutebook*, ed. Carol MacClintock (Wellesley, MA: Broude Brothers, 1965), pp. 120-123; and Lodovico Agostino, *L'echo et enigmi musicali a sei voci* (Venice: Alessandro Gardano, 1581), pp. 14-18 RISM $1581^5$ (as a canzona for five voices).

[41] Dalla Gostena announced this association on the title page of his *Il libro primo di madrigali a quattro voci* (Venice: Angelo Gardano, 1582).

[42] Dalla Gostena's *Ohimé lasso* was included in Monte's *Il terzo libro De Madrigali à quattro voci* (Venice: Heirs of Girolamo Scotto, 1585). See Brian Mann, *The Secular Madrigals of Filippo di Monte, 1521-1603* (Ann Arbor, MI: UMI Research Press, 1983), pp. 7, 21, 457 n. 67.

composer in the utilization and manipulation of a well-known model, or to emulate that tradition in which his musical education was formed.

It was not uncommon practice for composers in the sixteenth century to draw from an exemplary model for a new work.[43] Typically the new composition and the model share the same text. Among the explanations that have been given by scholars for this phenomenon is the desire of one composer to pay homage to, compete with, or to emulate the work of another composer. Compositional modeling is an important feature in several of Molinaro's pieces, which draw upon the exemplary works of his contemporaries, including works with material borrowed from the music of Dalla Gostena.[44]

Molinaro's *Il terzo libro de motetti à cinque voci* published in 1609 contains three settings of the text of *O sacrum convivium*, two by Molinaro and one by Dalla Gostena, that are related by general characteristics in the settings and through melodic quotation. The *exordiums* of all three versions in this book begin with four of the five voices singing the first syllable of text homophonically in breves and moving to a chord based on the fourth scale degree on the second syllable followed by a repetition of the entire first phrase of text. In one of his settings Molinaro uses a distinctive four-note motive on the word *recolitur* that was borrowed

[43] The literature on this topic is voluminous. The following discussions are restricted primarily to this concept in the Renaissance. Among the recent and earlier discussions on imitation, compositional modeling, and parody, see Lewis Lockwood, 'On 'Parody' as Term and Concept in 16th-Century Music', in *Aspects of Medieval and Renaissance Music: A Birthday Offering to Gustave Reese,* ed. Jan Larue (New York: W.W. Norton; reprint New York: Pendragon Press, 1978), pp. 560-575; Howard Mayer Brown, 'Emulation, Competition, and Homage: Imitation and Theories of Imitation in the Renaissance', *Journal of the American Musicological Society*, 35 (1982), 1-48; J. Peter Burkholder, 'Johannes Martini and the Imitation Mass of the Late Fifteenth Century', *Journal of the American Musicological Society*, 38 (1985), 470-523; Gary Tomlinson, *Monteverdi and the End of the Renaissance* (Berkeley: University of California Press, 1987), pp. 33-57; Fromson, *Imitation and Innovation*; Glenn Watkins, *Gesualdo: The Man and His Music*, 2nd ed. (Oxford: Clarendon Press, 1991), pp. 305, 325-359; Fromson, 'A Conjunction of Rhetoric and Music'; Lionel Pike, *Hexachords in Late-Renaissance Music* (Brookfield, Vt.: Ashgate, 1998), pp. 101-180; Michael Tilmouth – Richard Sherr, 'Parody', in *The New Grove Dictionary of Music Online,* ed. L. Macy (Accessed 15 November 2002), http://www.grovemusic.com; J. Peter Burkholder, 'Modeling', in *The New Grove Dictionary of Music Online* ed. L. Macy (Accessed 10 December 2002), http://www.grovemusic.com; Sarah M. Stoycos, 'Uncovering the 'Hidden and Buried' Models in Lasso's Early Madrigal', Paper presented at the annual meeting of the American Musicological Society, Columbus, Ohio, 1 November 2002.

[44] For a discussion of the concept and practice of *imitatio* in the music of Molinaro see Poulos, *The Life and Sacred Music of Simone Molinaro*, pp. 194-239.

Ex. 3. Dalla Gostena. *O sacrum convivium* (1609), mm. 9-13.

Ex. 4. Simone Molinaro. *O sacrum convivium* (1609), mm. 12-14.

Ex. 5. Dalla Gostena. *O sacrum convivium* (1609), mm. 13-16.

Ex. 6. Simone Molinaro. *O sacrum convivium* (1597), mm. 16-21.

from his uncle's version on the same word (exs. 3 and 4). The motive consists of two pitches, the first sung three times followed by a rising interval of a minor or major second that occurs imitatively in Dalla Gostena's setting on *e"-f"* in the cantus and altus parts, *a'-b*$^{b}$ in the quintus and bassus, and *c'-d'* in the tenor. The motive is used with the identical shape and contour in Molinaro's version presented in the altus on *e'-f'* in augmentation, *g'-a'* in the cantus, and on *c'-d'* in the quintus. The phrases in both examples converge at the words *passionis ejus* on an identical octave cadence on D. A second setting of this text by Molinaro in the same collection utilizes the borrowed material in an inverted form.

Other melodic quotations from Dalla Gostena's version occur in Molinaro's *O sacrum* setting from the 1597 *Motectorum*. Molinaro fashioned a melody in the cantus of his motet at the words *memoria passionis ejus* (ex. 6) based upon the altus part of Dalla Gostena's motet (ex. 5). The prime similarities are the opening notes on C-D (*c'-d'* in the Dalla Gostena version transposed up to *c"-d"* in the Molinaro version) on the first two syllables, the leap to an agogically accented F at *passionis*, and an eventual stepwise descent to C# in both examples. The borrowed melody is elaborated with an added leap and melisma at the word *ejus* that extends the lyrical contour of the line. A quotation from this section of the melody was also adopted in Molinaro's setting of the same text published in 1605.[45]

As he had done in his writings and with his editorial endeavors Molinaro evoked in music the memory of his esteemed uncle. The strands of the teacher's music are woven into that of the student's and reflect the bonds of Molinaro's devotion to his uncle. Molinaro's Latin dedication to the Doge signified his goal to succeed to the position of chapel master in San Lorenzo; an aspiration that was motivated by his desire to honor and emulate the legacy of his uncle and mentor.

UNIVERSITY OF CINCINNATI
USA – Cincinnati, Ohio 45221
poulosps@email.uc.edu

[45] This quotation is found in Molinaro's *Concerti ecclesiastici a due et a quatro voci nelli quali si contiene Messa, Motetti & Magnificat in tutti li otto Toni con la sua partitura per l'organo* (Venice: Ricciardo Amadino, 1605; RISM M 2937).

## APPENDIX

I. Simone Molinaro's dedication letter to Matteo Senarega[46]

SERENISSIMO REIPUBLICAE GENUENSIS DUCI MATTHAEO SANAREGAE [*sic*] SIMON MOLINARIUS S.

Tanta est virtutum, quibus ubique terrarum, Serenissime Dux, nominis tui fama pervagatur, magnitudo, & praestantia; ut laudum tuarum praeconia, vel nemo prorsus, vel tua solius eloquentia celebrare possit; non modo, quod istum dignitatis gradum obtines omnium sanè, qui in civitate deferuntur, & maximum, & honorificentissimum: sed magis etiam, quod in te sunt ea, quibus dignitatem mereris, nec tam dignitatis ornaris honore, quam tu ipse dignitatem tua dignitate exornas. Itaque summam gloriae meritorumque tuorum amplitudinem, quam mihi nullo pacto verbis amplecti licet, silentio potius, quam inani oratione colendam censeo. Tantum à tua summa, ac singulari humanitate etiam atque etiam peto, ut has meas Musicae lucubratiunculas ad rerum sacrarum celebrationem, & ritum pertinentes, quas sub tui splendore nominis emittendas iudicavi; ea frontis hilaritate, qua caetera tibi gratiora soles, libeat accipere. Quis enim hos tibi inscriptos Musicae concentus minus convenire dixerit, qui suavissimum, ac prope incredibilem honestatis concentum sentiat, quem ex consonanti praeclararum actionum tuarum varietate virtutum omnium in tuo pectore residens chorus modulatur, & agit? Ne asperneris igitur, vir amplissime, hoc qualecunque munusculum illustre quidem, ac perpetuum quoddam meae erga te egregiae voluntatis, observantiaeque pignus & argumentum; quod si tibi arrisisse, tuique testimonij laude honostatum [*sic*] fuisse intellexero; & mei laboris uberrimum fructum coepisse videbor, & ad maiora propediem, quae iam instituta habeo, perficienda vehementius incitabor. Vale.

*SIMONE MOLINARO SENDS HIS GREETINGS TO MATTEO SENAREGA, THE MOST SERENE DUKE OF THE REPUBLIC OF GENOA.*

*So great, most Serene Duke, is the magnitude and excellence of your virtues, in every part of the world which the fame of your reputation has reached, that either nobody at all, or your very own eloquence alone, could celebrate the making public of your glories, not only, because you hold that position of authority which is of course both the greatest and most honorific of all which are awarded in the city, but even more so, because in your person are those qualities by which you deserve that position, and you are not so much adorned by the honor of your position as adorn in yourself the position by your own natu-*

[46] Cantus of RISM M 2930, p. 2. The spelling of the Latin letters used in the printed dedication letter has been updated in accordance with modern values, i.e. 'ubique' for 'vbique', 'praestantia' for 'praeftantia', etc.

*ral position. And so I consider that I should reverence the utmost amplitude of your glory and merits, which I may in no manner express by words, rather by silence than by meaningless speech. This alone again and again I seek from your utmost and singular benevolence, that you may be pleased to accept these worthless nocturnal musical compositions of mine, which are intended for the celebration of sacred events and the liturgy, and which I judged should be sent forth under the splendor of your name, with the same joy on your brow with which you are wont to accept other offerings which are more pleasing to you. For who would claim that the musical compositions inscribed herein are unfitting for you, who are aware of the sweetest and almost unbelievable harmony of your own goodness, and whom a choir of all the virtues, residing in your heart, hymns and inspires with all the consistent variety of your illustrious actions? Do not therefore, most noble man, despise this bright little gift of mine, however unworthy it be, which is a sort of everlasting pledge and proof of my outstanding goodwill and respect towards you; if I learn that you have smiled favourably on it and that it has been honoured by the praise of your testimony, I shall both consider that I have gained a most abundant fruit for my labor and I shall be encouraged all the more eagerly to complete greater tasks in the future, which I have already conceived.*

## II. Motet Texts of the *Motectorum quinis, et missae denis vocibus, liber primus* (1597)[47]

*Recogitandis donis tuis* (source of text unknown)
Recogitandis donis tuis et annis meis
conterantur quaeso Domine viscera mea
et duro sic expressa dolore perennes fontes
excitent lachrimarum tu dele tu lava tu miserere

*Erravi sicut ovis* (first line from Psalm 119. 176; source of second line of text unknown)
Erravi sicut ovis quae periit; quaere servum tuum
pro quo, ut non periret mori dignatus es, et voluisti.

*Miser factus sum* (Psalm 37. 7)
Miser factus sum, et curvatus sum, usque in finem,
tota die contristatus ingrediebar.

*Domine, ne in furore tuo arguas me*, Prima Pars (Psalm 6. 2-4)
Domine, ne in furore tuo arguas me,
neque in ira tua corripias me.
Miserere mei Domine,

[47] The spelling of Latin letters in the motet texts has been updated in accordance with modern values standardized in the *Liber Usualis*, i.e. 'Jesu' for 'Iesu', 'vivos' for 'viuos', etc.

quoniam infirmus sum:
sana me, Domine,
quoniam conturbata sunt ossa mea.
Et anima mea
turbata est valde,
sed tu, Domine, usquequo?

*Convertere Domine*, Secunda pars (Psalm 6. 5-6)
Convertere Domine
et eripe animam meam:
salvum me fac propter
misericordiam tuam.
Quoniam non est in morte qui memor sit tui:
in inferno autem quis confitebitur tibi?

*Laboravi in gemitu meo*, Tertia pars (Psalm 6. 7-8)
Laboravi in gemitu meo
lavabo per singulas noctes lectum meum
lacrimis meis stratum meum rigabo.
Turbatus est a furore oculus meus
inveteravi inter omnes inimicos meos.

*Omnes gentes plaudite* (Psalm 46. 2-3)
Omnes gentes plaudite manibus,
Jubilate Deo in voce exultationis.
Quoniam Dominus excelsus,
terribilis rex magnus super omnem terram.

*Quae est ista quae progreditur* (lines 1-3 Song of Solomon 6:9; source of remaining text unknown)
Quae est ista quae progreditur
Quasi aurora consurgens
Pulchra ut luna electa ut sol.
Haec est Domina mundi
Gaudium paradisi solatium Angelorum
Curramus ergo ad eam et dicamus:
Ave gratia plena.

*Virgo mater* (source of text unknown)
Virgo mater sponsa filia Regis Regum omnium.
Tu nos rege, tu nos fove, tu nos amantes suscipe
et qua refulges gratia Paradisum nobis aperi.
Culpas nostras hilari vultu deprecans.
Namque pace tua ni peccaret homo.
Nec tu semper Virgo Dei Filium genuises et hominem.

*O sacrum convivium* (Magnificat Antiphon, Second Vespers, Liber Usualis, p. 959)

O sacrum convivium
in quo Christus sumitur
recolitur memoria
passionis ejus.
Mens impletur gratia
et futurae gloriae
nobis pignus datur.
Alleluia.

*Versa est in luctum* (Job 30. 31, 30; 6. 16)
Versa est in luctum cithara mea
et organum meum in vocem flentium.
Cutis mea denigrata est super me
et ossa mea aruerunt.
Parce mihi, Domine,
nihil enim sunt dies mei.

# INDICES

## 1. INDEX NOMINUM SELECTORUM[1]



[1] Composuere D. Sacré & N. Gabriëls.

## 2. INDEX CODICUM MANU SCRIPTORUM[2]



[2] Composuit D. Sacré.